PRIMER   MATTHEW CRAVEN

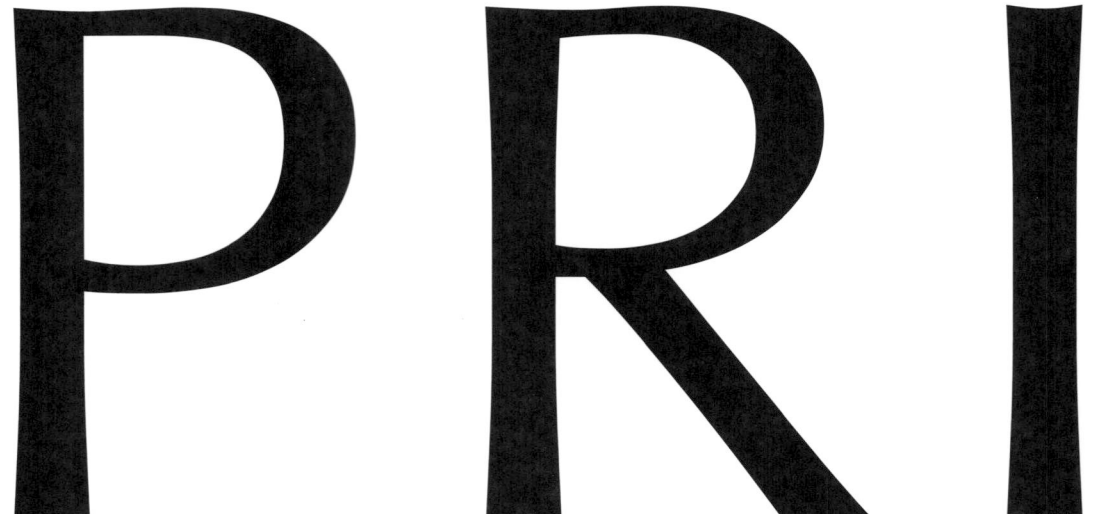

First published in the United States of America in 2018 by Anthology Editions, LLC. 87 Guernsey Street, Brooklyn, NY 11222. anthologyeditions.com. Copyright © 2018 Anthology Editions, LLC. Editor: Mark Iosifescu. Art Director: Bryan Cipolla. Design: Nicholas Law. Proofreader: Chris Peterson. First Edition. ARC 058. Printed in China. ISBN: 978-1-944860-18-9. Library of Congress Control Number: 2018946712

MER

MATTHEW CRAVEN

Anthology Editions, New York

FOREWORD

Leslie Jones

Buried in used-bookstore basements and packed away in local library and school district storerooms are the materials for Matthew Craven's art. Craven cuts up old encyclopedias, textbooks, and generally antiquated picture books that once told the Western history of global art and culture. He clips out images of ancient statues and architecture from cultures as distinct as those of Greece and China, of folk art from regions as distant as Eastern Europe and the American Southwest, and of objects as far apart chronologically as Neolithic hand tools and modern sculpture.

Far closer in time are the reproductions themselves, which date roughly from the 1950s through the early 1970s, when black and white predominated and what color images there were had a distinctly matte (rather than glossy) quality. As one would imagine, in the age of the Internet these books are disappearing, and have become harder to find. Craven likens his process to that of a collector: "Digging for books is like digging for records" (which he also collects)[1]—and it's "so much more fun to find a new book than to go and buy a new tube of paint."[2] The works' paper supports, too, are collected by Craven, and are mostly versos of movie posters from the same period that carry the bends, tears, and stains of age and, like the images, are also remnants of commercial printing's past. In his unique brand of collage, Craven repurposes bygone printed matter to meaningful and visually compelling effect.

Oftentimes, Craven recomposes the art historical snippets on the poster sheets as if laying tesserae or letterpress type. All together they create patterns reminiscent of decorative mosaics or textiles, while others appear to follow the registration lines of a page and thereby evoke pictographs associated with many ancient languages. Affixed with spray adhesive, the images do not overlap as in conventional collage but interact visually as individuated elements so they can have, according to Craven, the "presence and power they deserve."

To that same end, Craven may choose to isolate a single image or pair of images and then embellish with patterns in colored pencil. Some patterns evoke the key motif on ancient Greek vases, or the zigzag typical of Native American textiles, resonating with the selected imagery. Others seem to have more in common with comic book graphics or, because of their underlying grid structure, the bitmap renderings of early video games. Woven together, the compositions are fanciful yet complex, like a lexicon of patterns past—a weaver's (or programmer's?) Esperanto.

Craven often repeats images within his compositions, which, while alluding to the reproductive quality of his source material, also evoke a sort of linguistic system or code. This reference to language is particularly interesting, since that is exactly what Craven leaves on the cutting room floor, so to speak. What he removes is the text or, in his words, the "Western dictation of history." Craven's pictorial revision of global art history is based largely on formal similarities across time, space, and cultures (not to mention the availability of materials and his own unique aesthetic sensibility)—what he describes simply as "things made by man." While a critique of Western imperialism is implied in his process, the work also summons universal notions of humankind's shared impulse to create.

This Anthology Editions publication, devoted to Craven's work over the past five years, returns much of the artist's source material to its original context: the book. As the title, *PRIMER*, suggests, the book offers an introduction to the artist's work, but it is far from a catalog in the usual sense. Working collaboratively by "cutting and pasting," using filters, and cropping, Craven, Anthology art director Bryan Cipolla, and designer Nicholas Law have created a new work of art that, in addition to offering this "revised" version of global art history and reaffirming the primacy of the codex as a source of Craven's creativity, provides a visual experience unique to the bound-and-printed page.

Leslie Jones is curator of prints and drawings at the Los Angeles County Museum of Art.

1. Unless otherwise noted, all quotations are from the author's interview with the artist on May 4, 2018.
2. Cited in Vivian Hua, "Matthew Craven Artist Interview: Getting Existential Through Pattern, History & Anthropology," *Redefine*, October 6, 2015, www.redefinemag.com/2015 /matthew-craven-artist-interview-existential-pattern-history-anthropology.

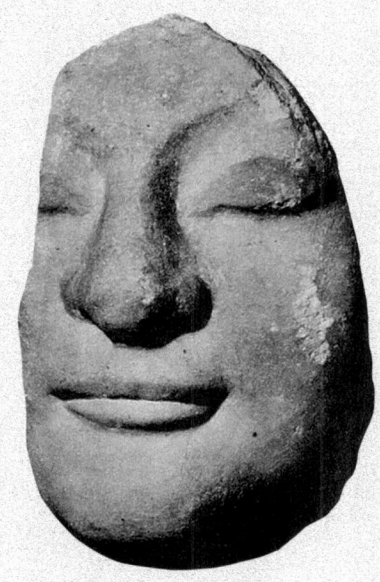

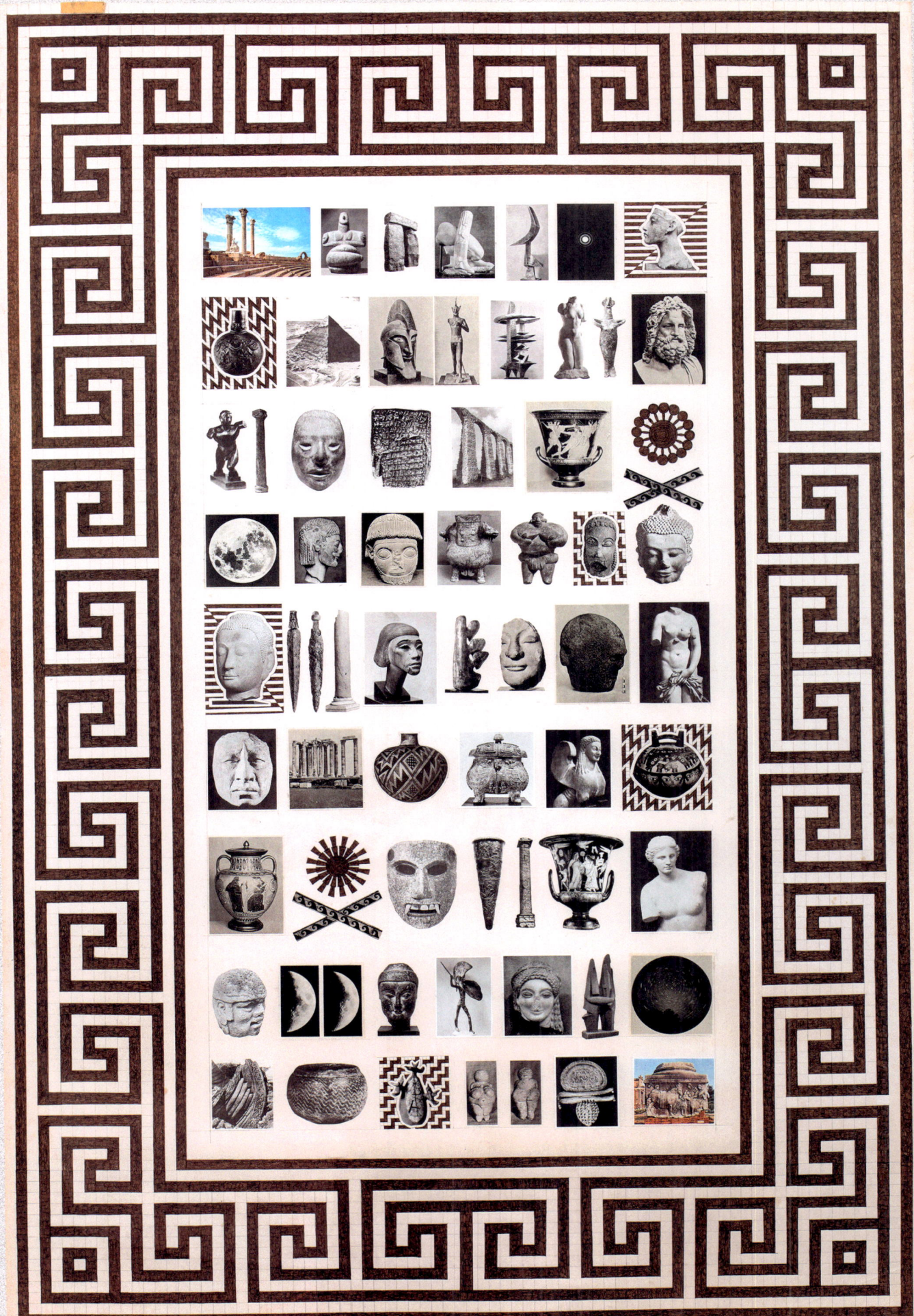

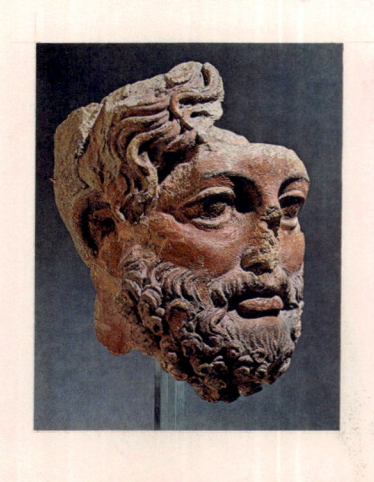
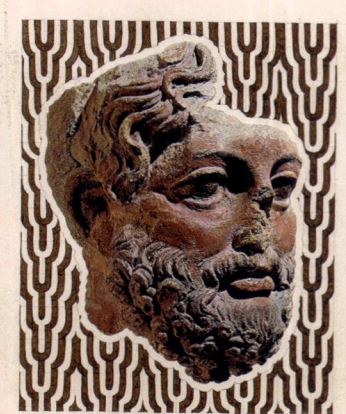
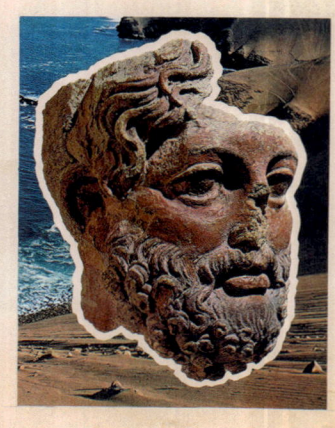
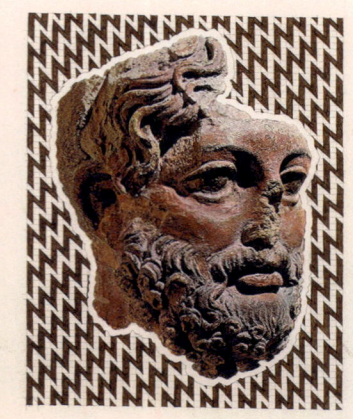
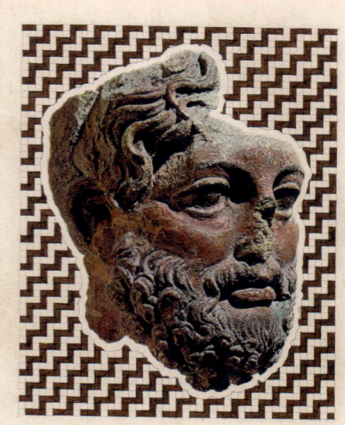

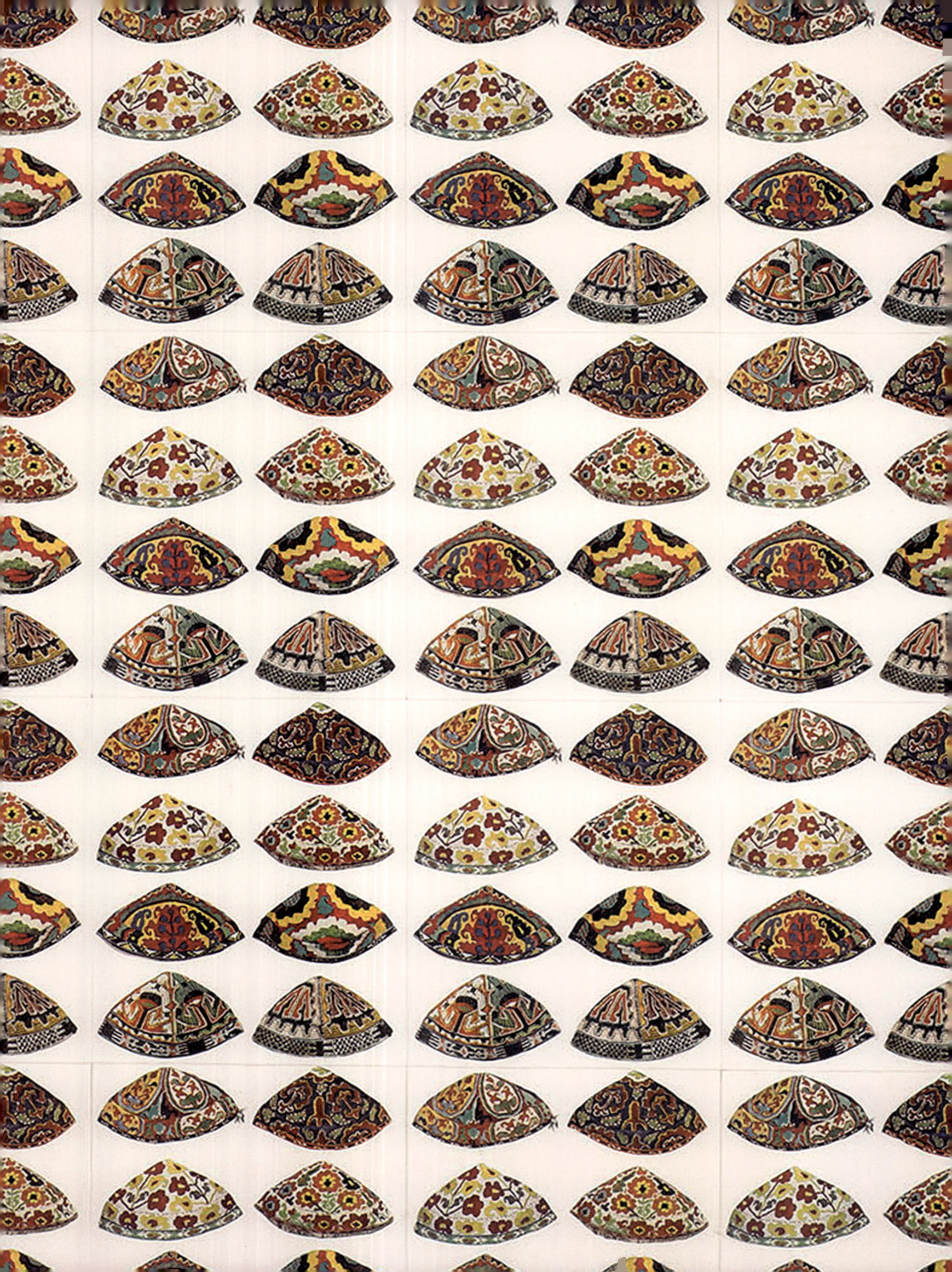

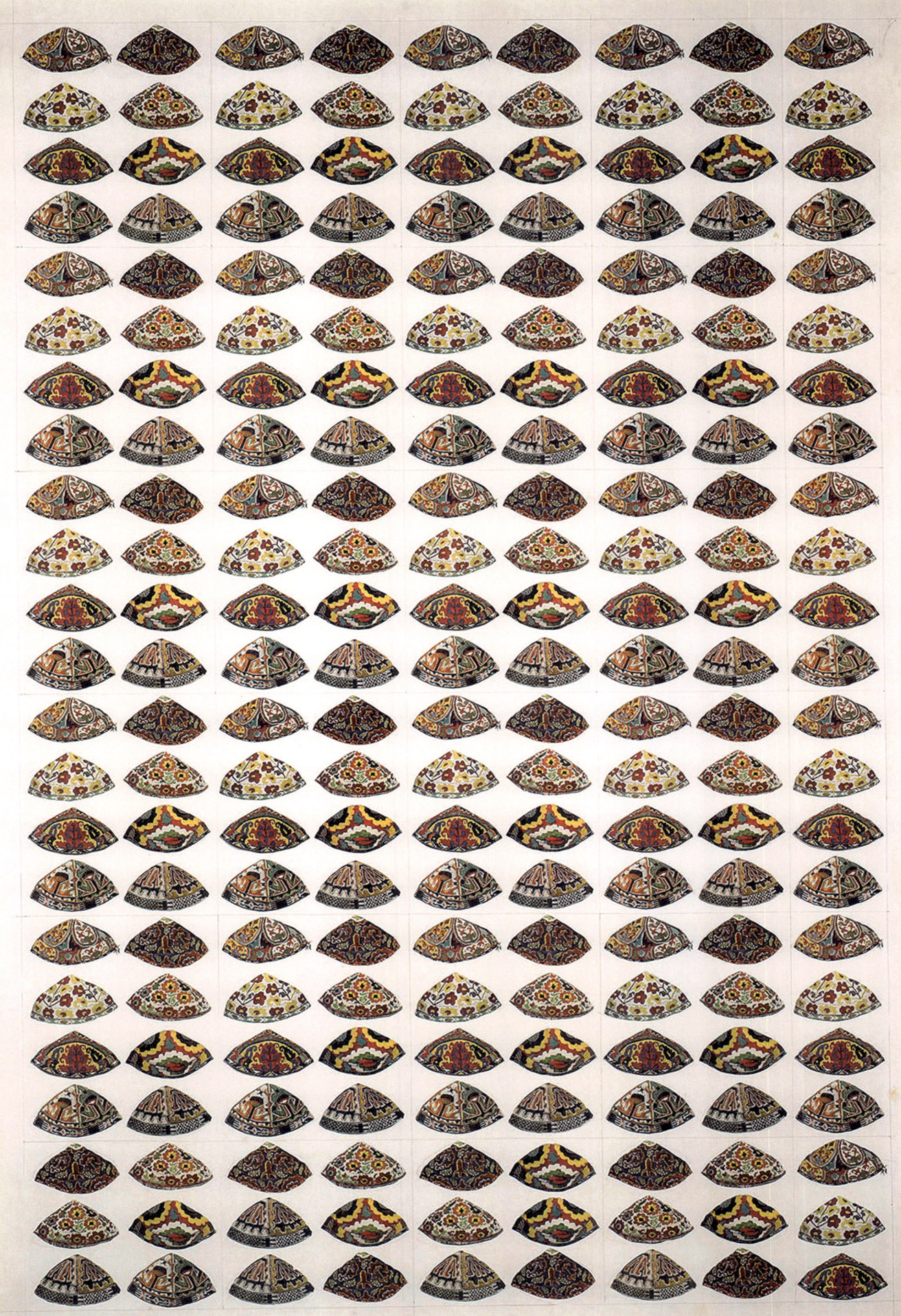

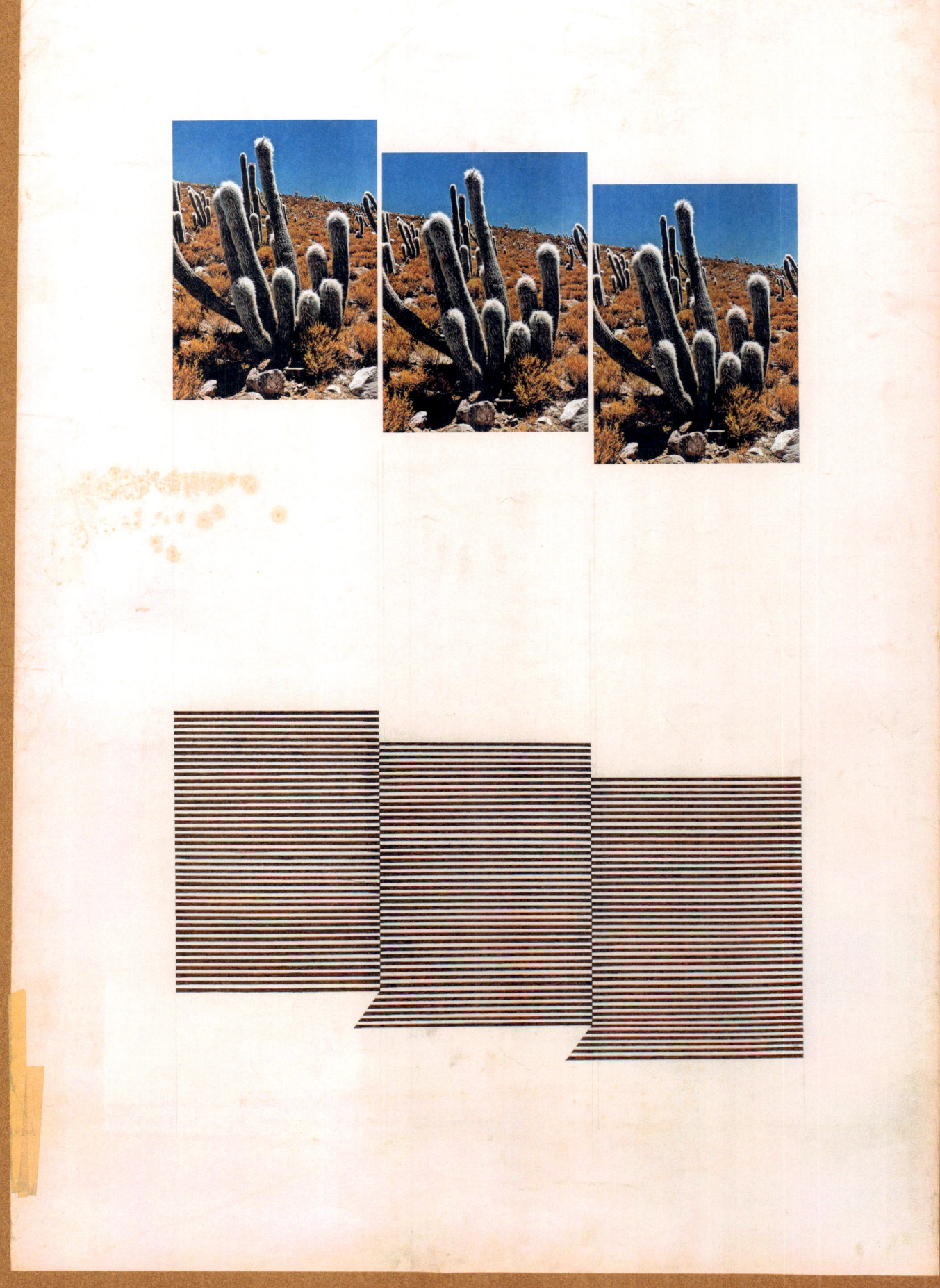

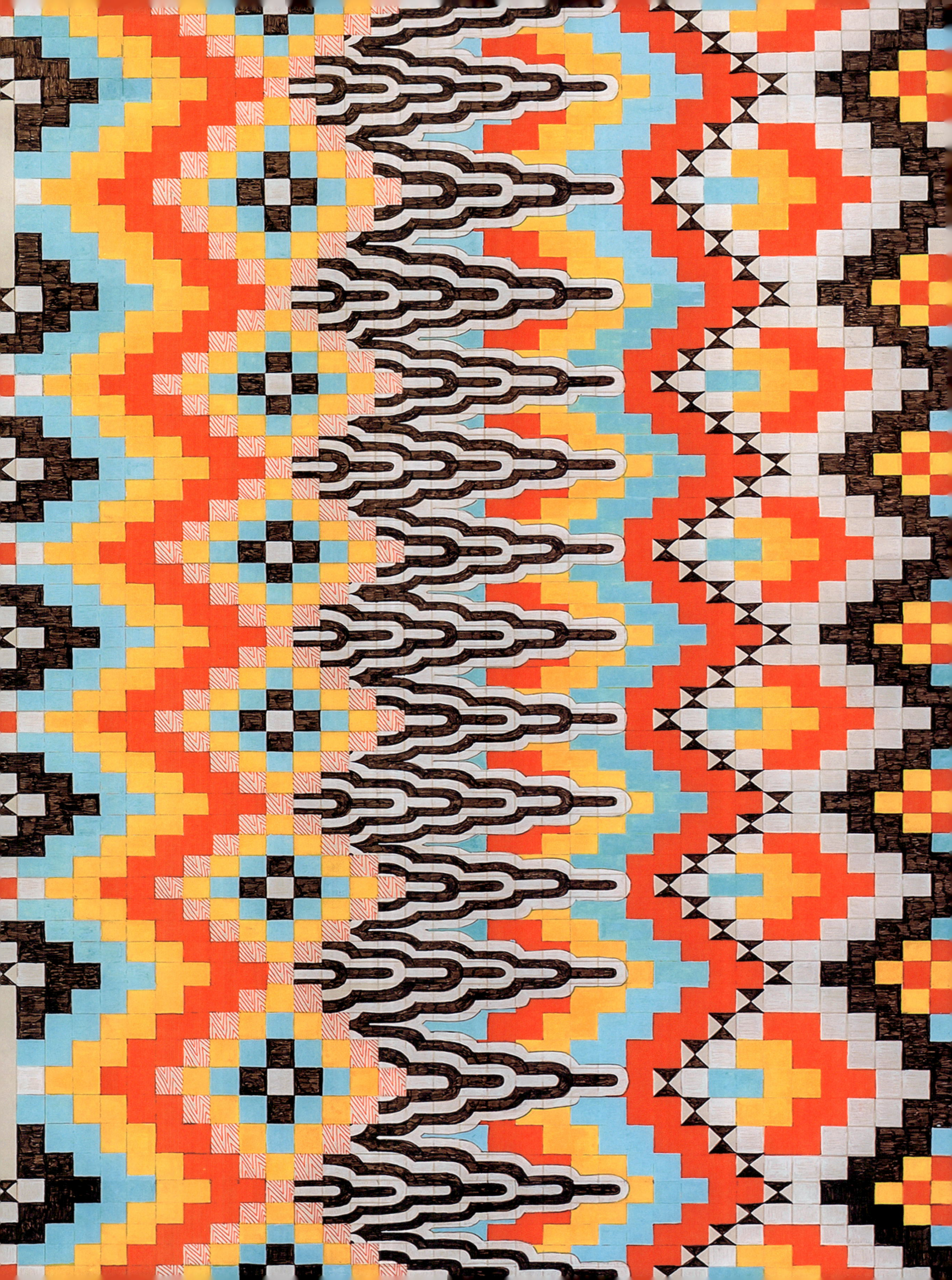

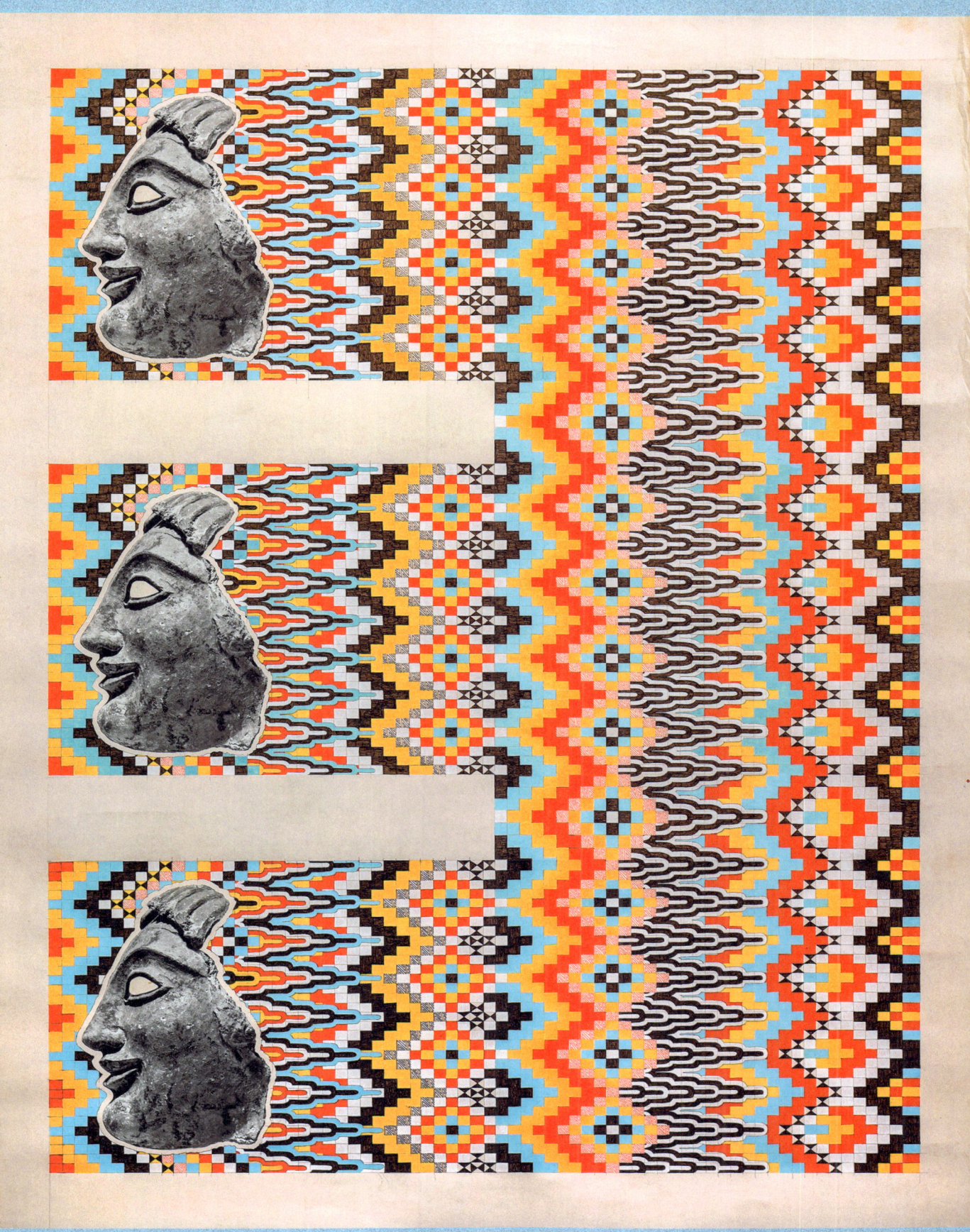

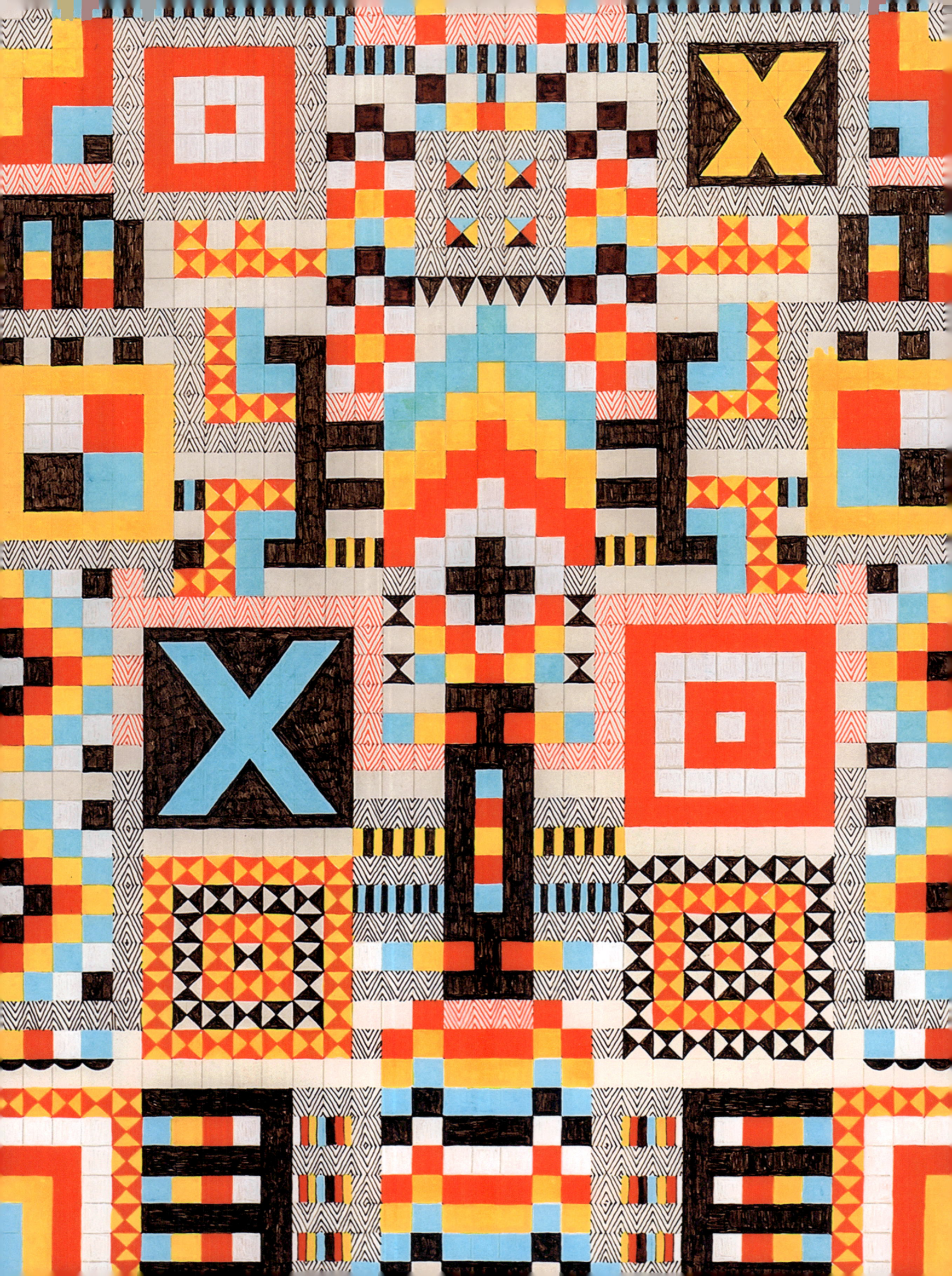

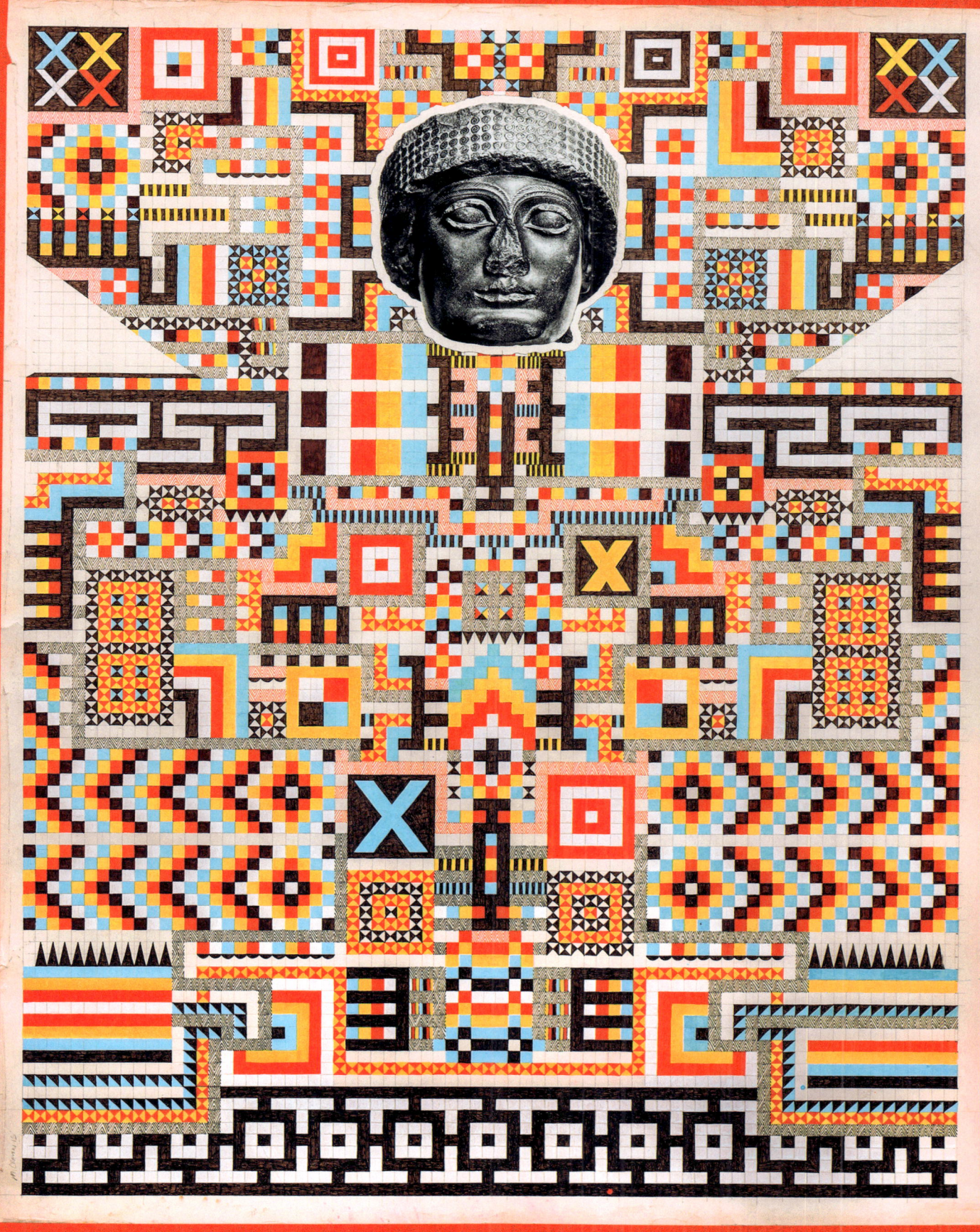

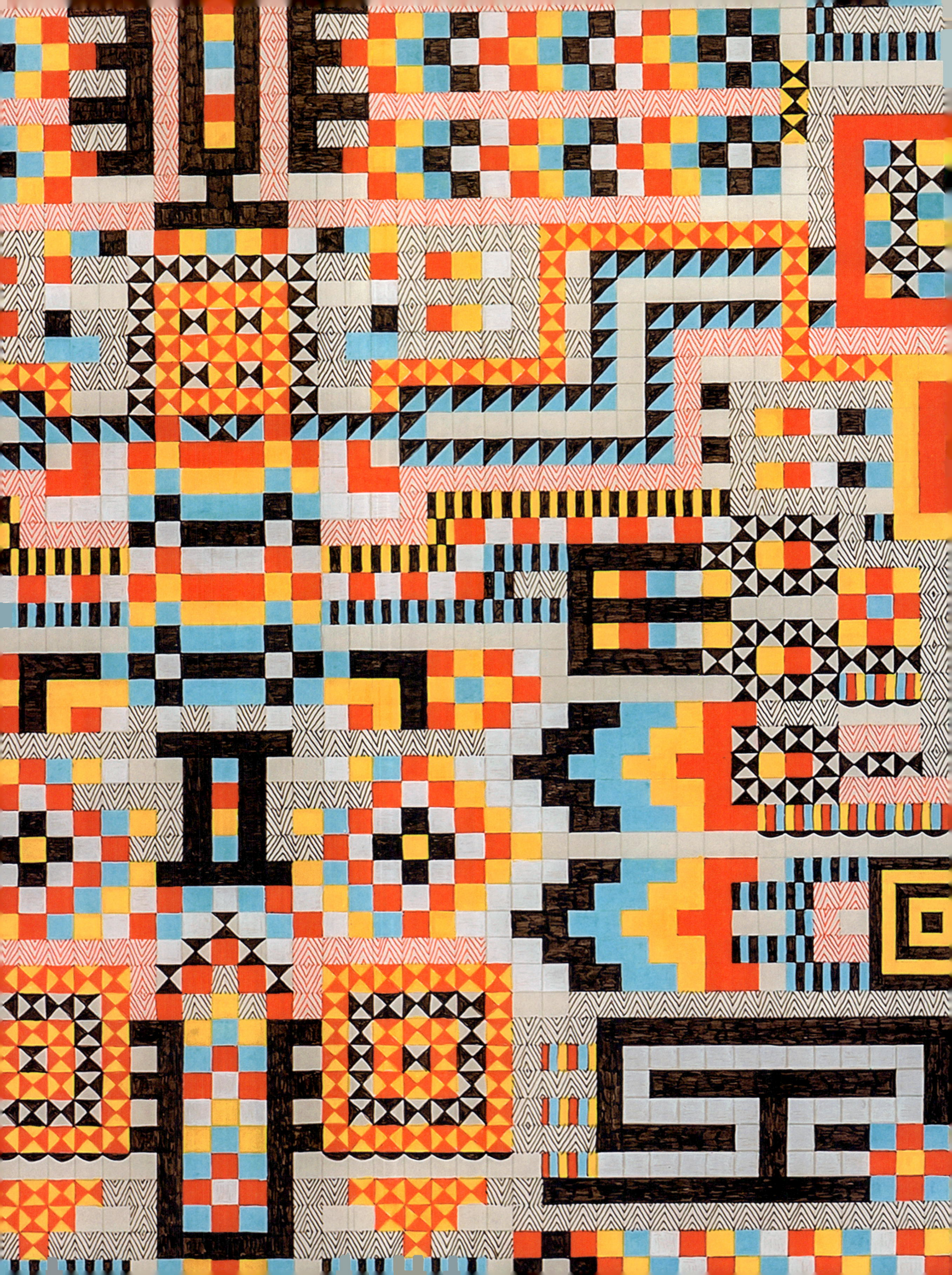

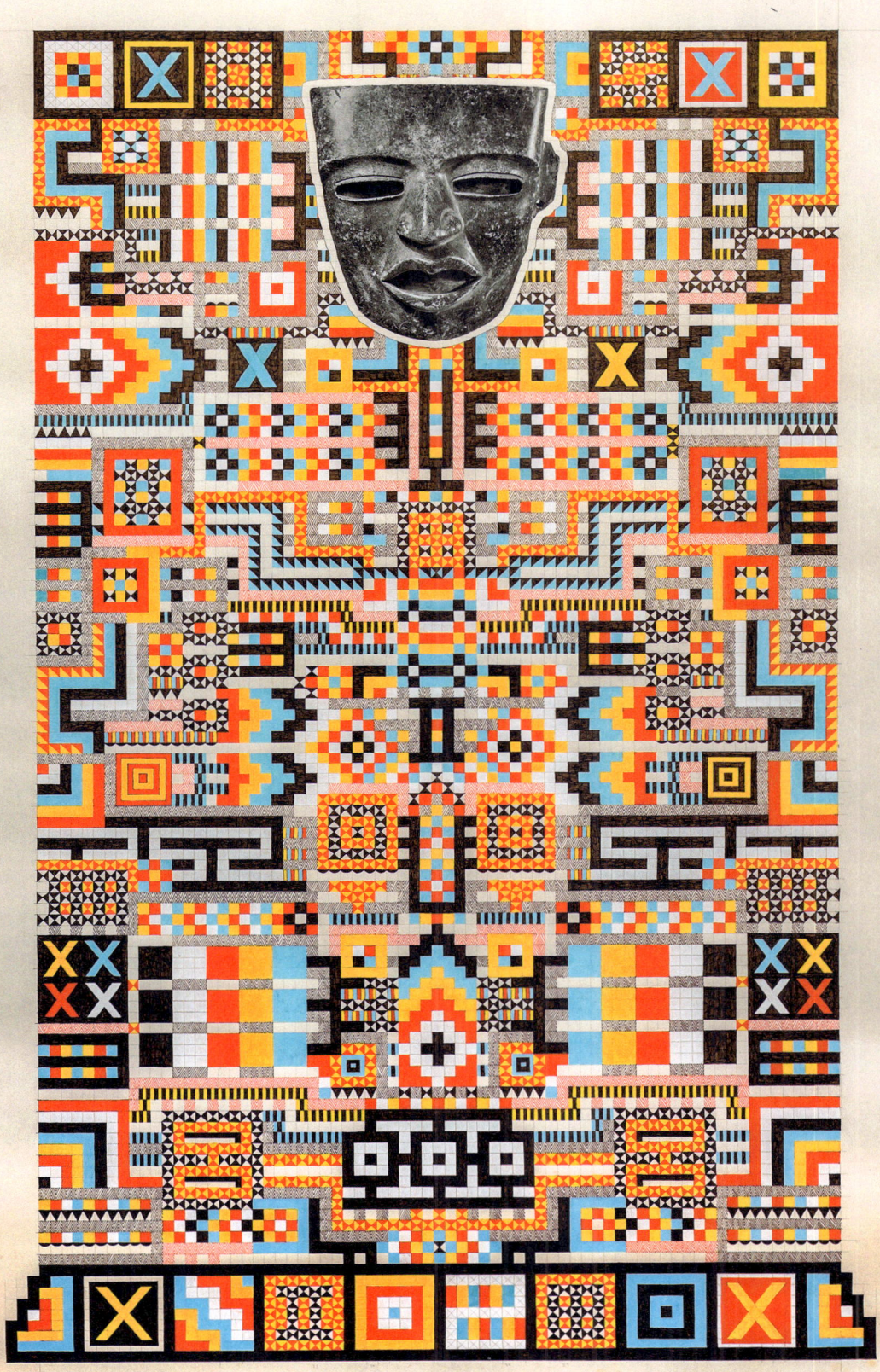

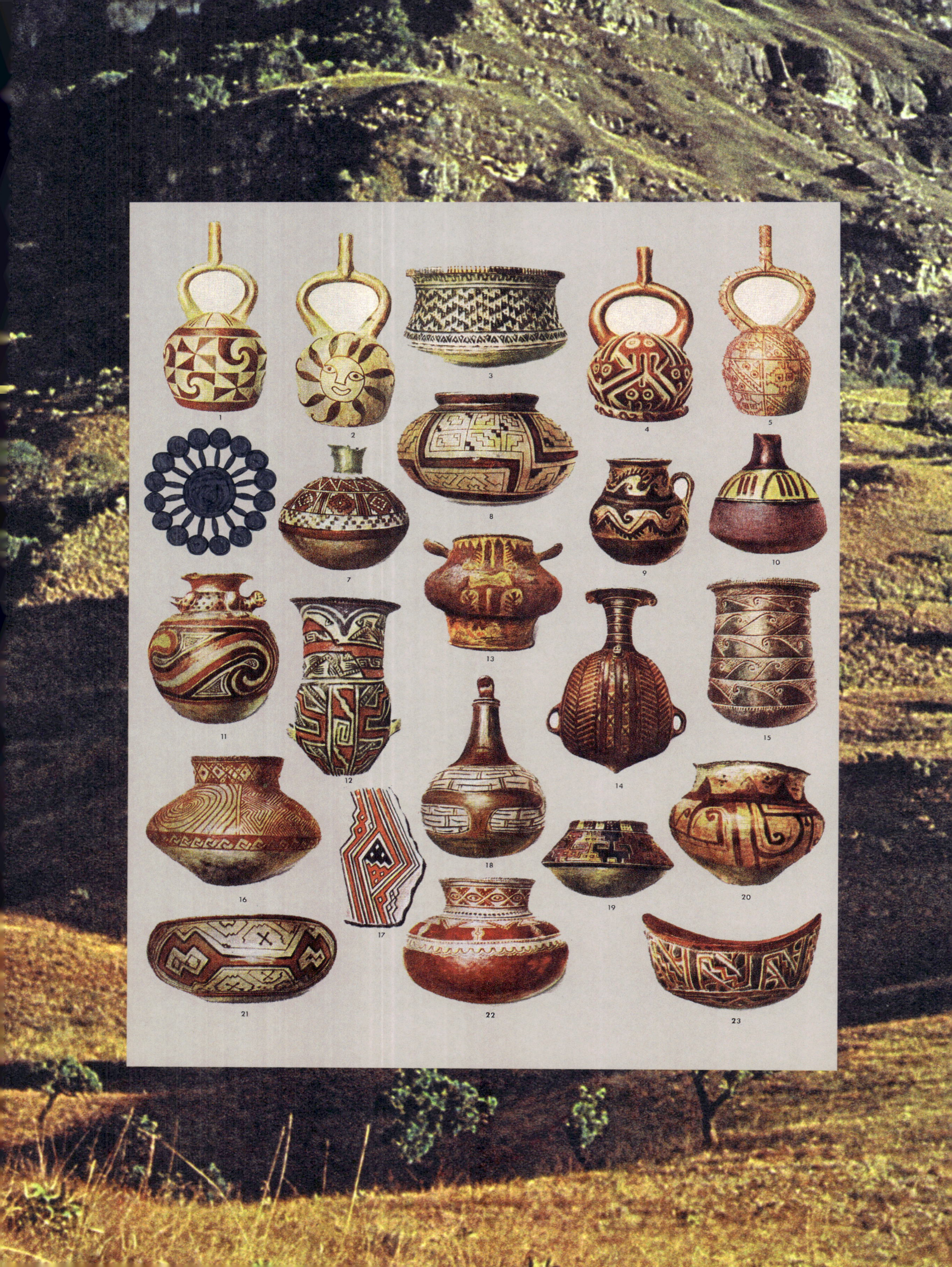

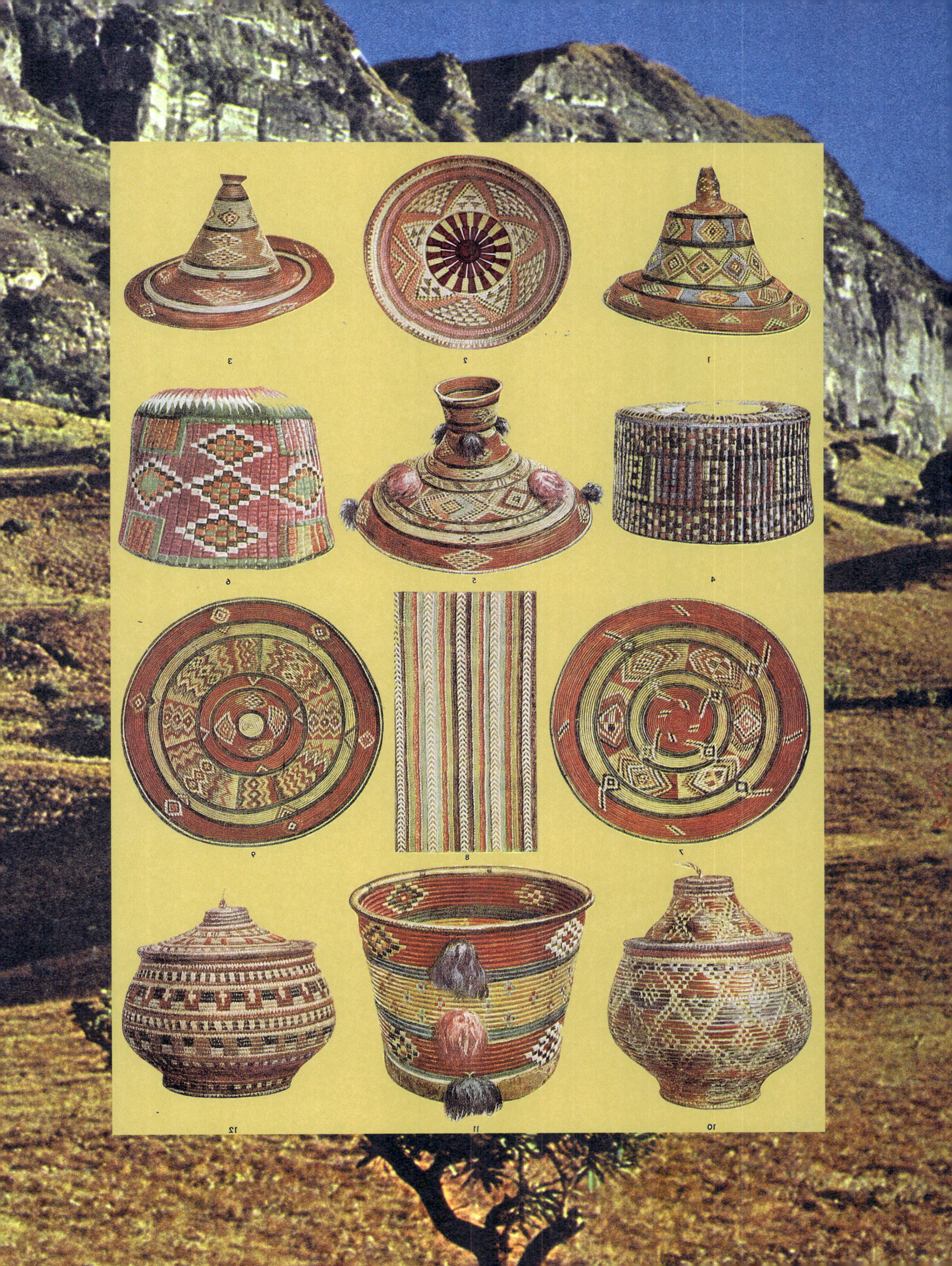

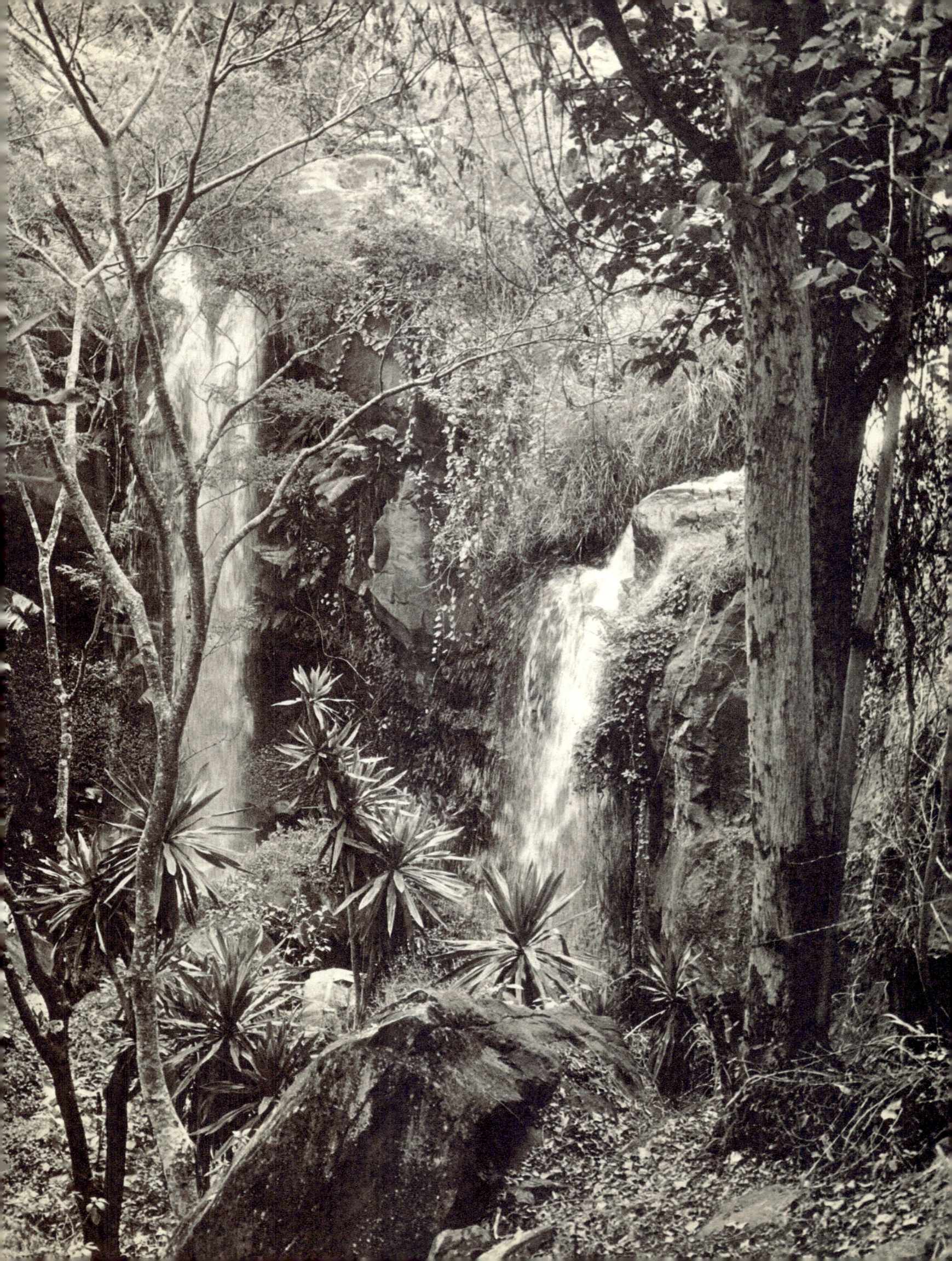

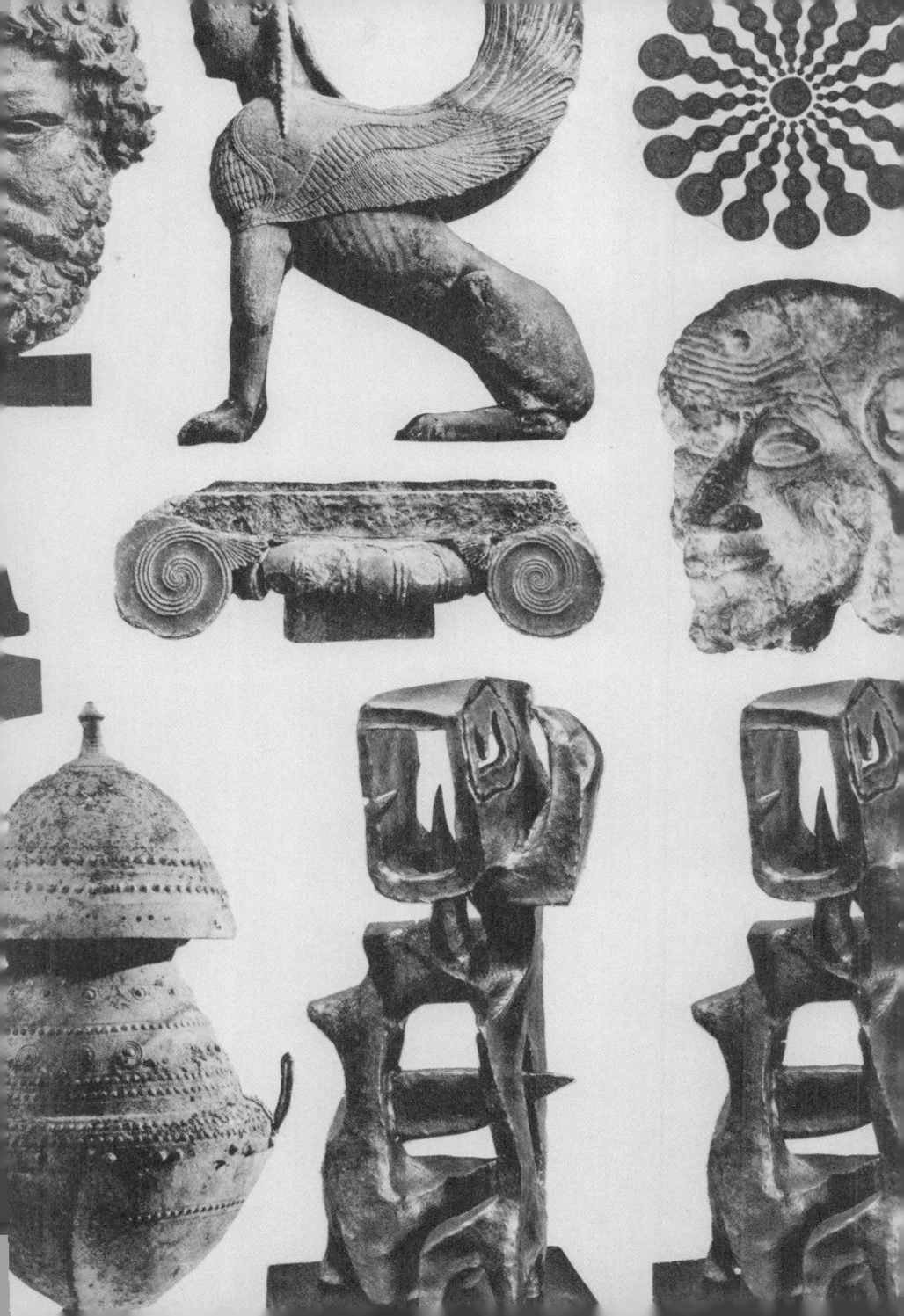

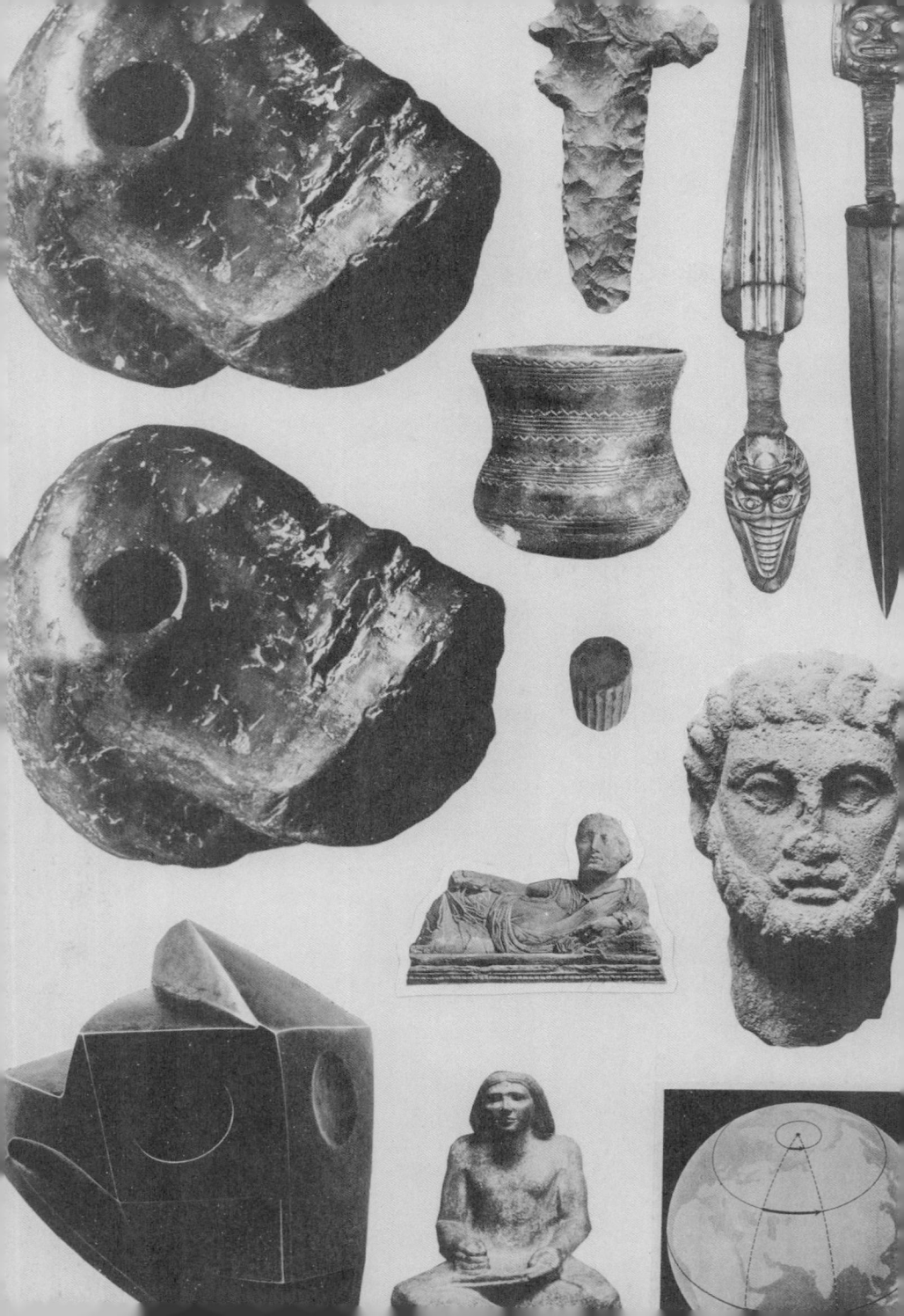

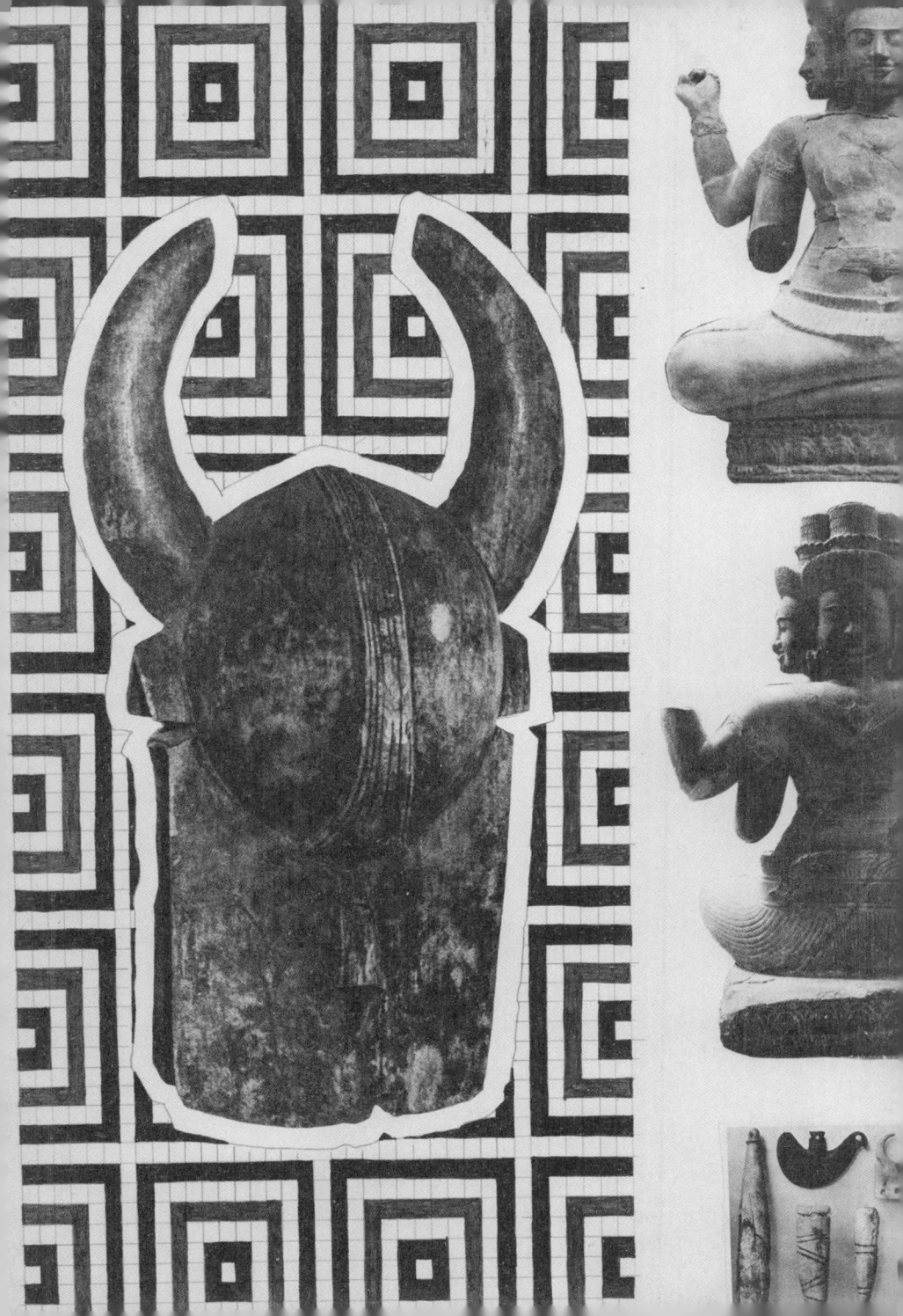

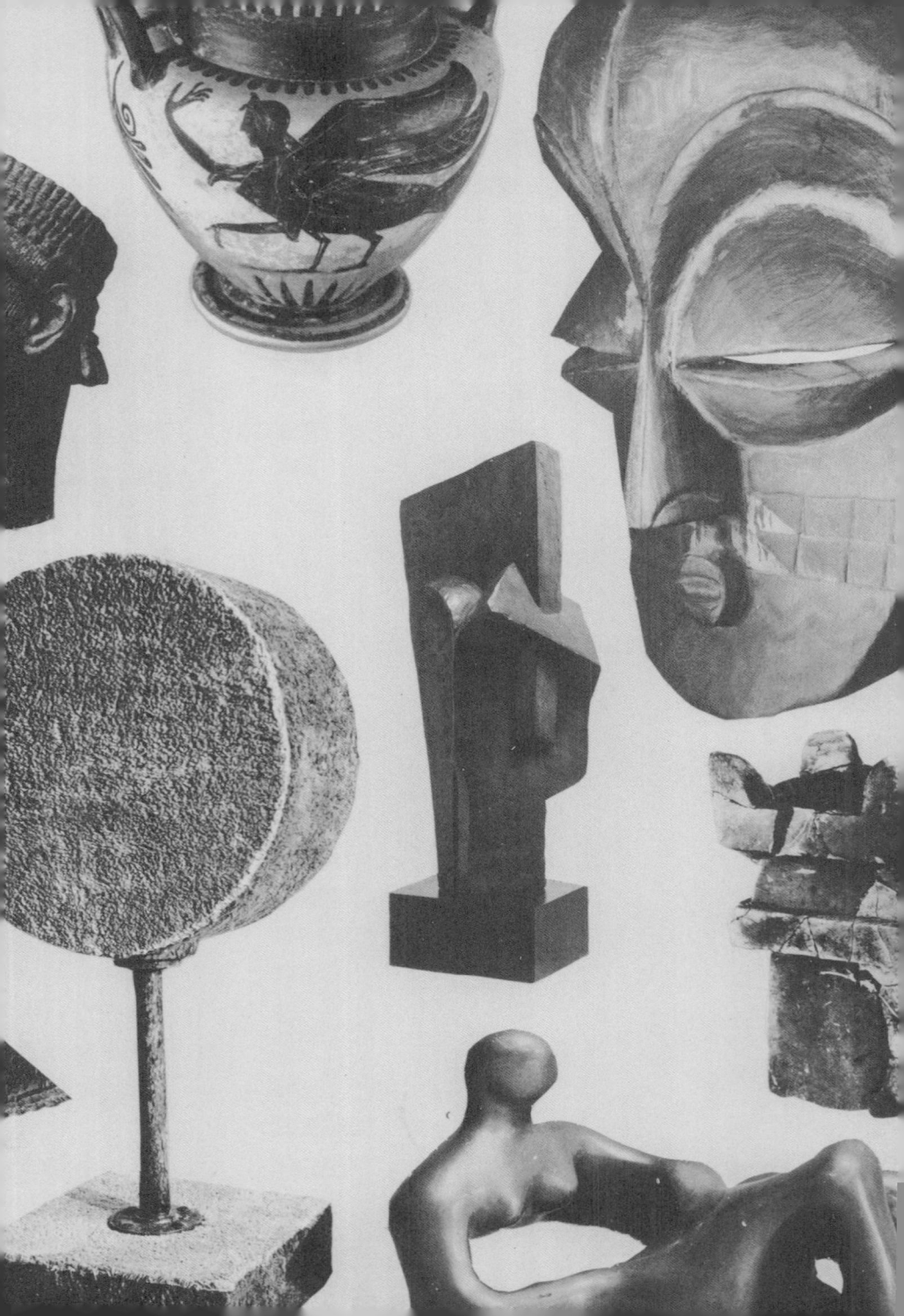

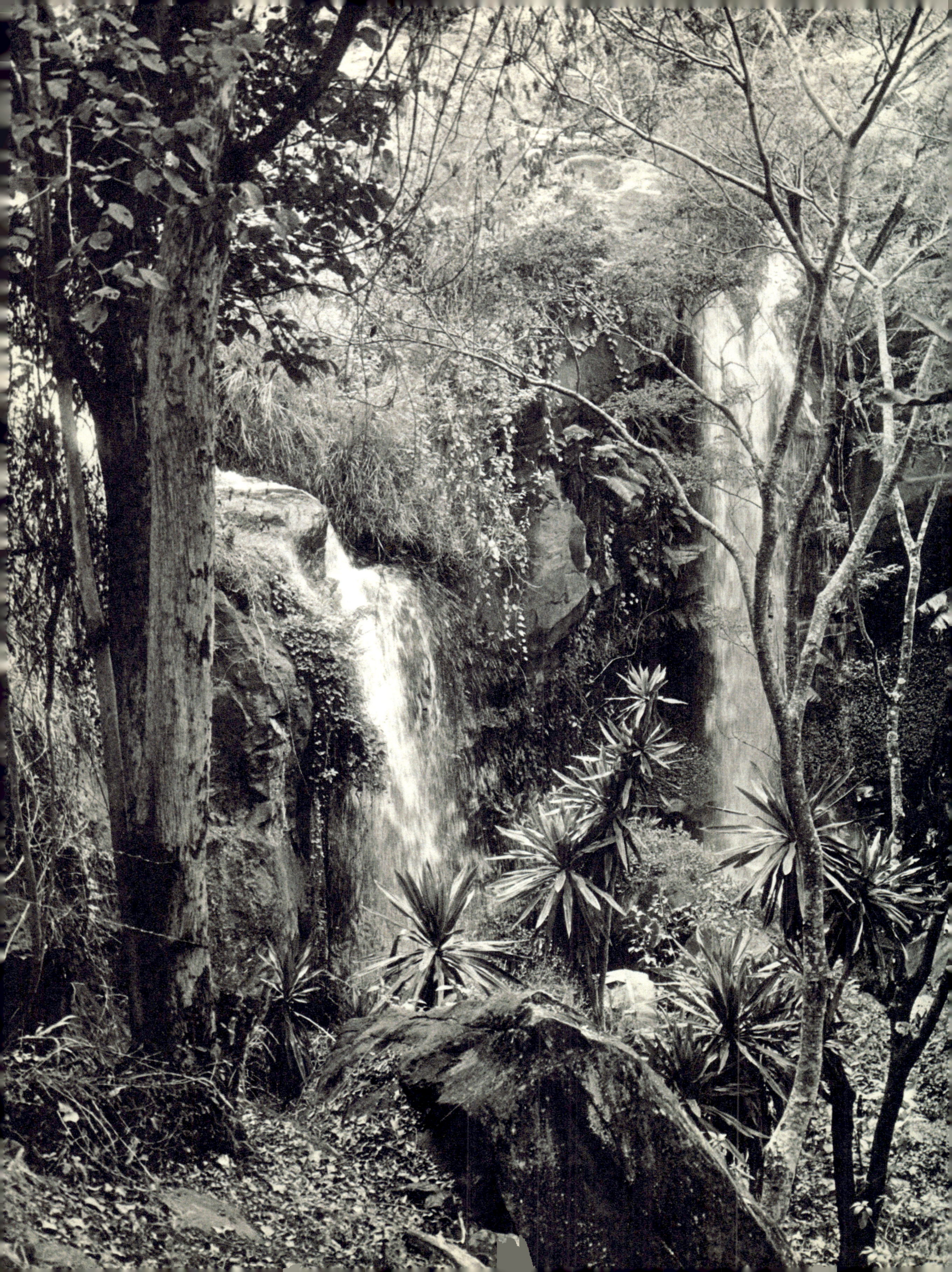

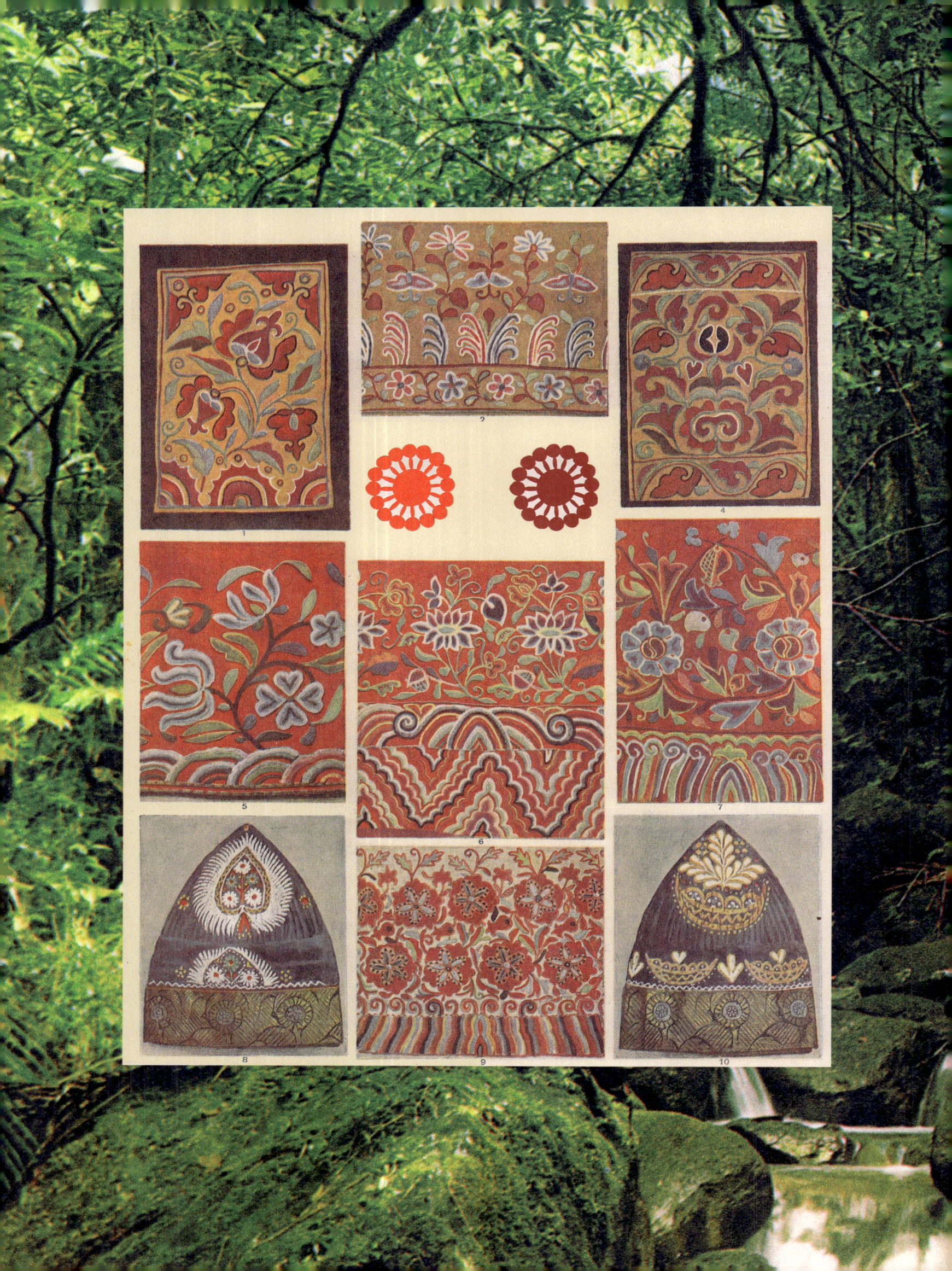

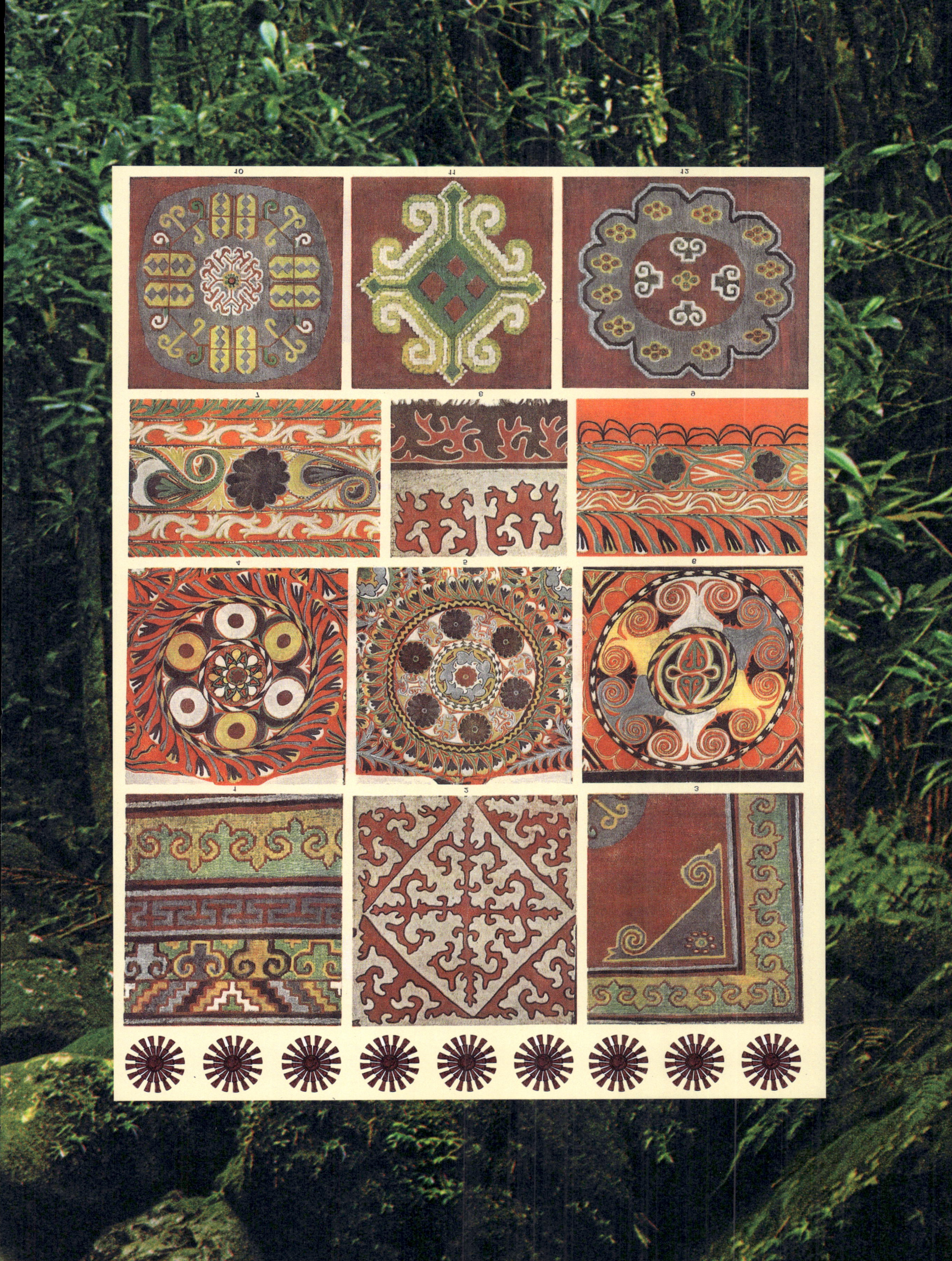

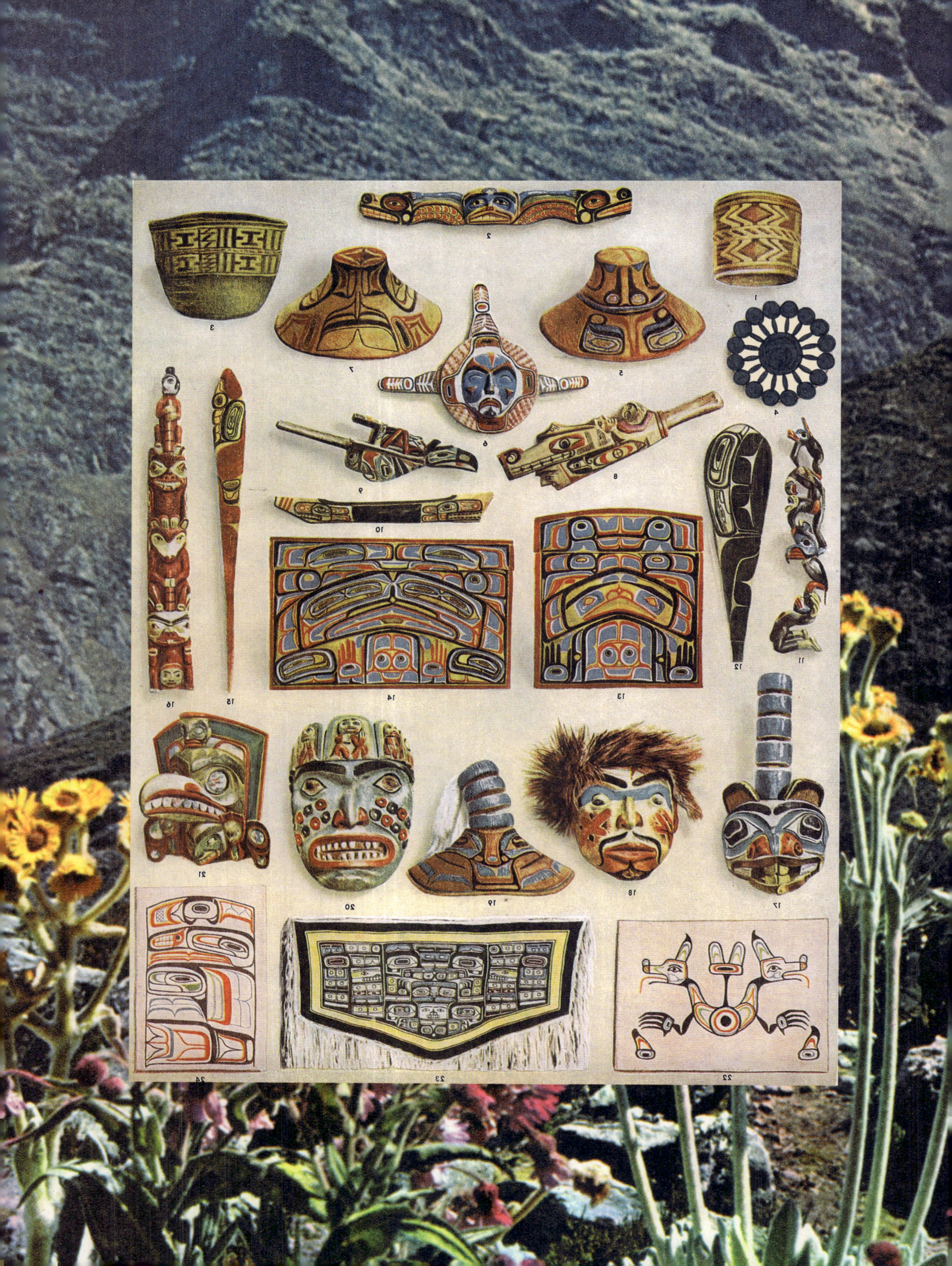

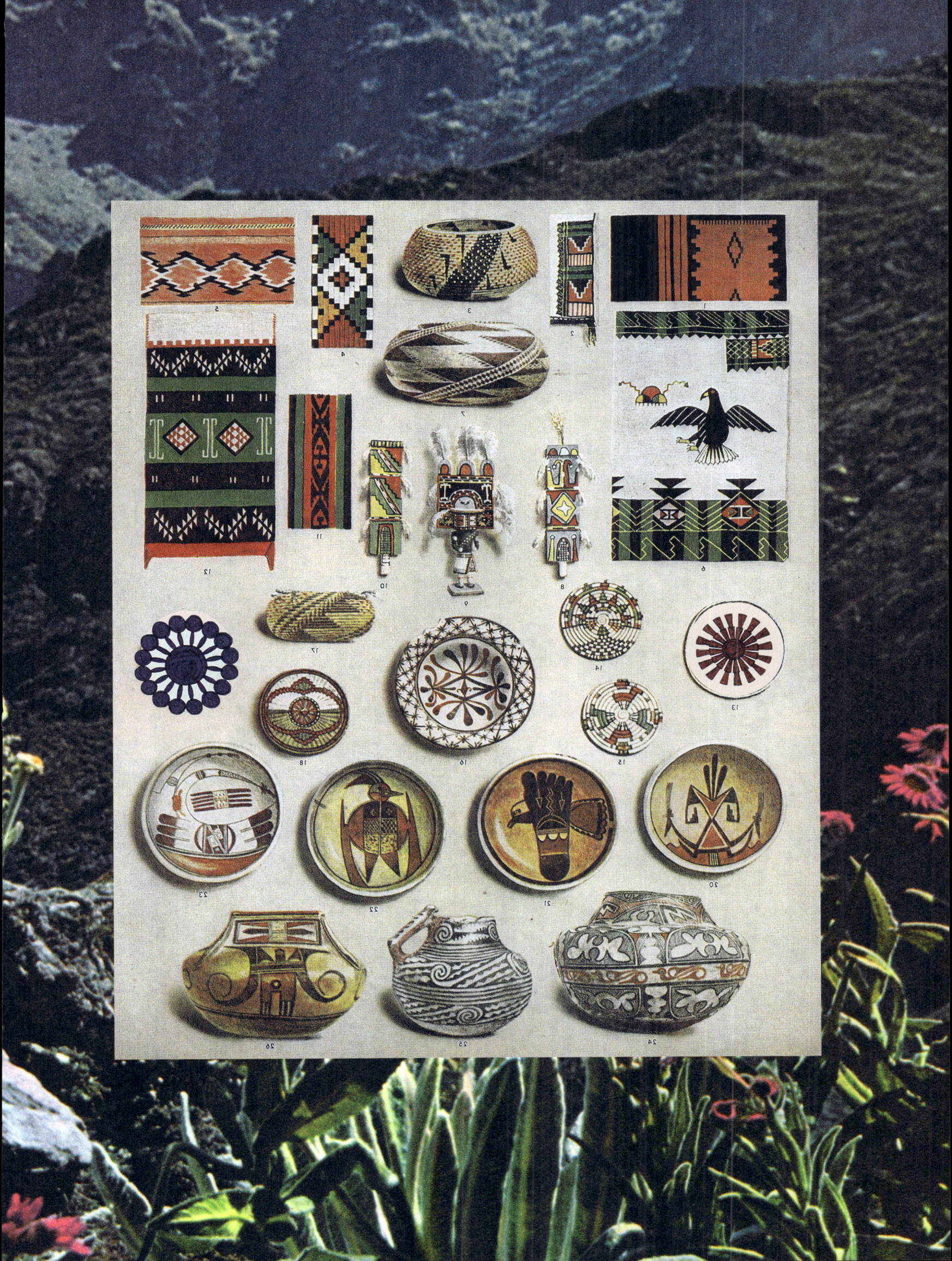

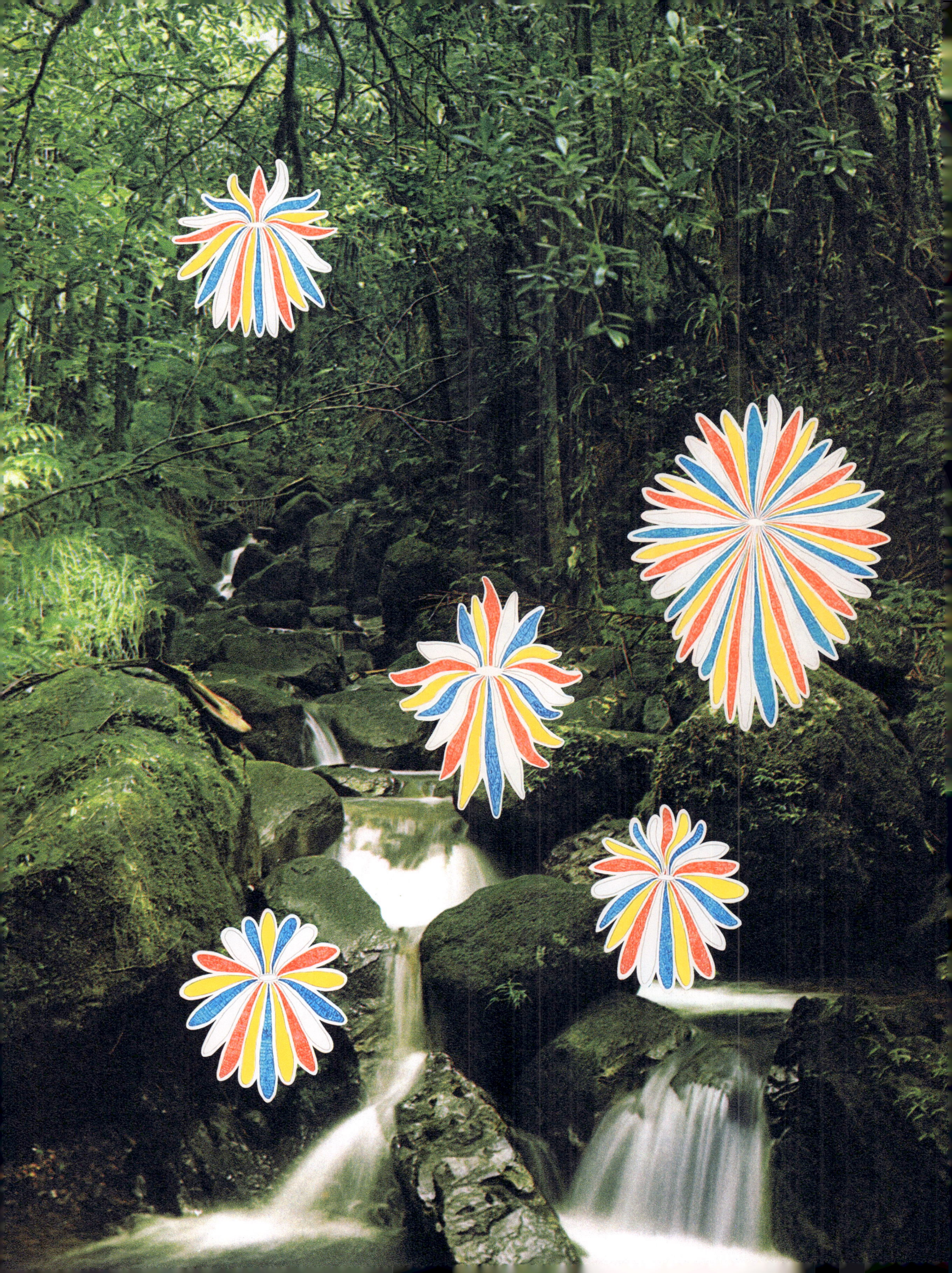

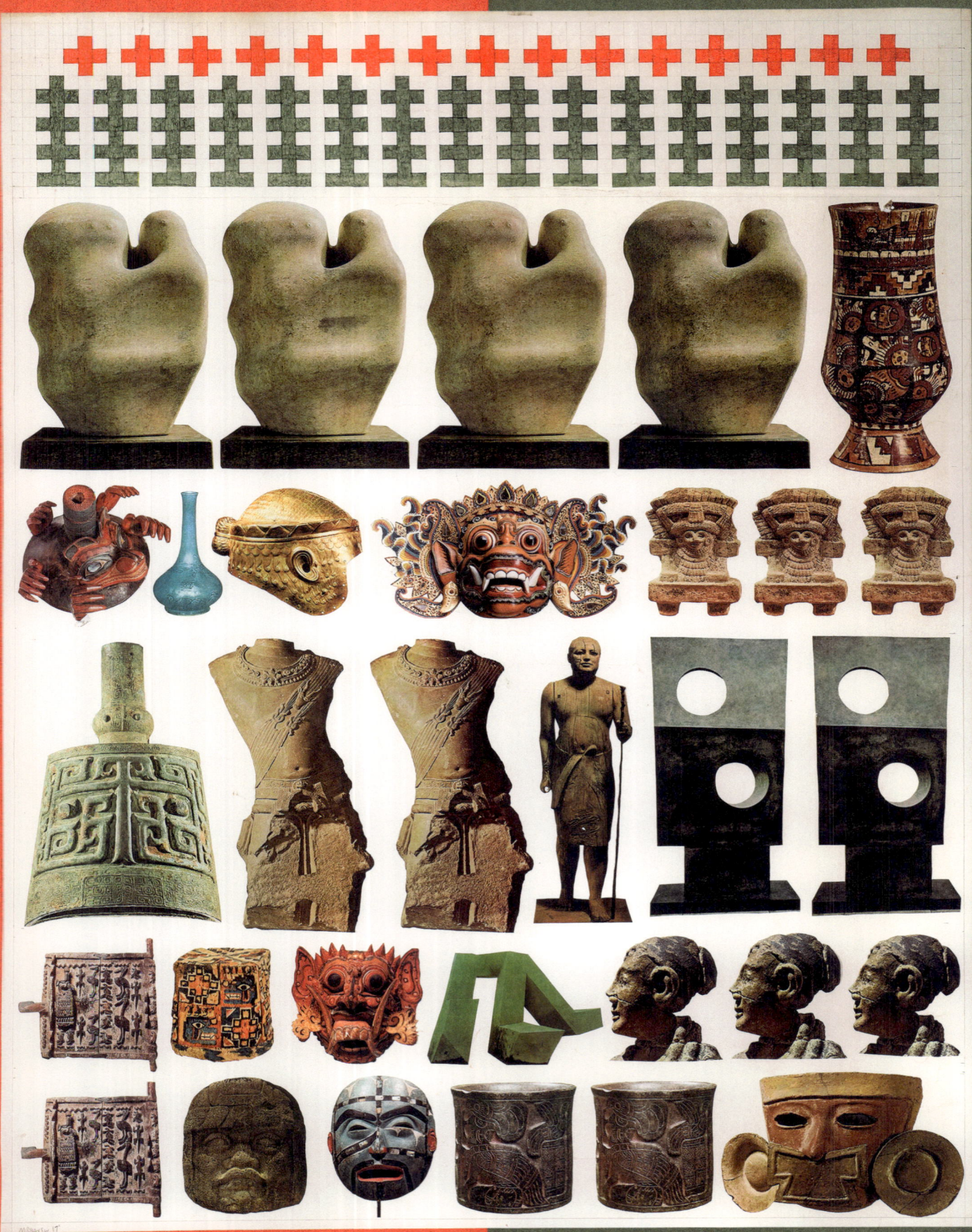

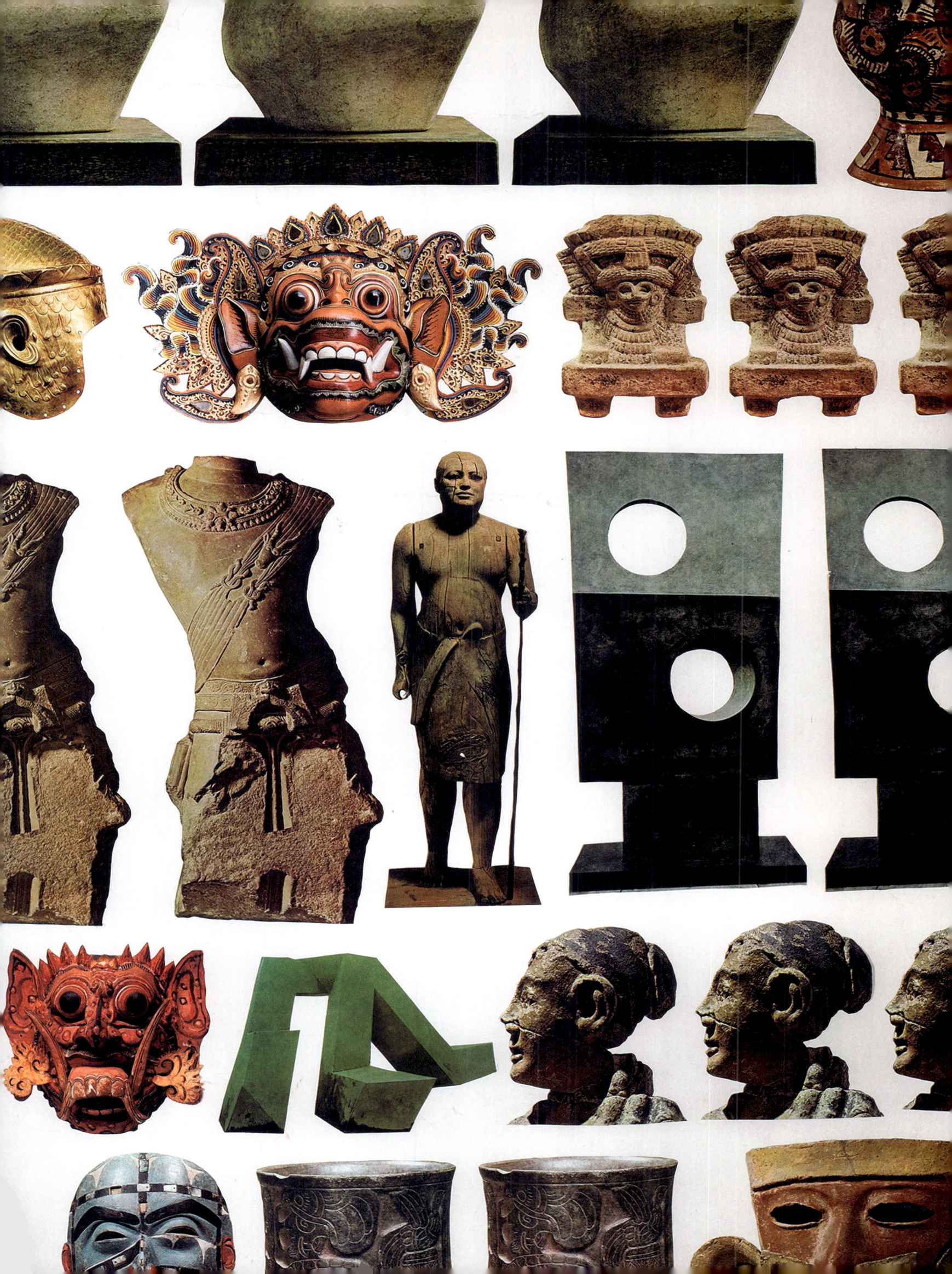

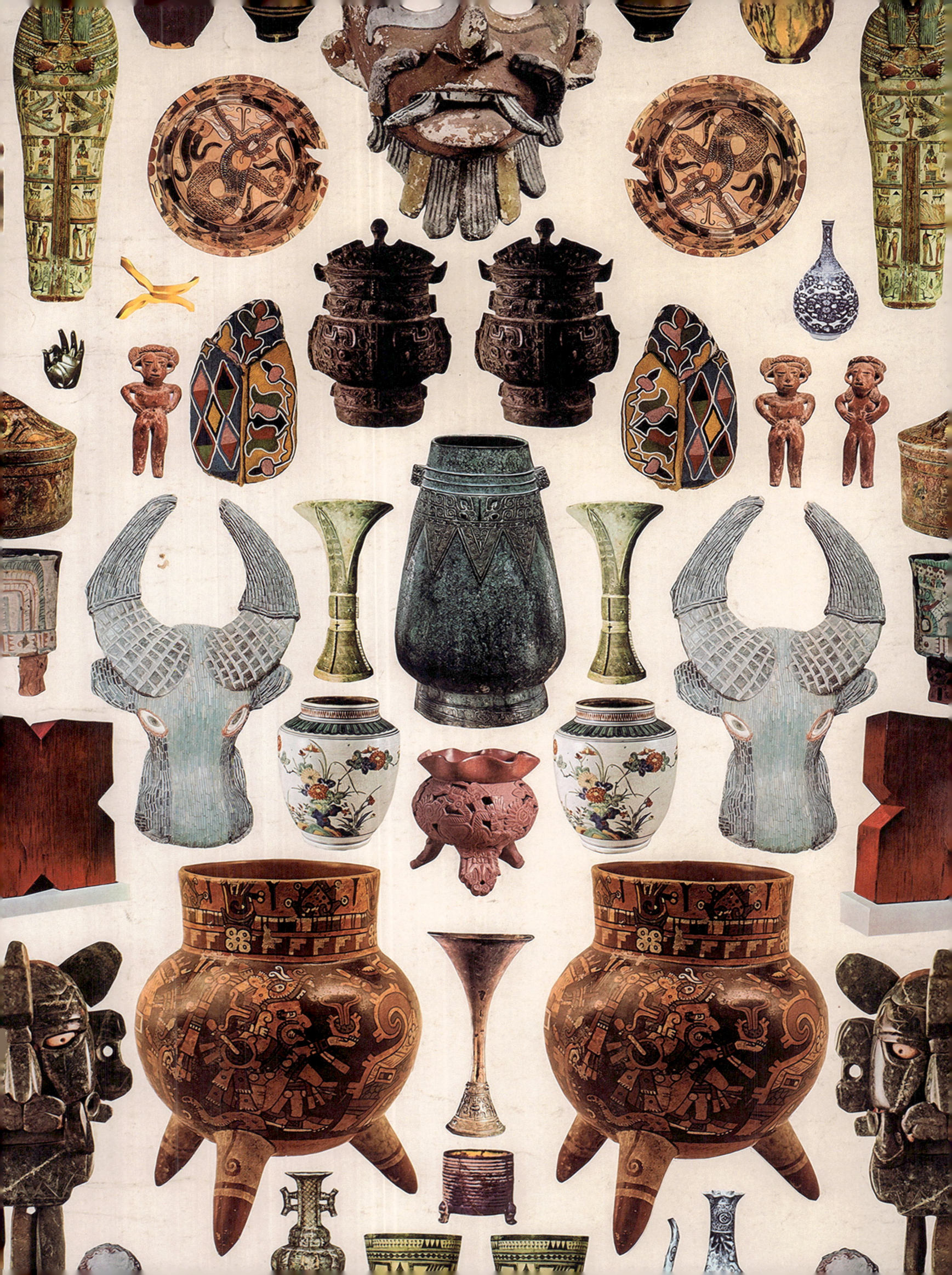

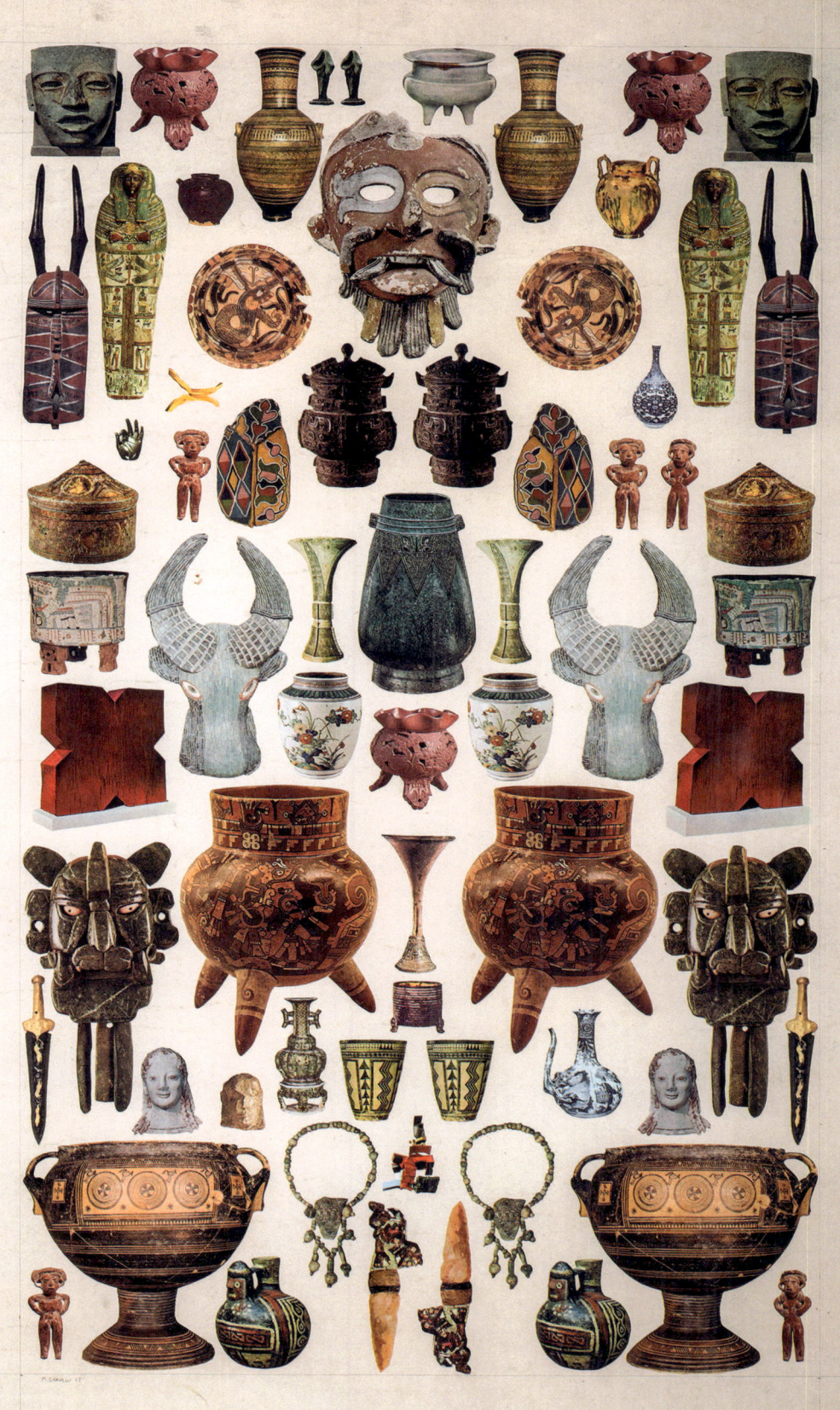

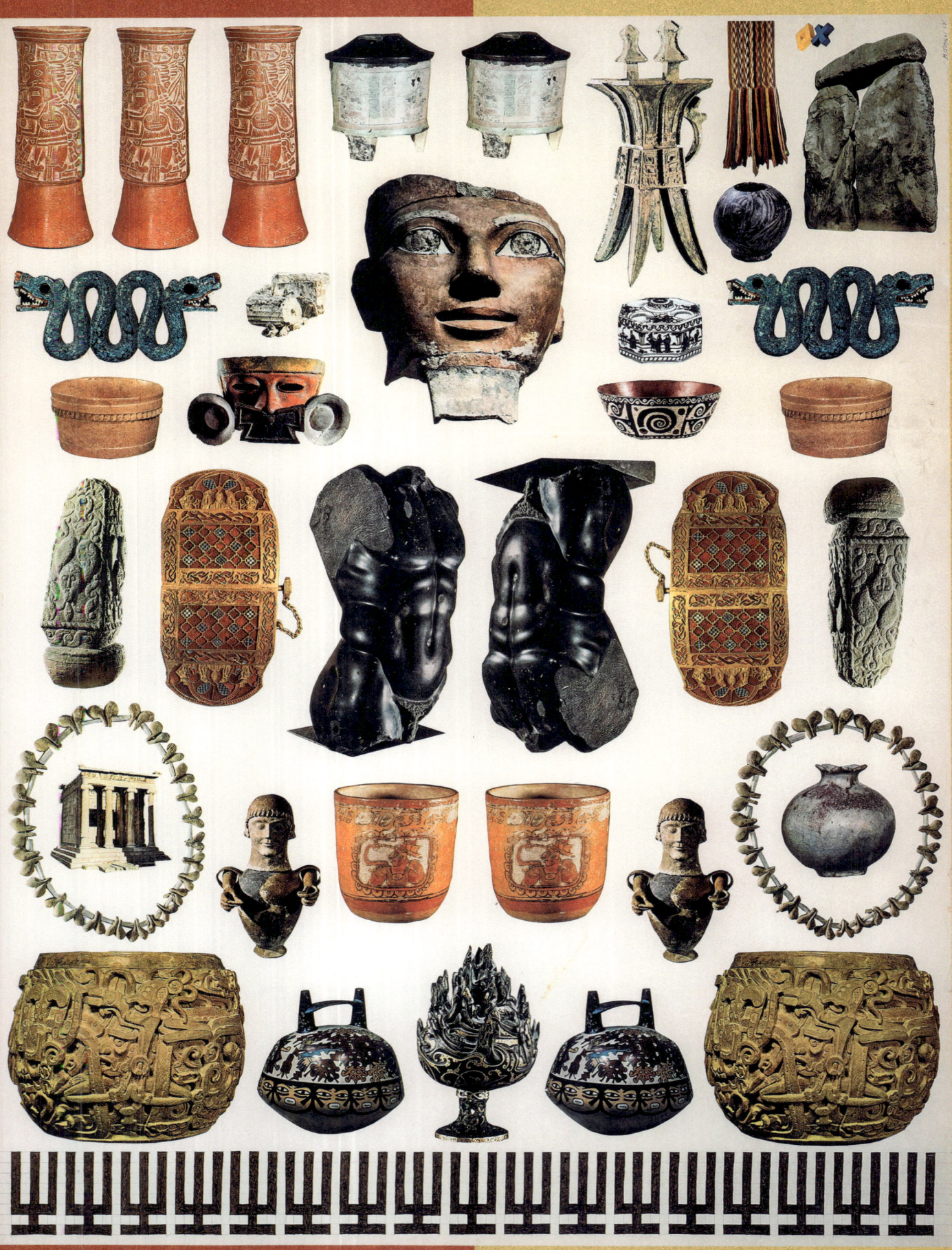

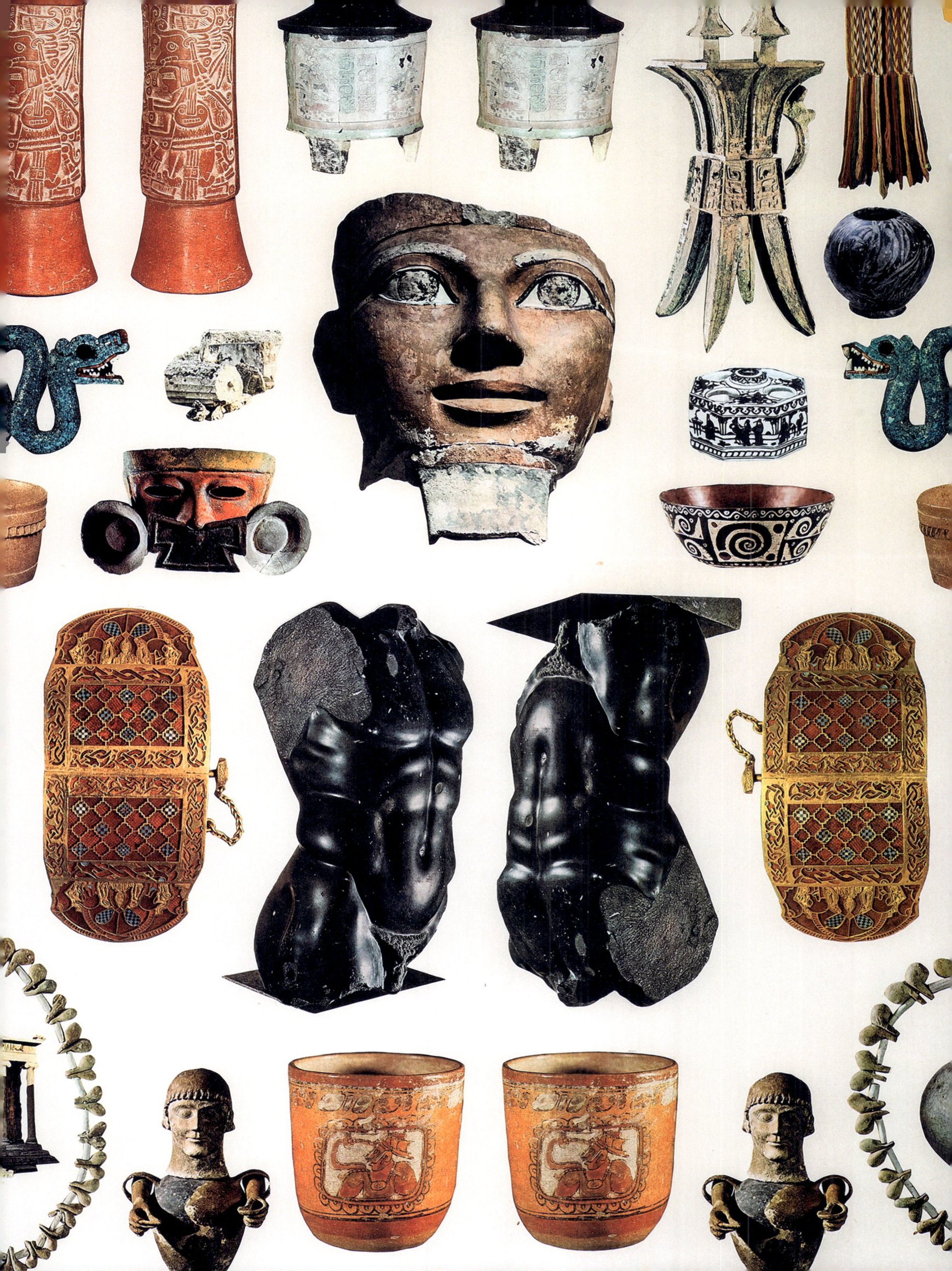

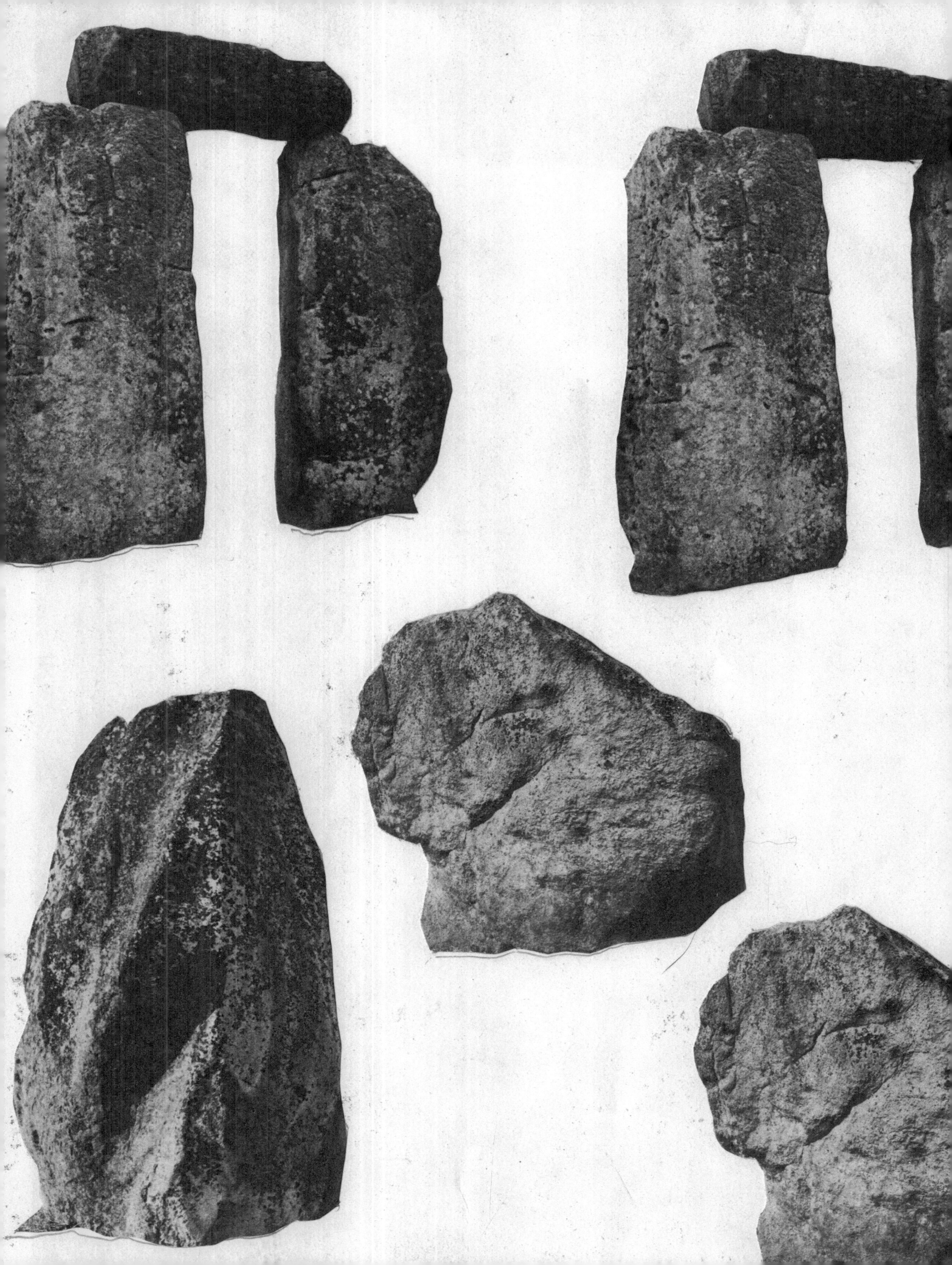

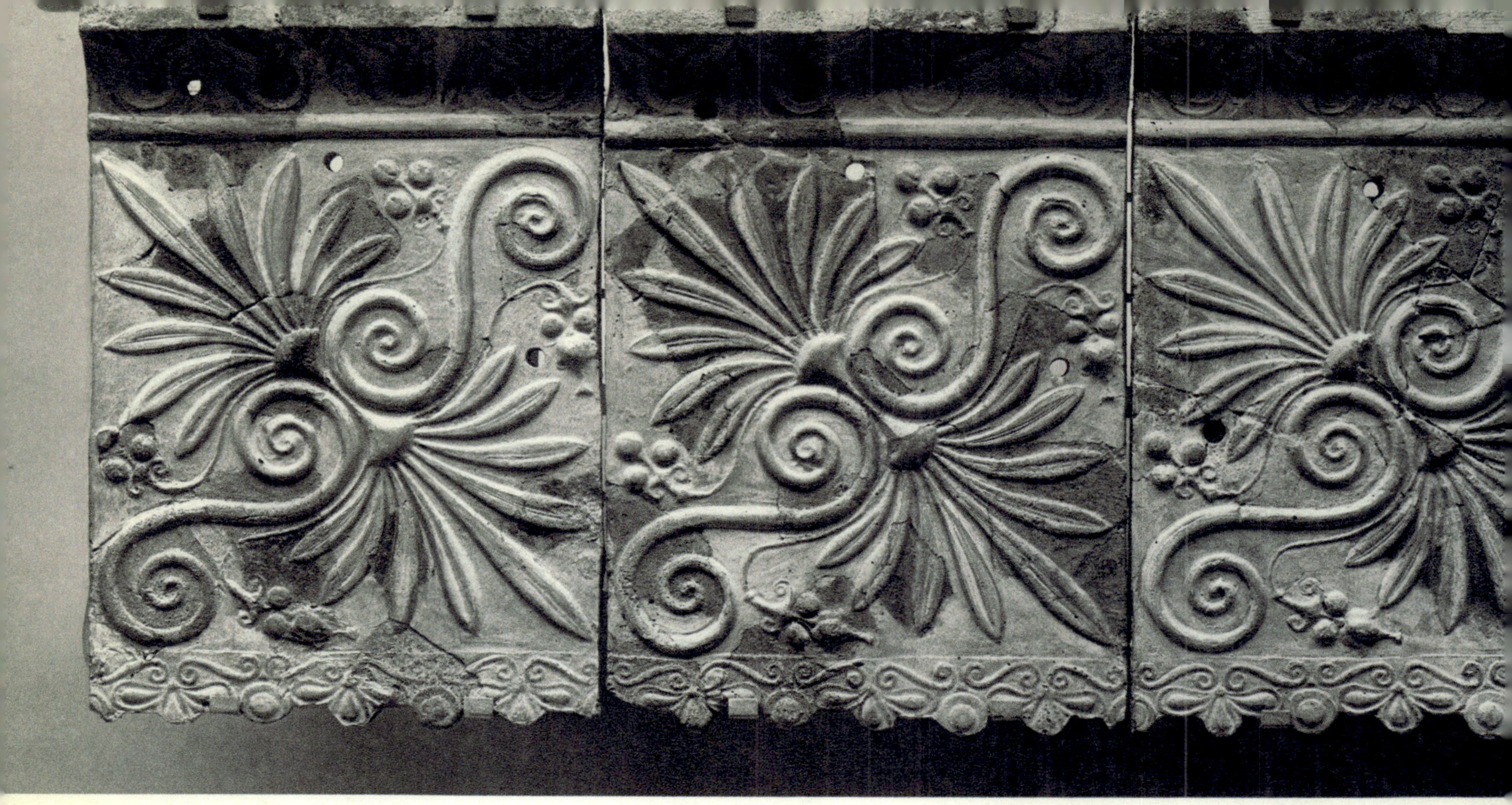

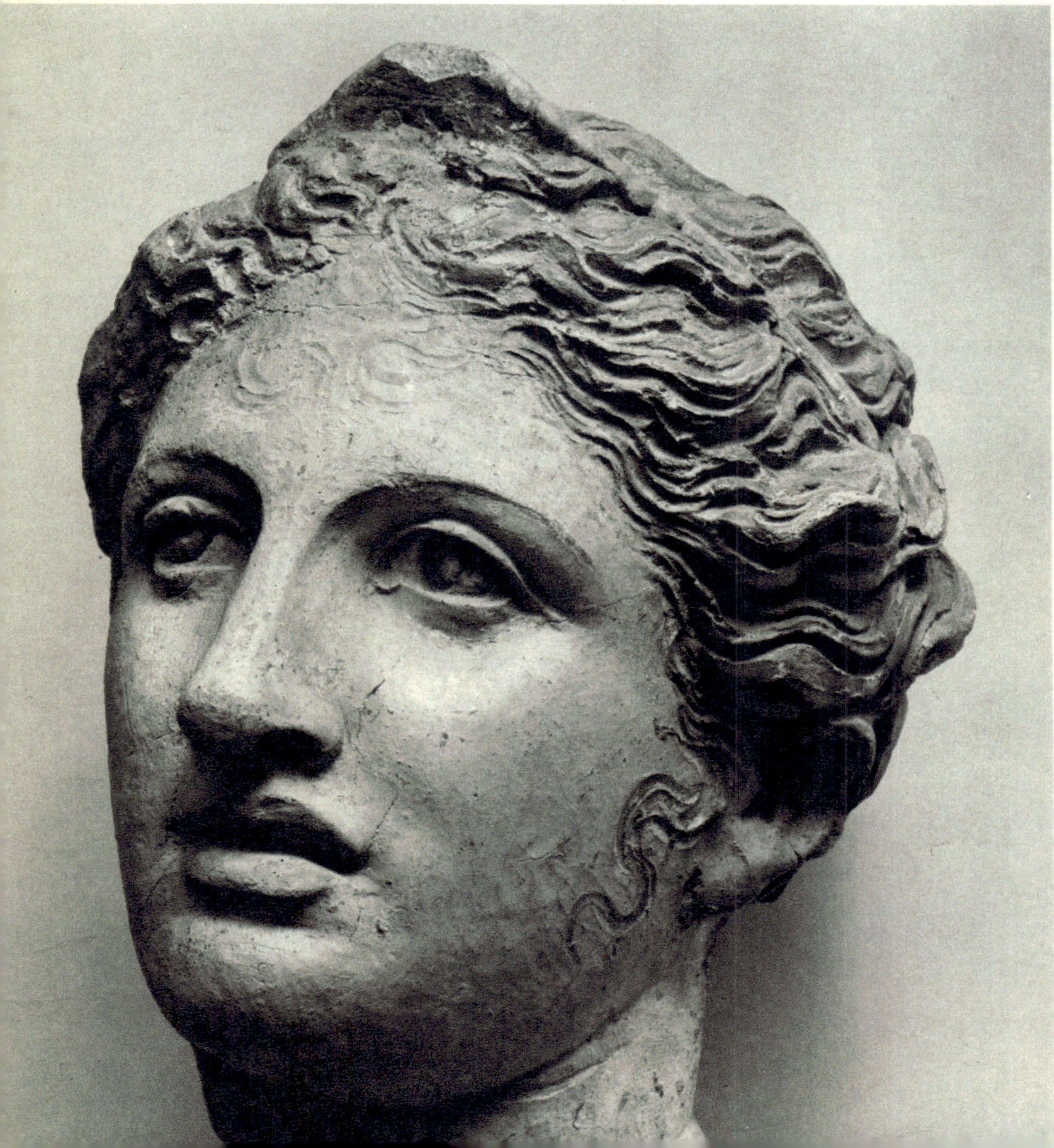

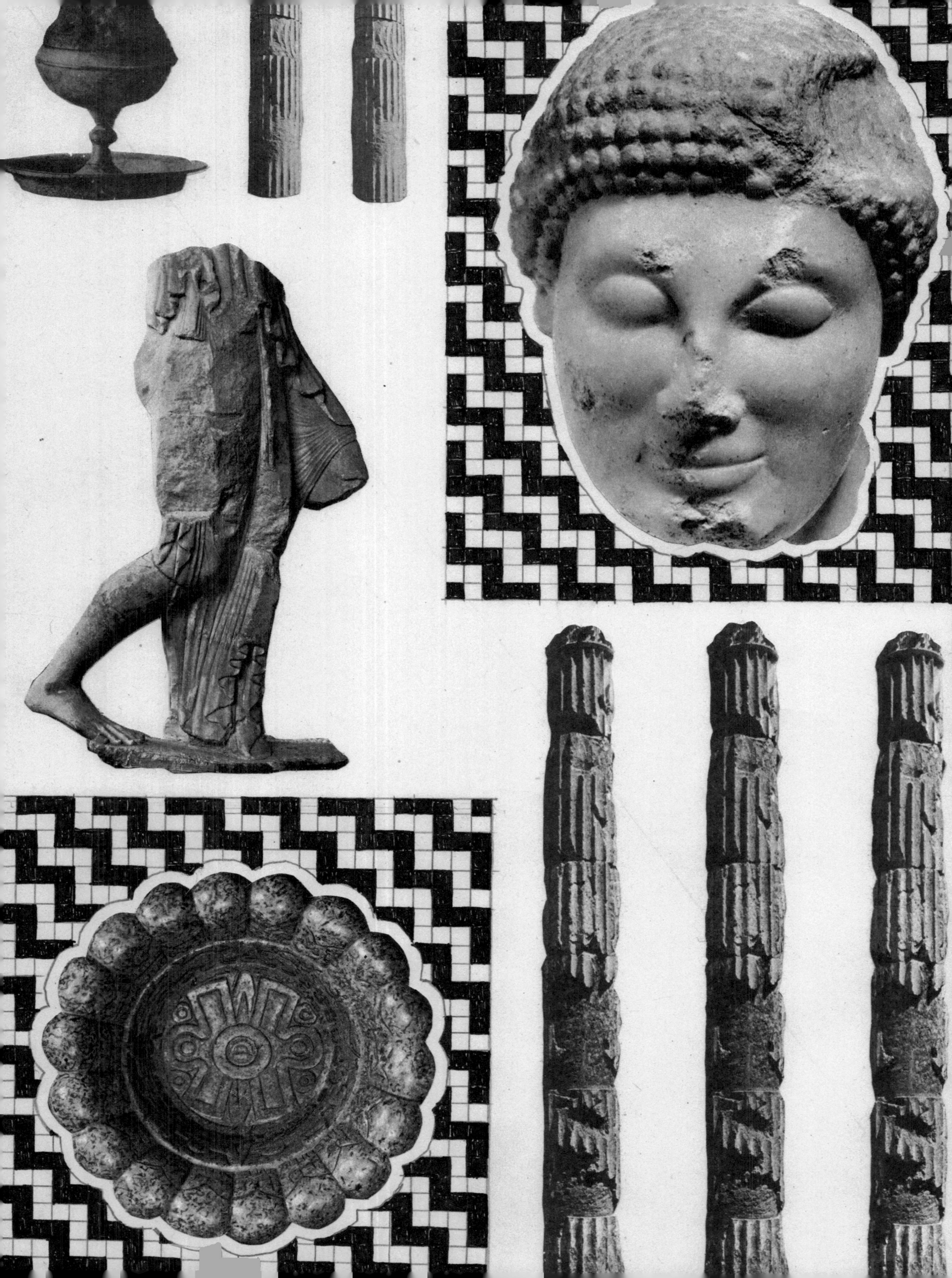

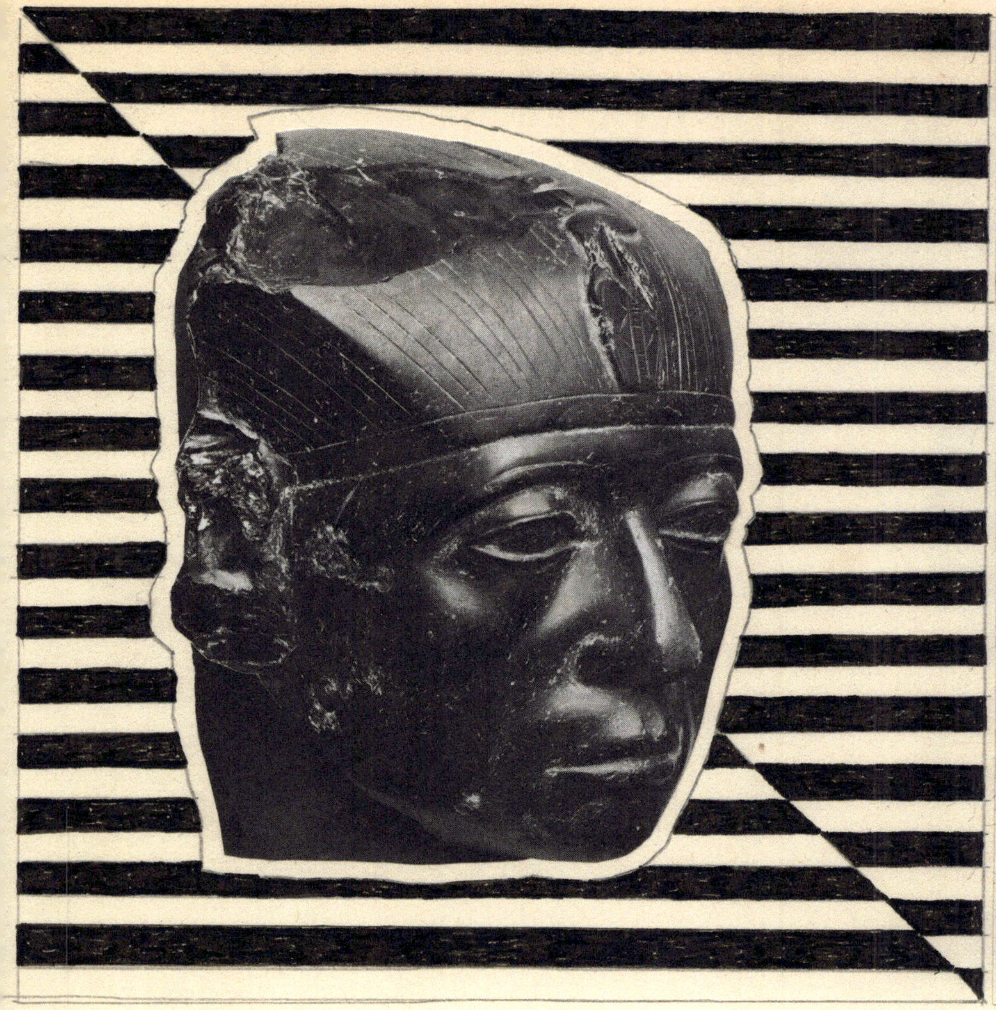

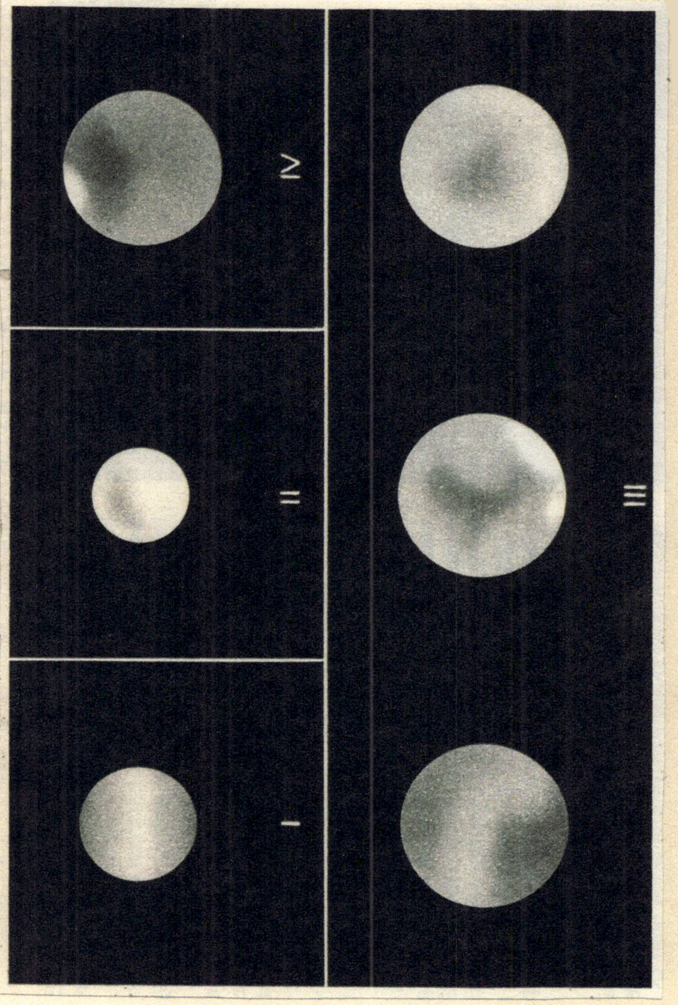
IV
II
III
I

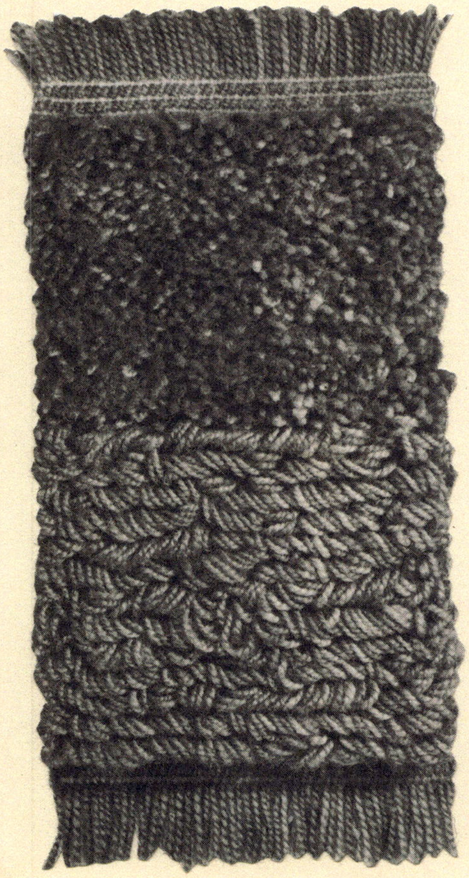

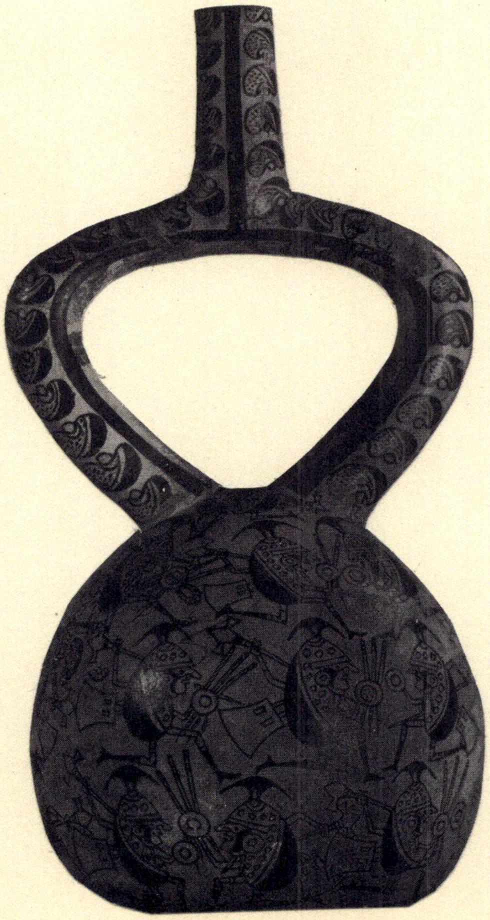

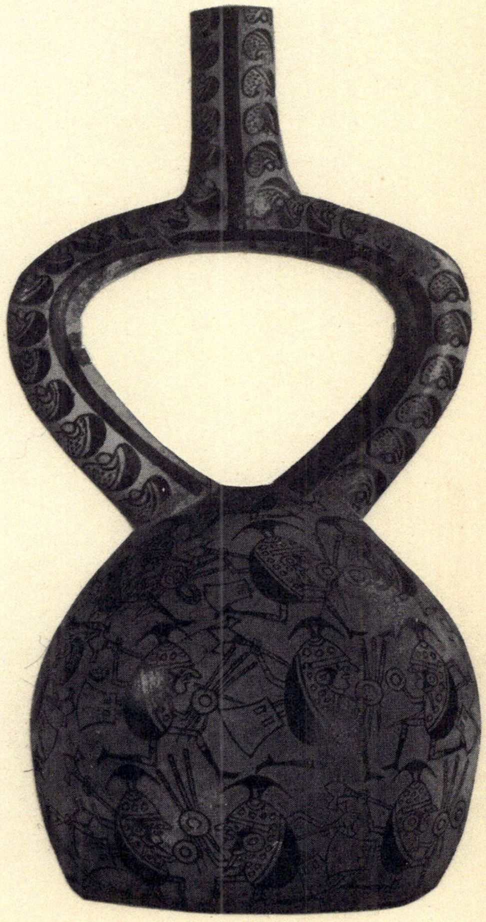

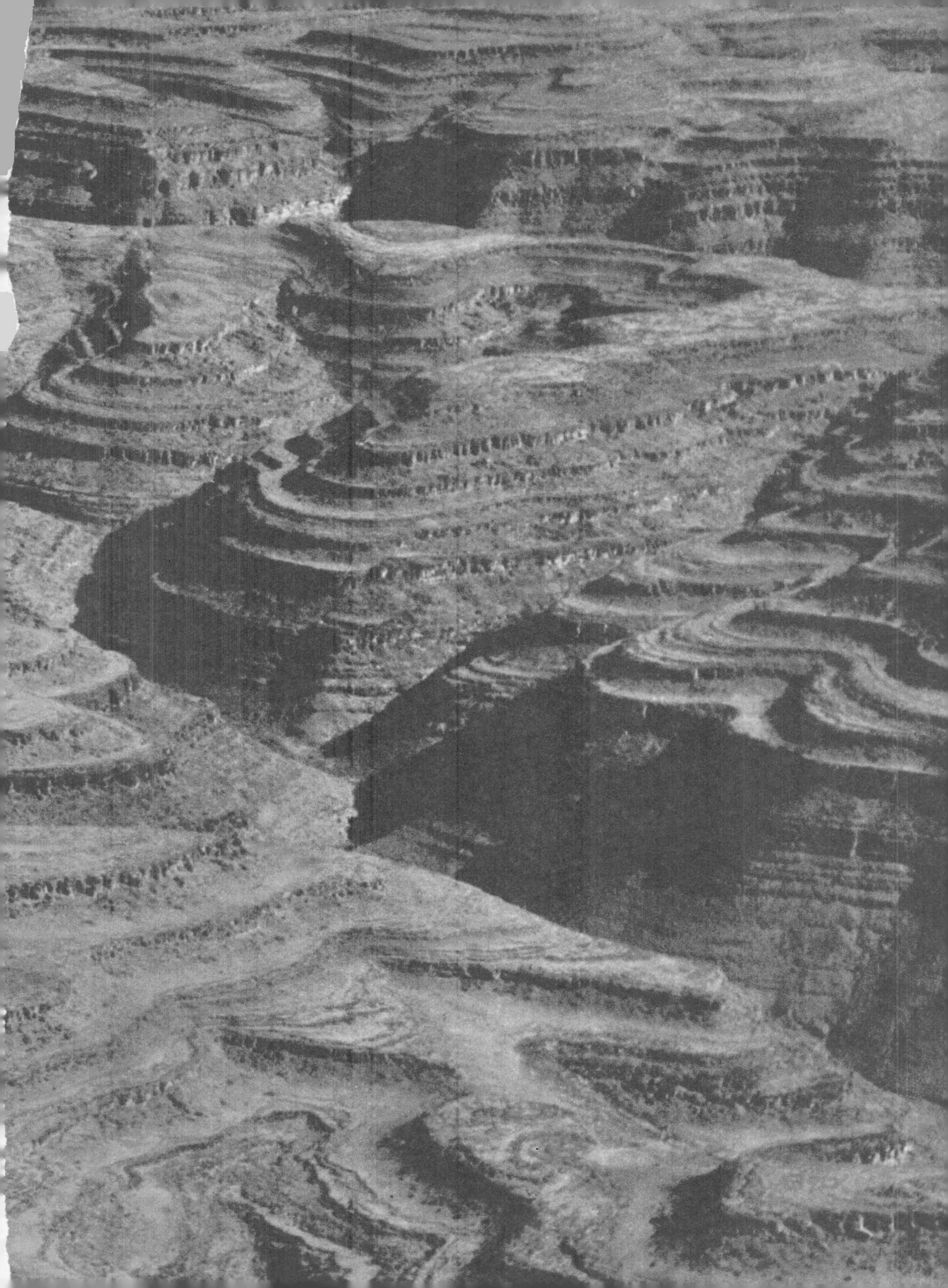

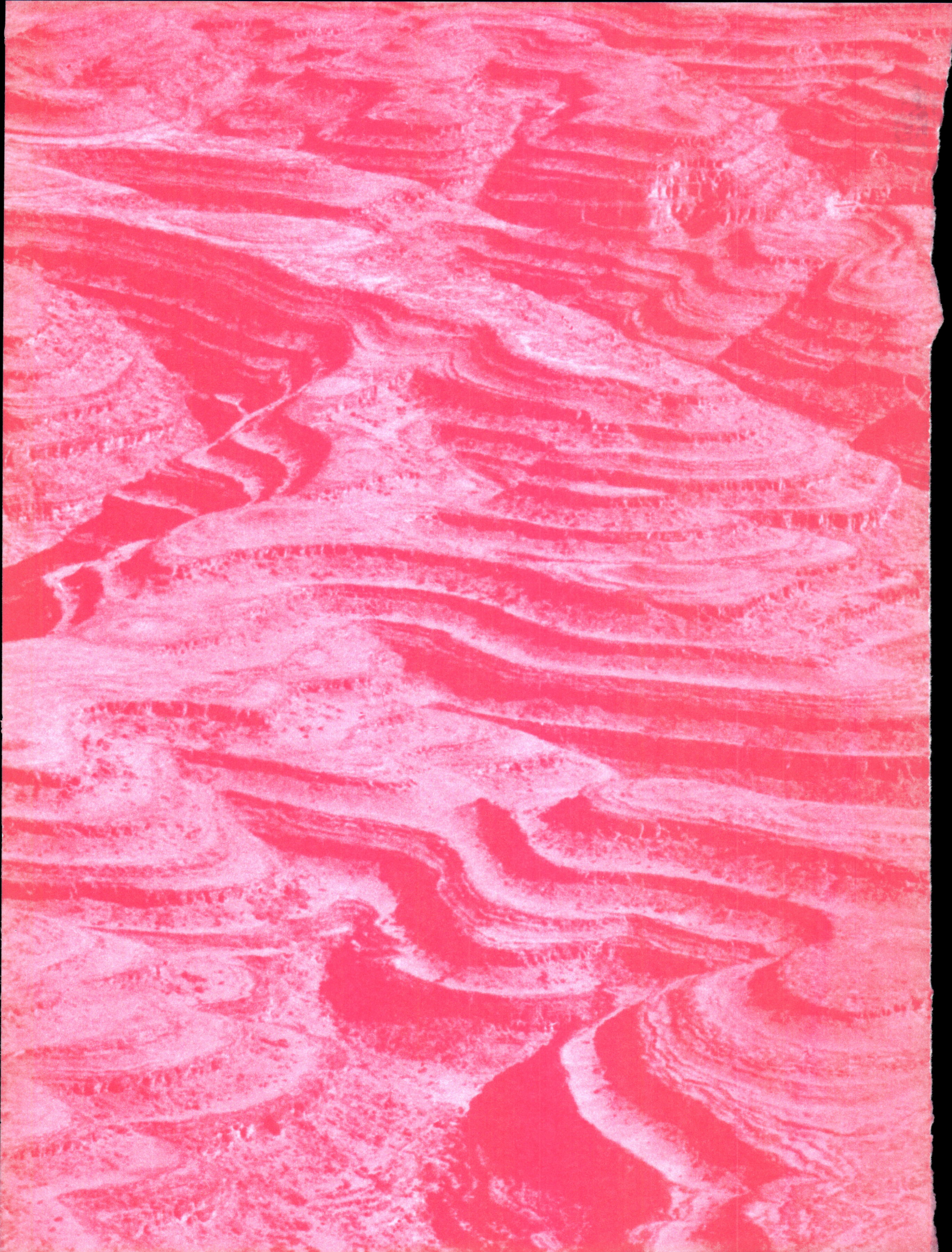

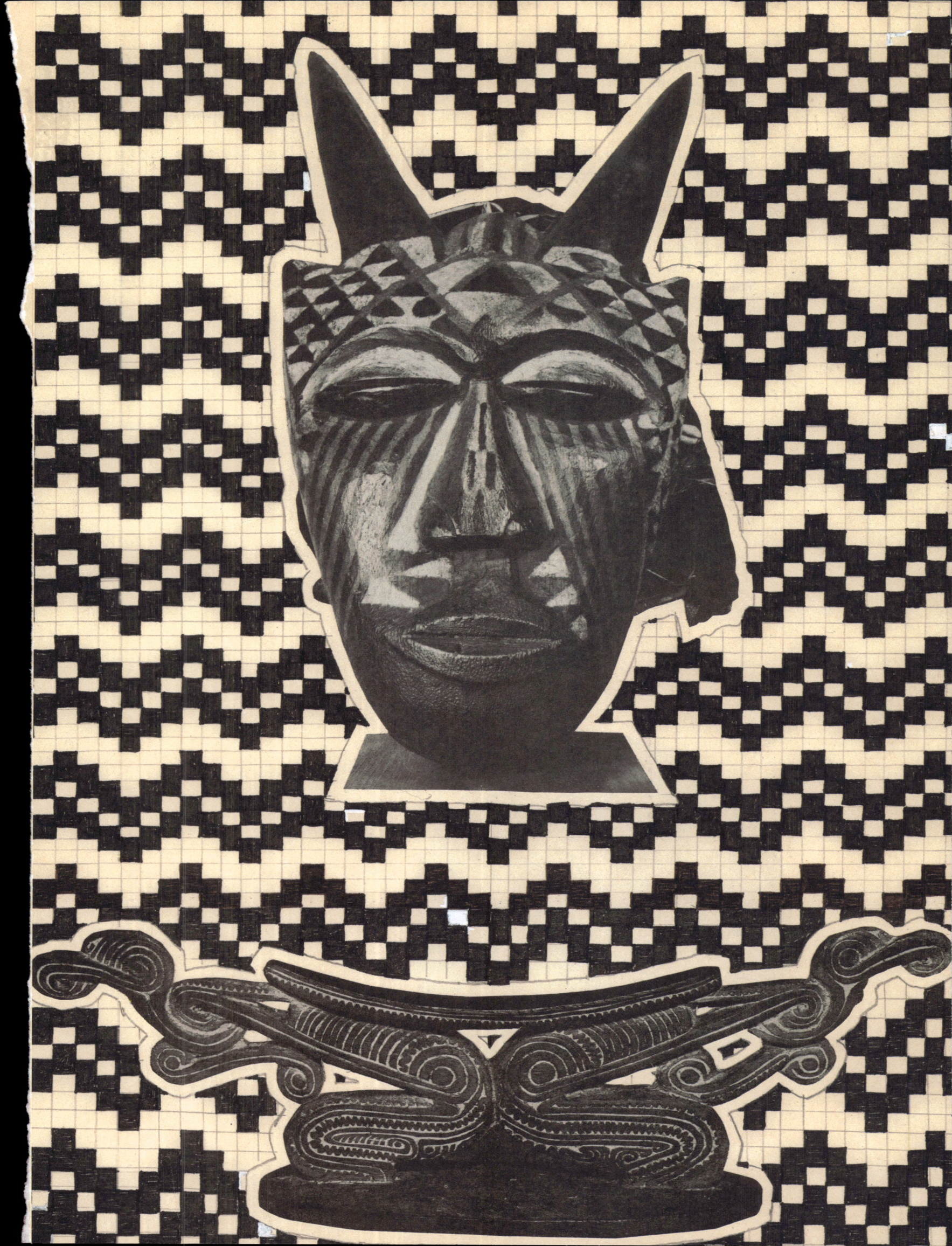

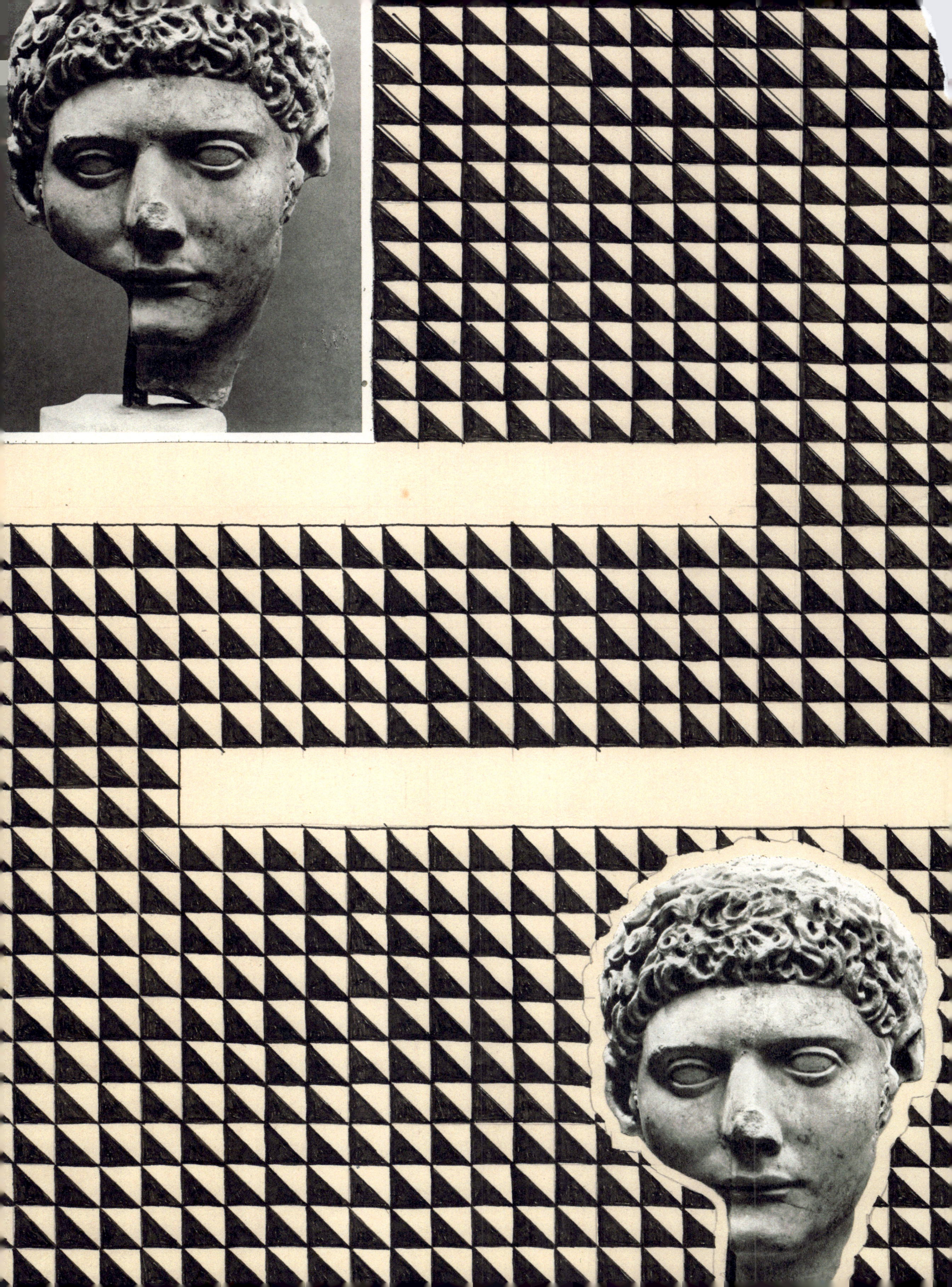

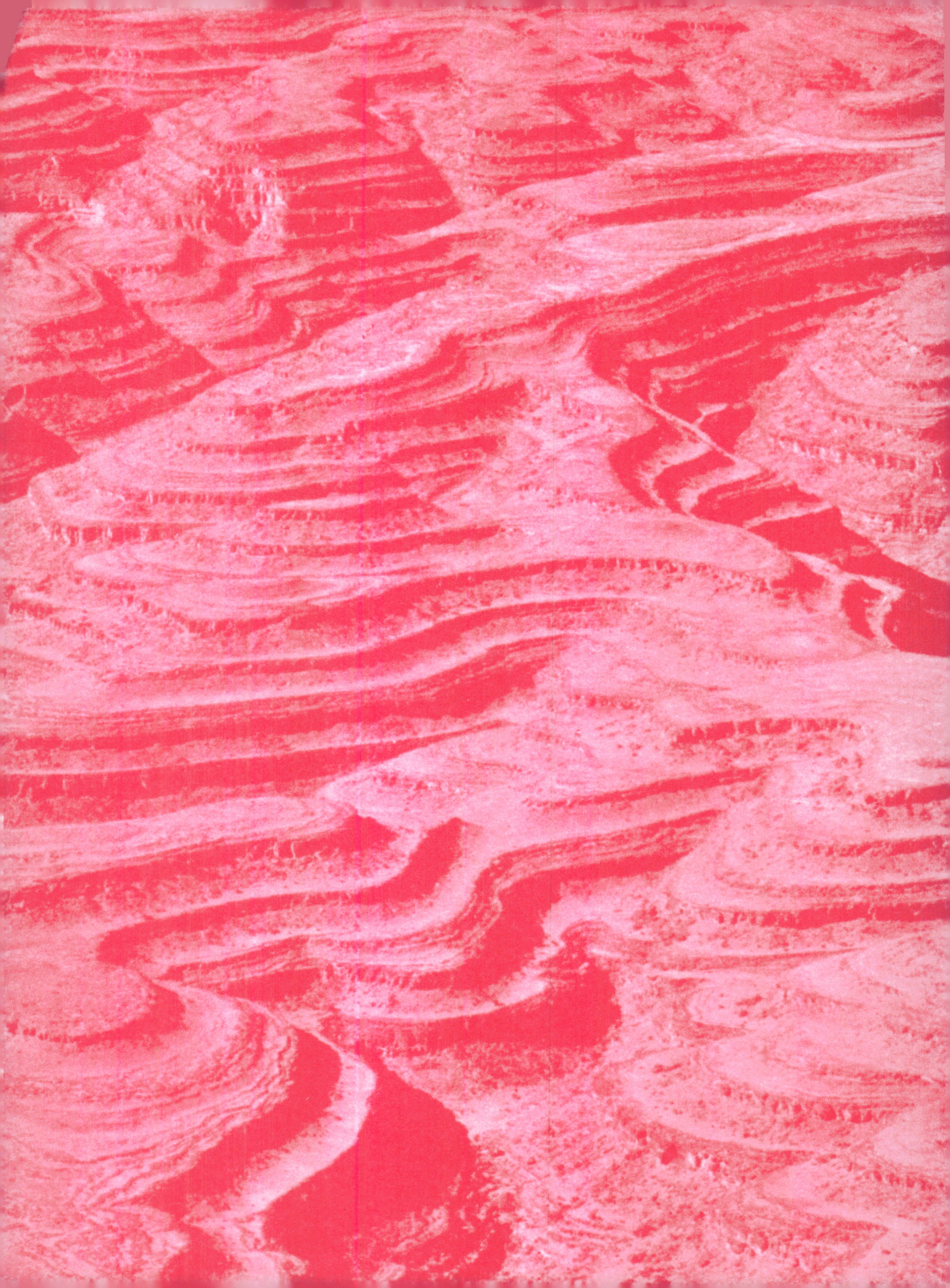

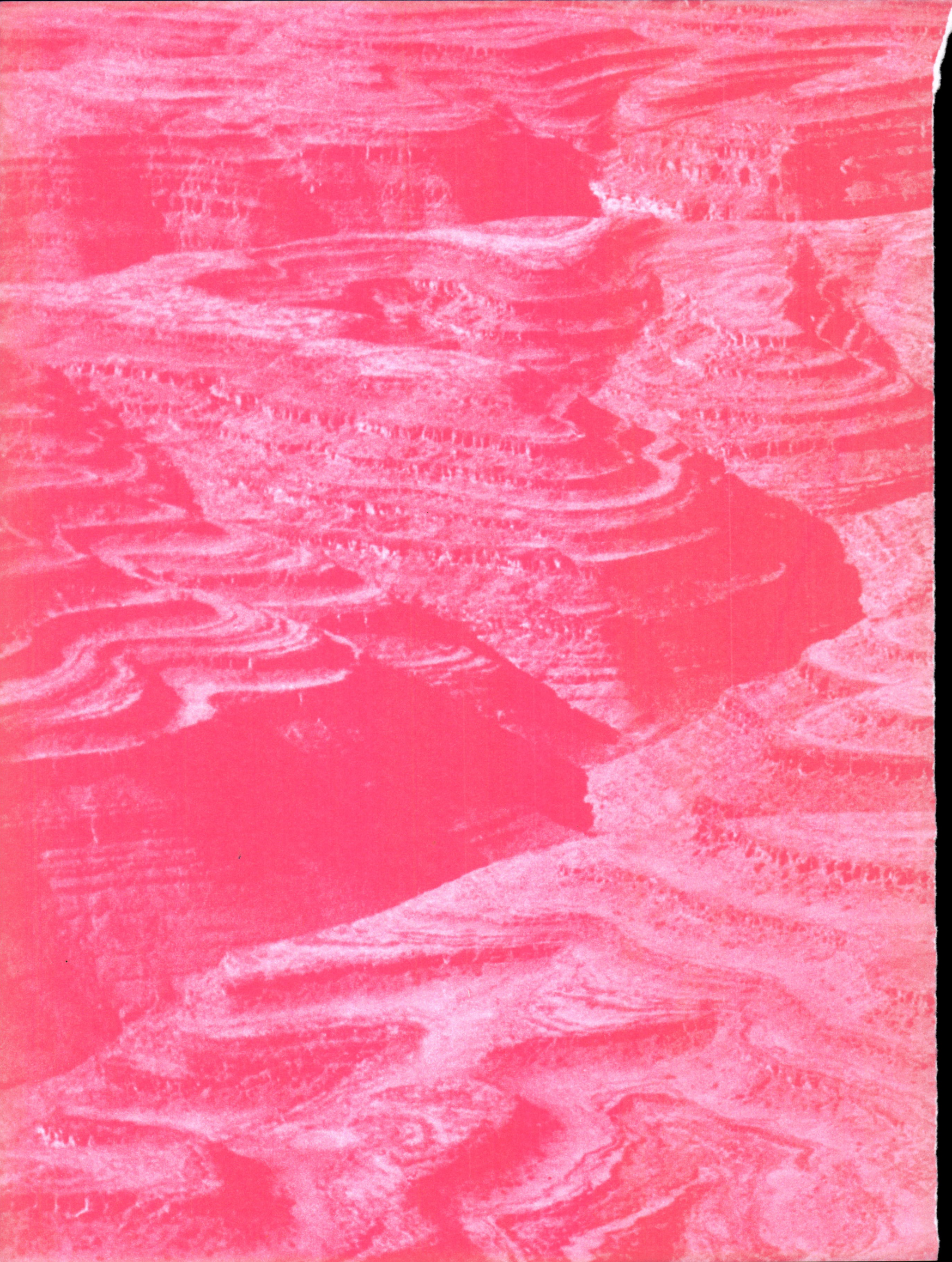

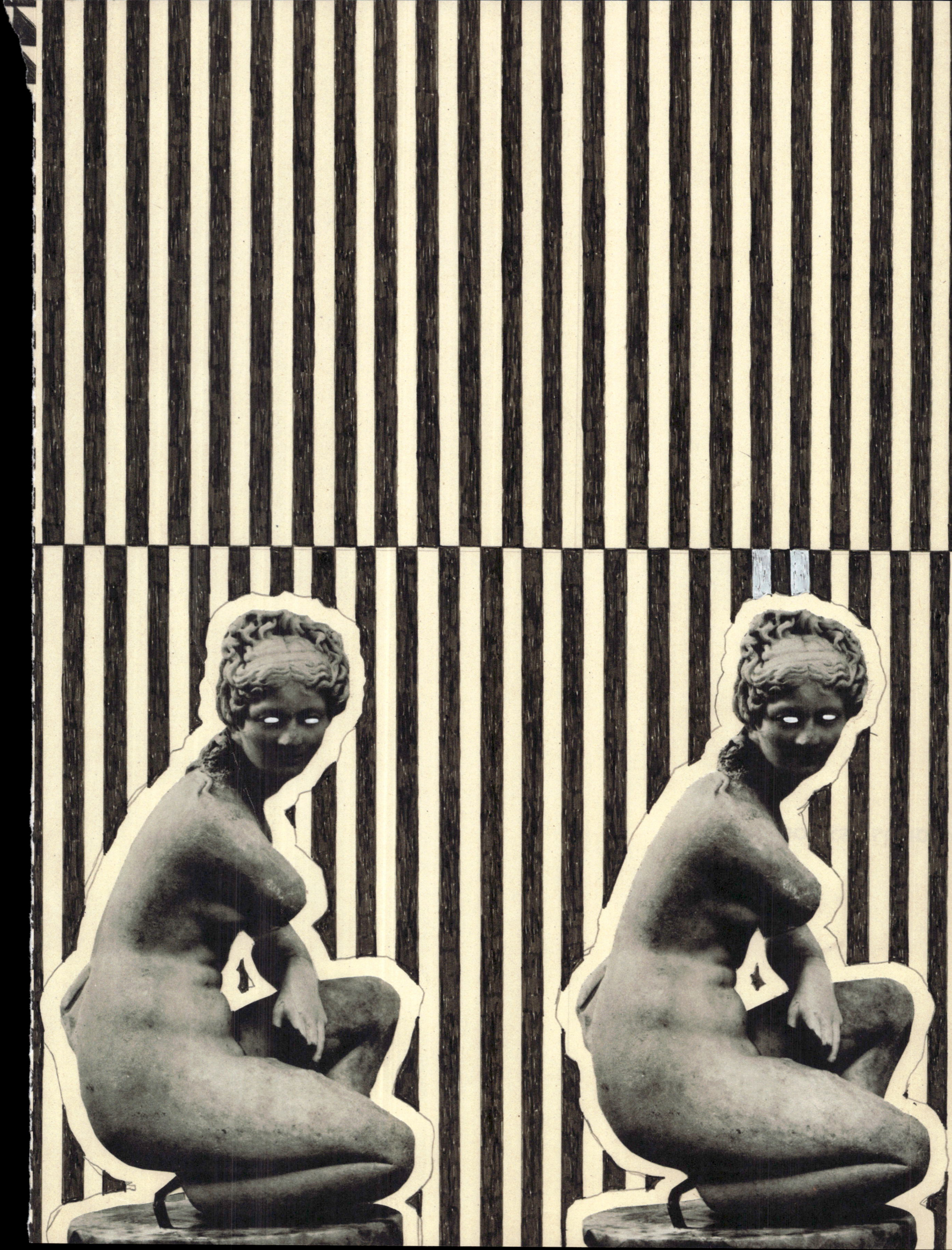

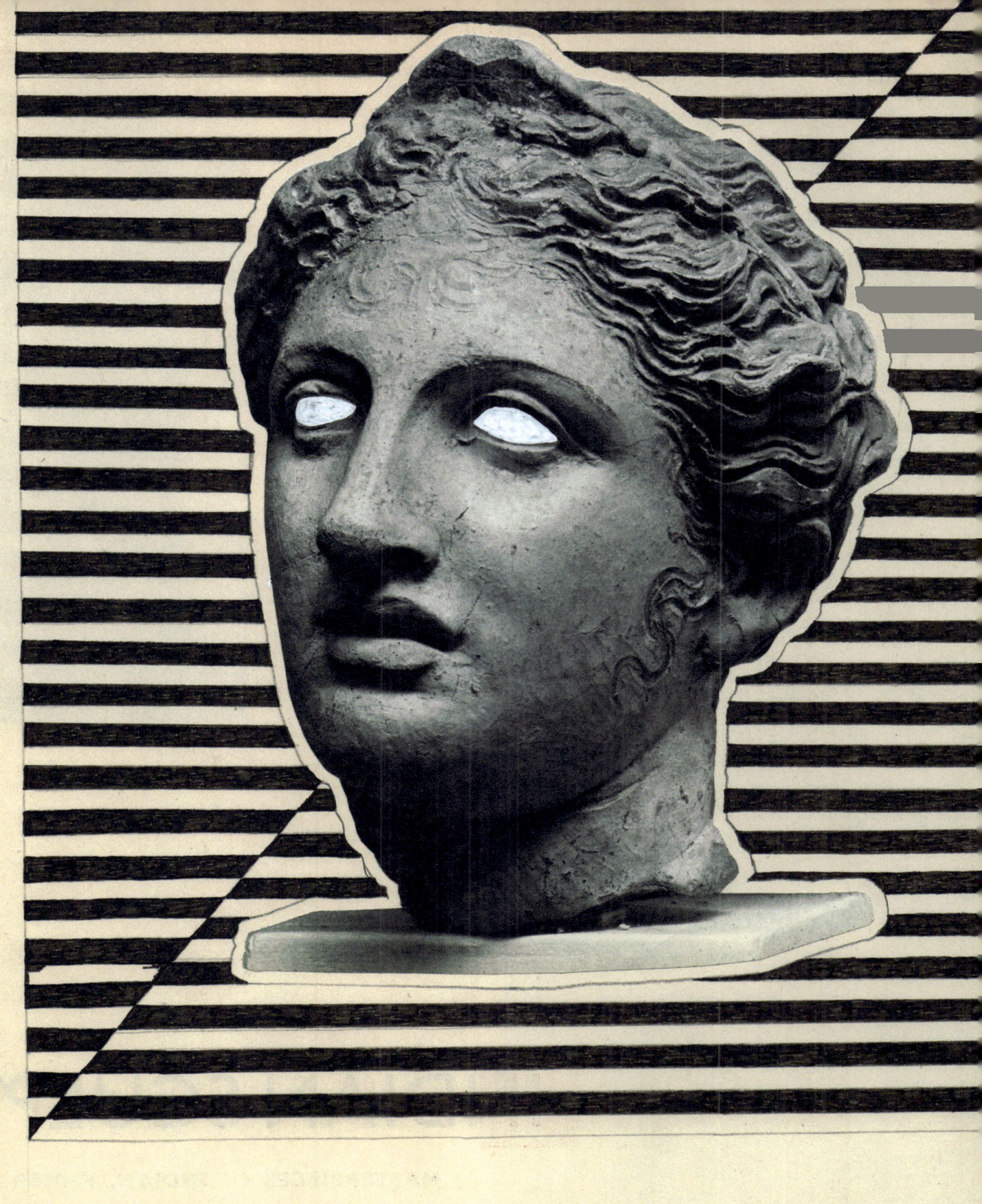

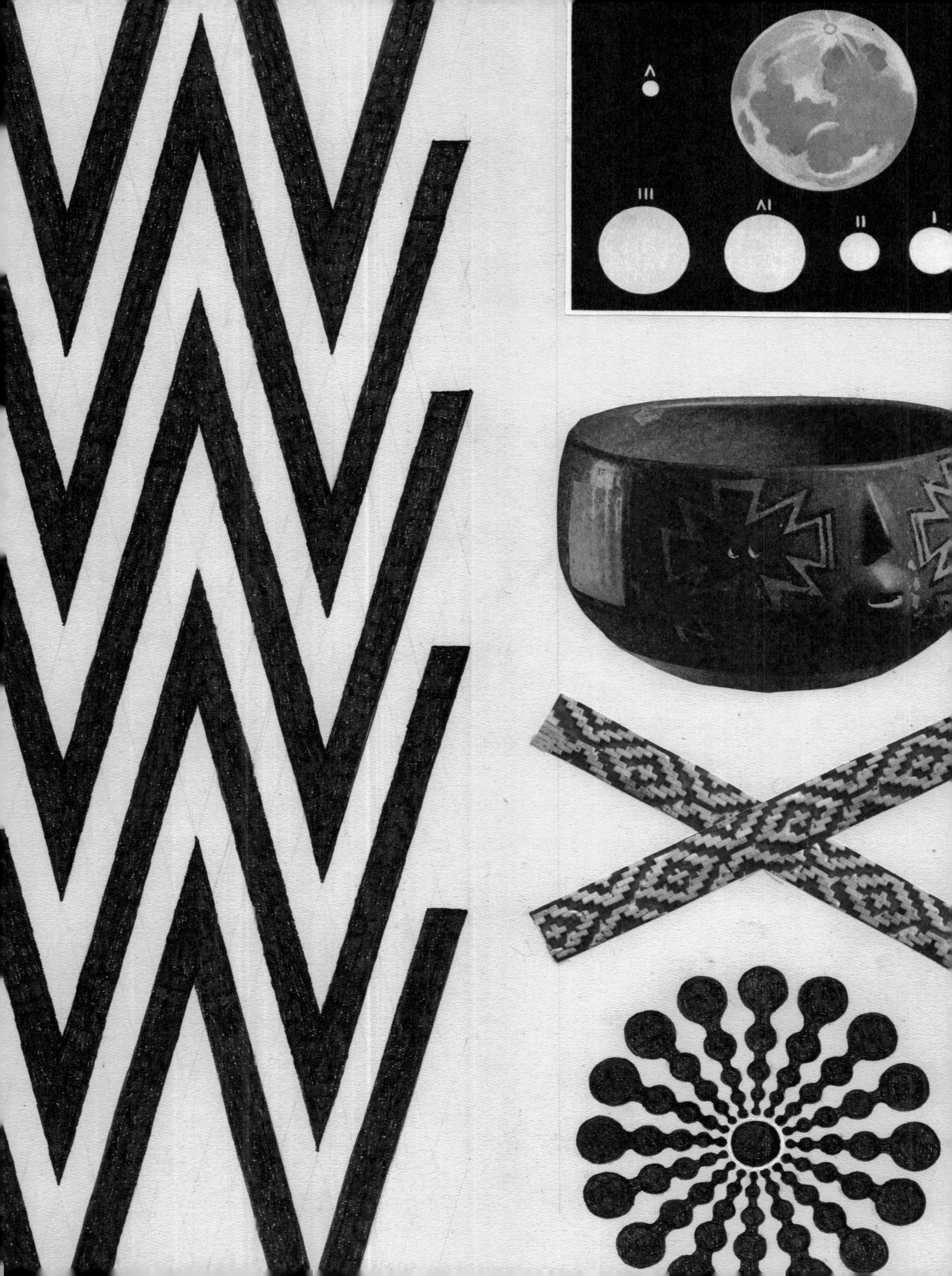

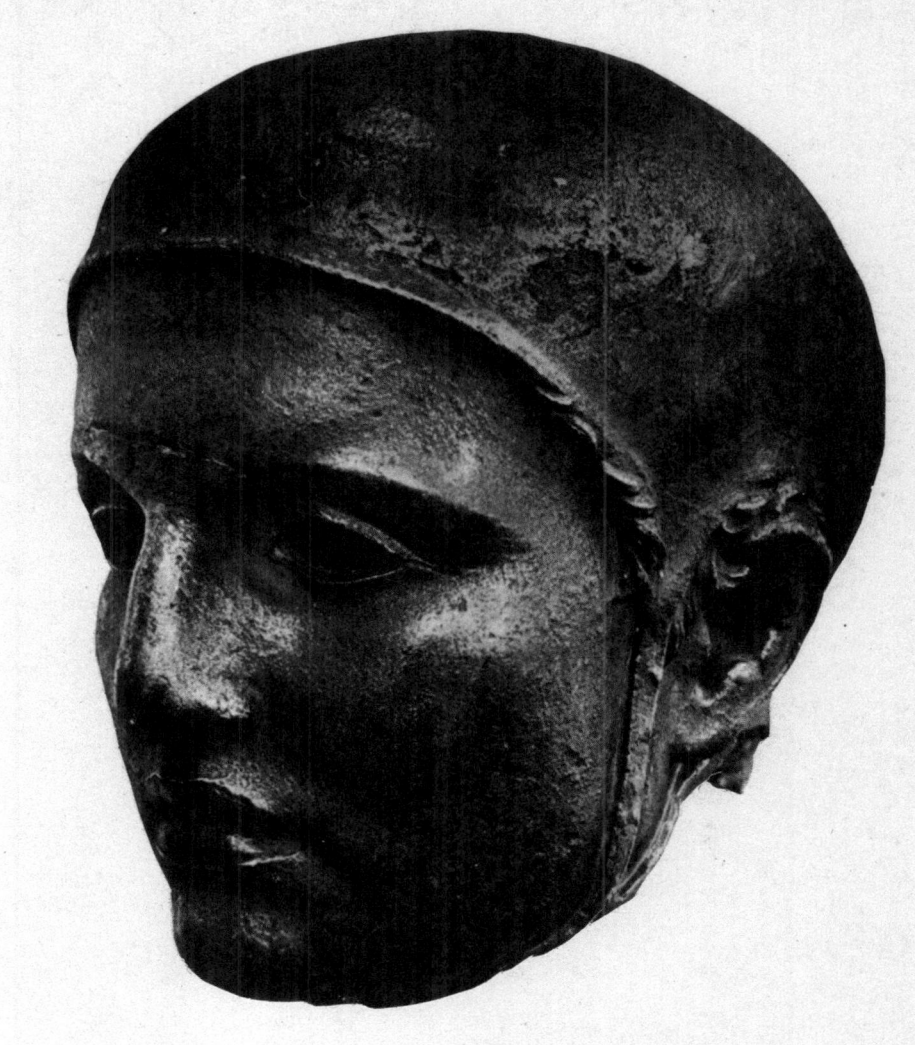

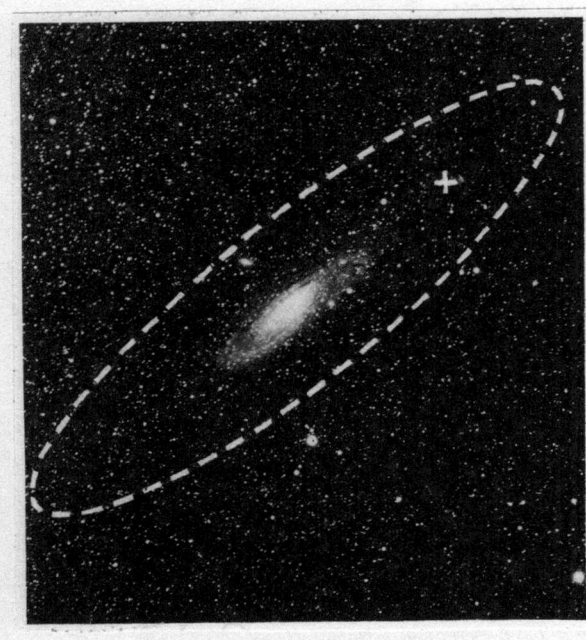

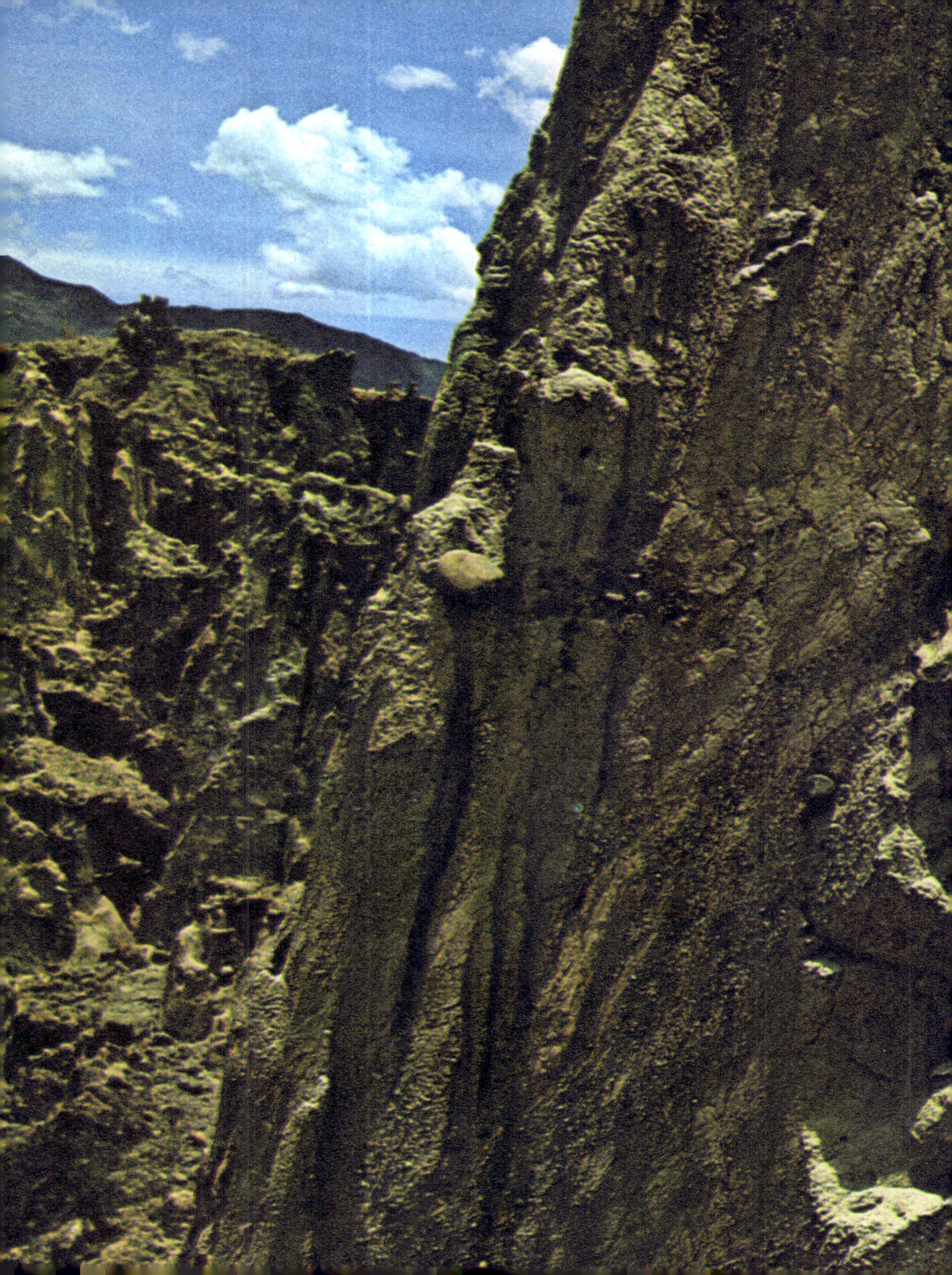

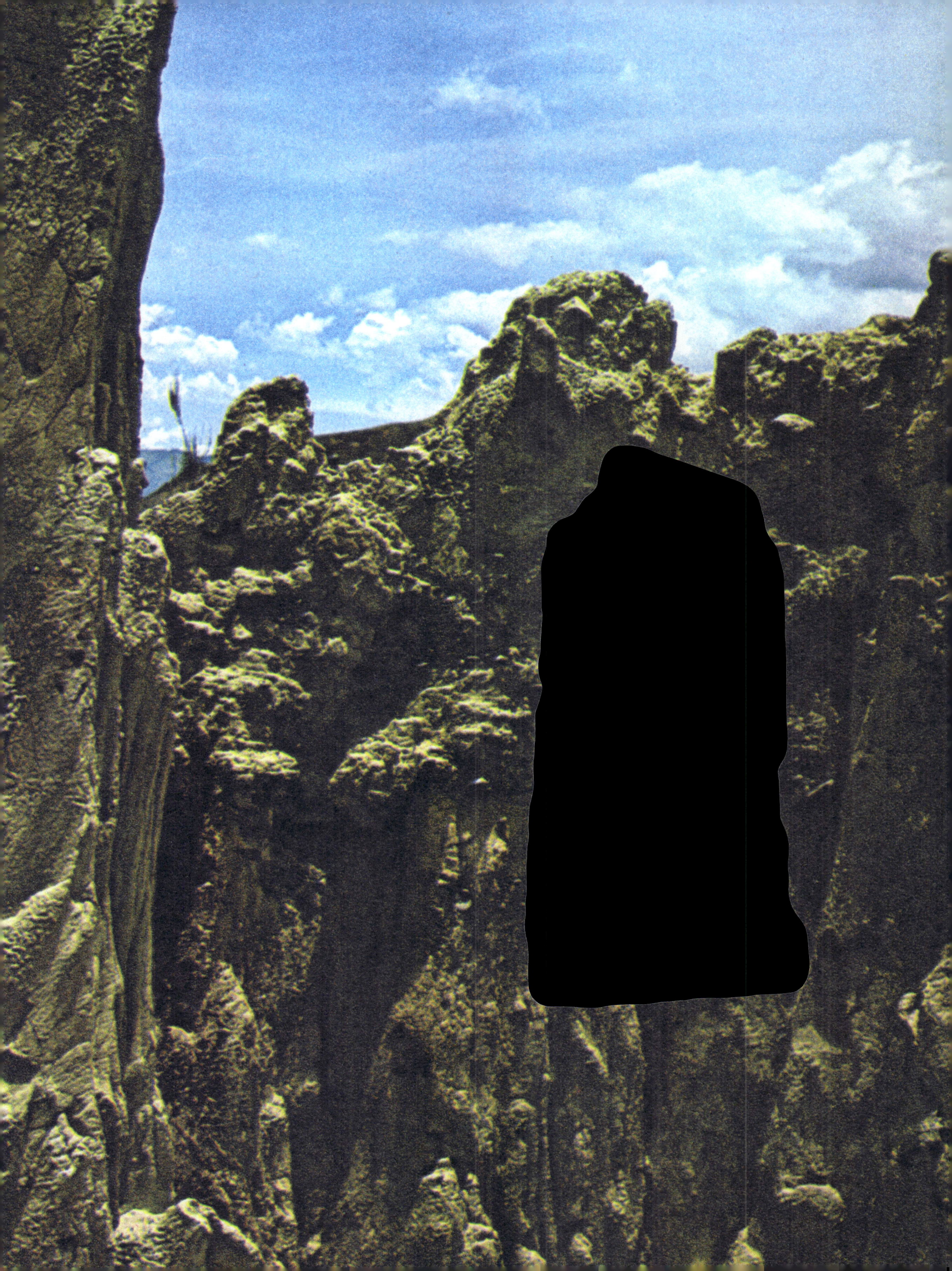

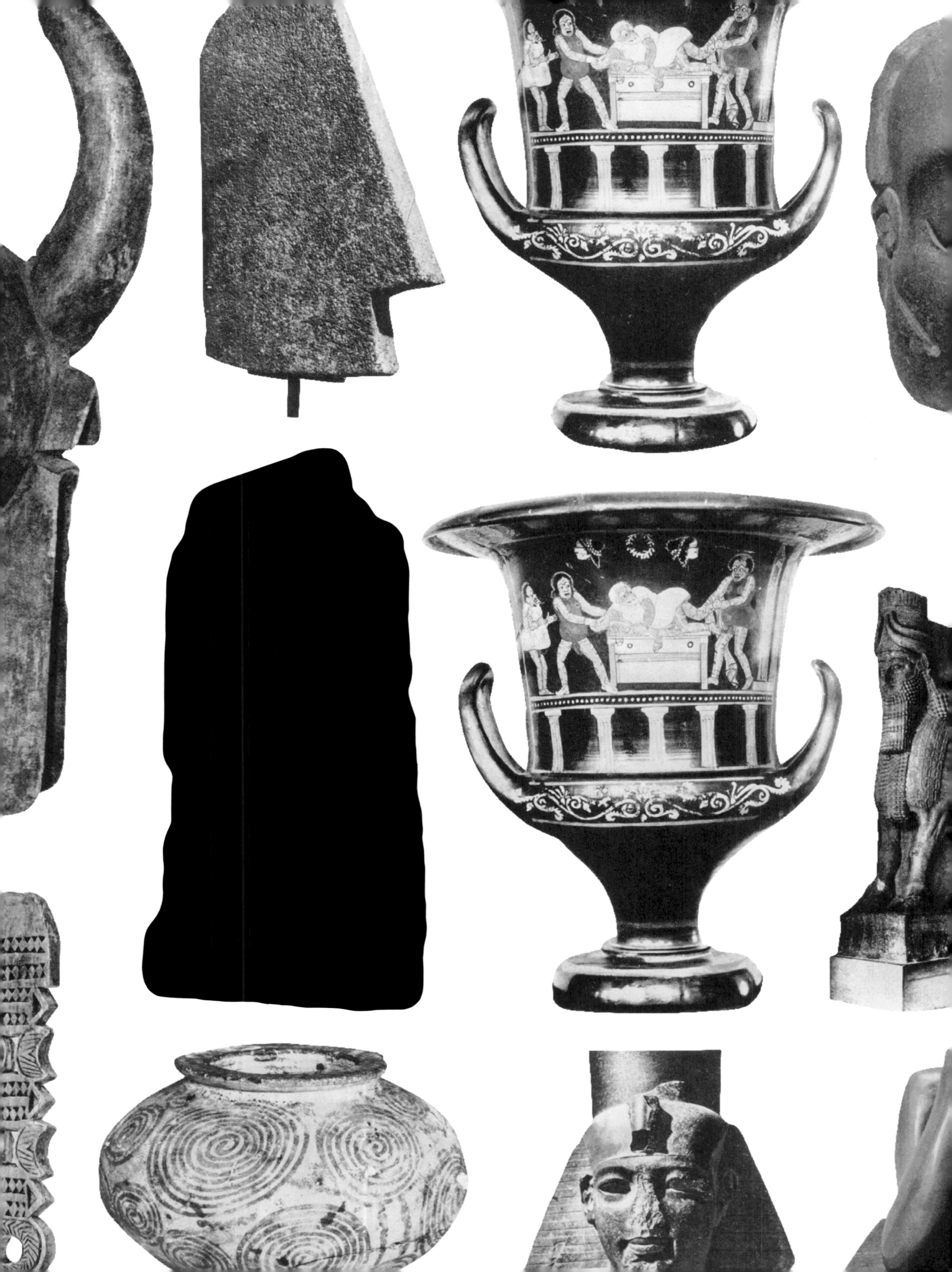

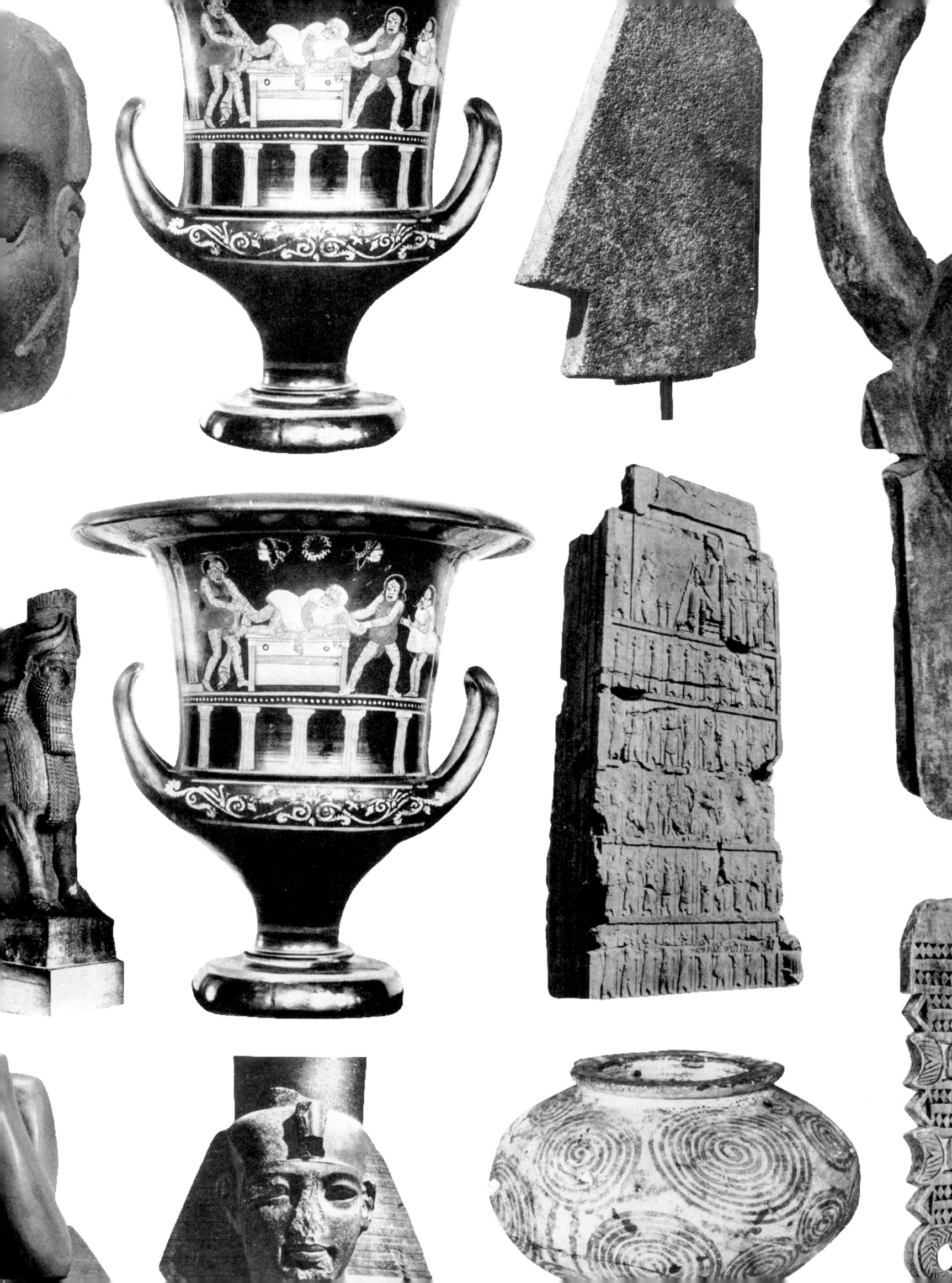

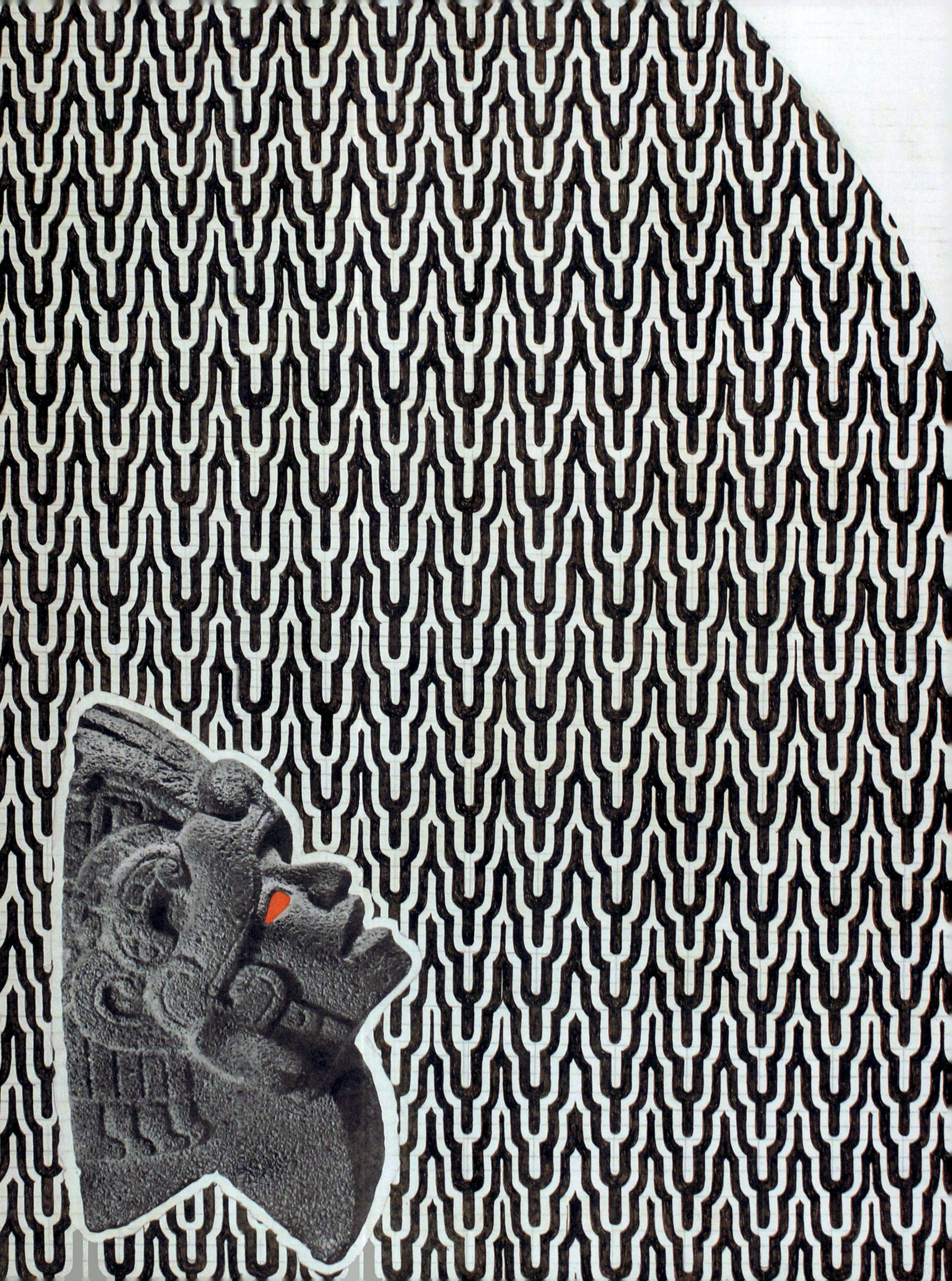

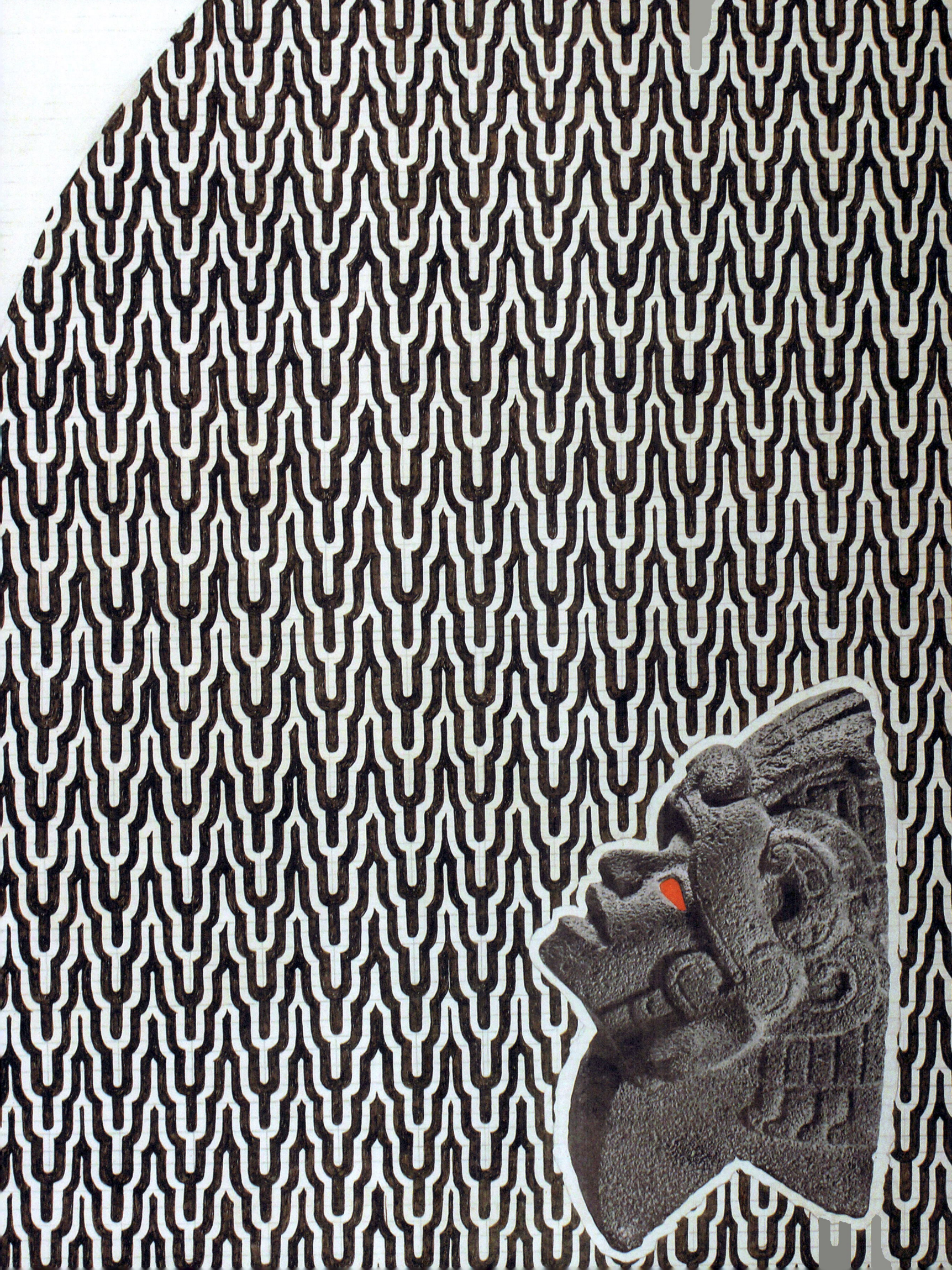

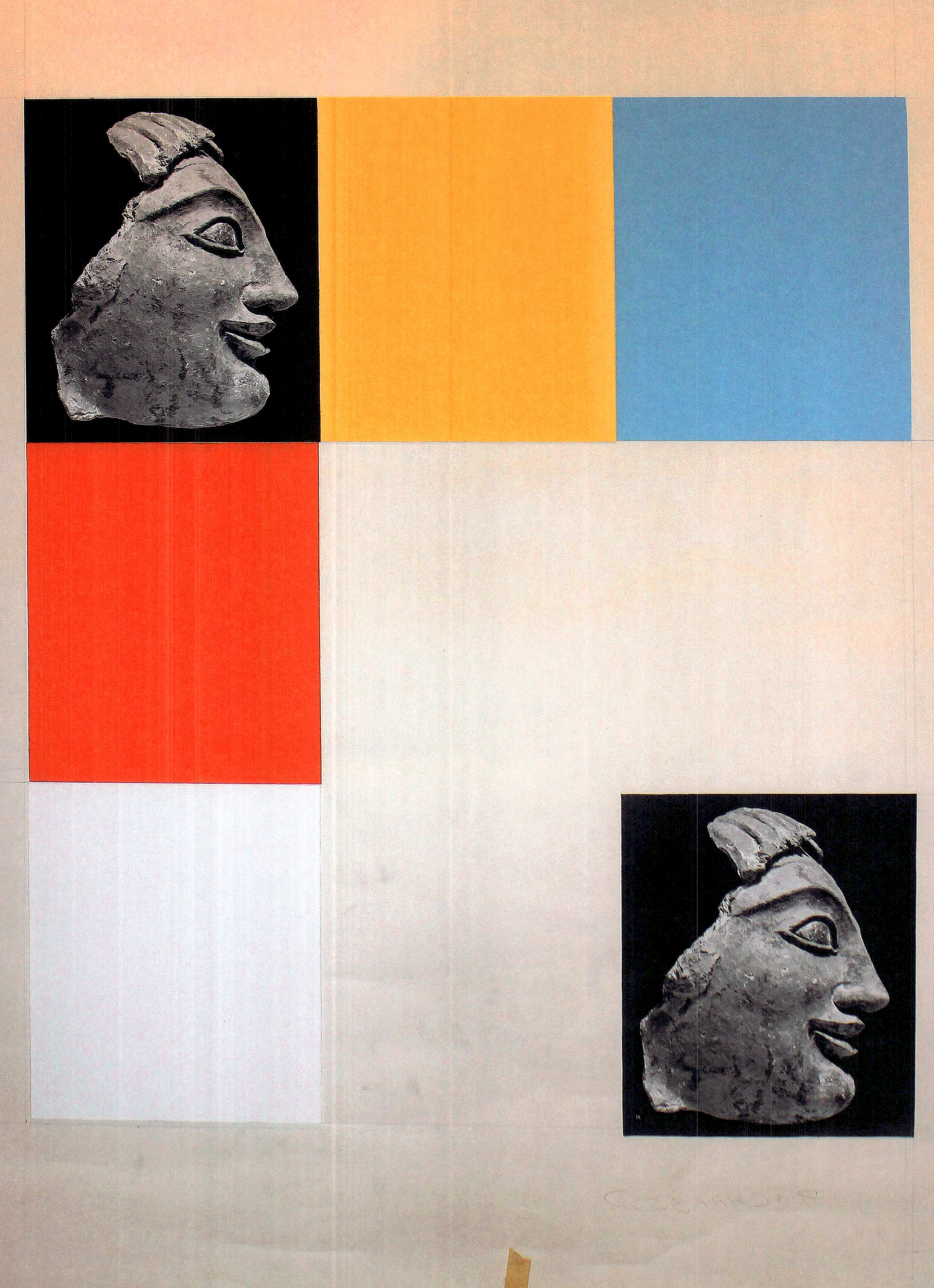

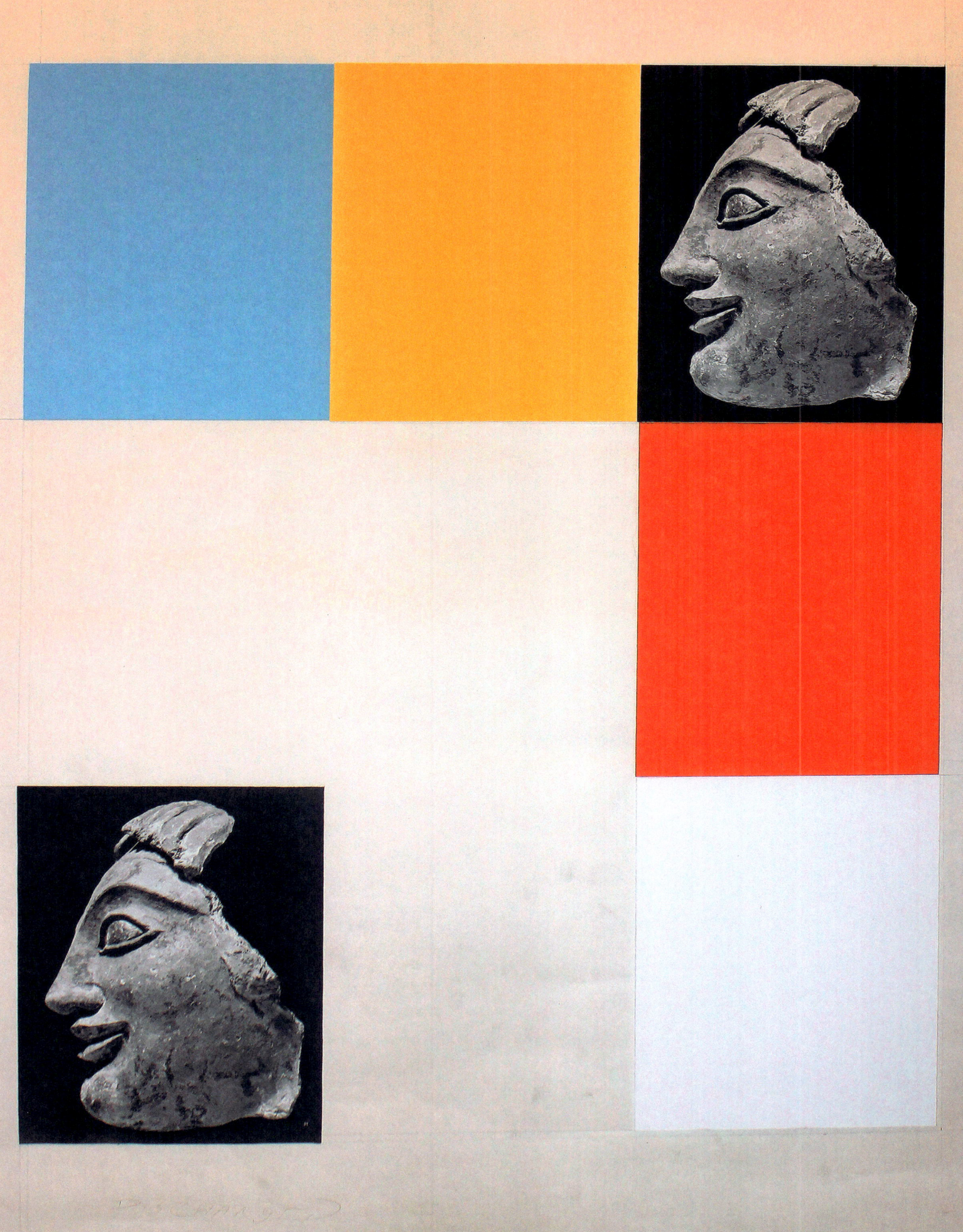

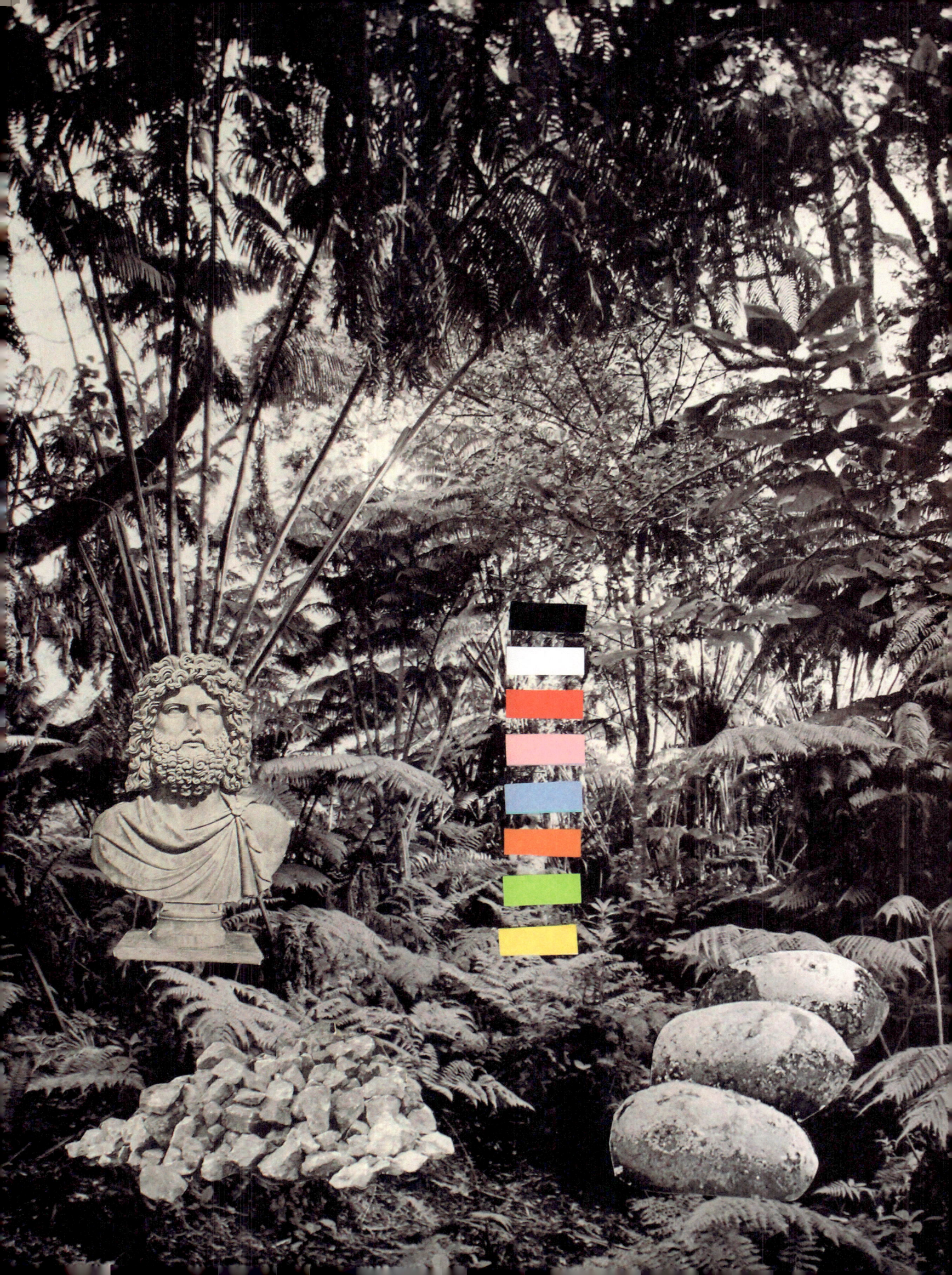

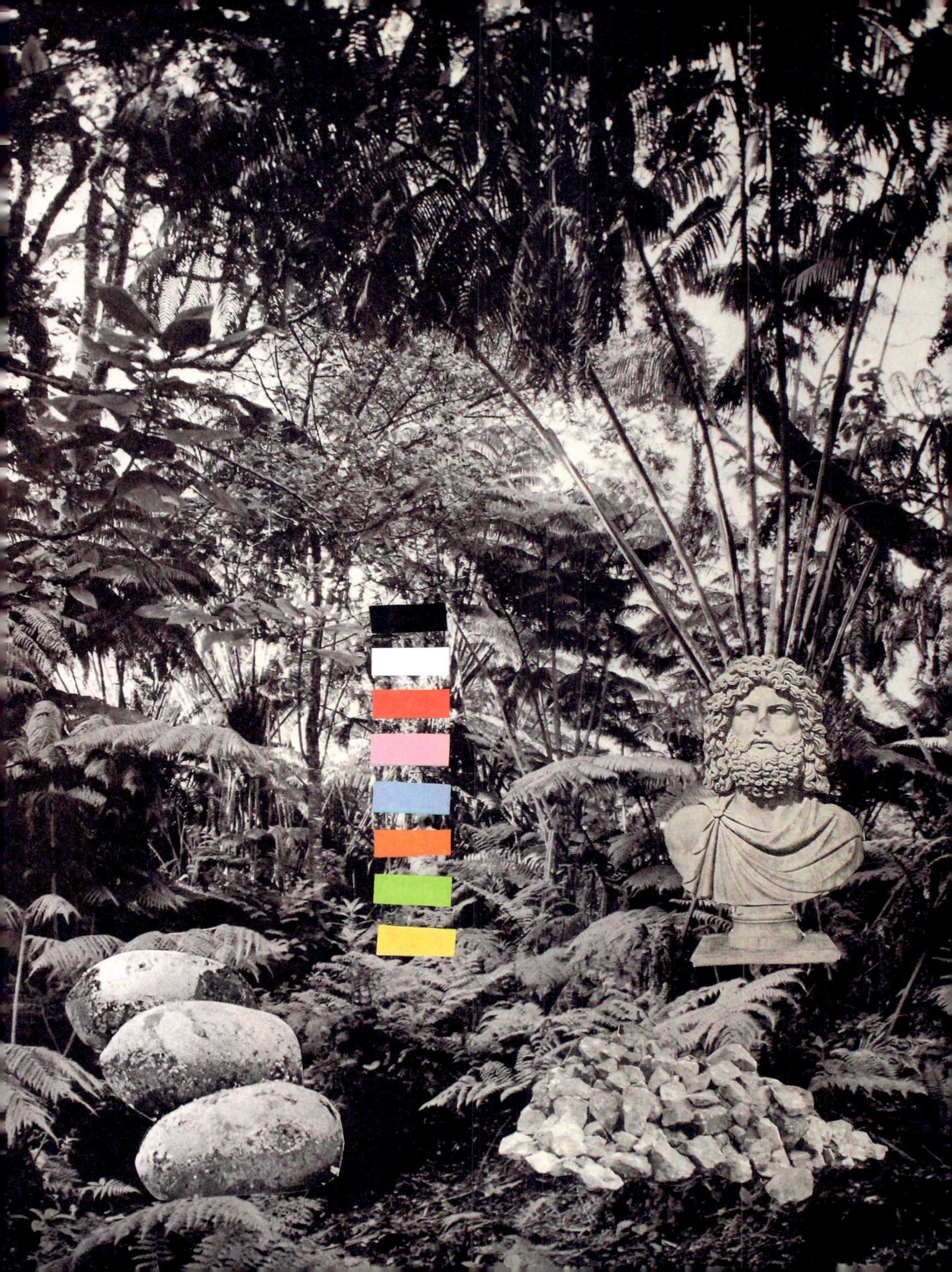

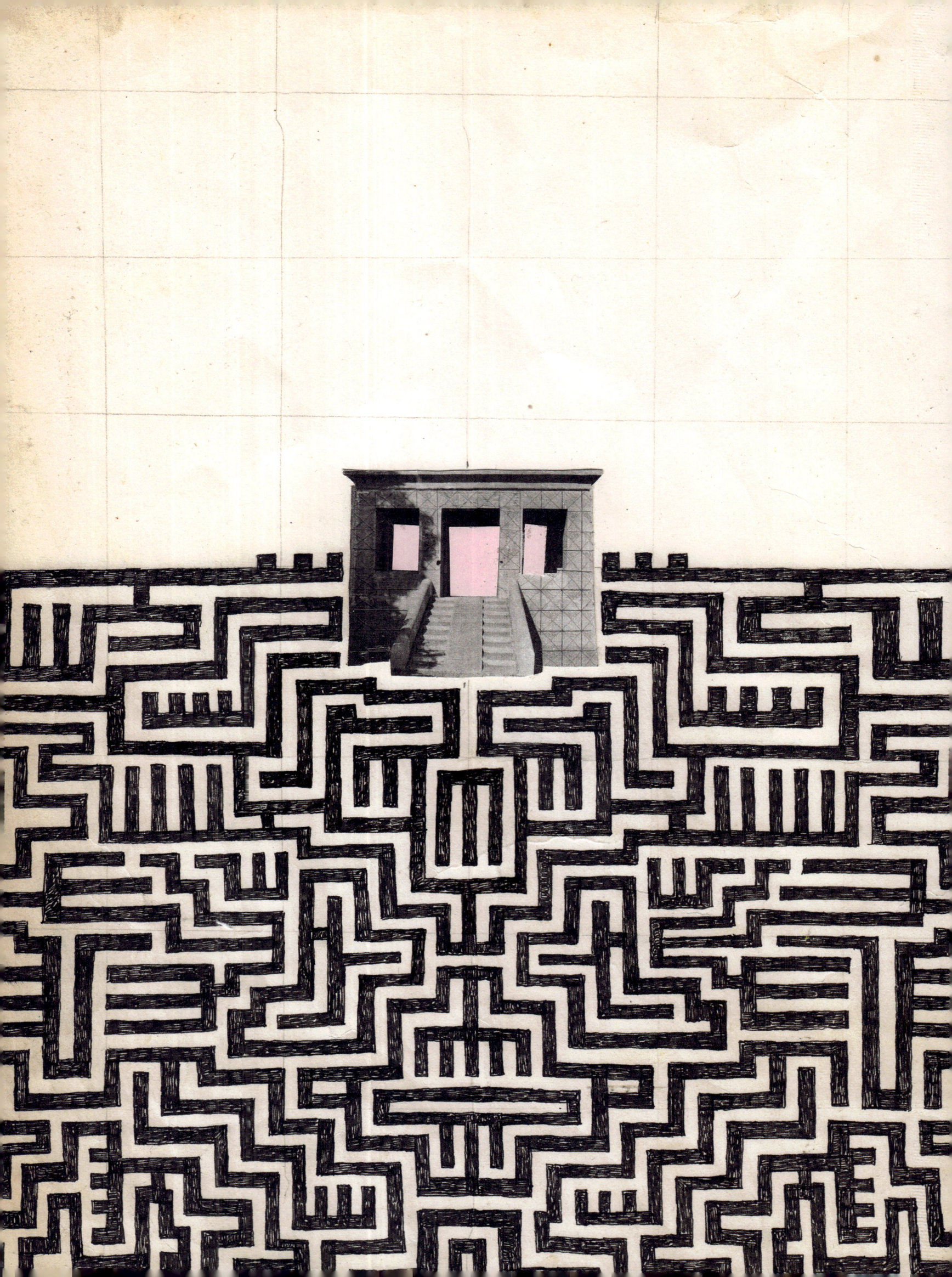

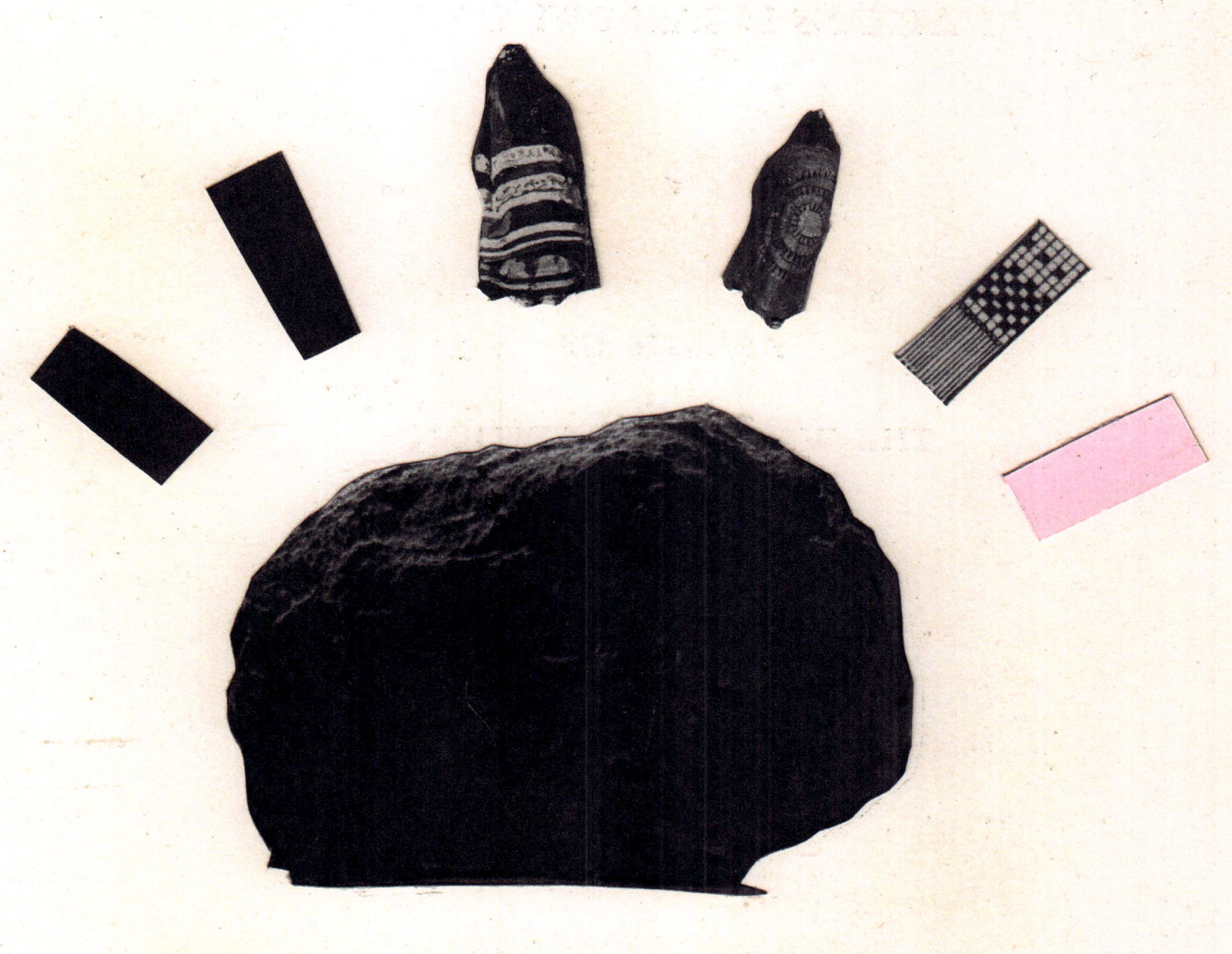

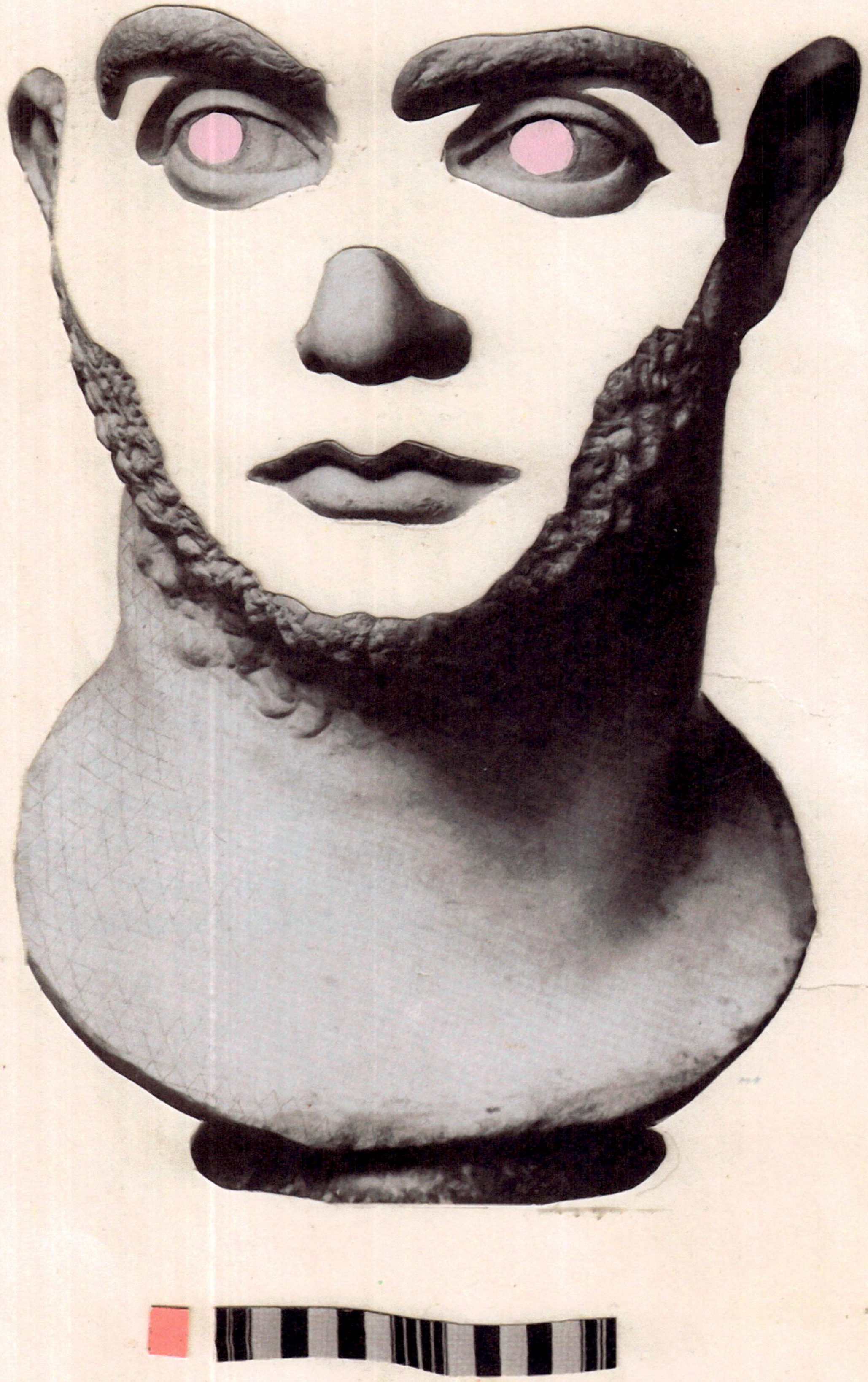

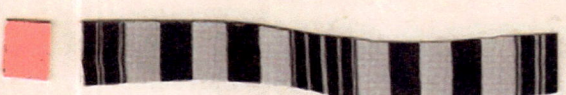

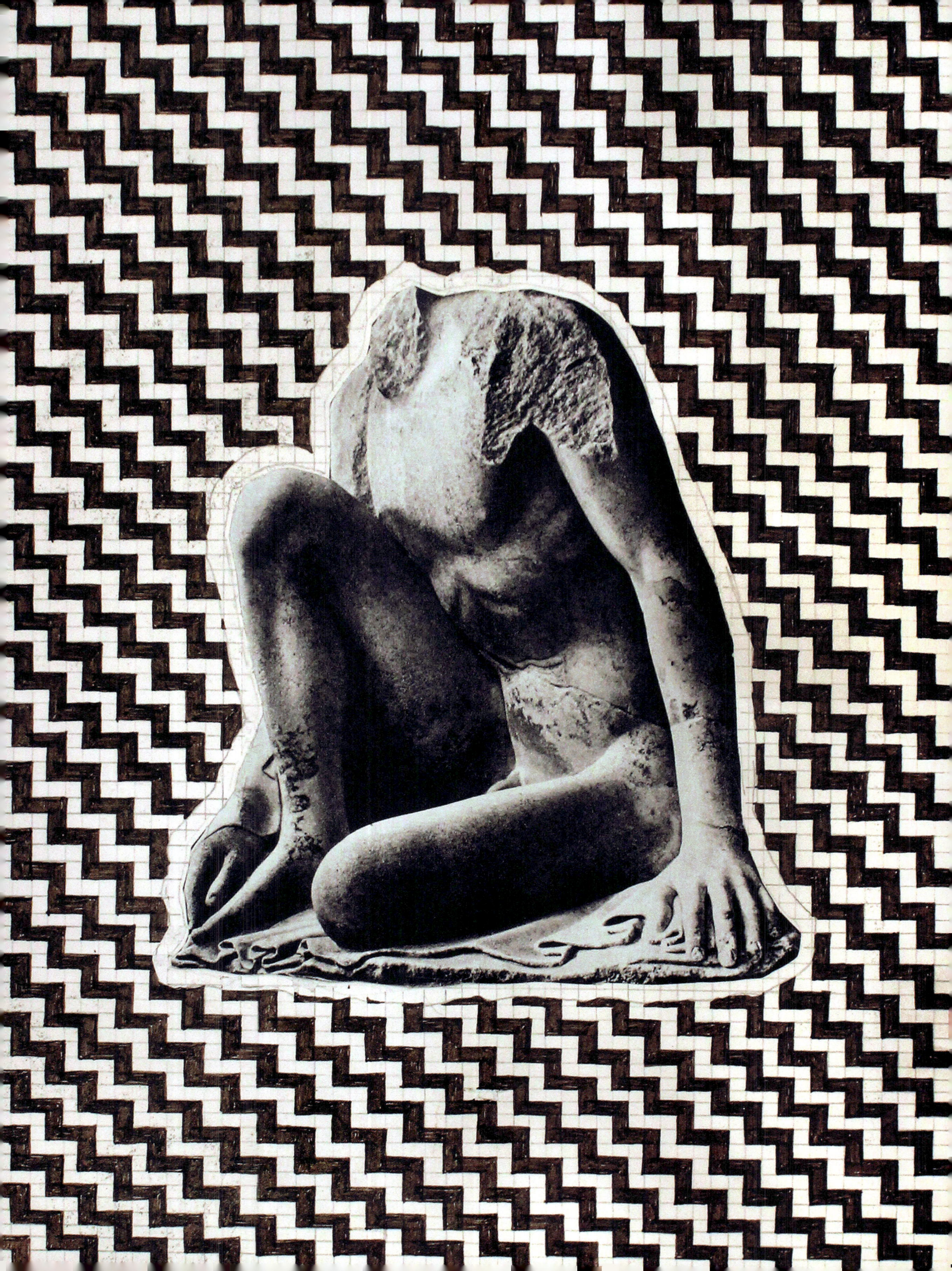

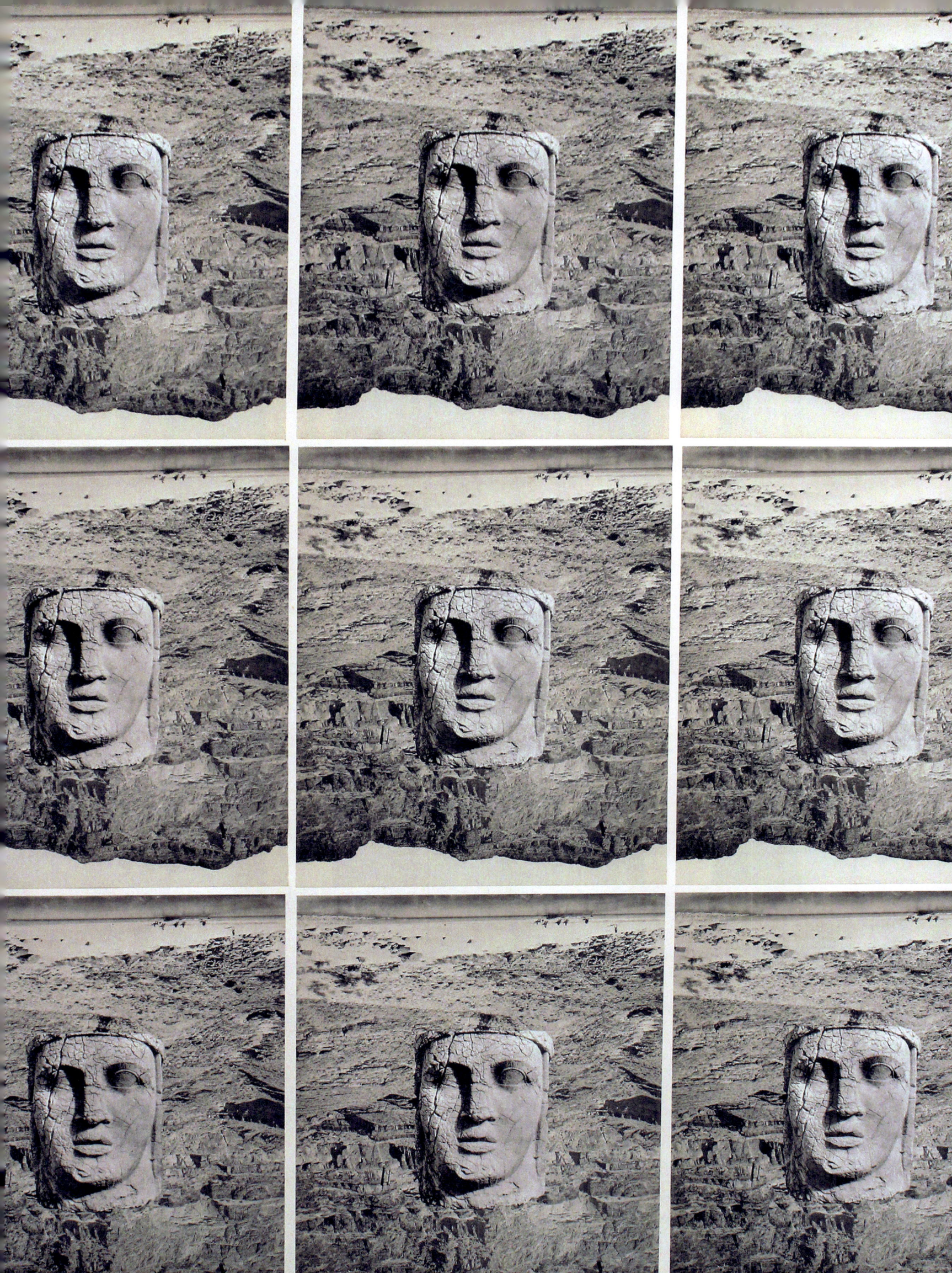

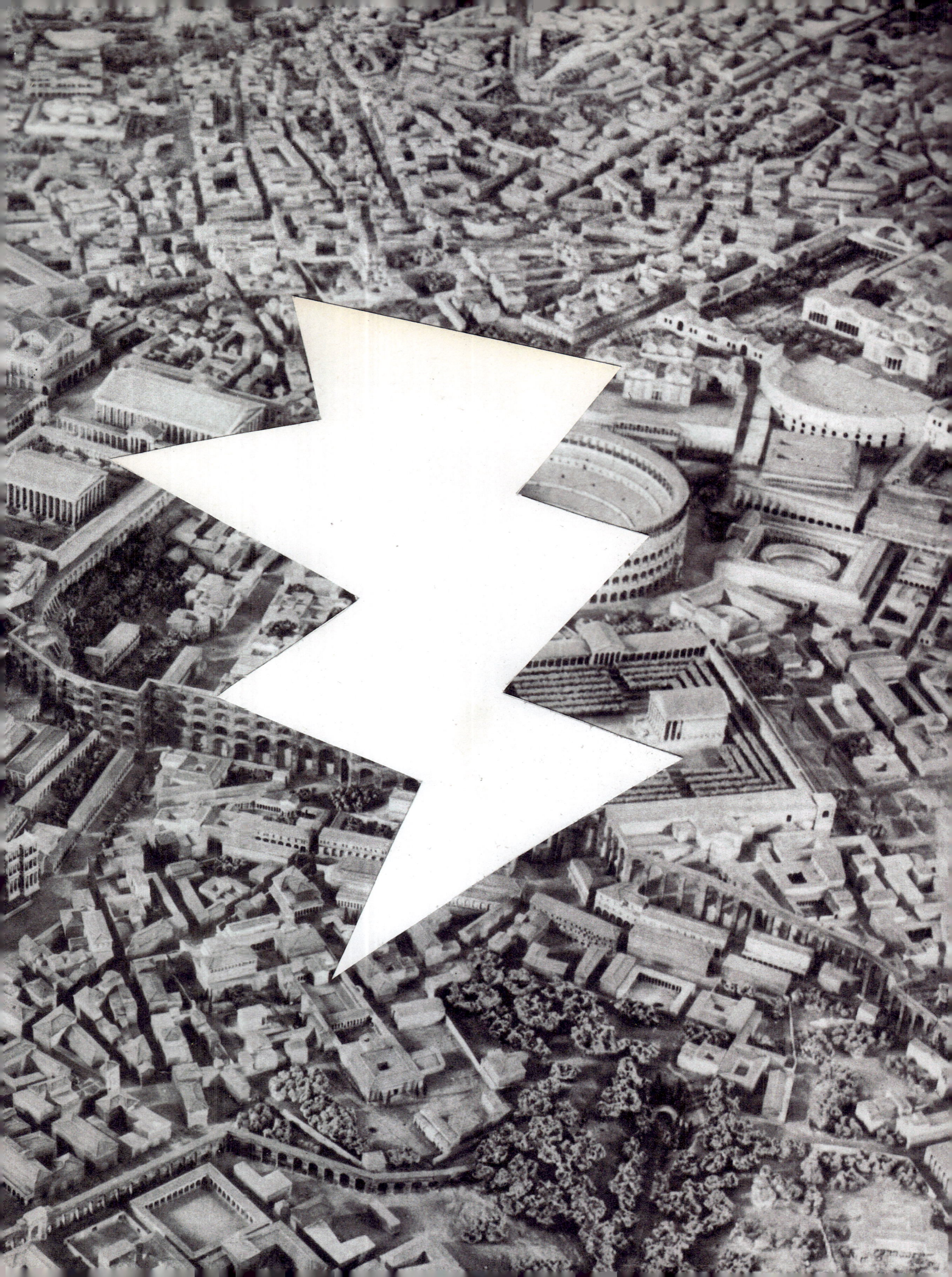

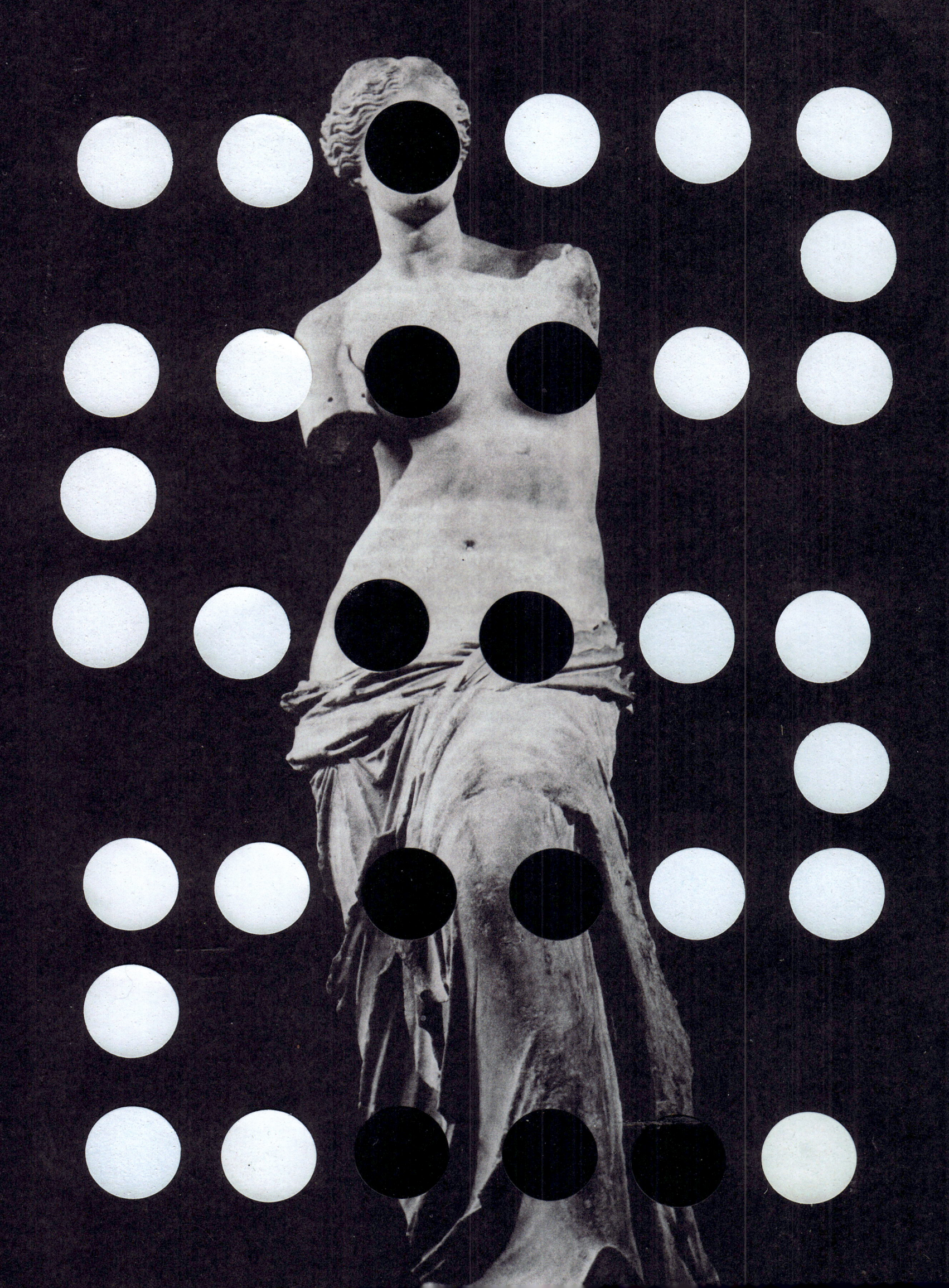

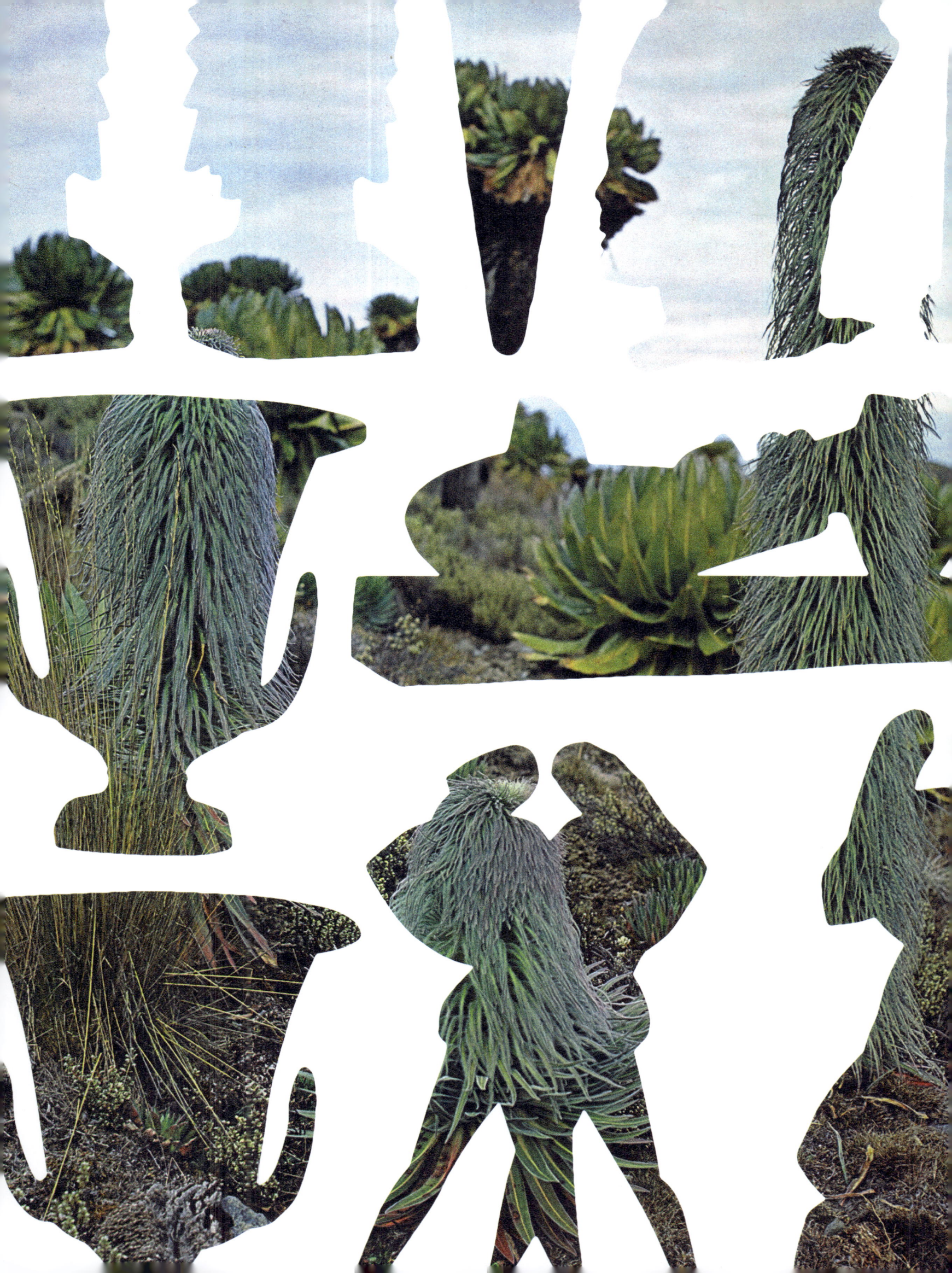

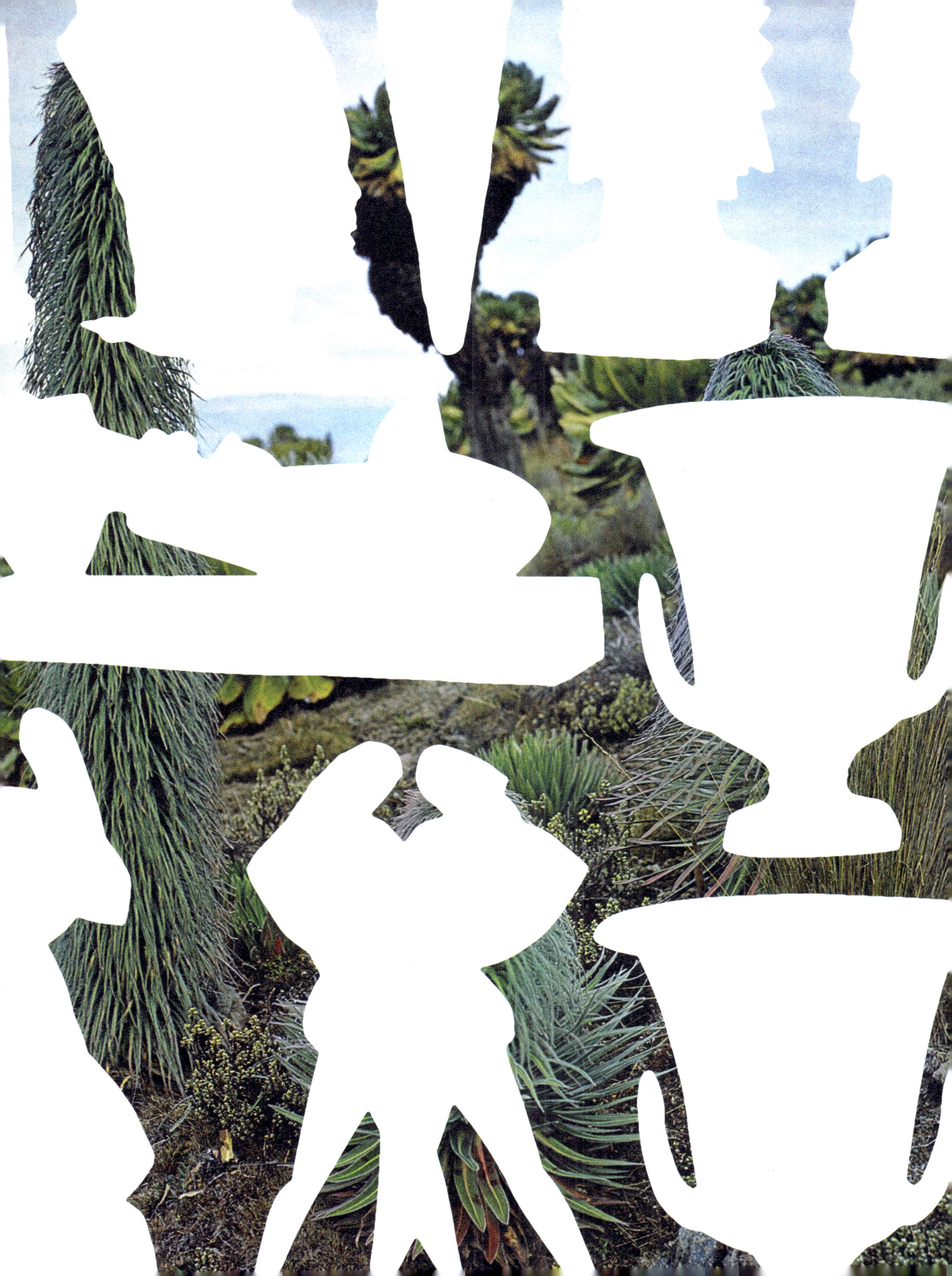

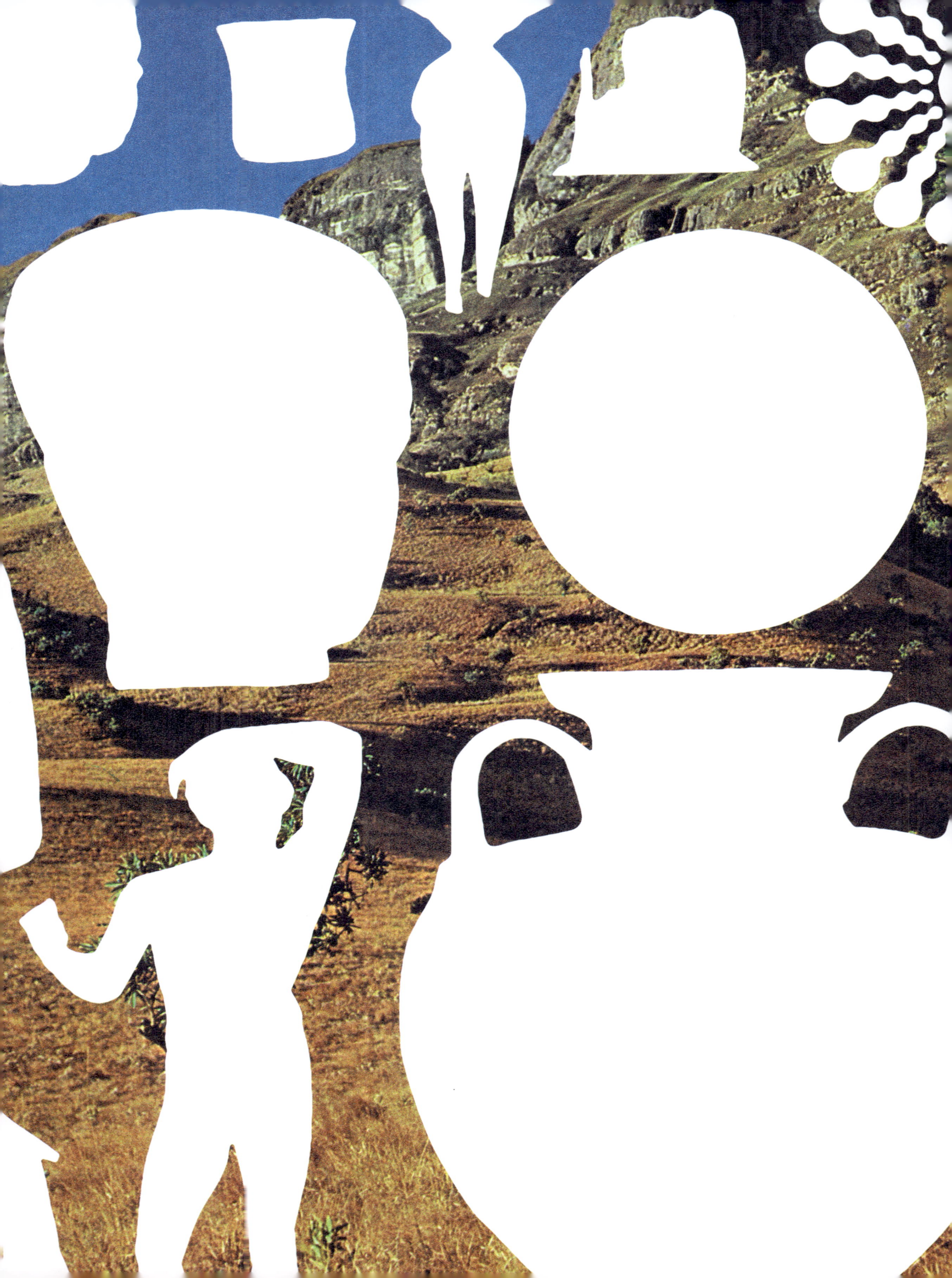

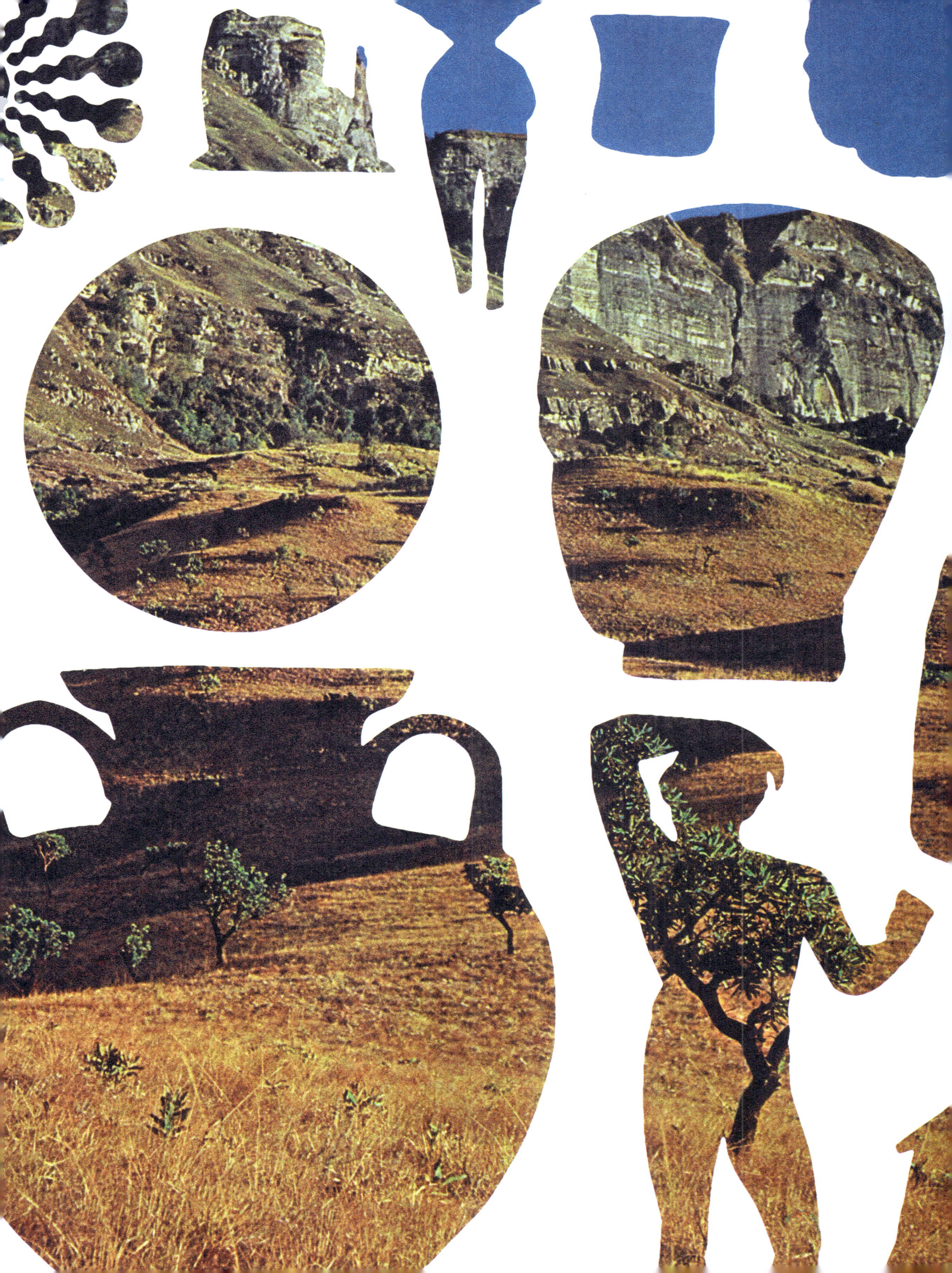

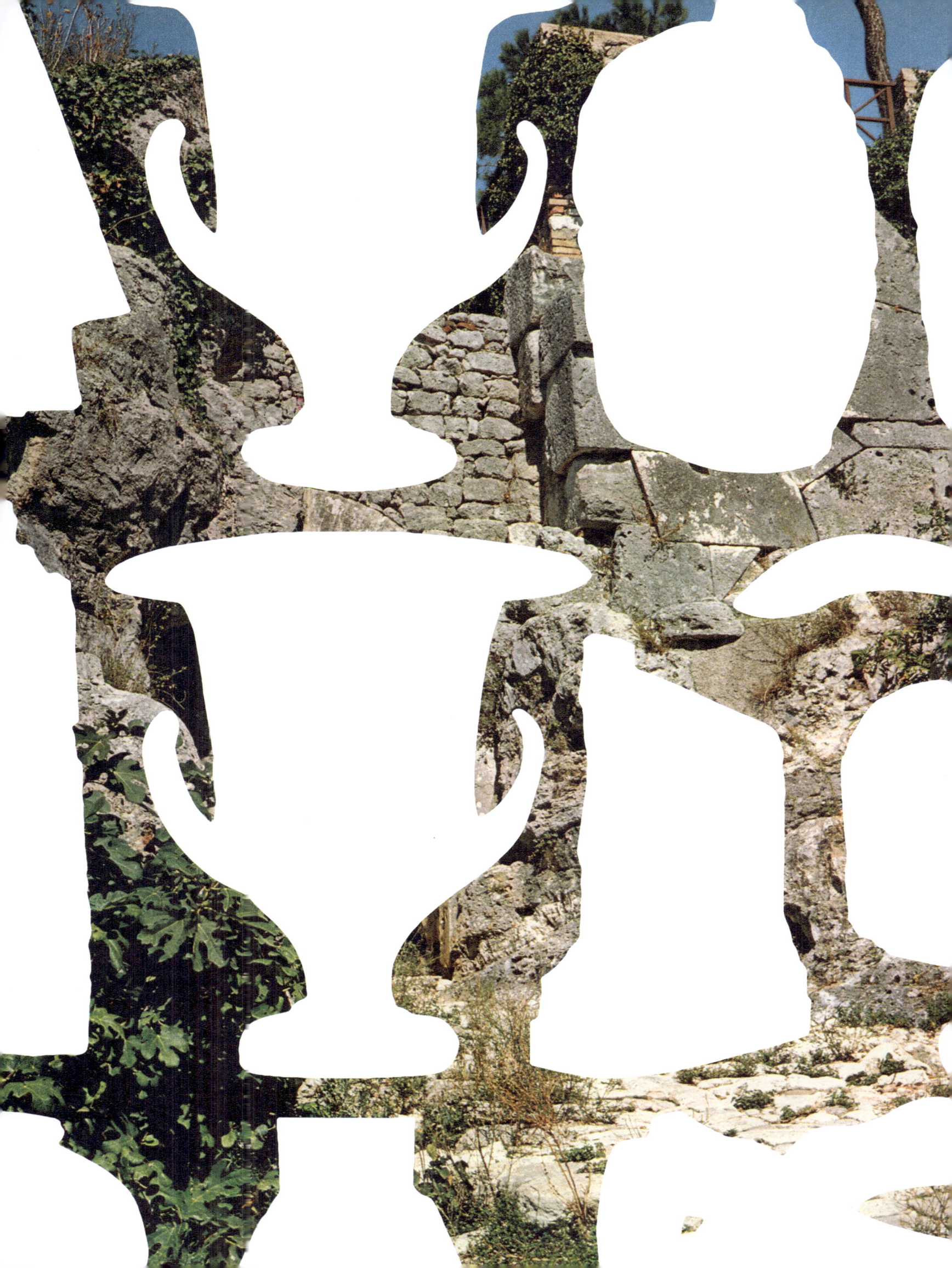

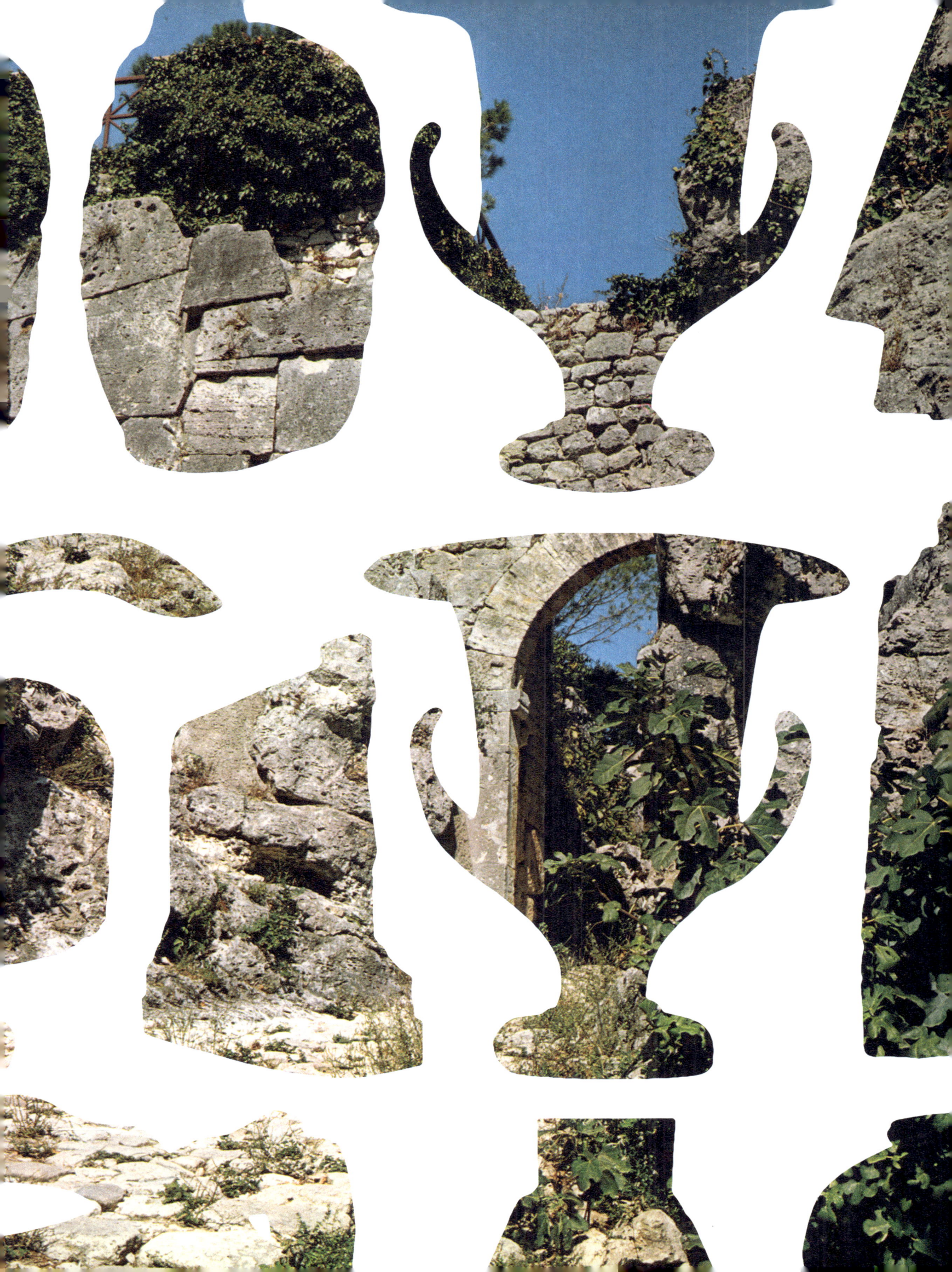

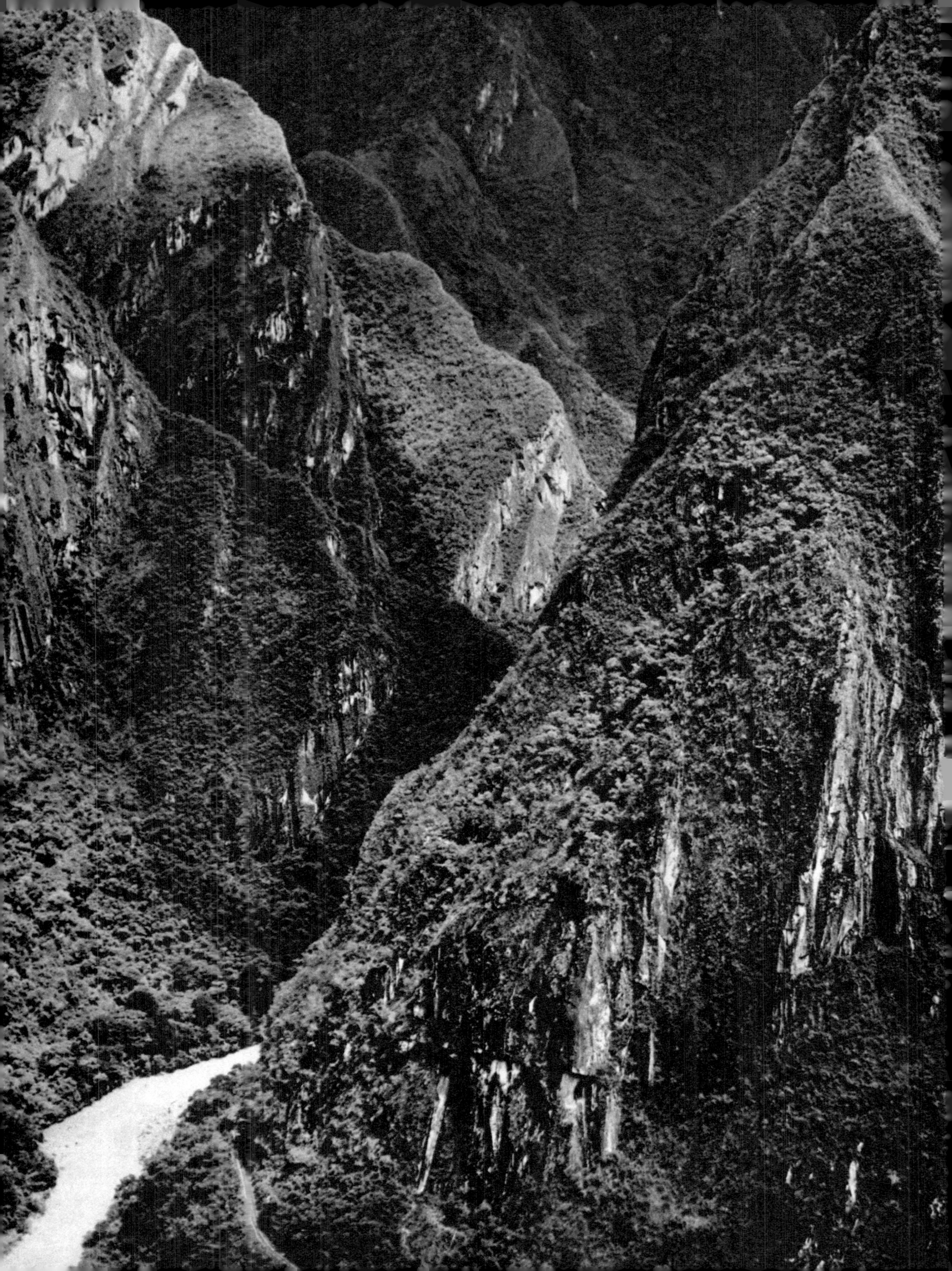

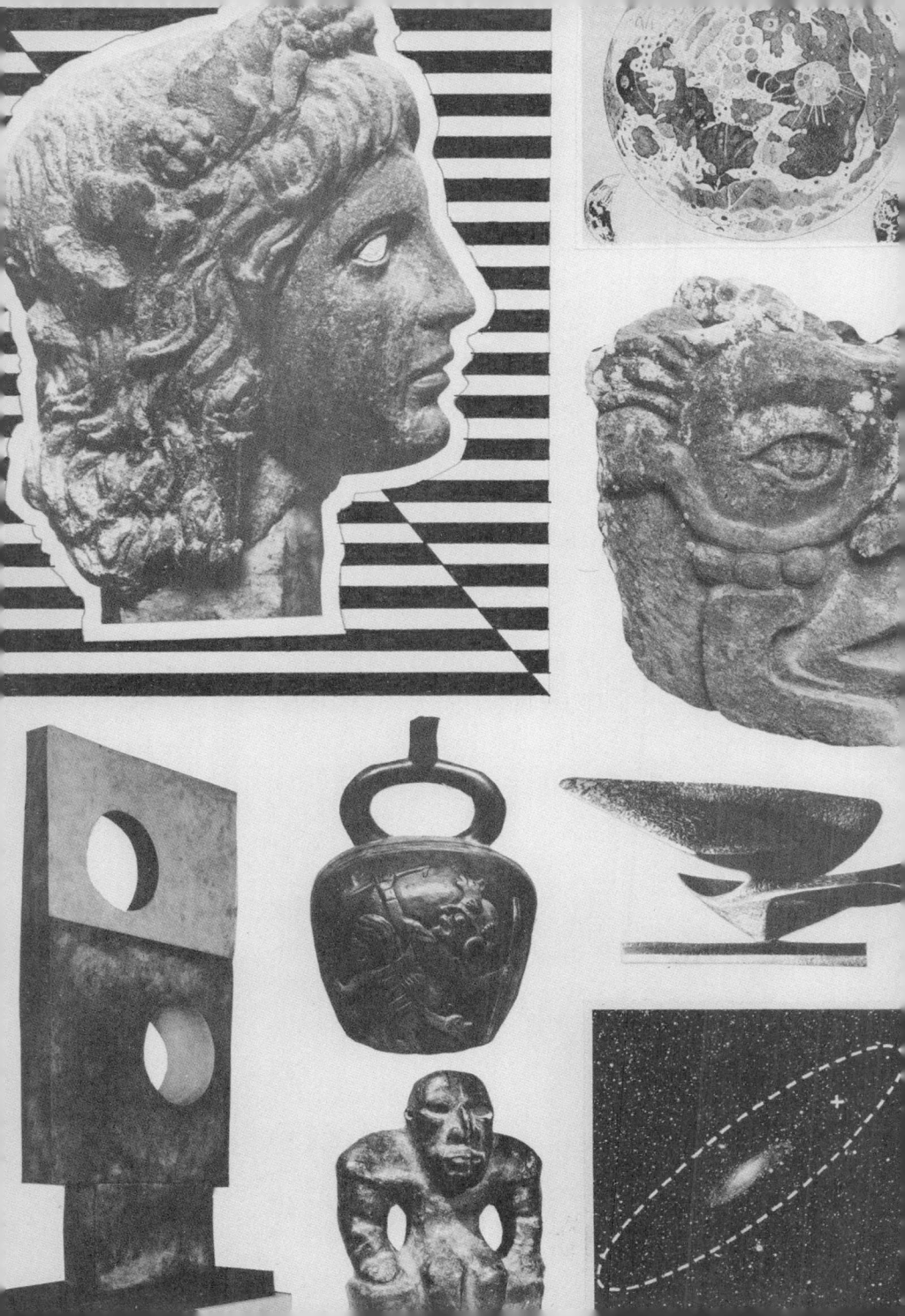

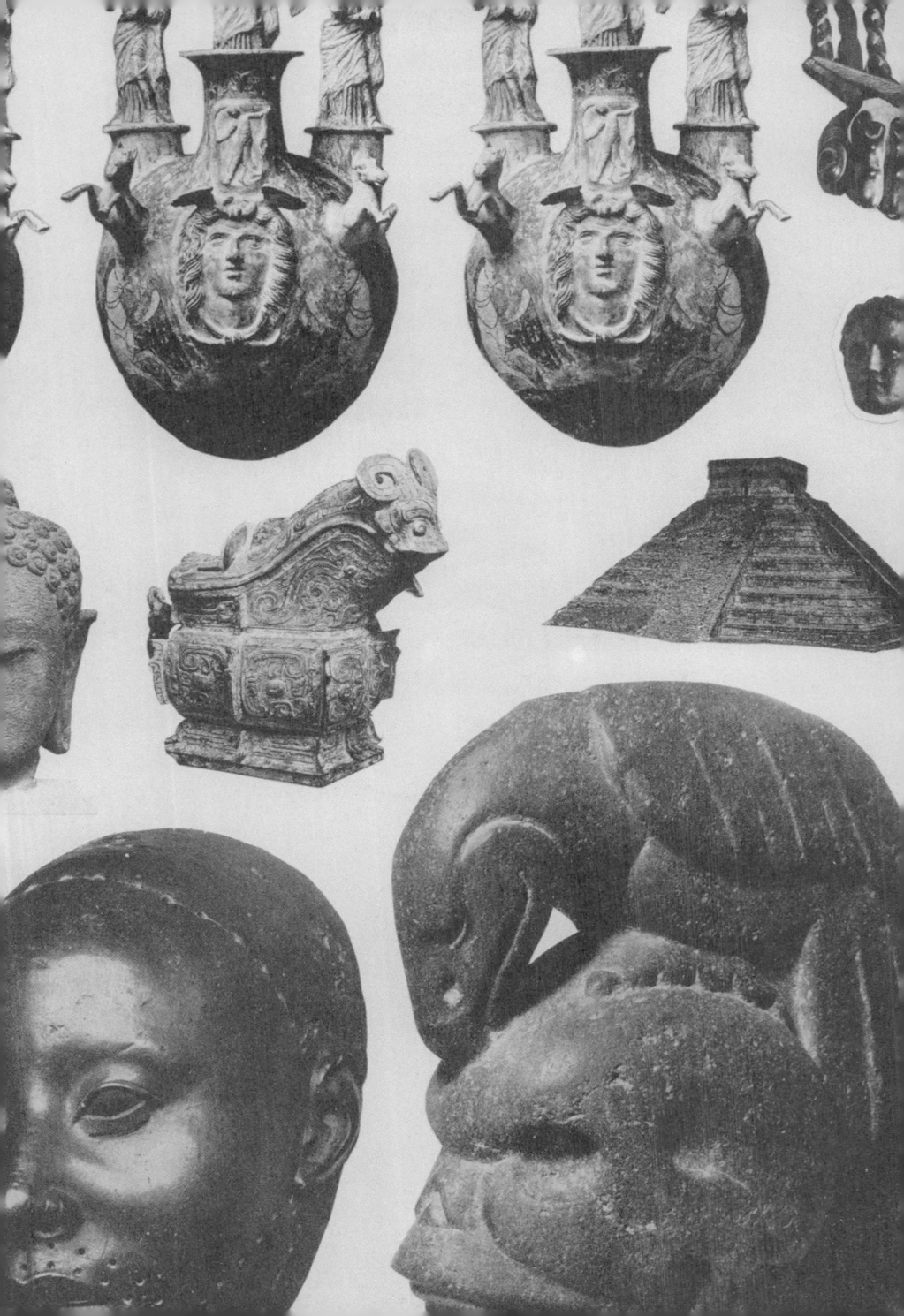

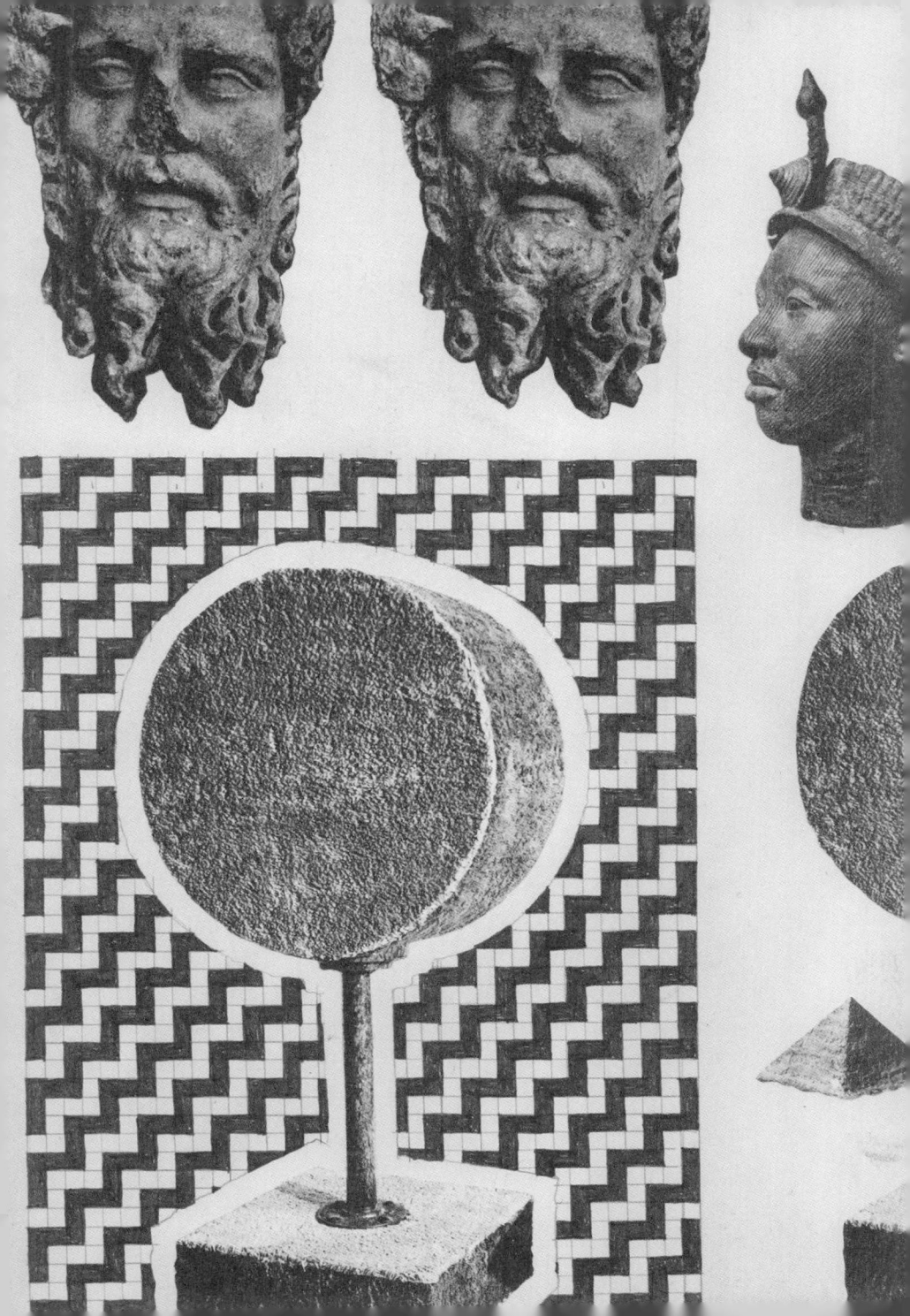

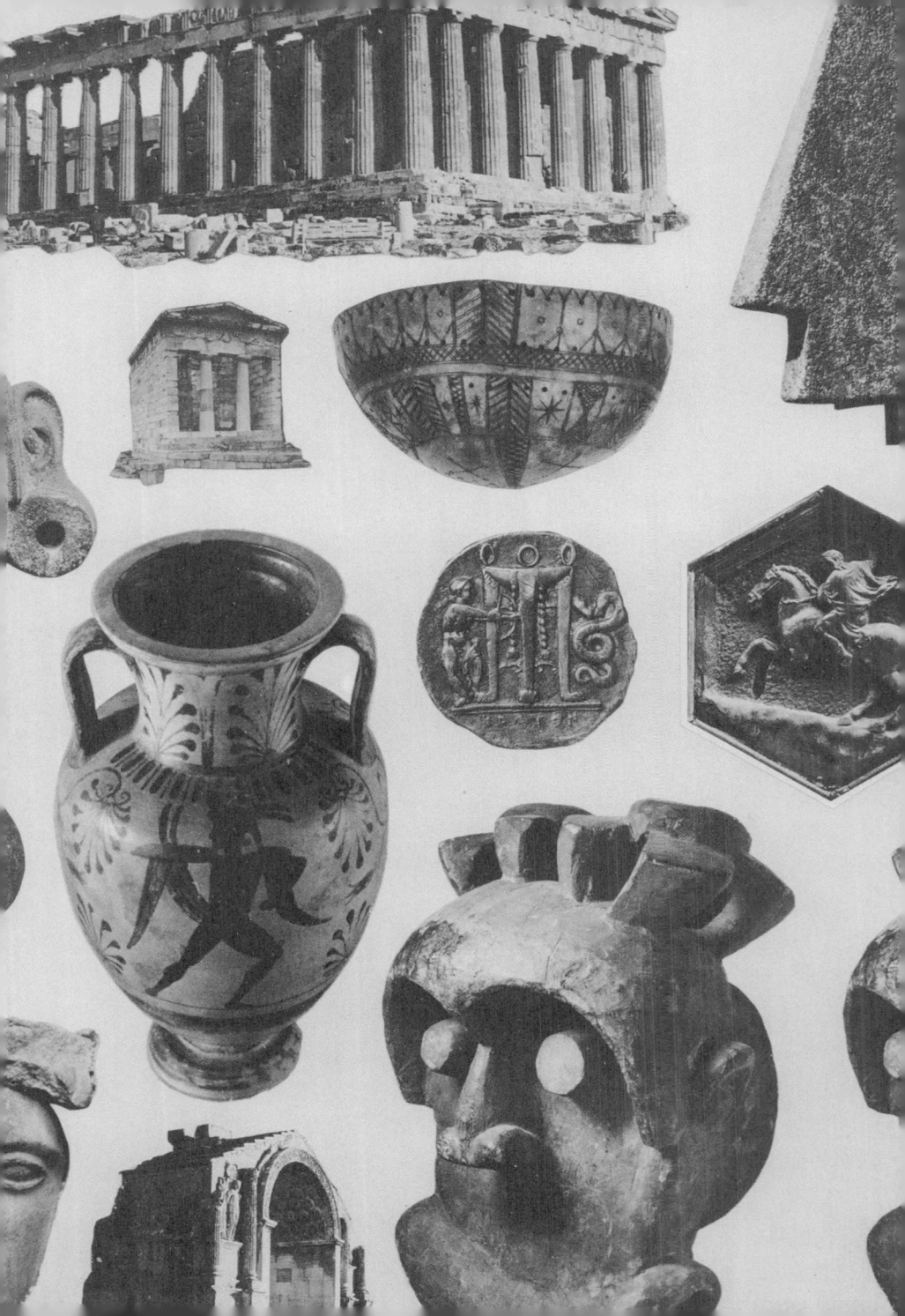

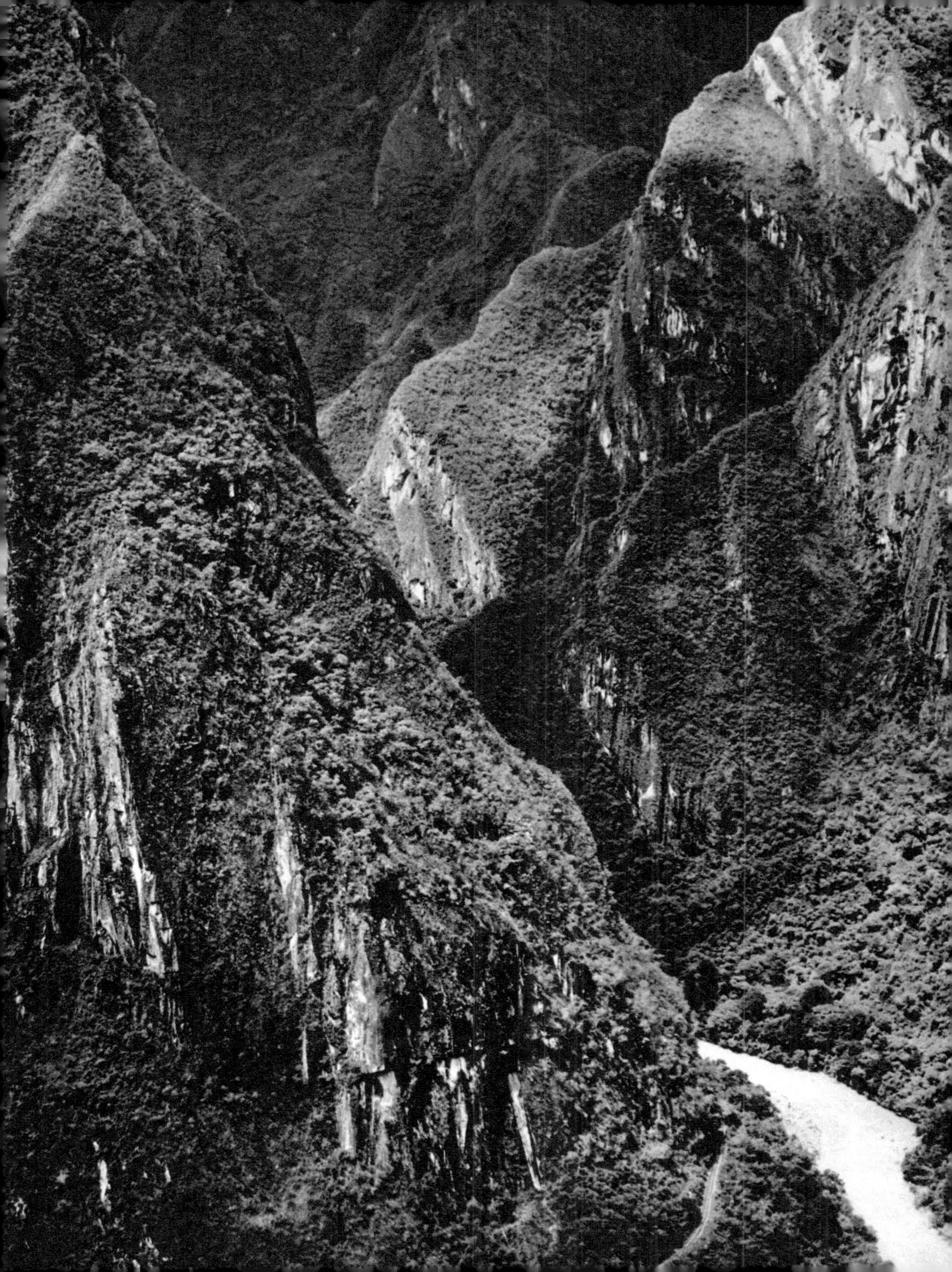

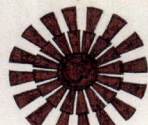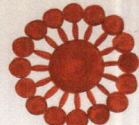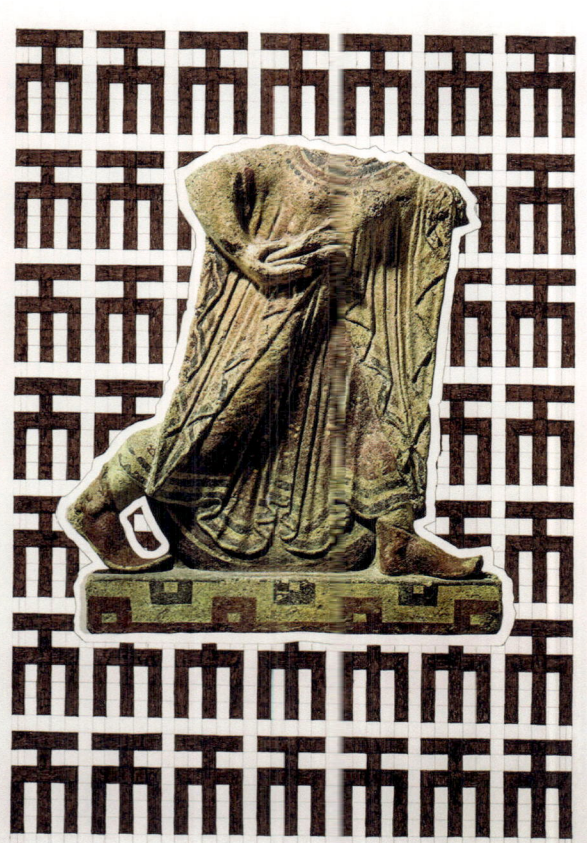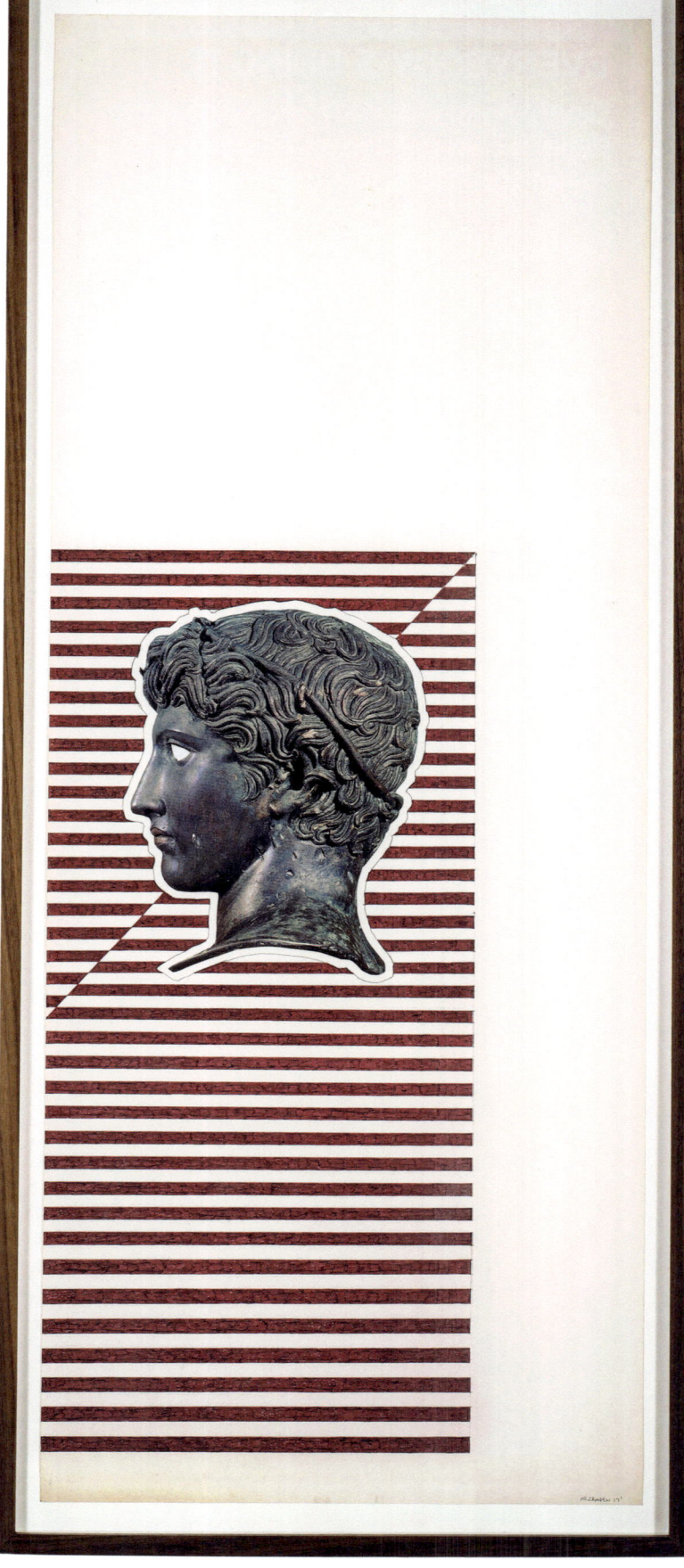

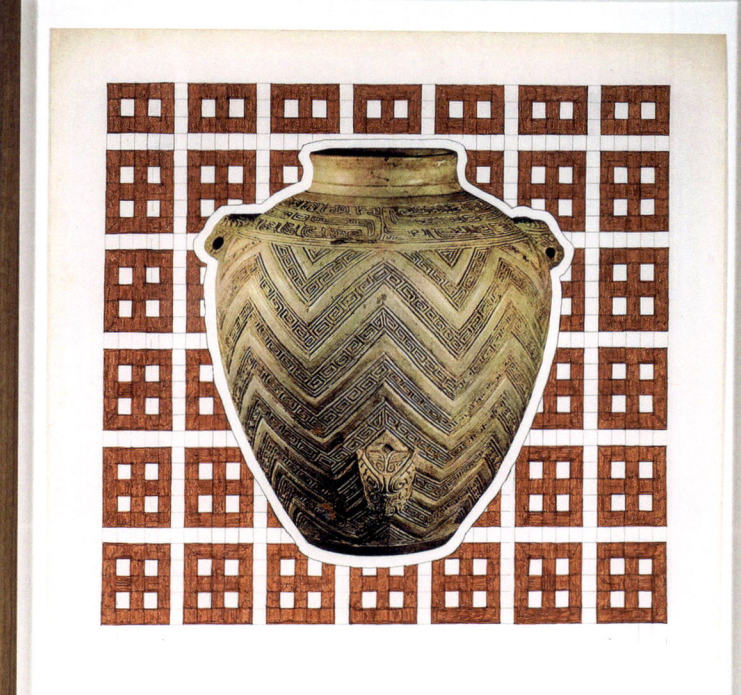

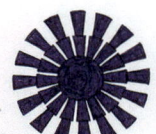
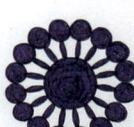
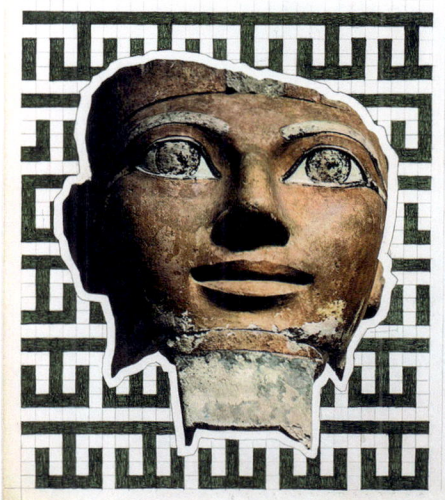

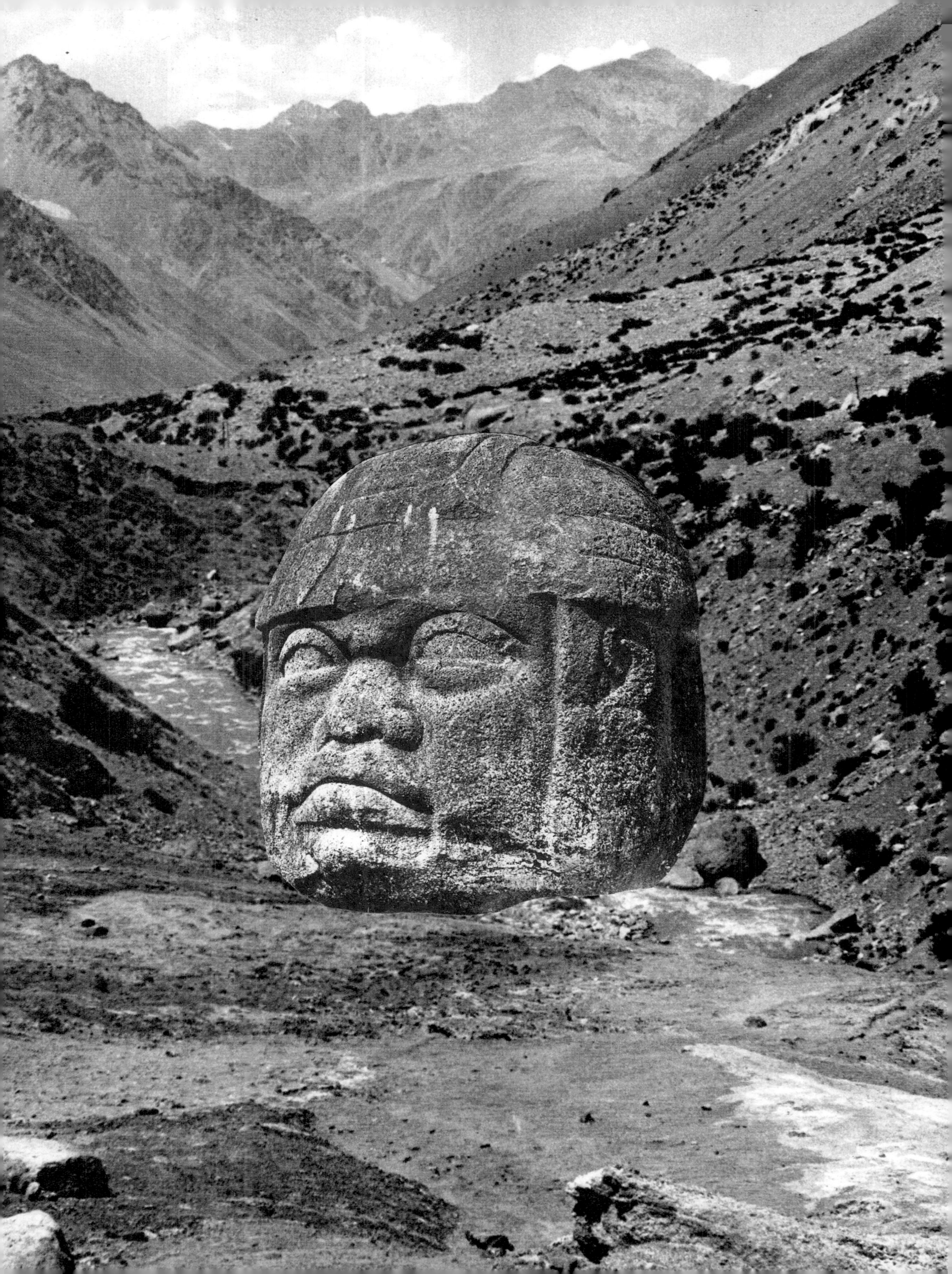

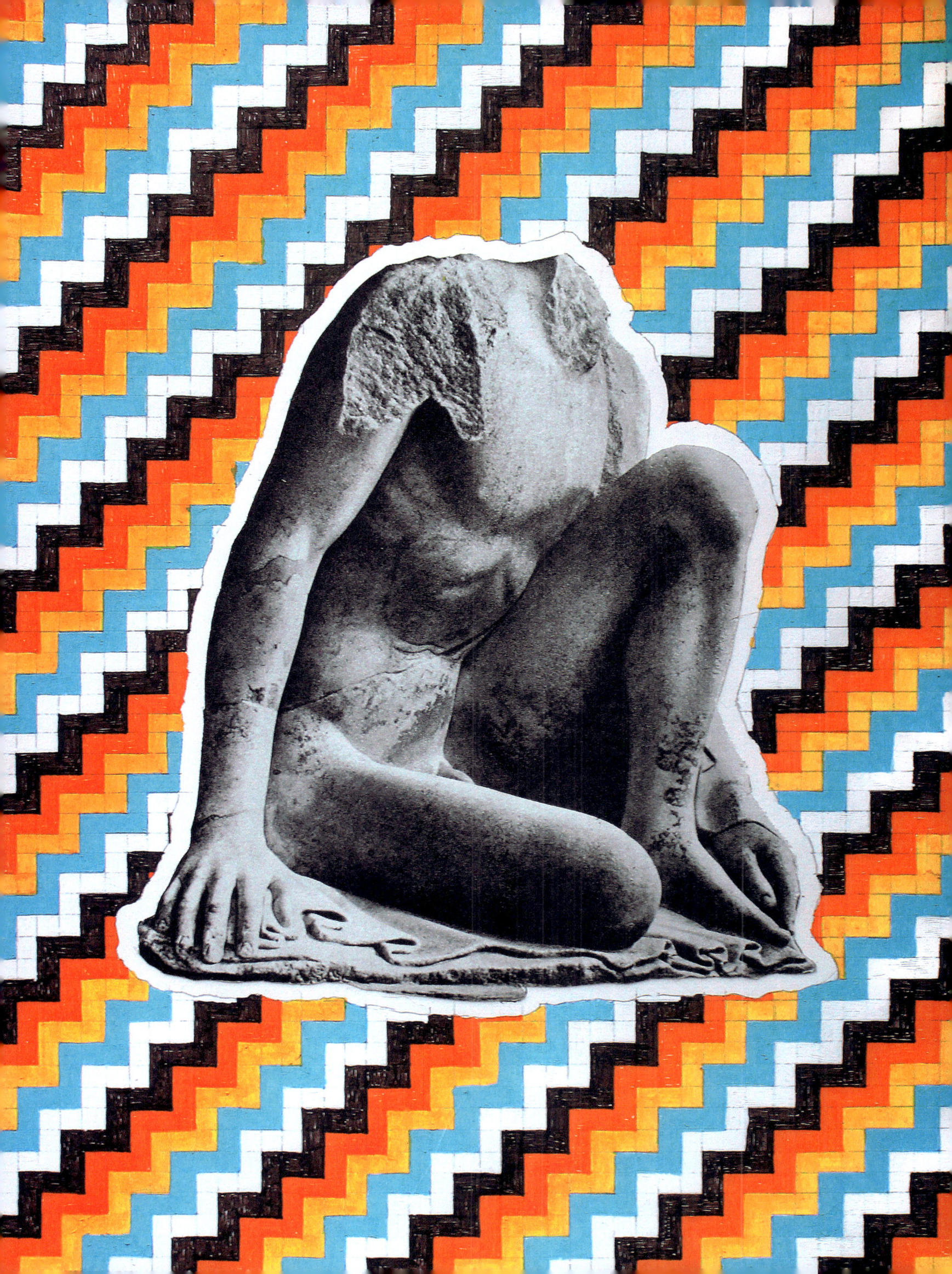

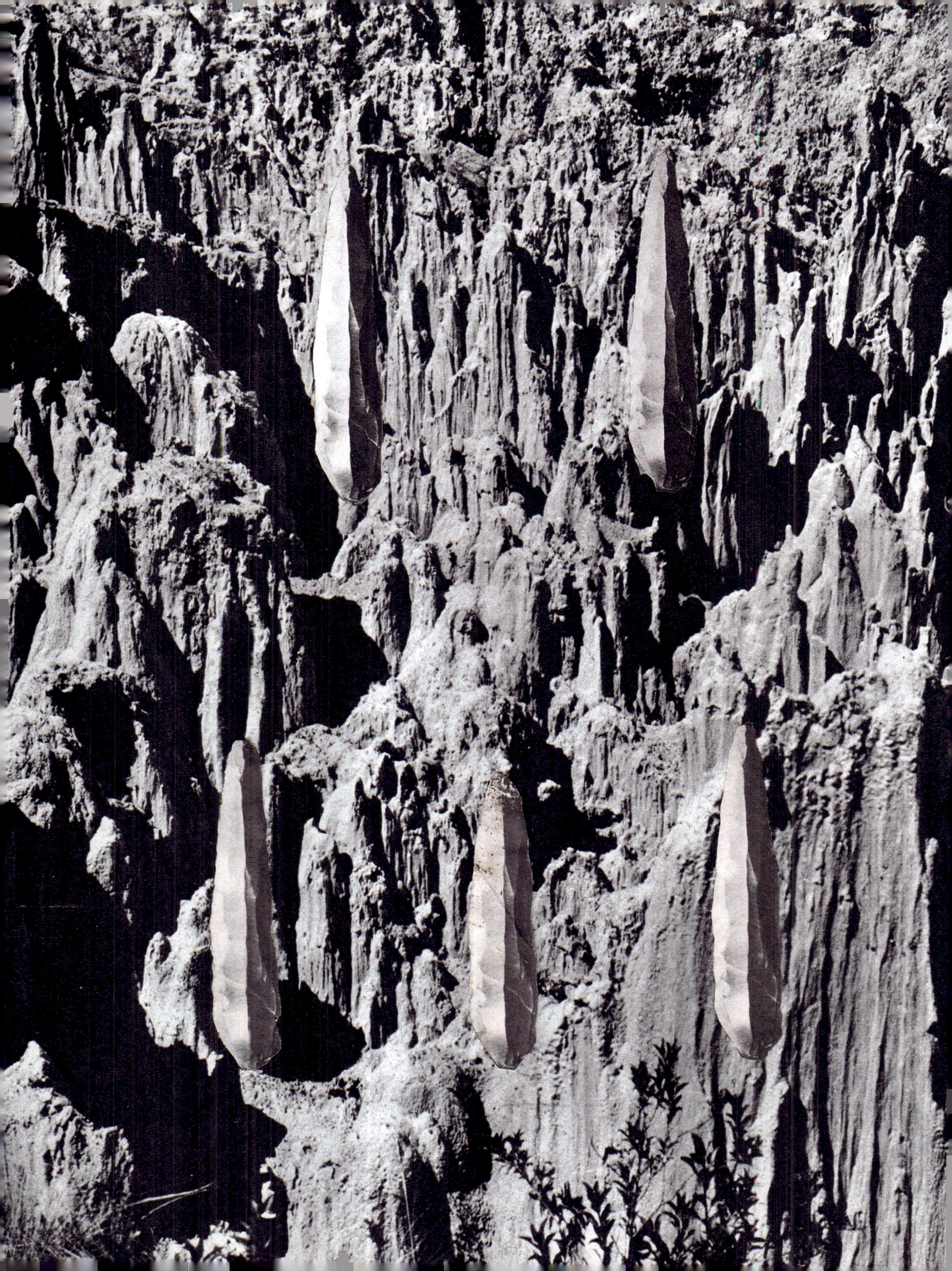

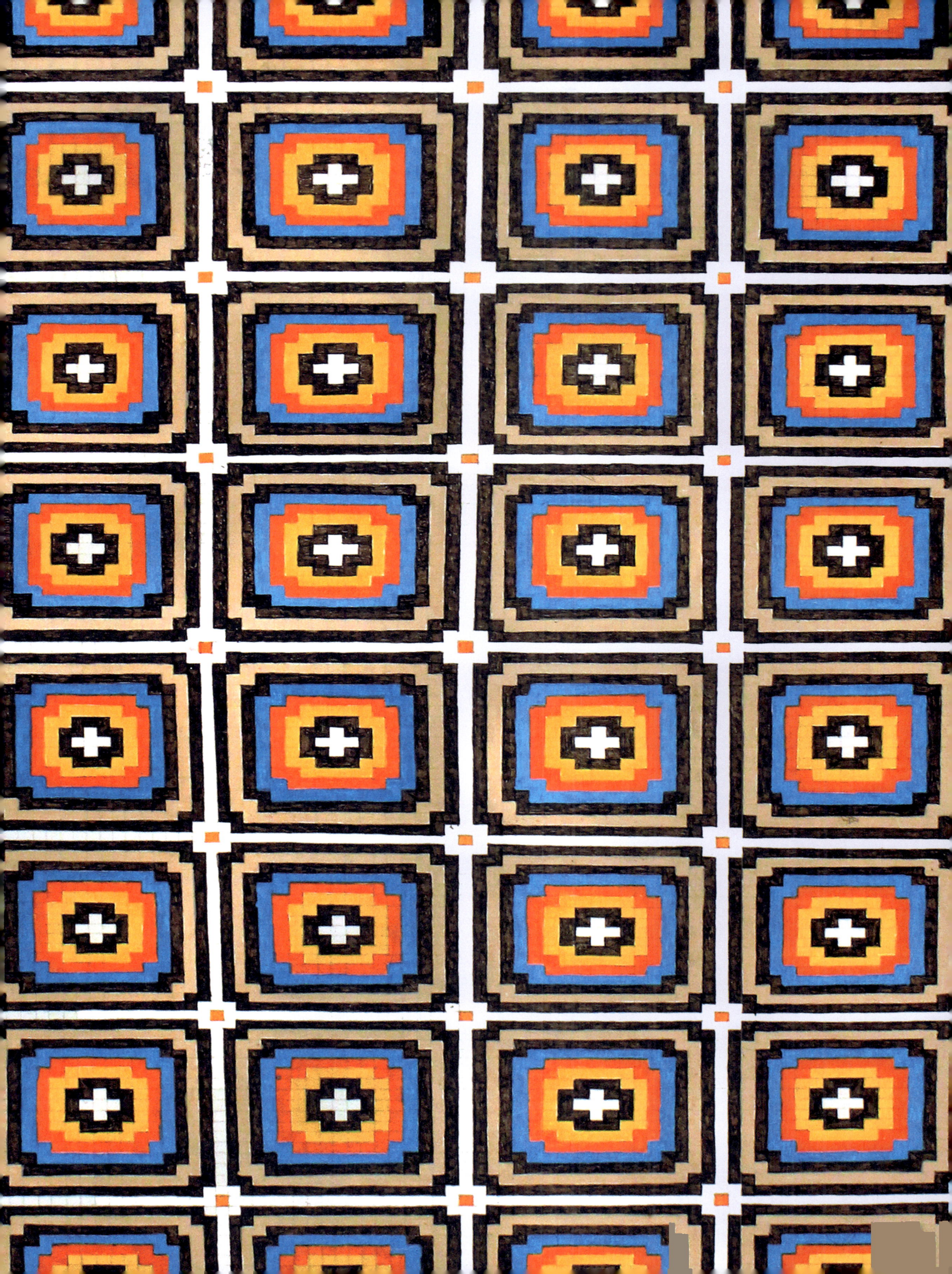

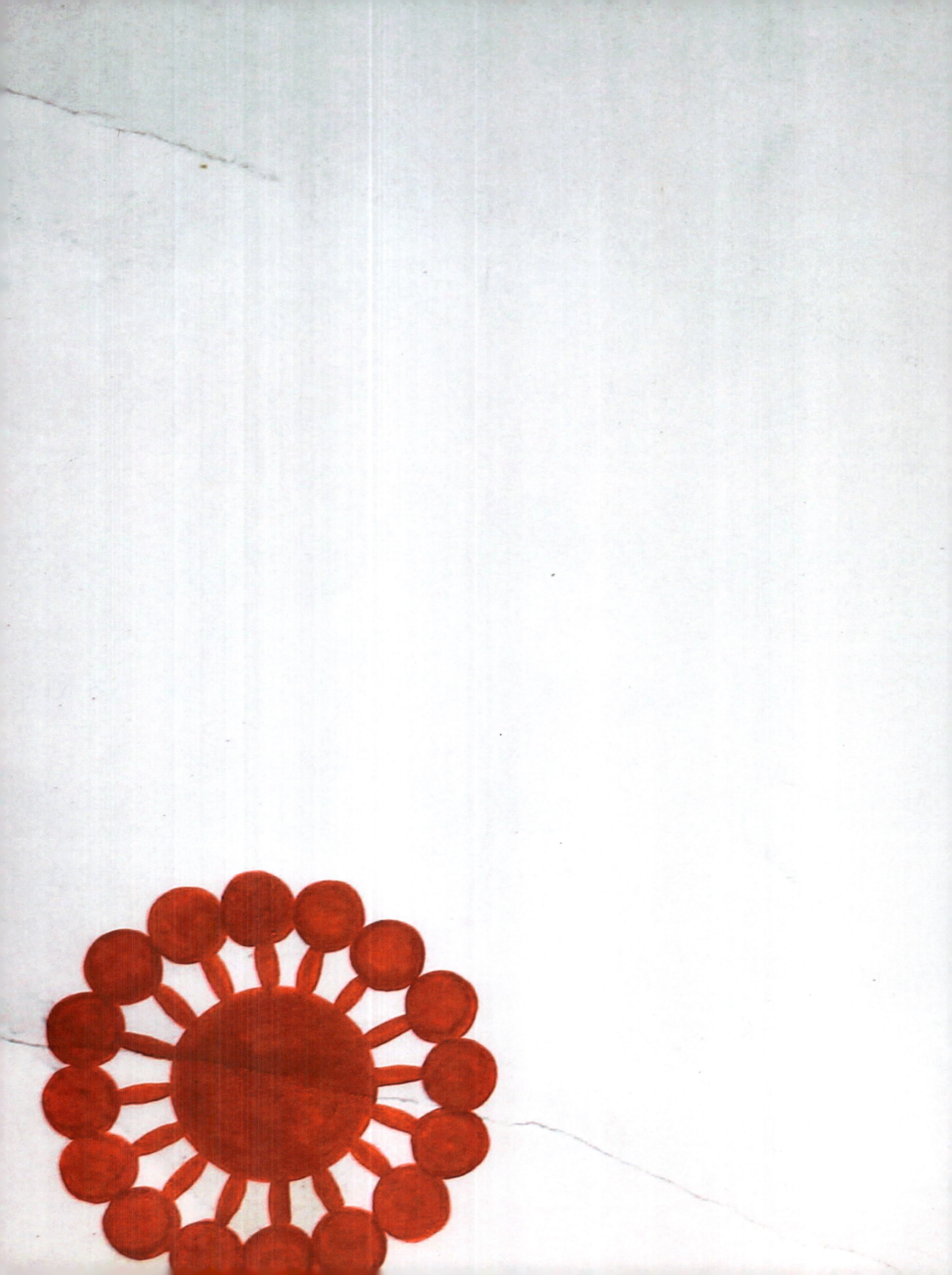

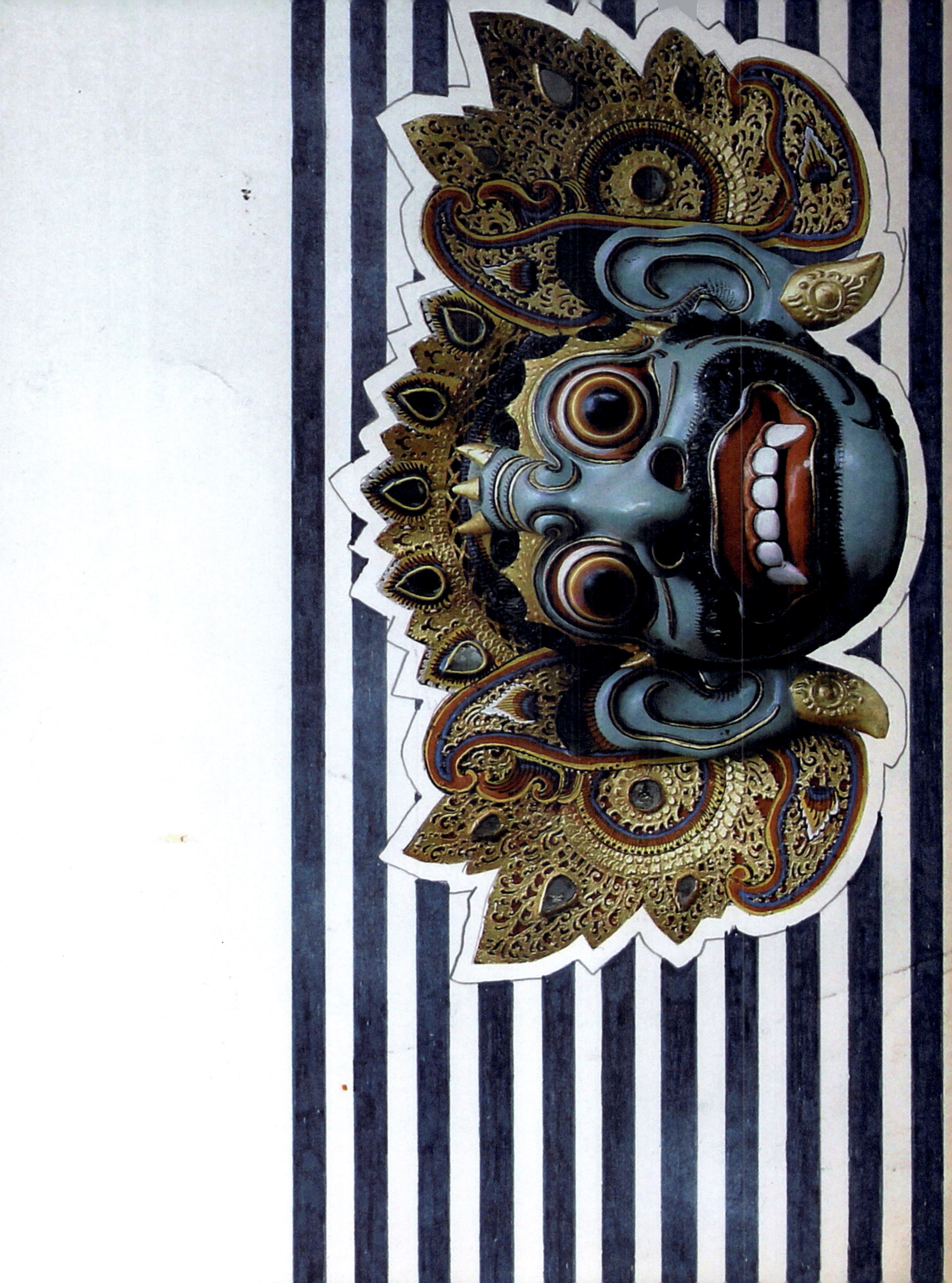

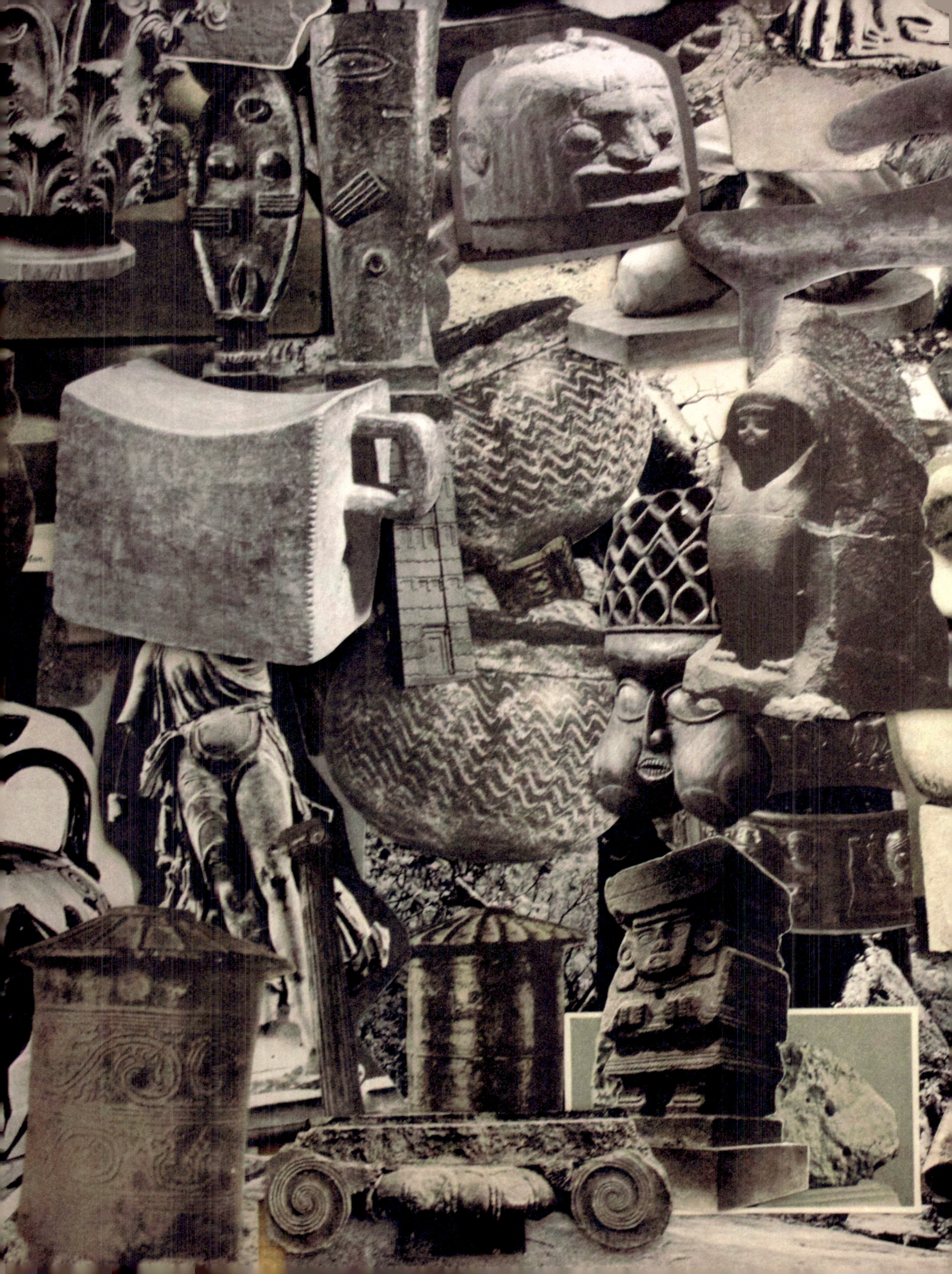

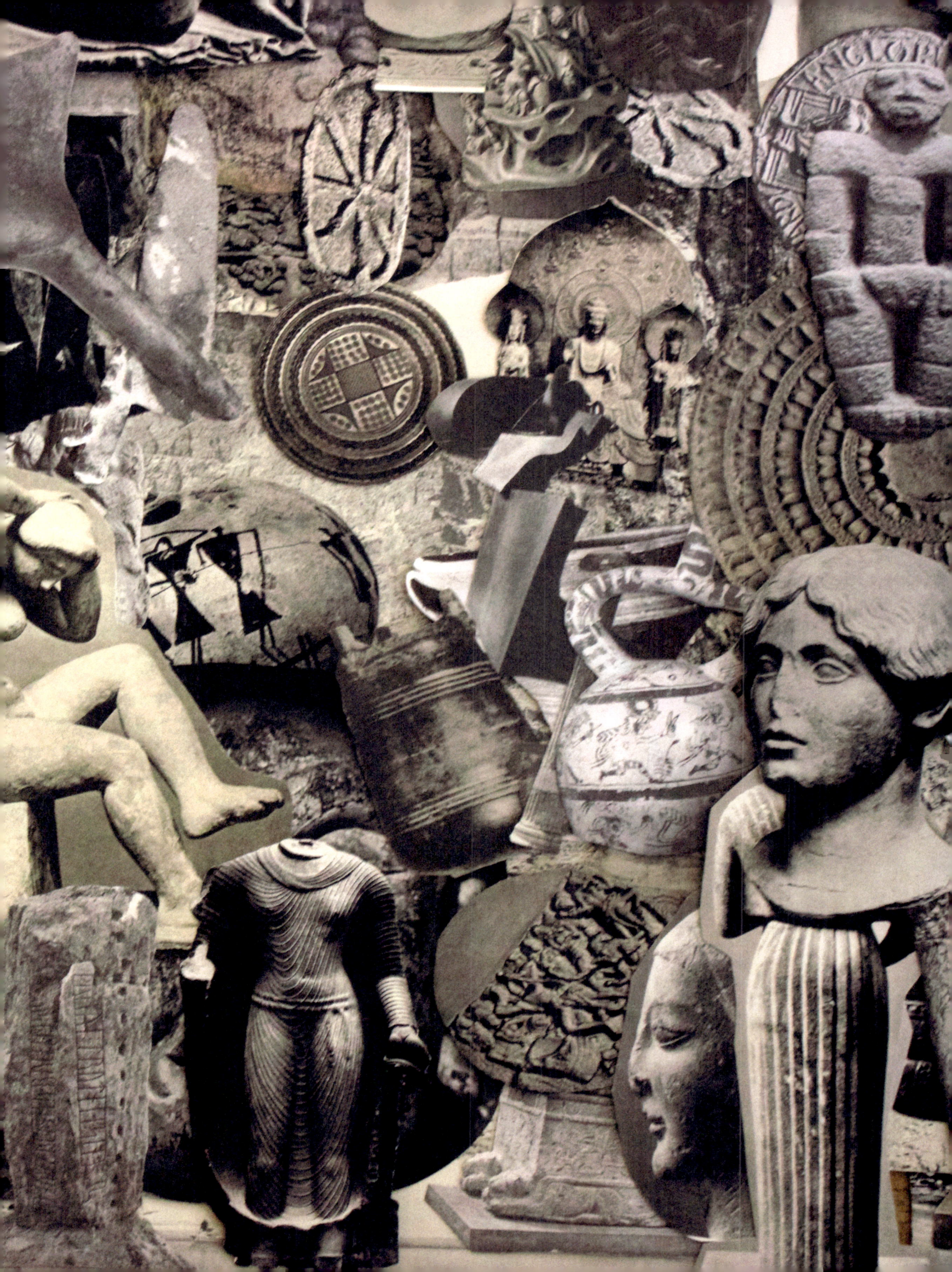

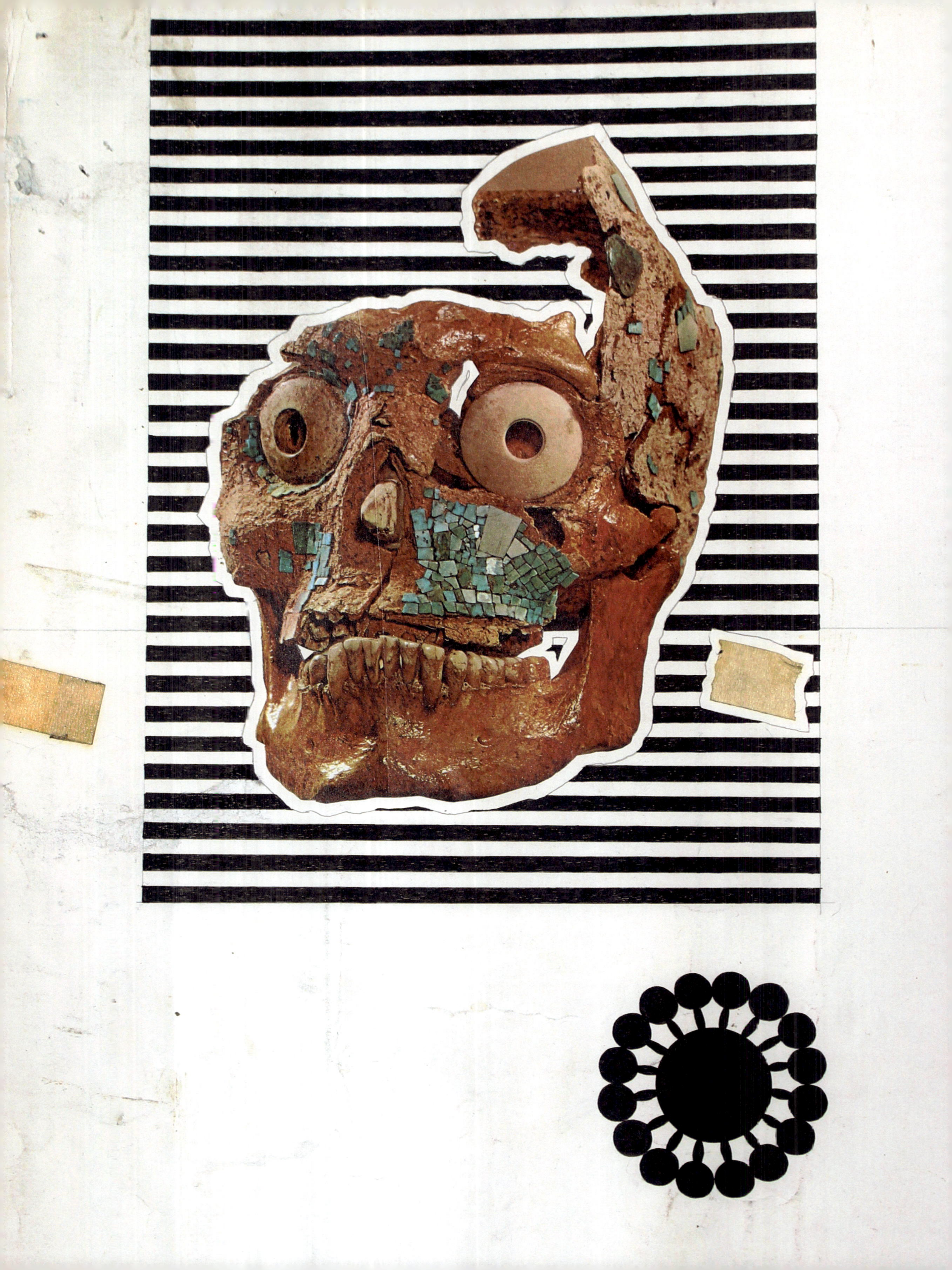

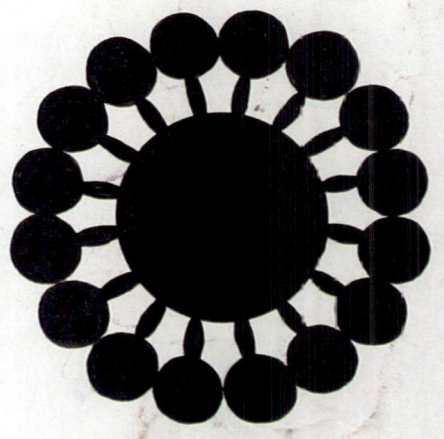

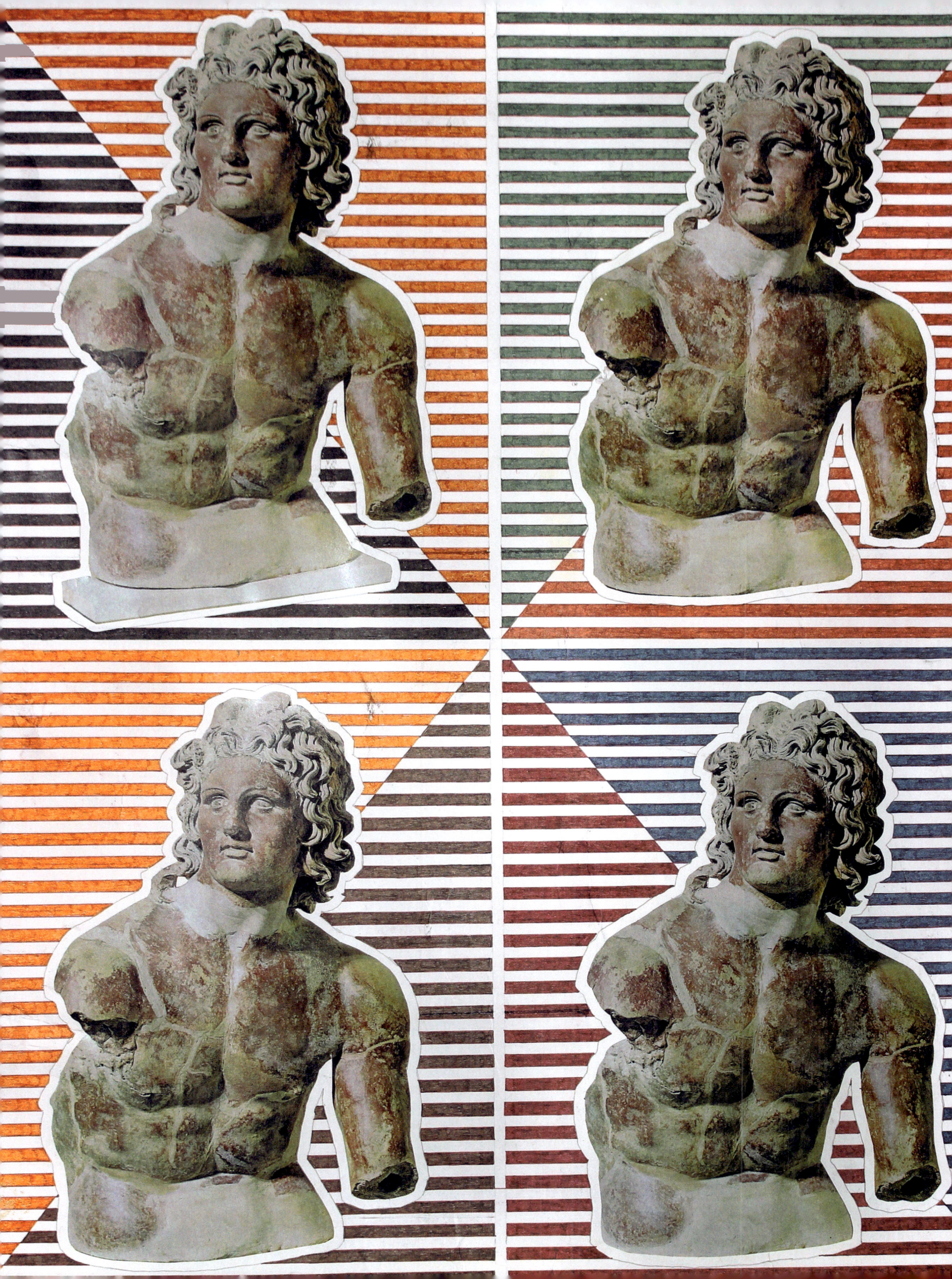

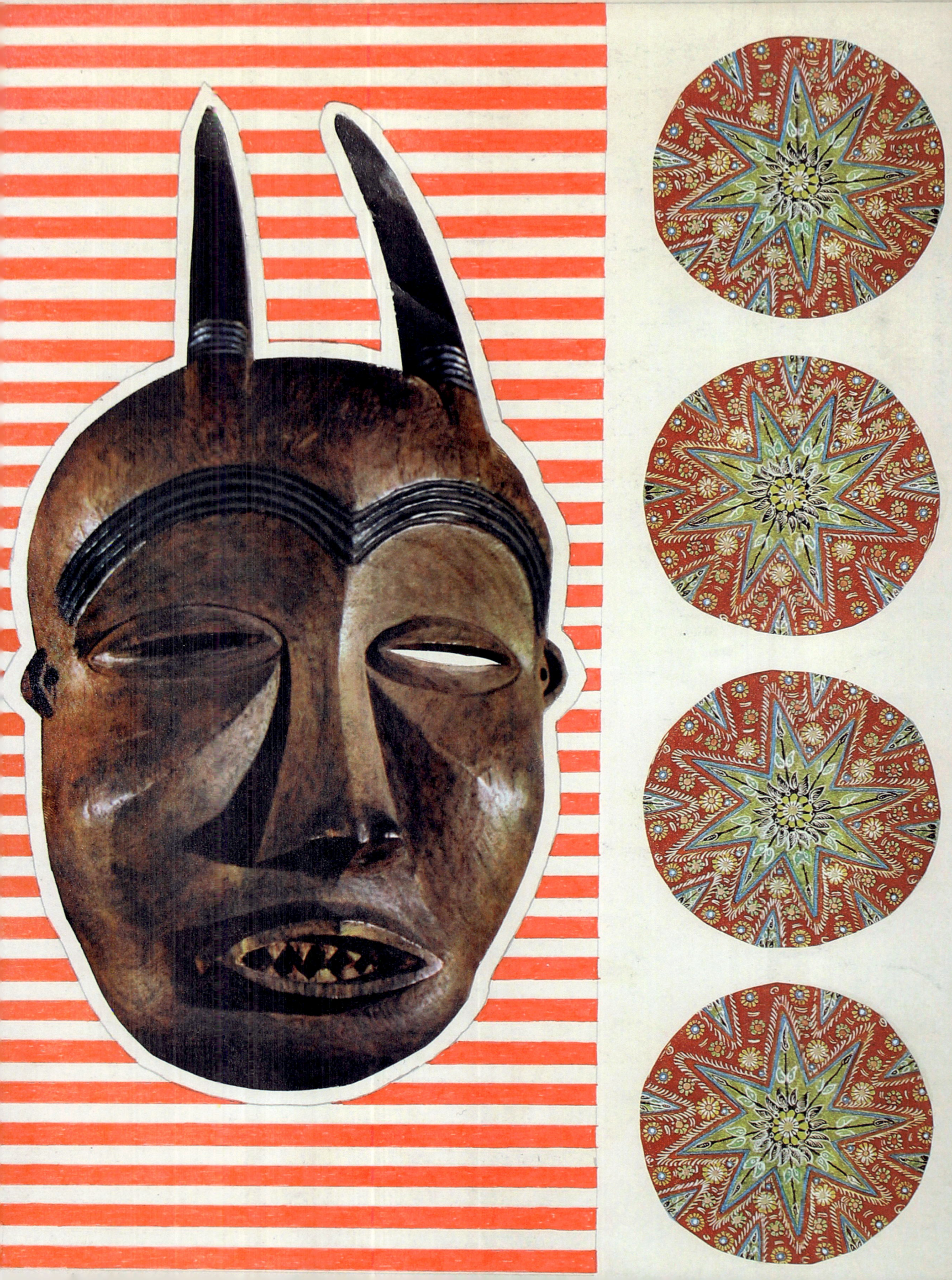

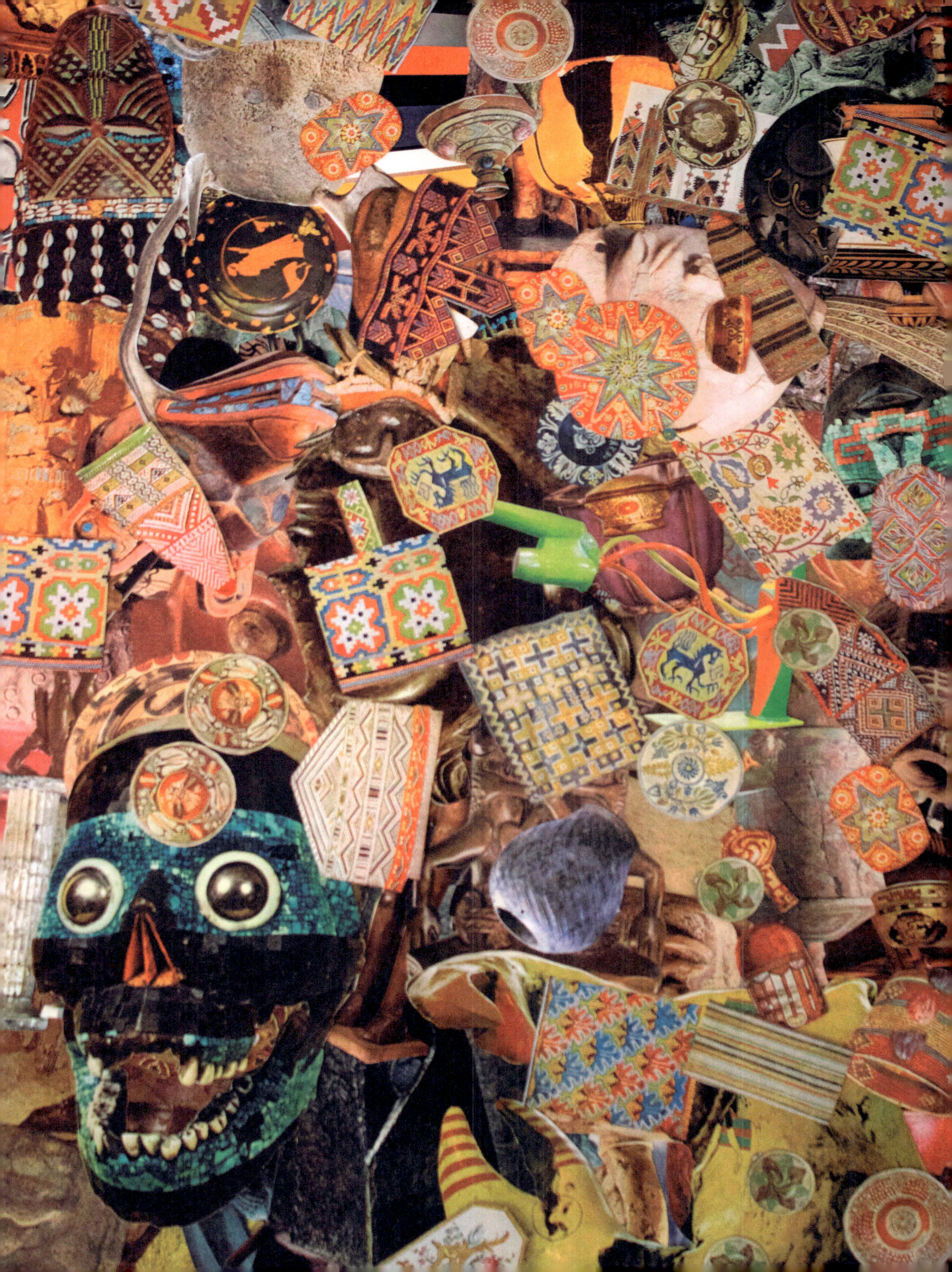

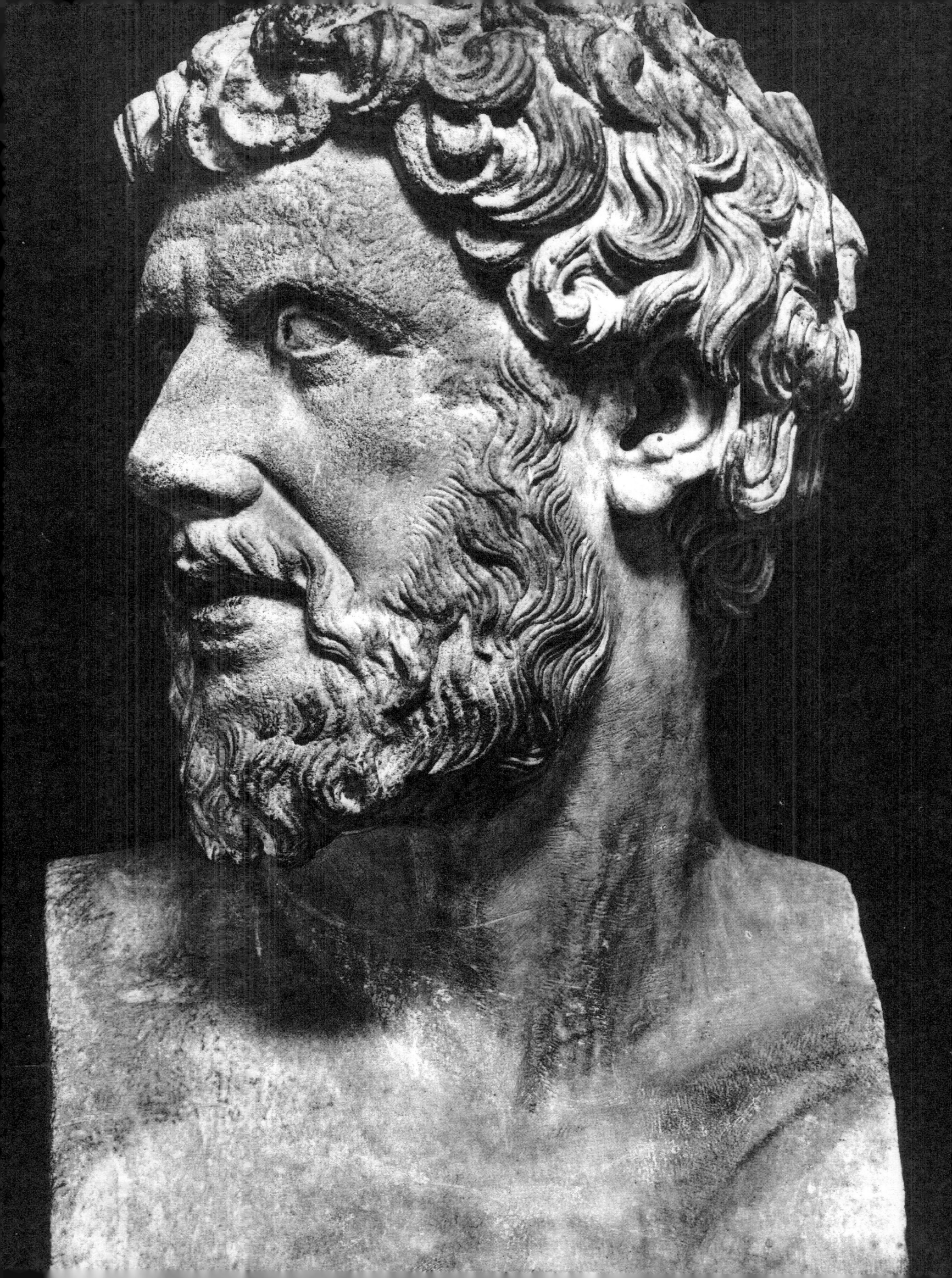

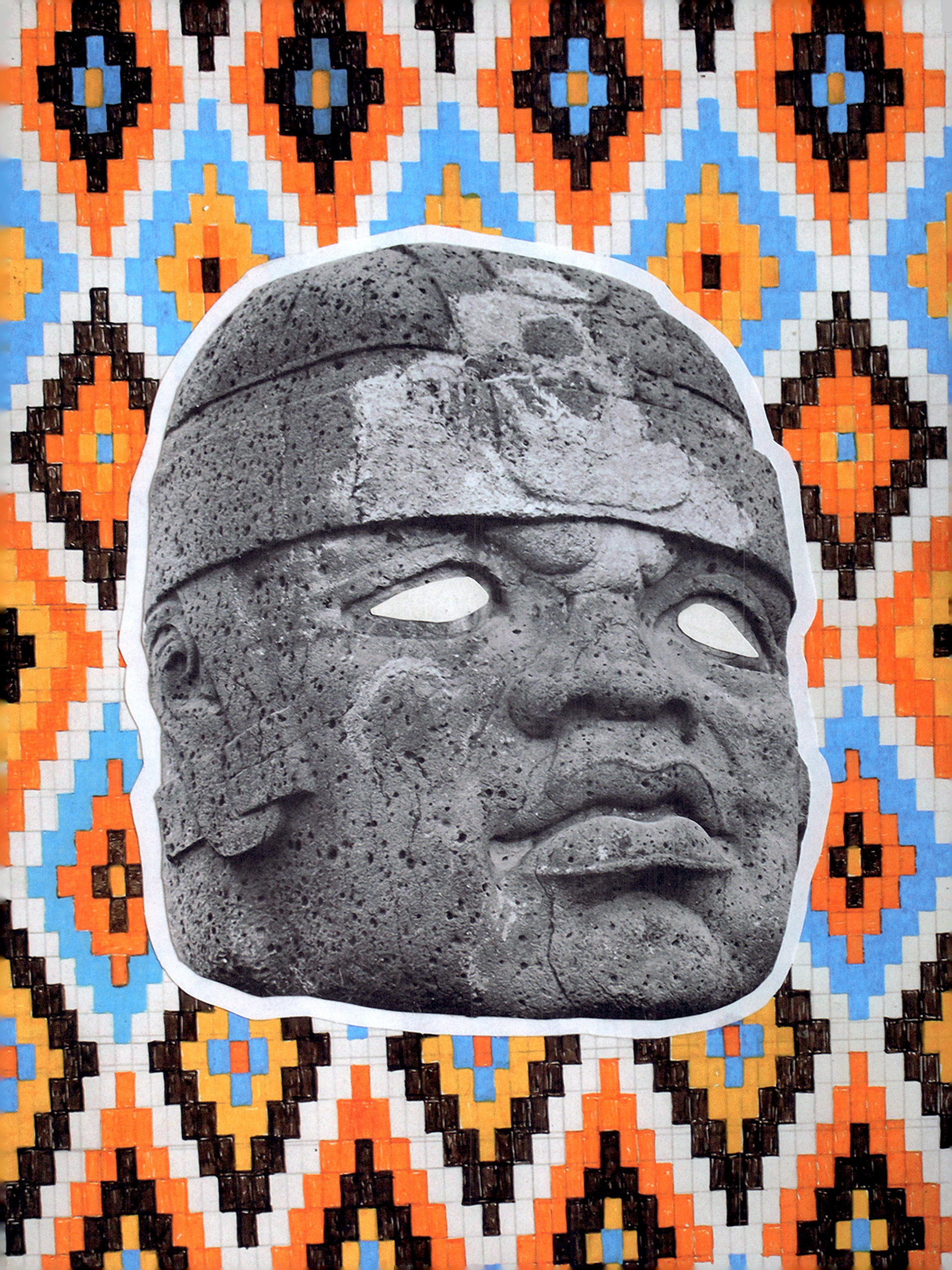

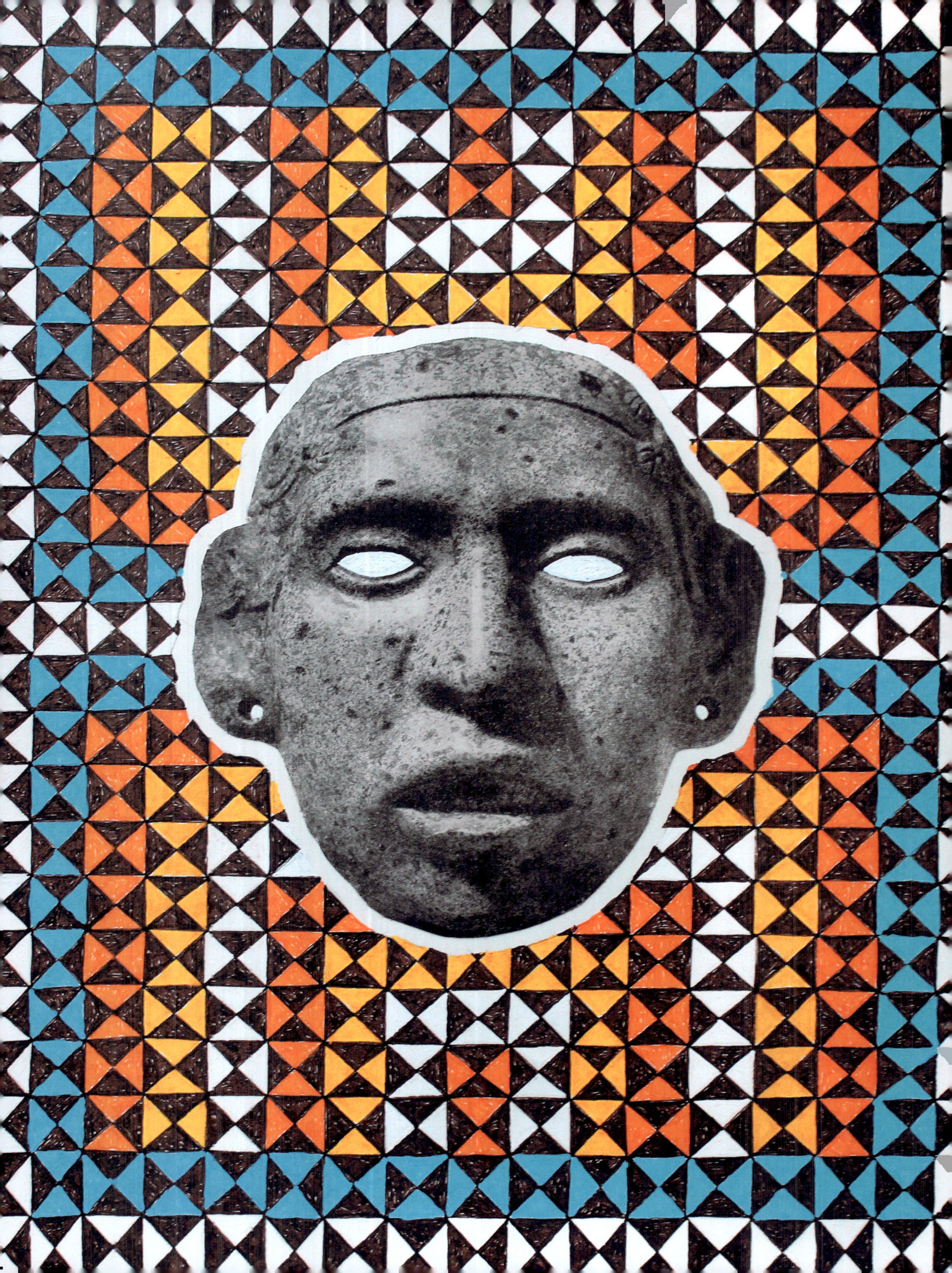

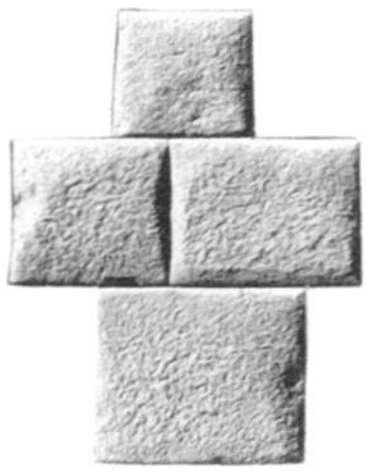
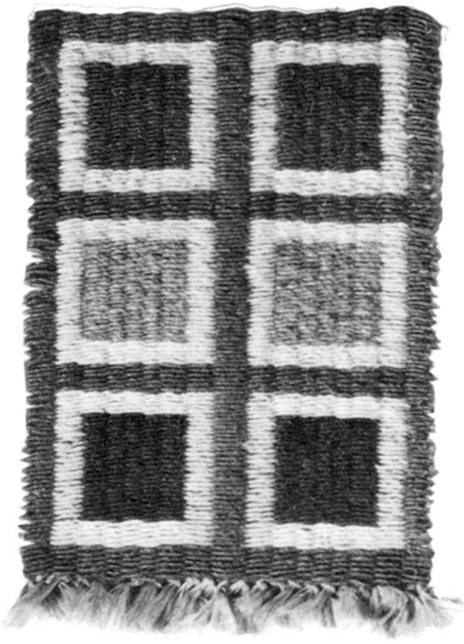
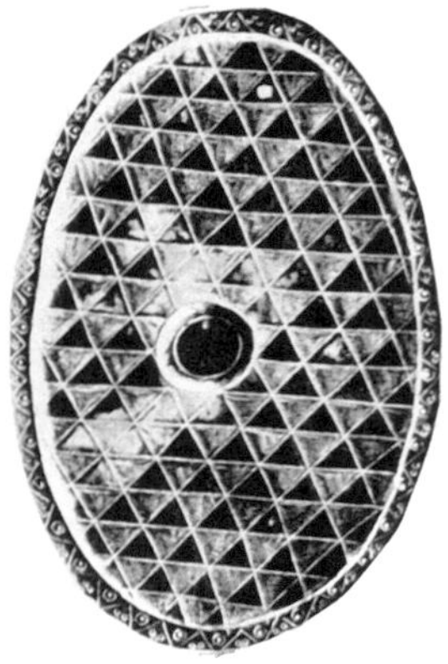
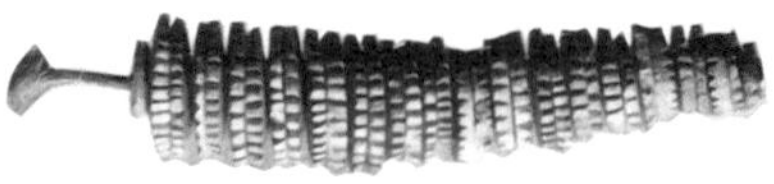
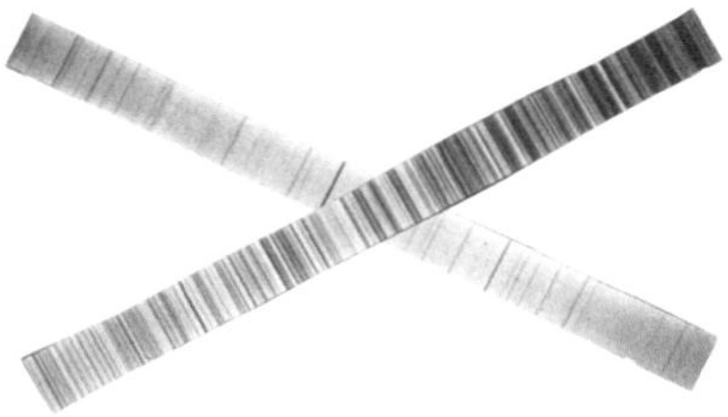
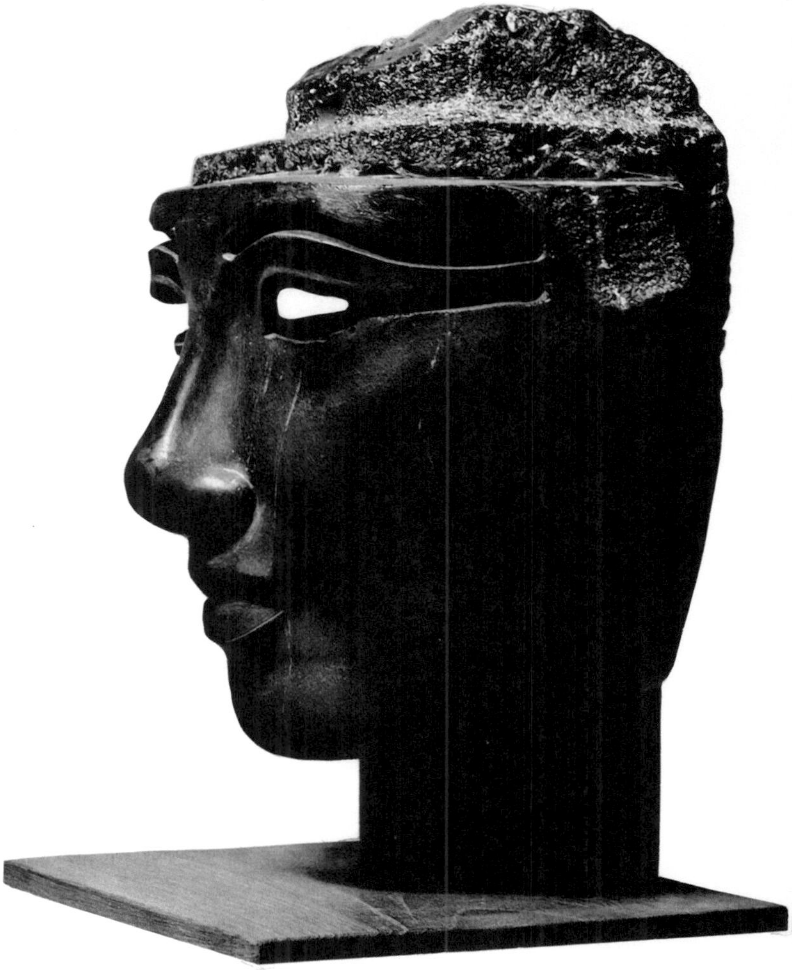
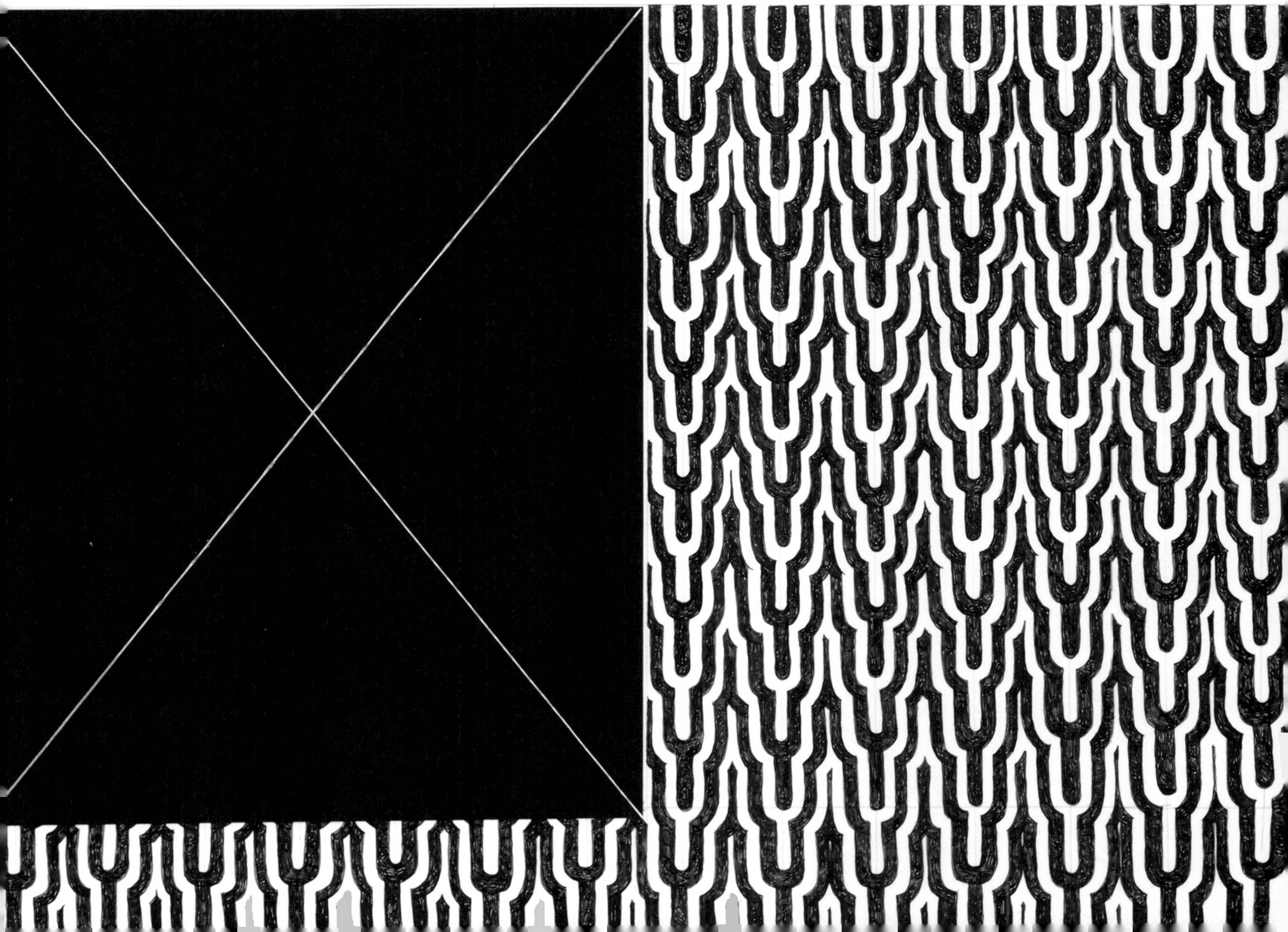

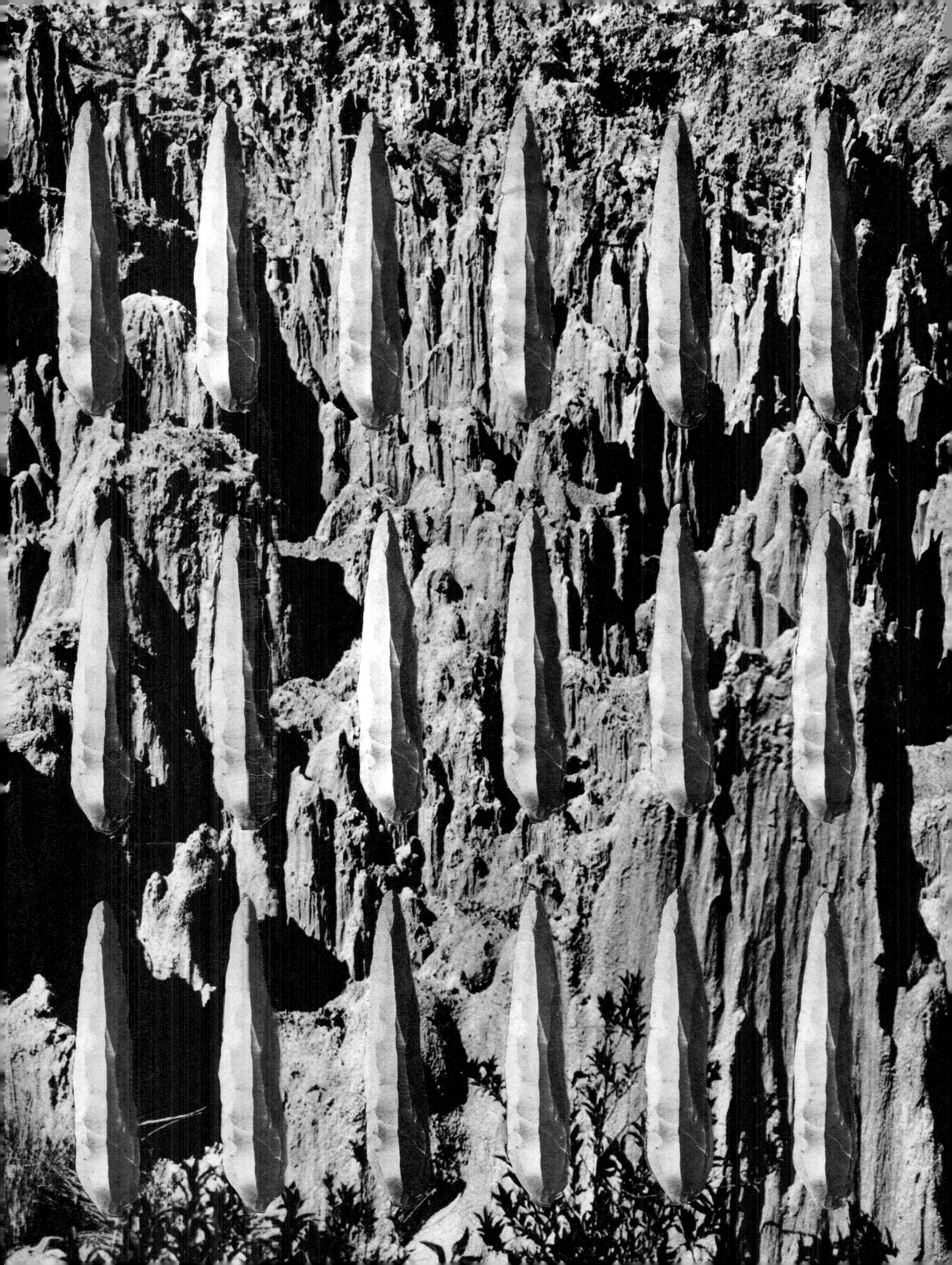

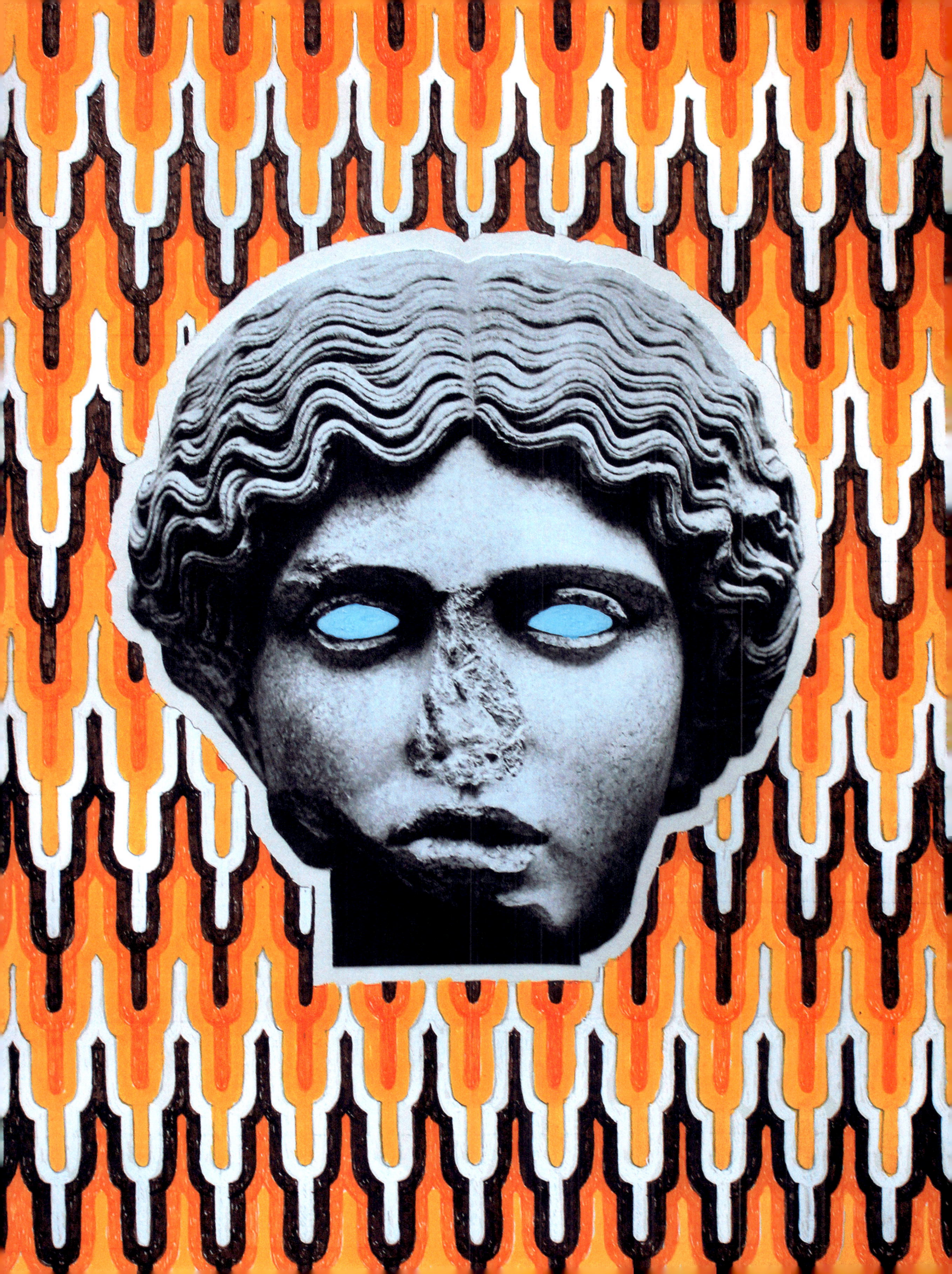

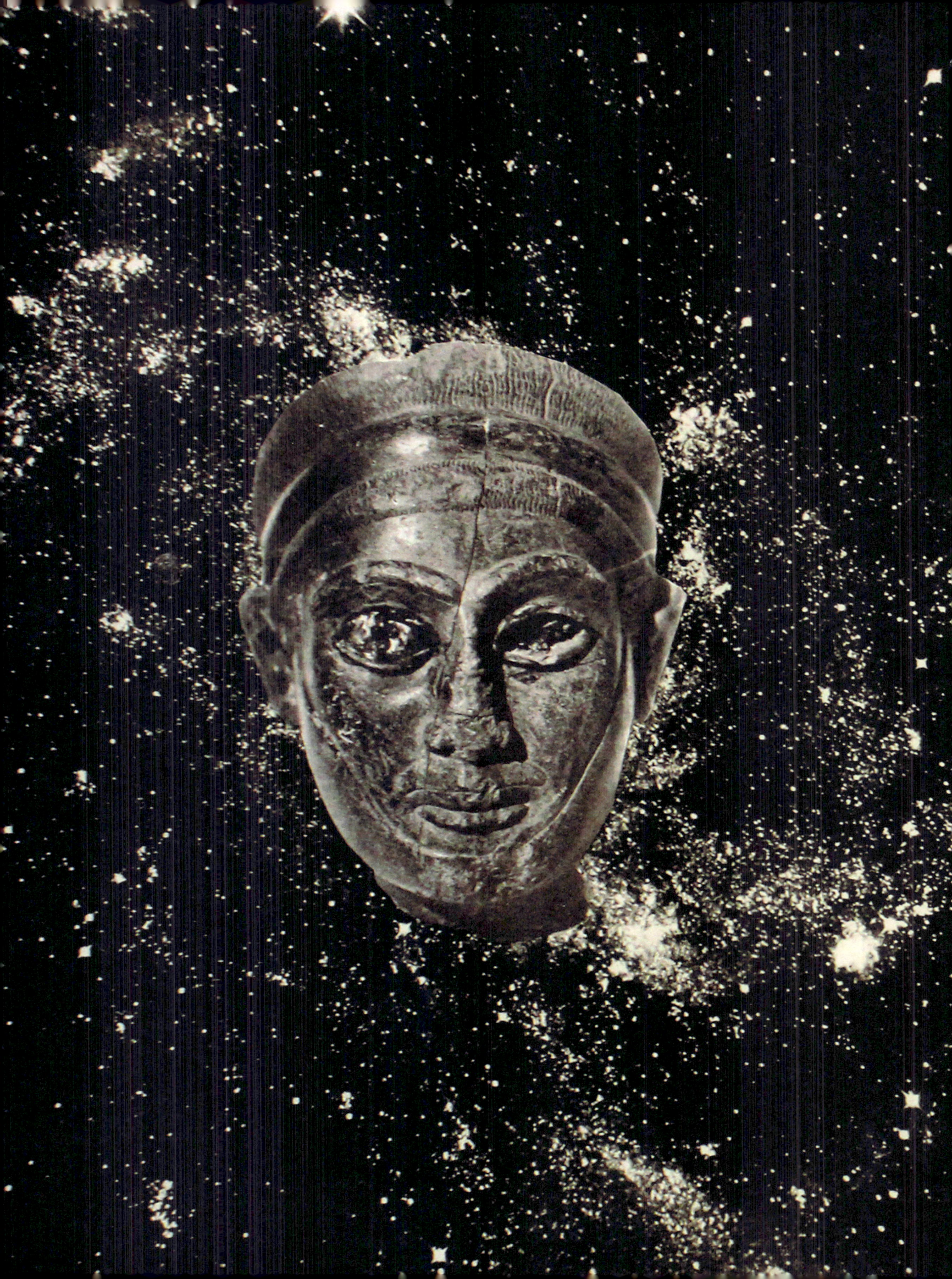

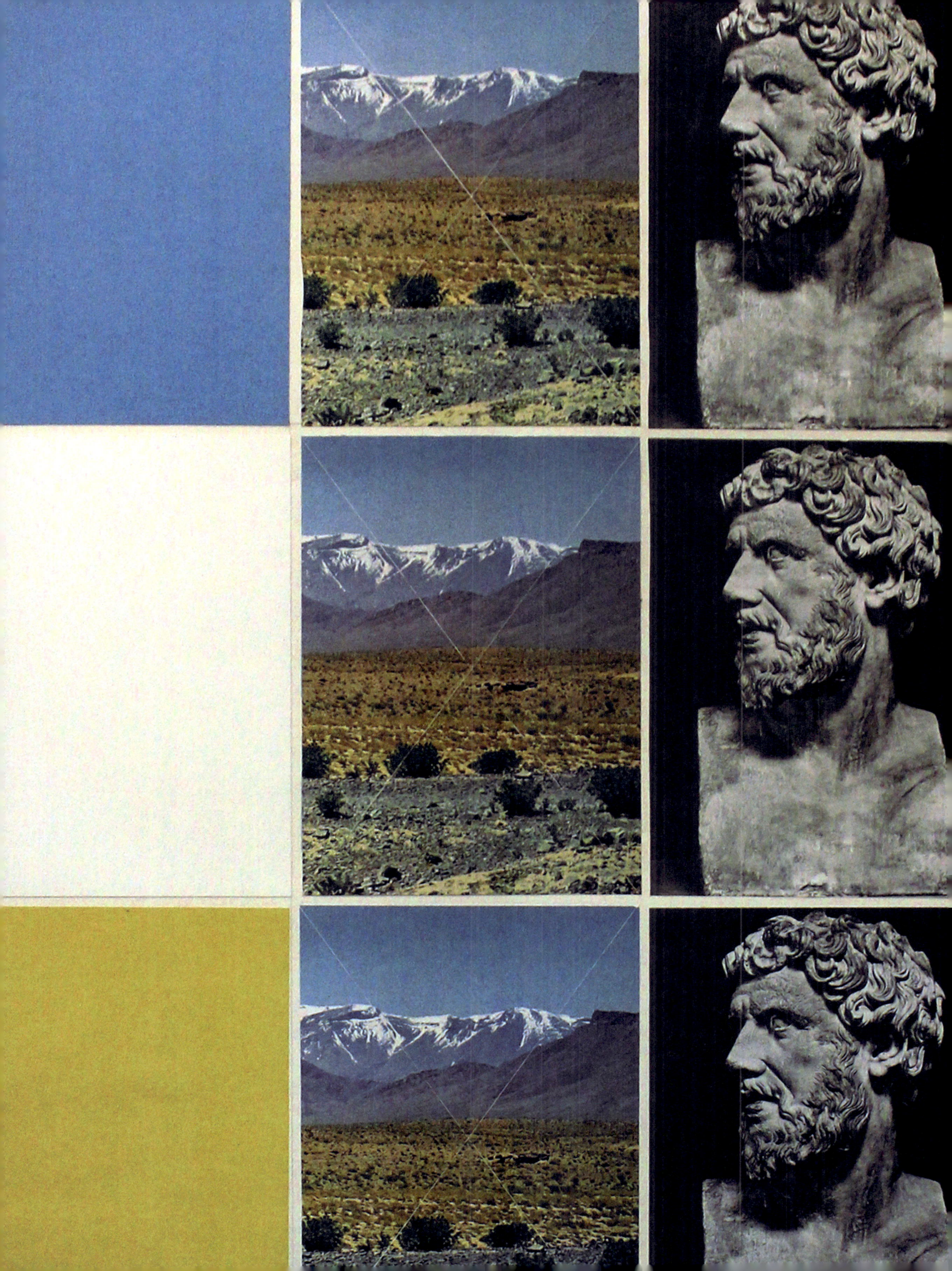

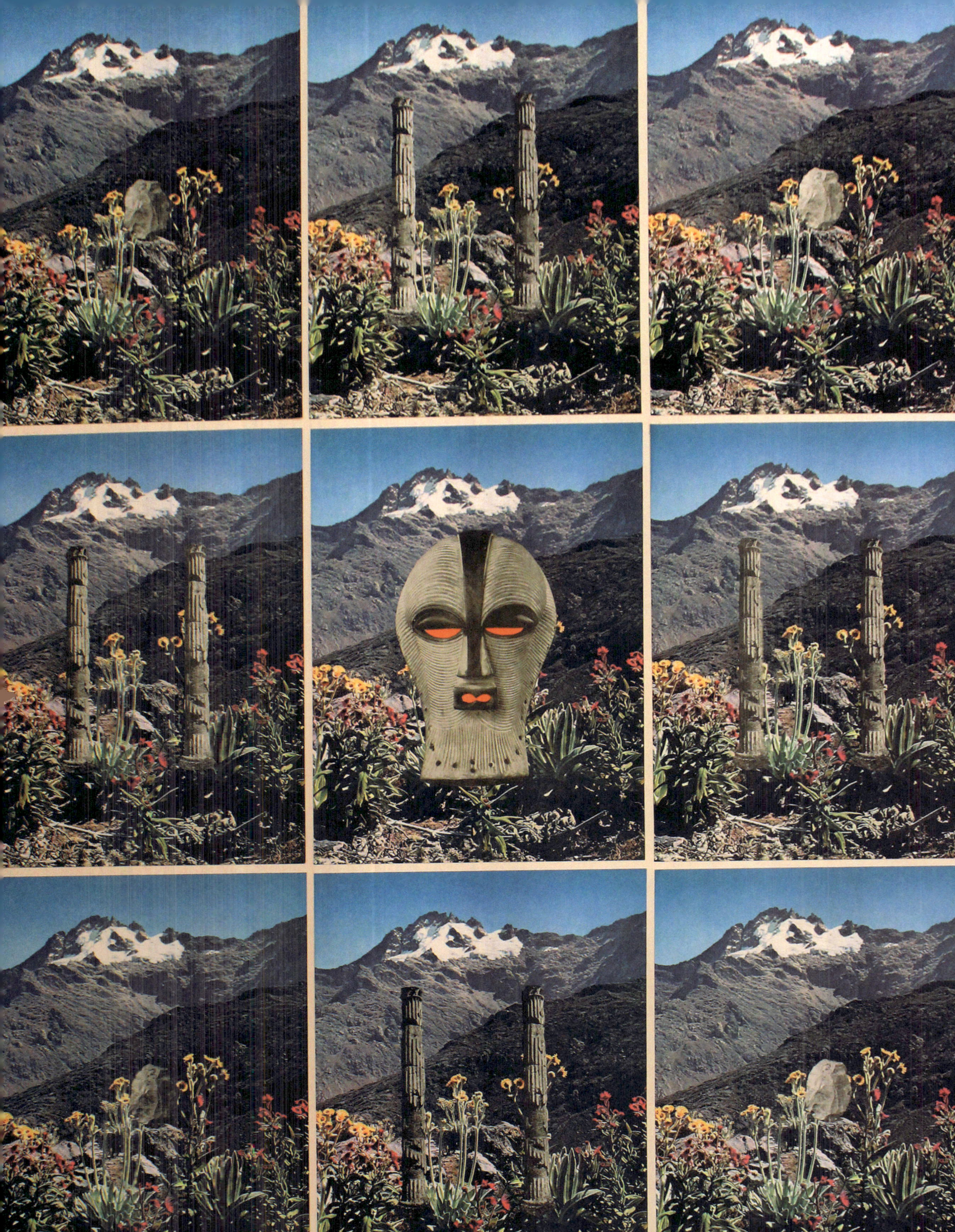

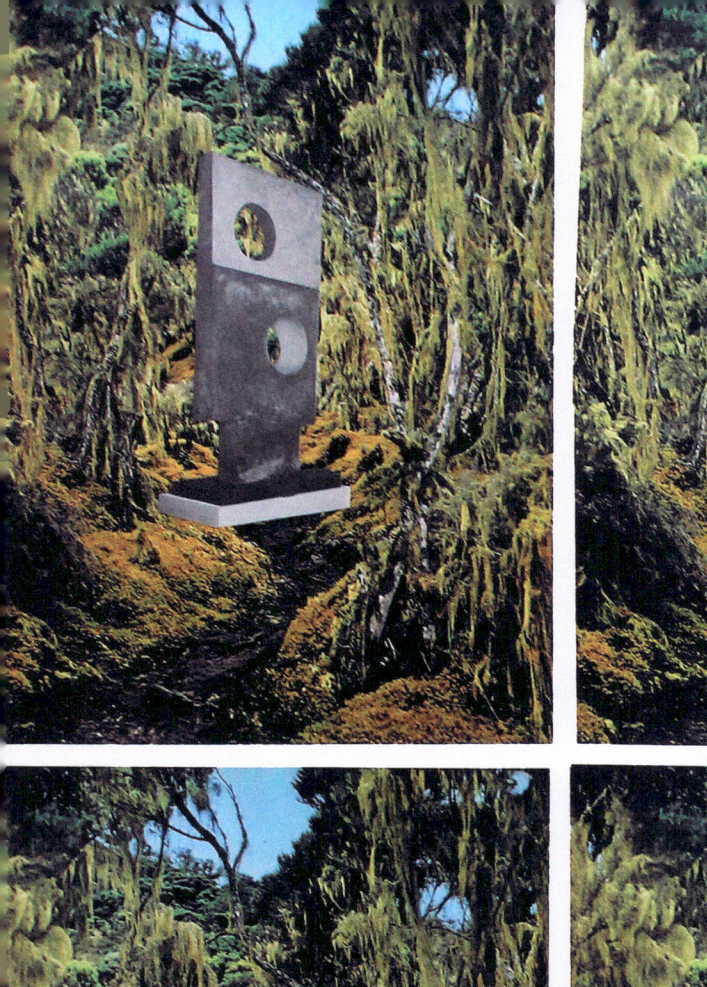
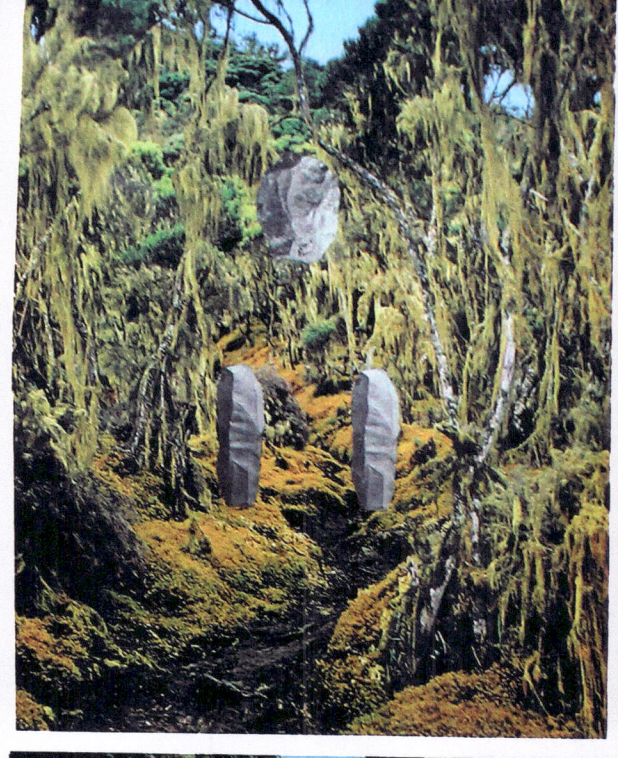
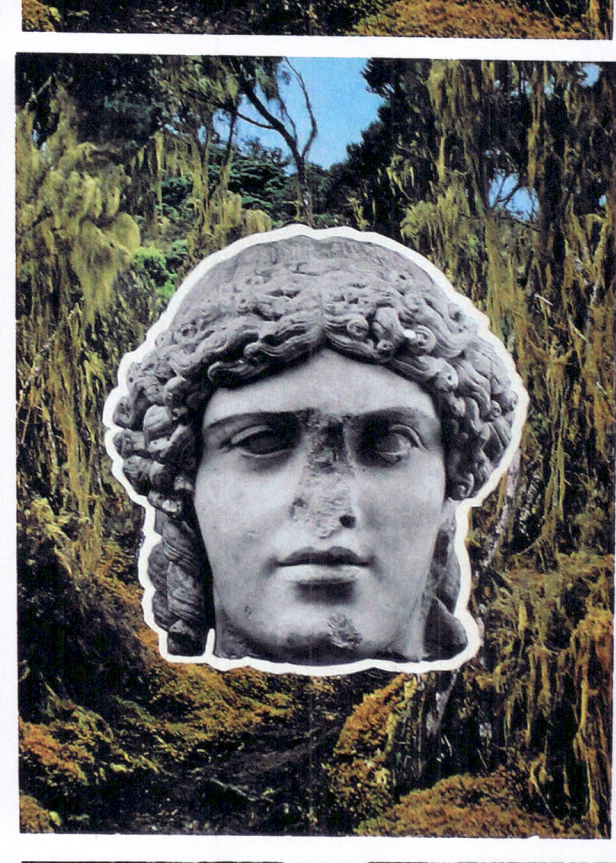
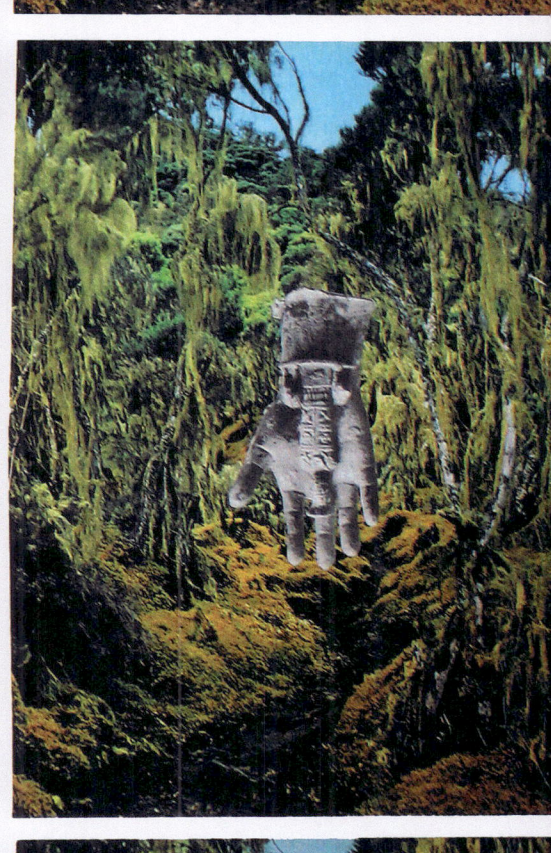
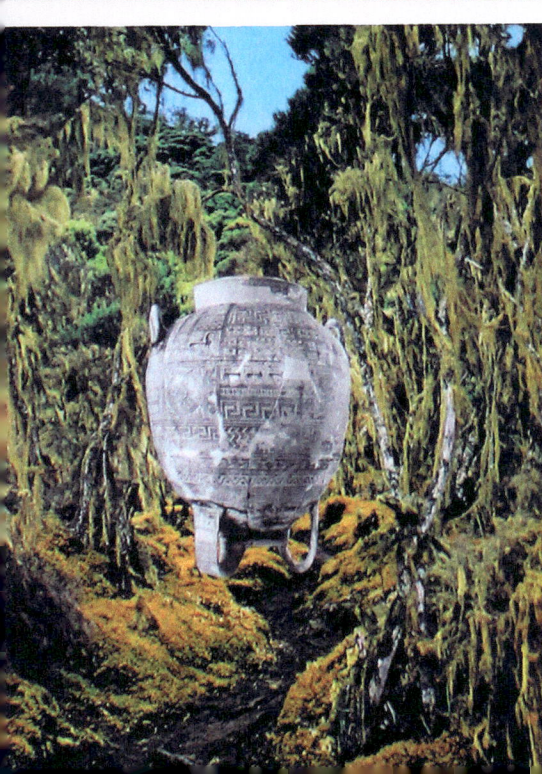
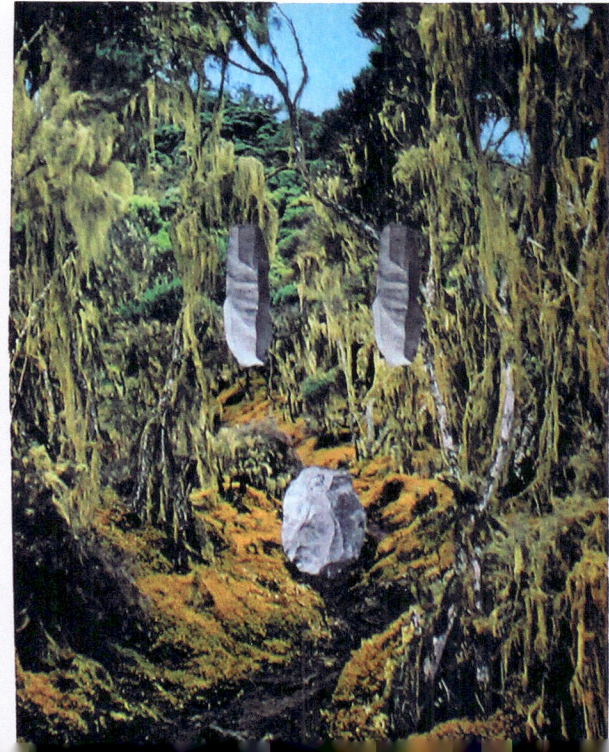
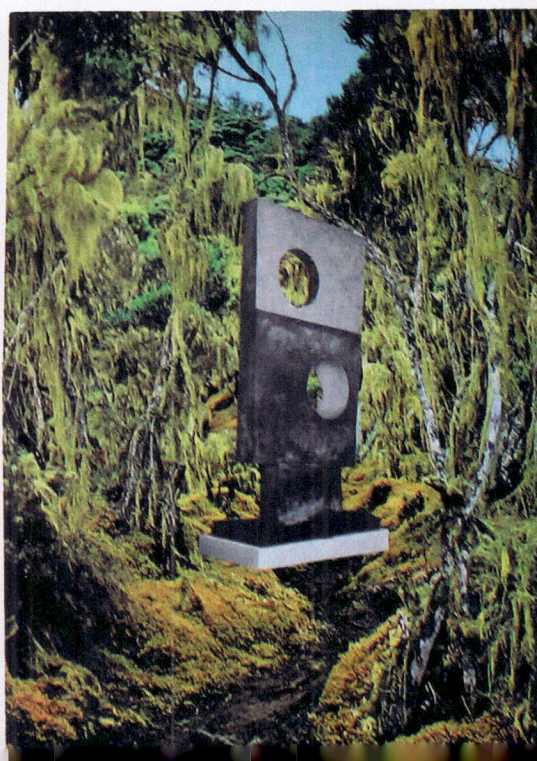

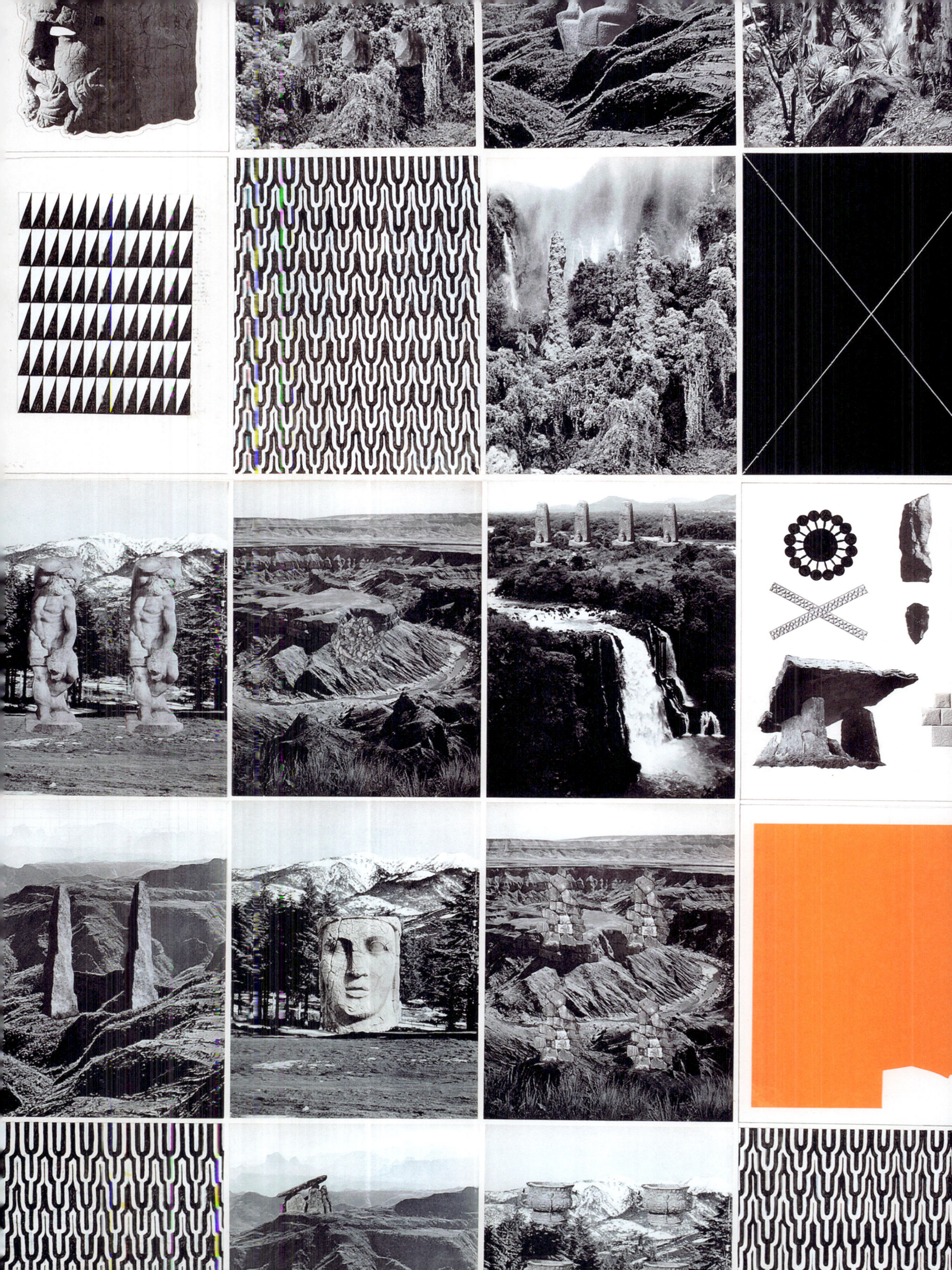

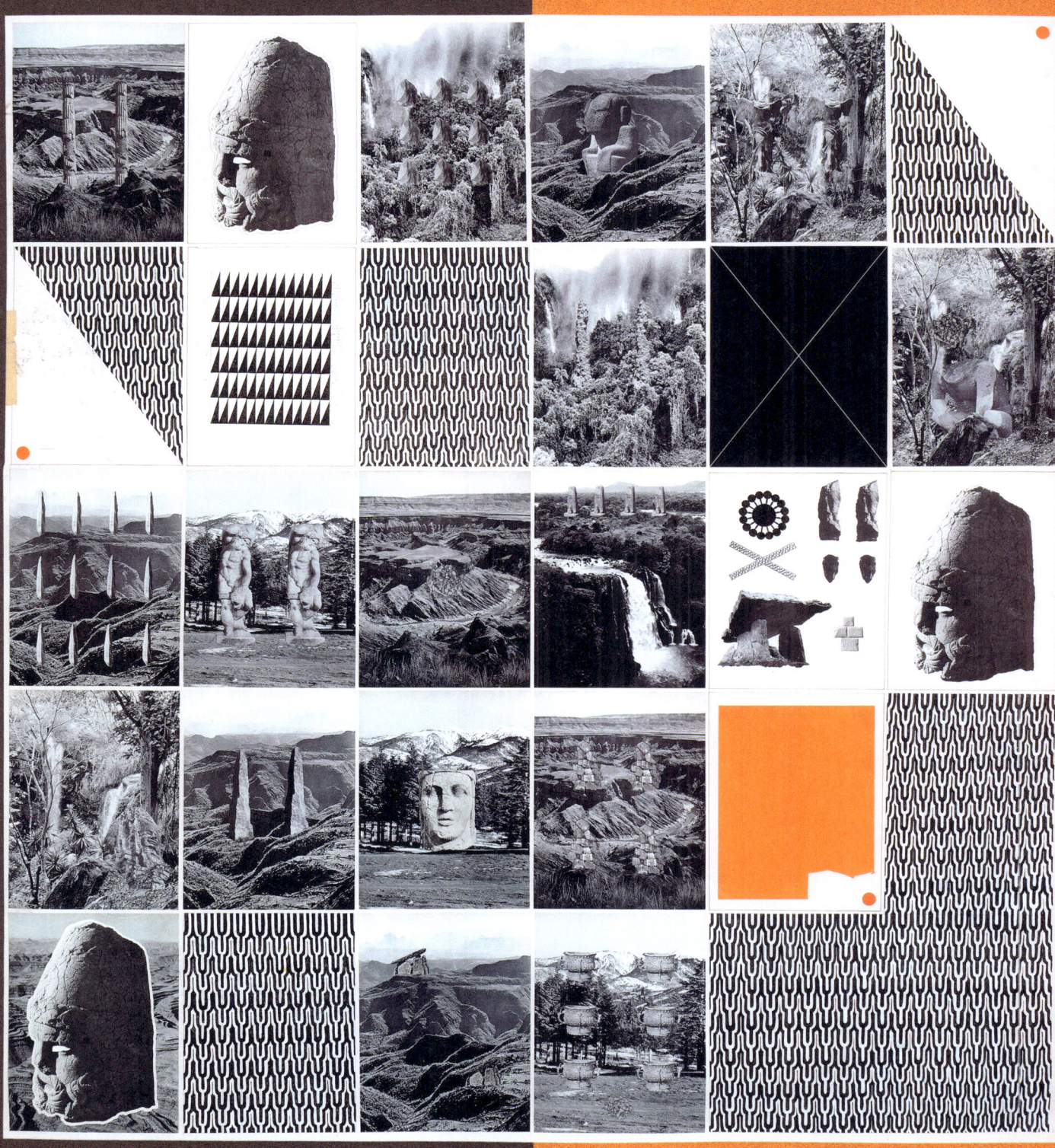

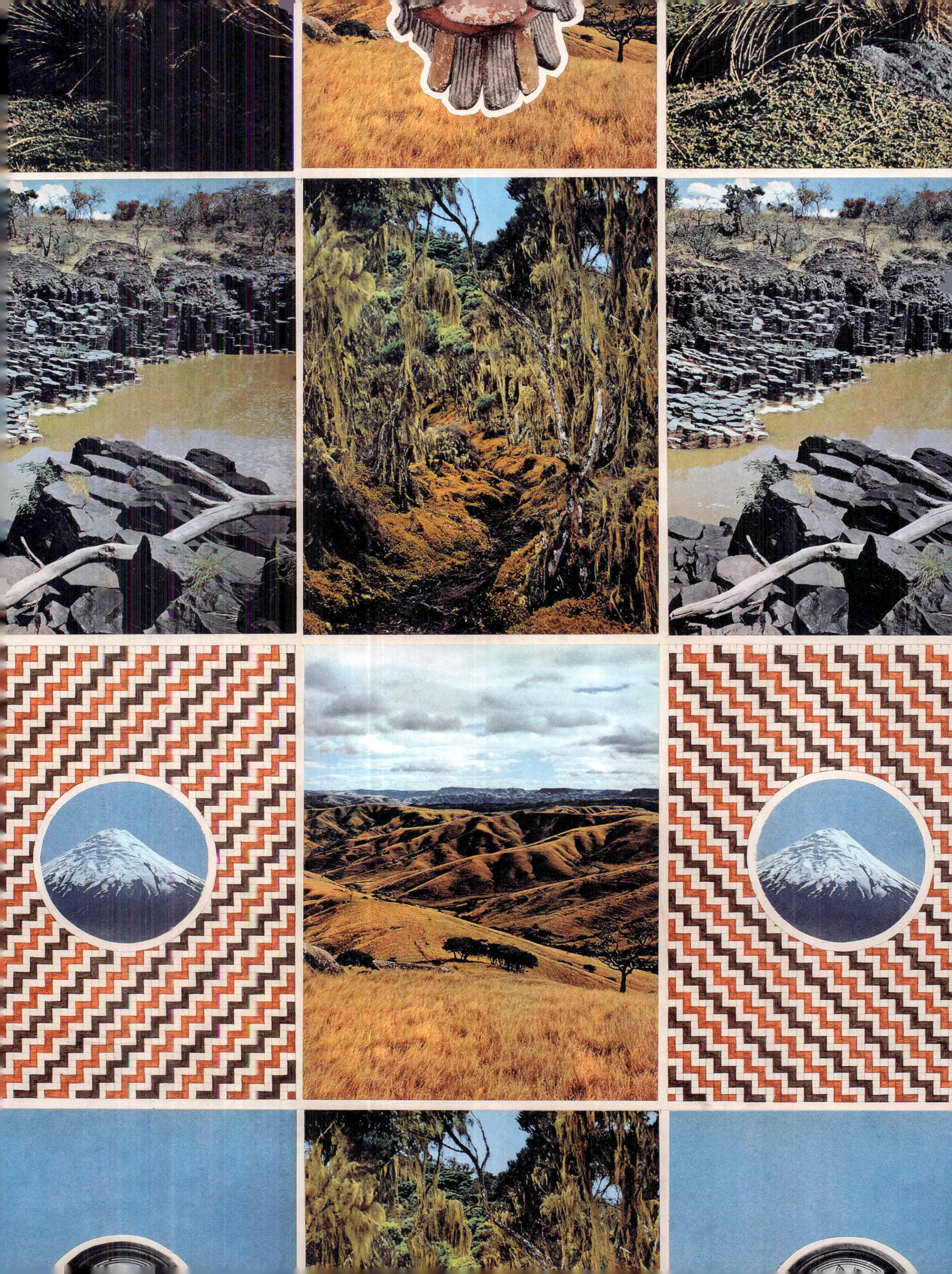

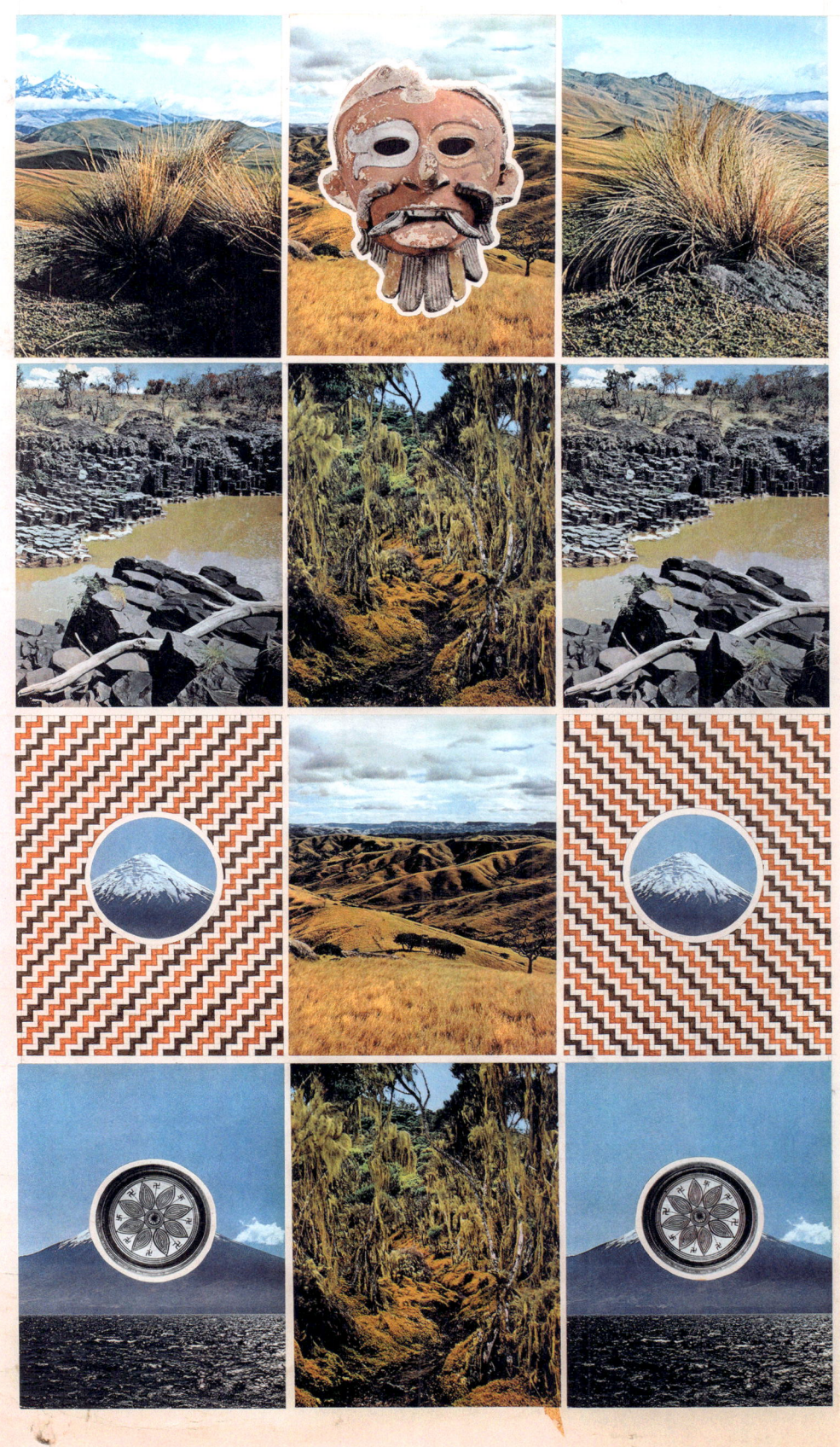

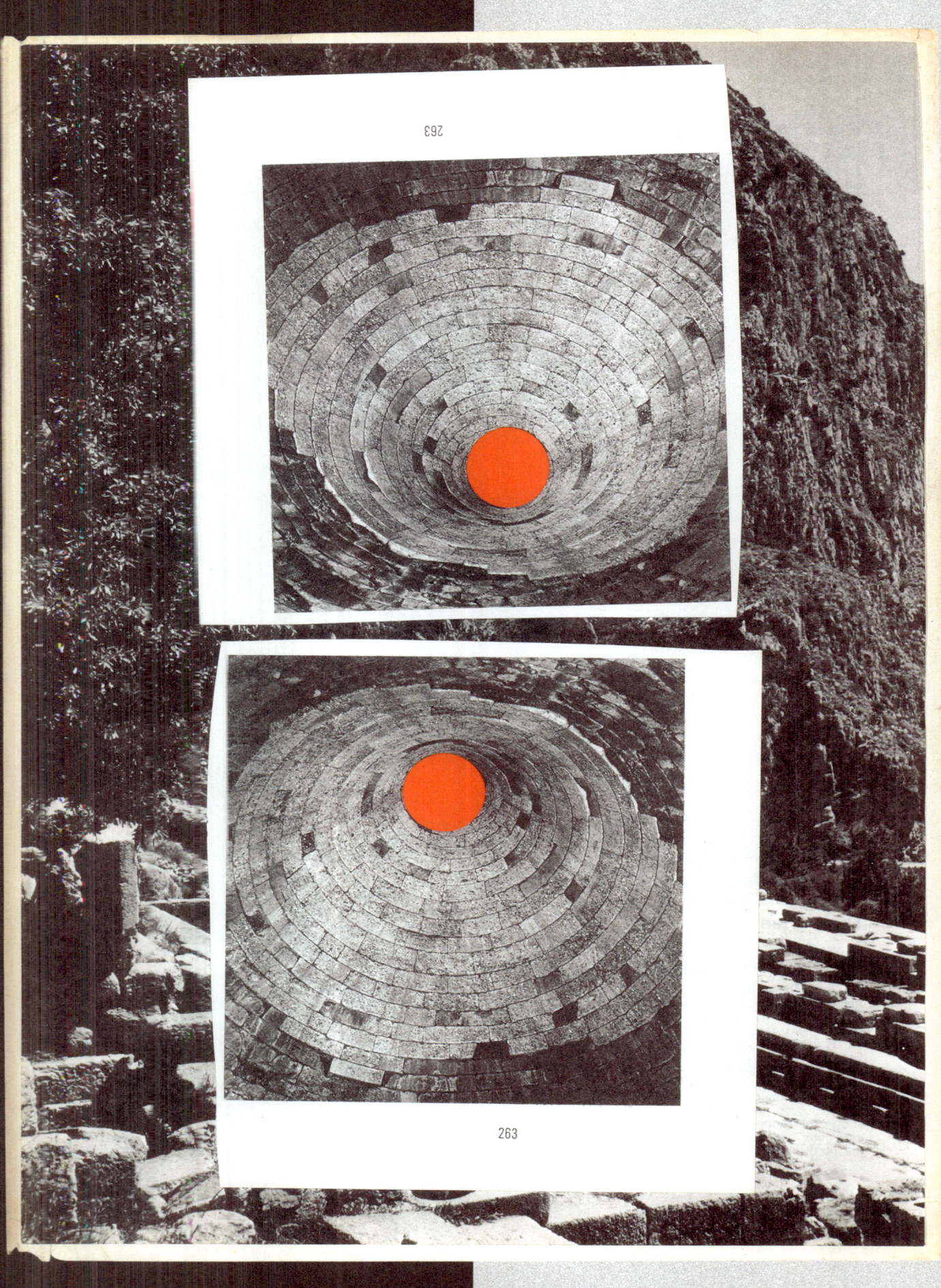

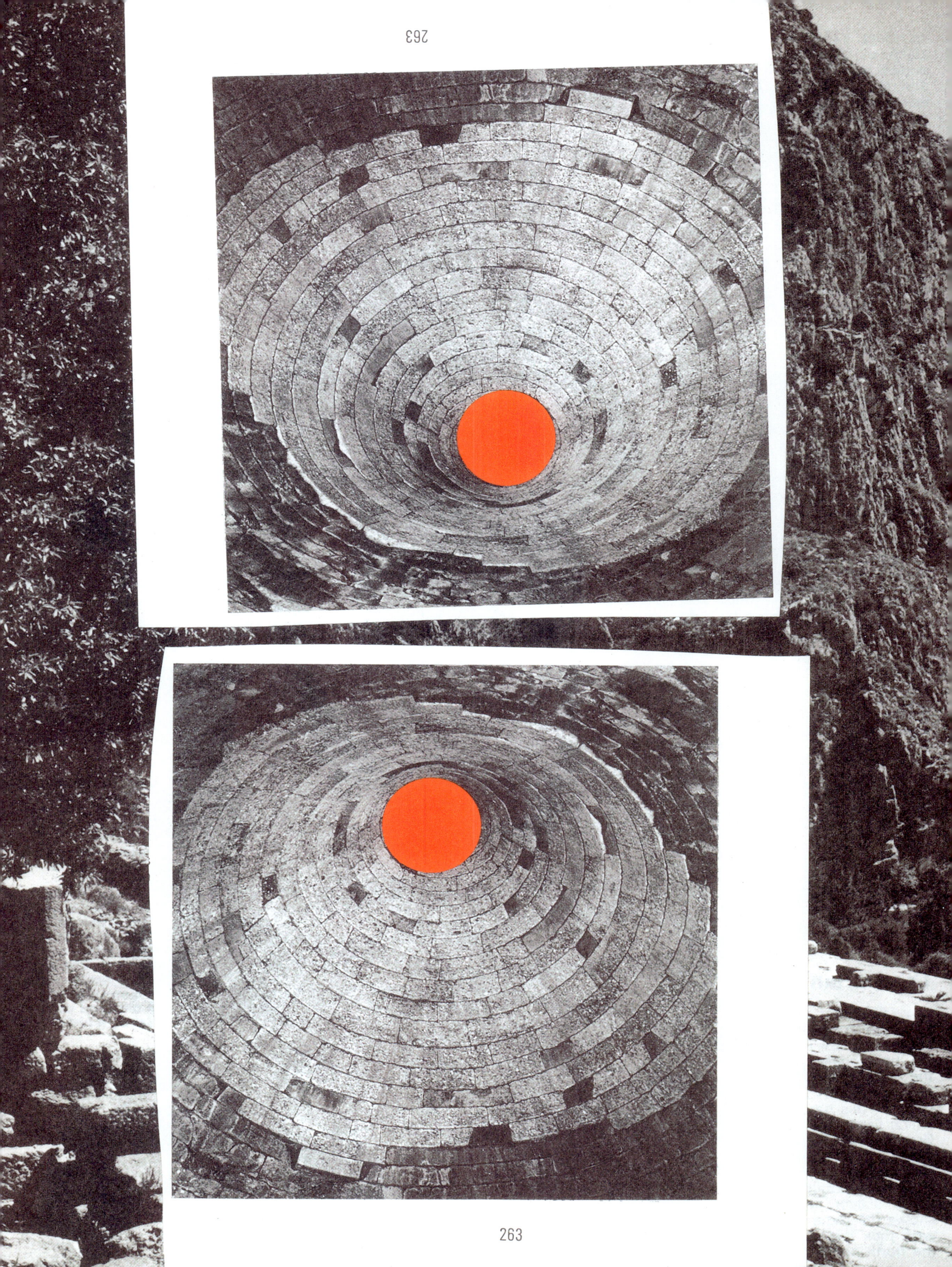

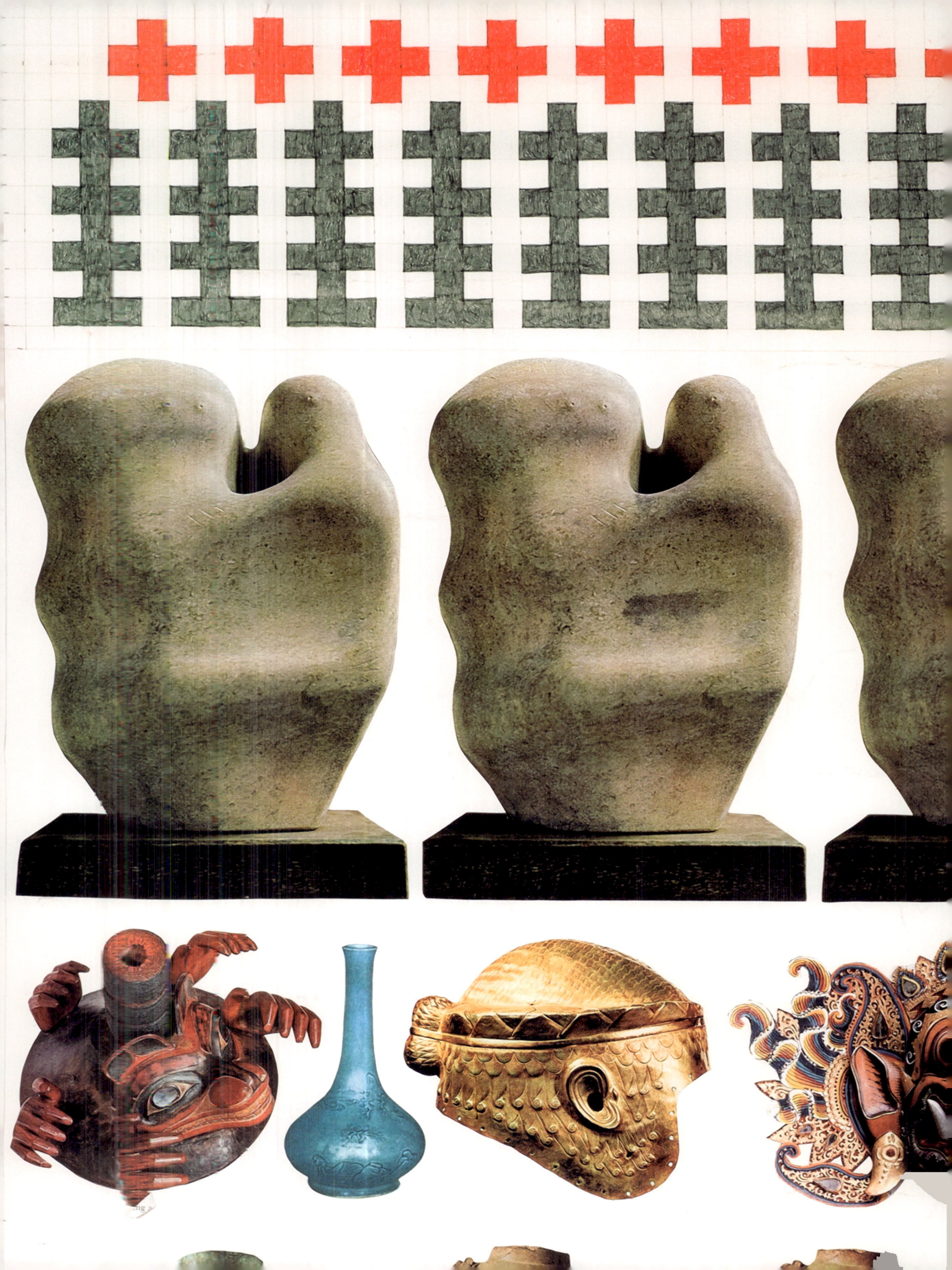

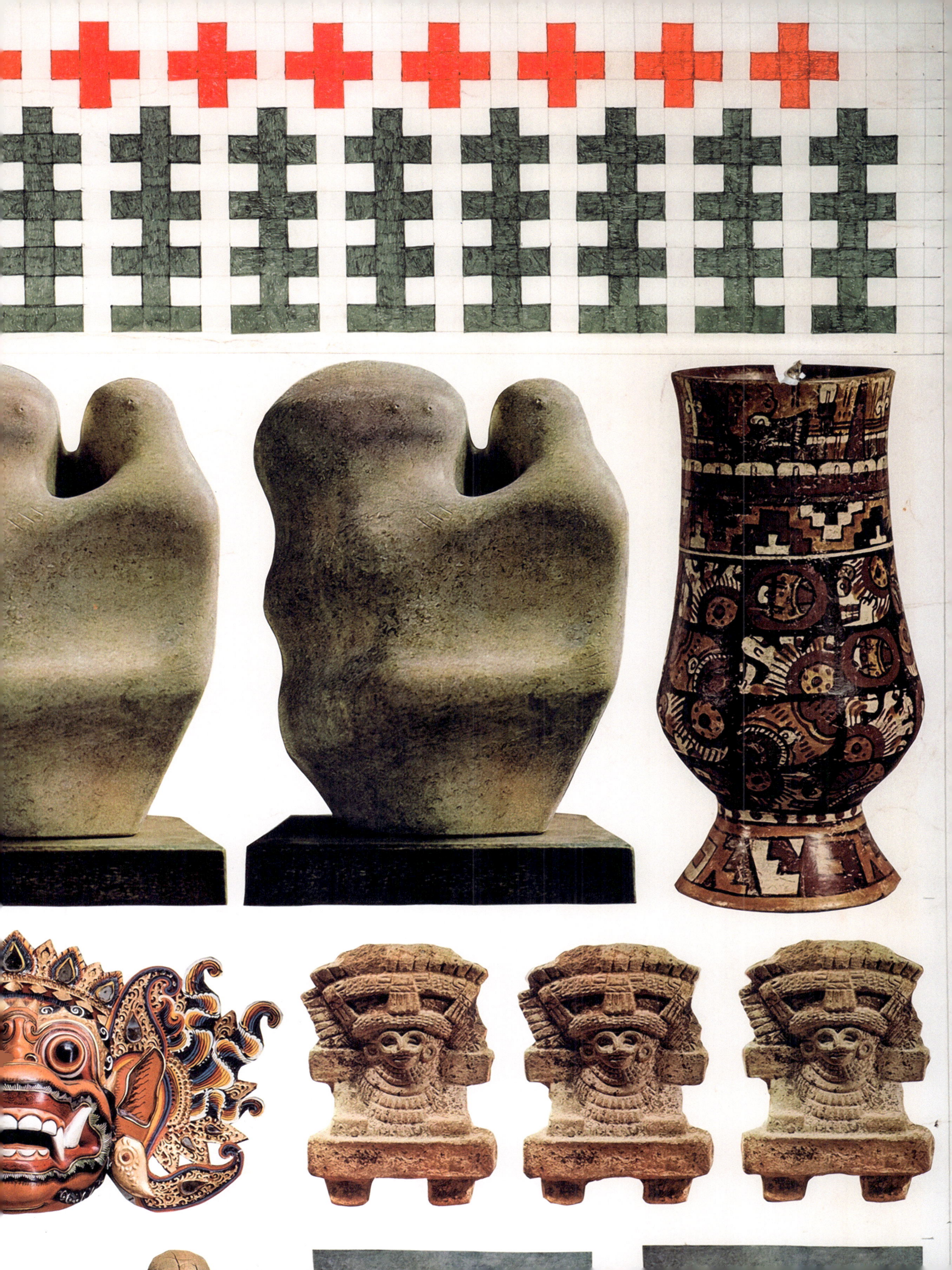

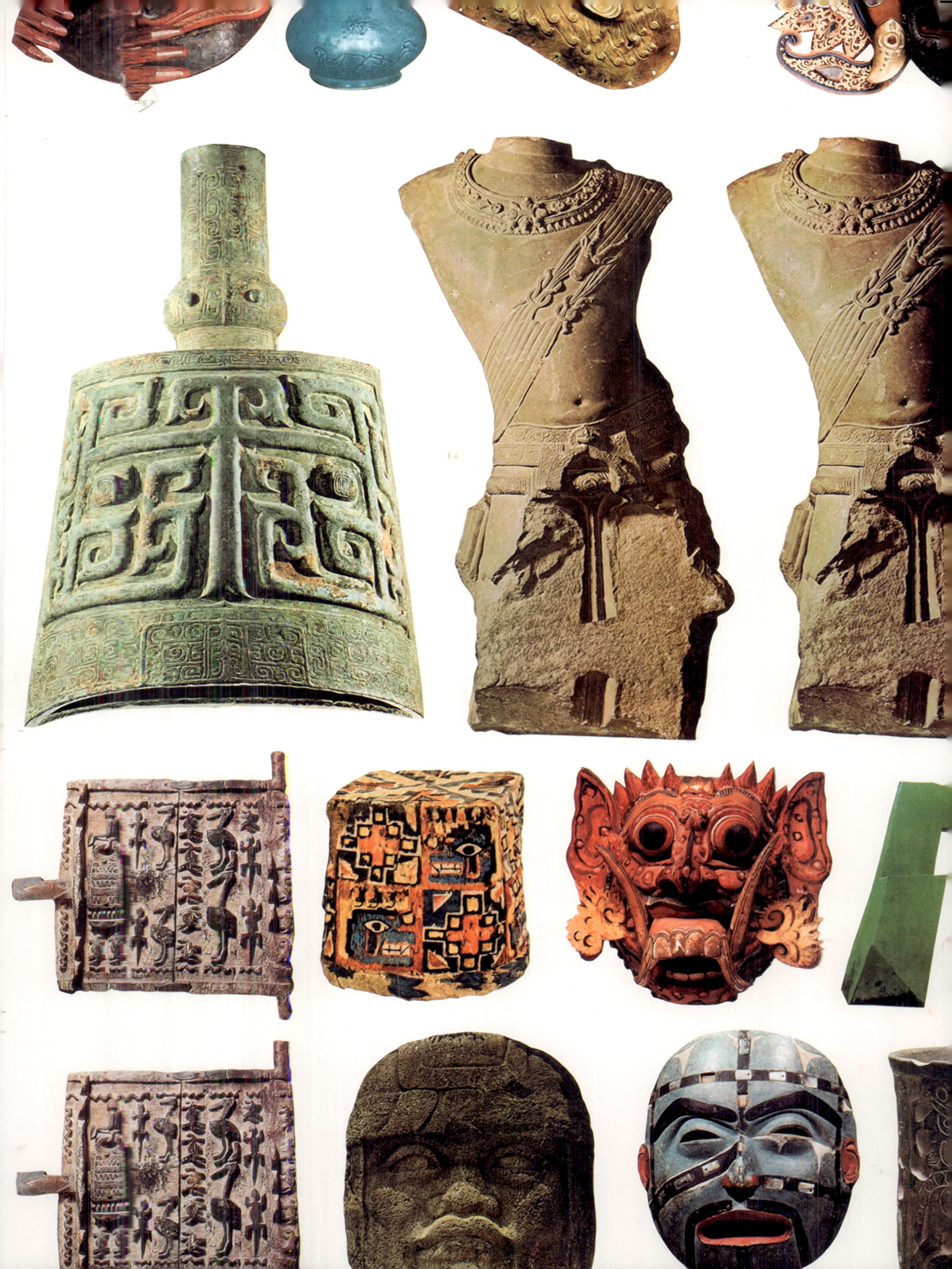

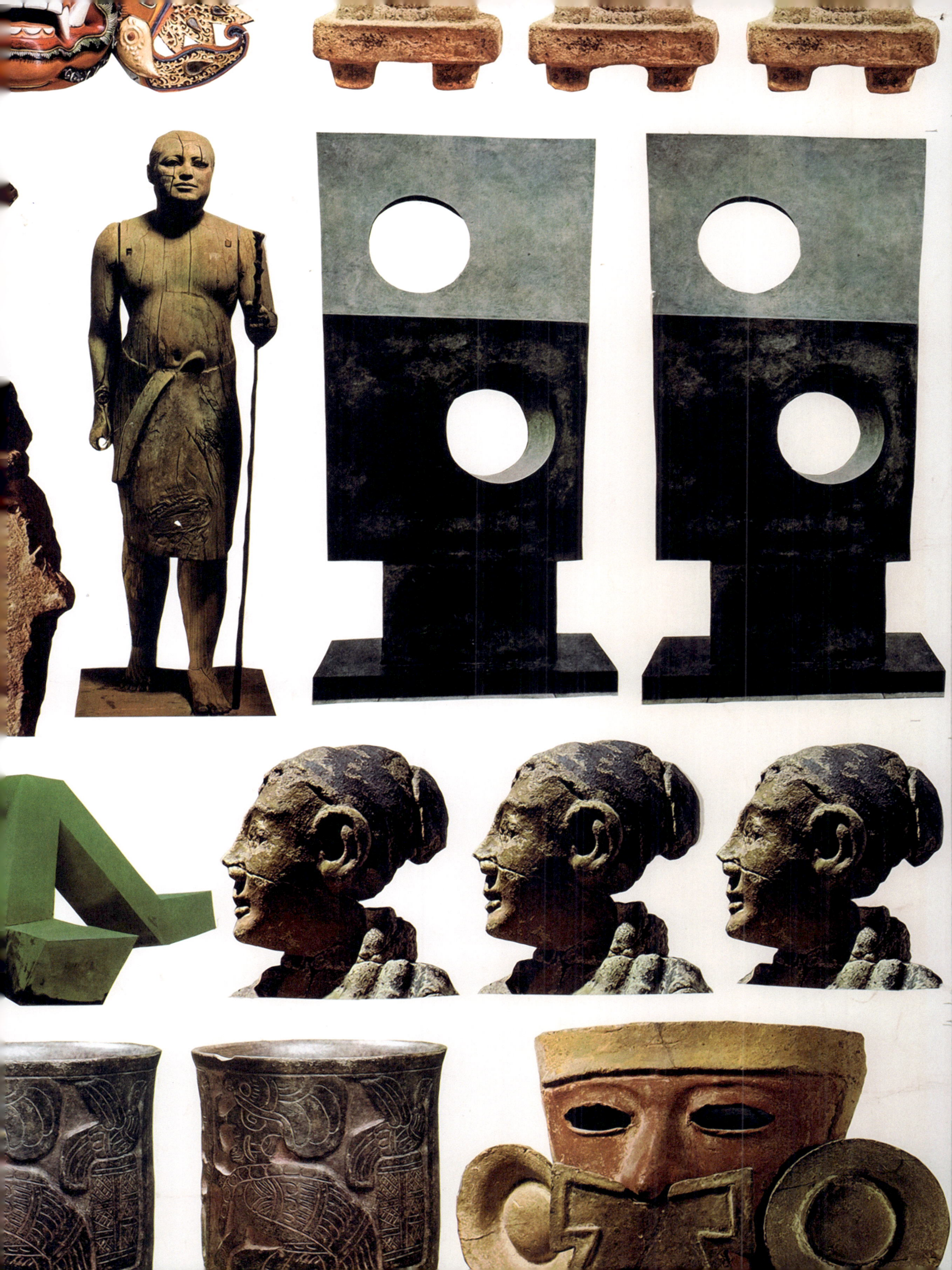

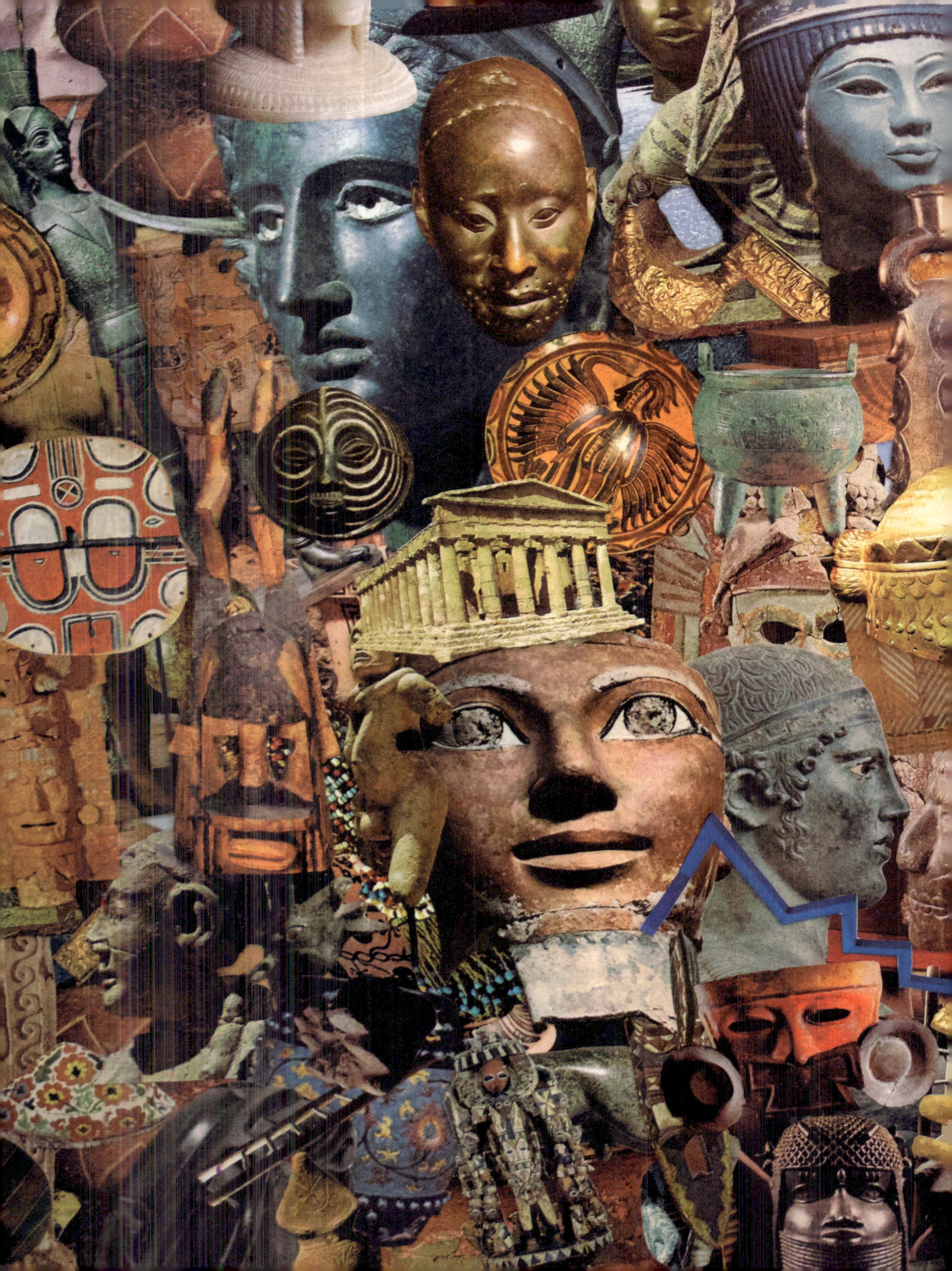

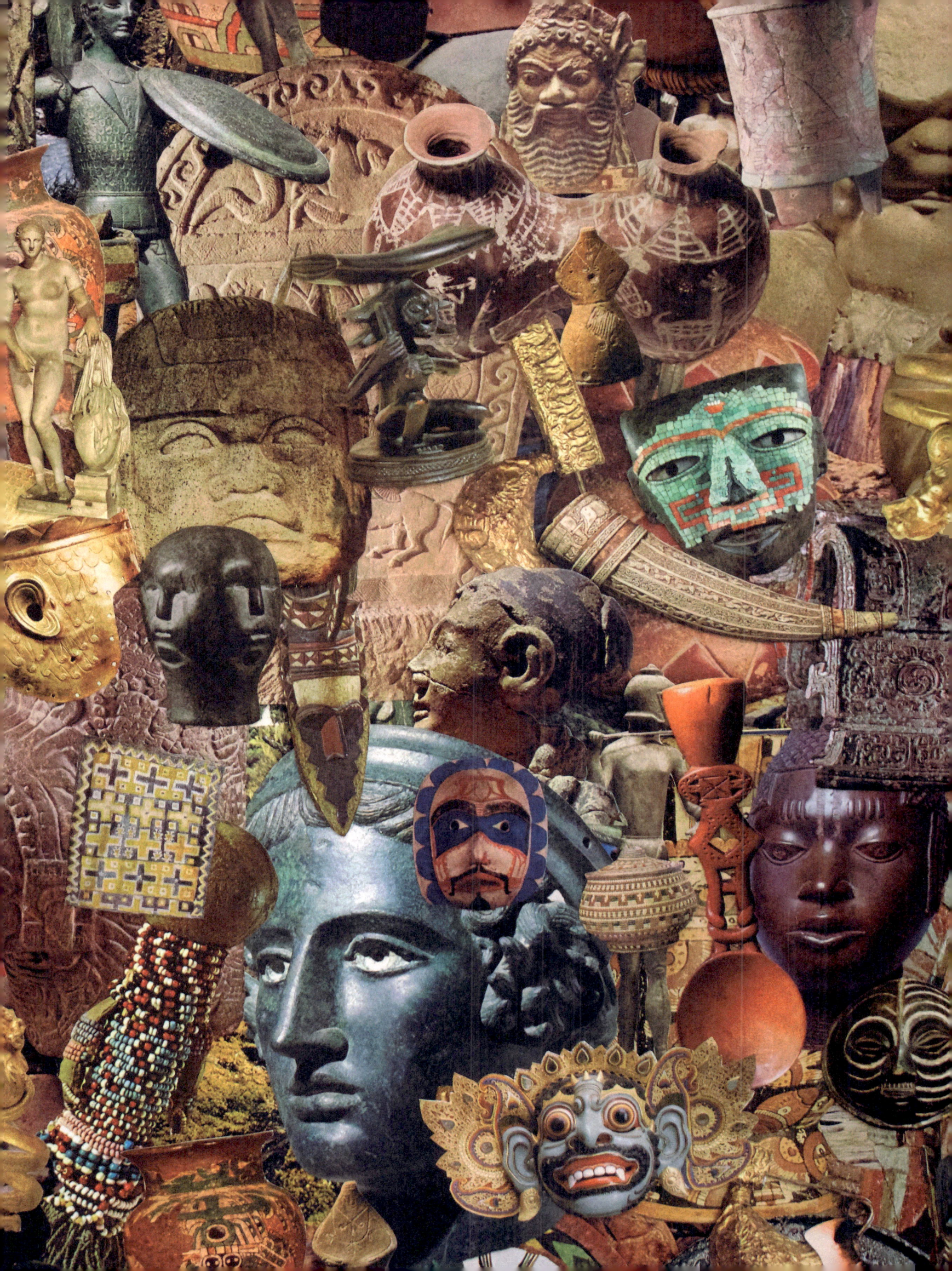

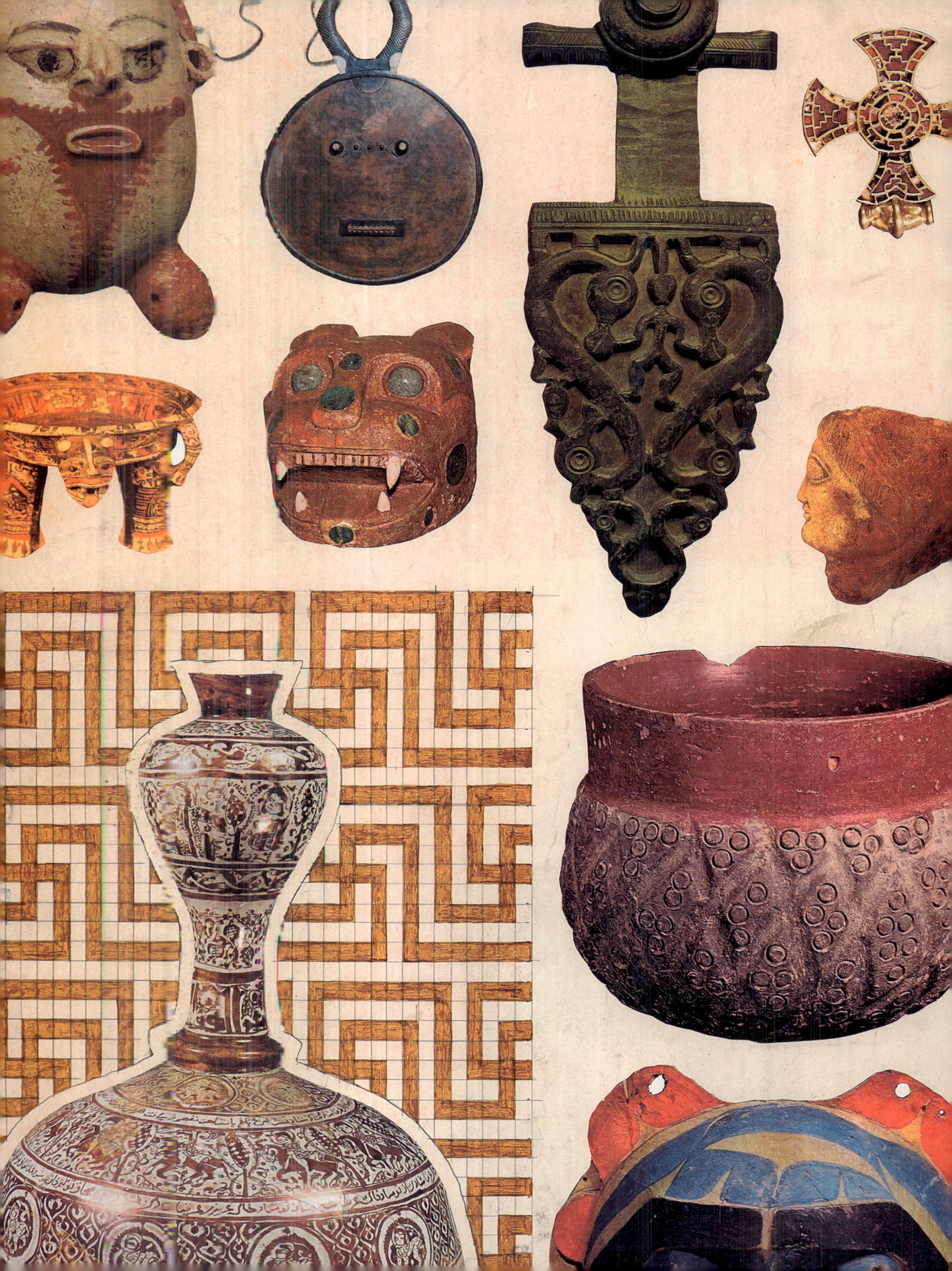

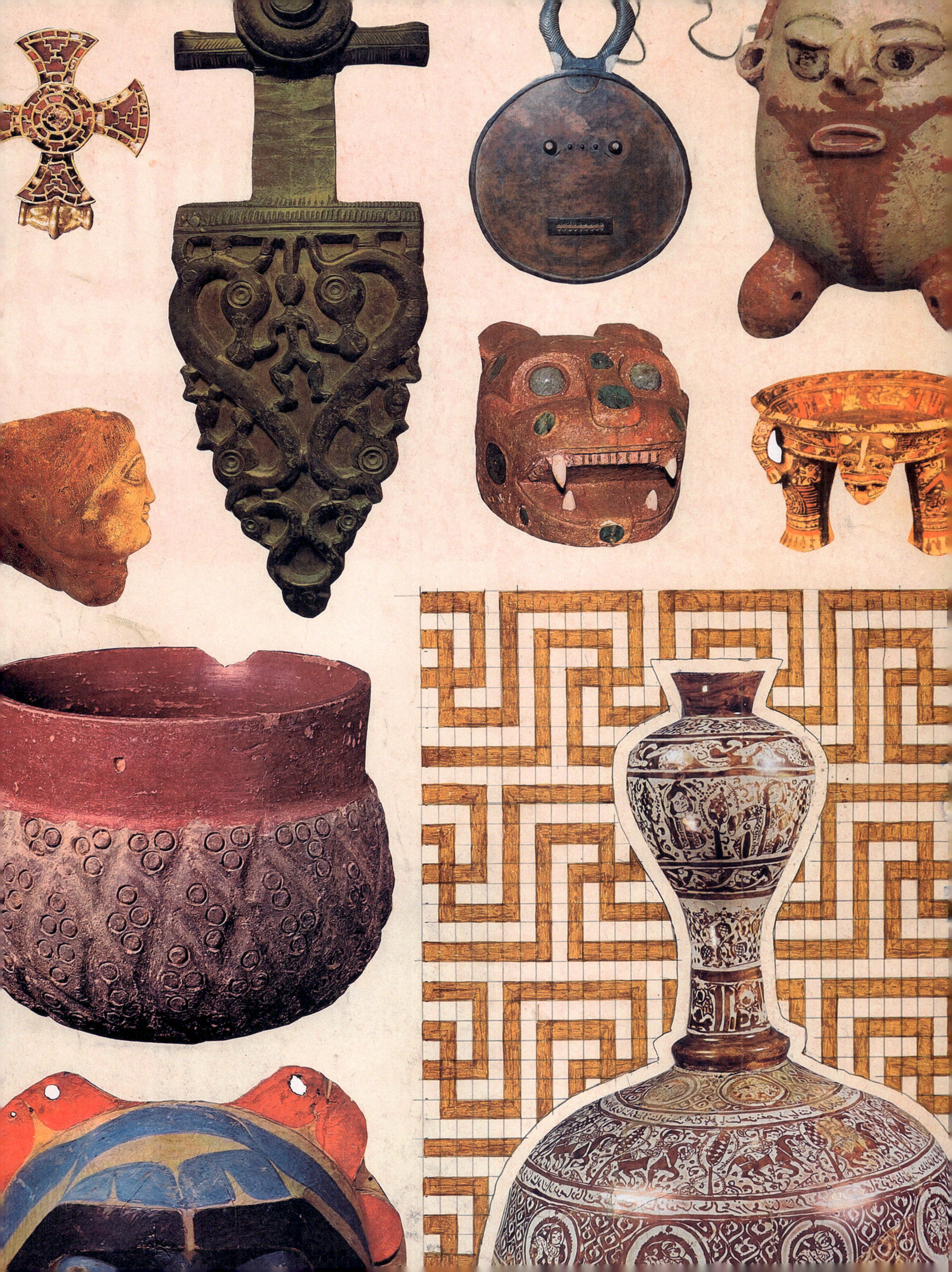

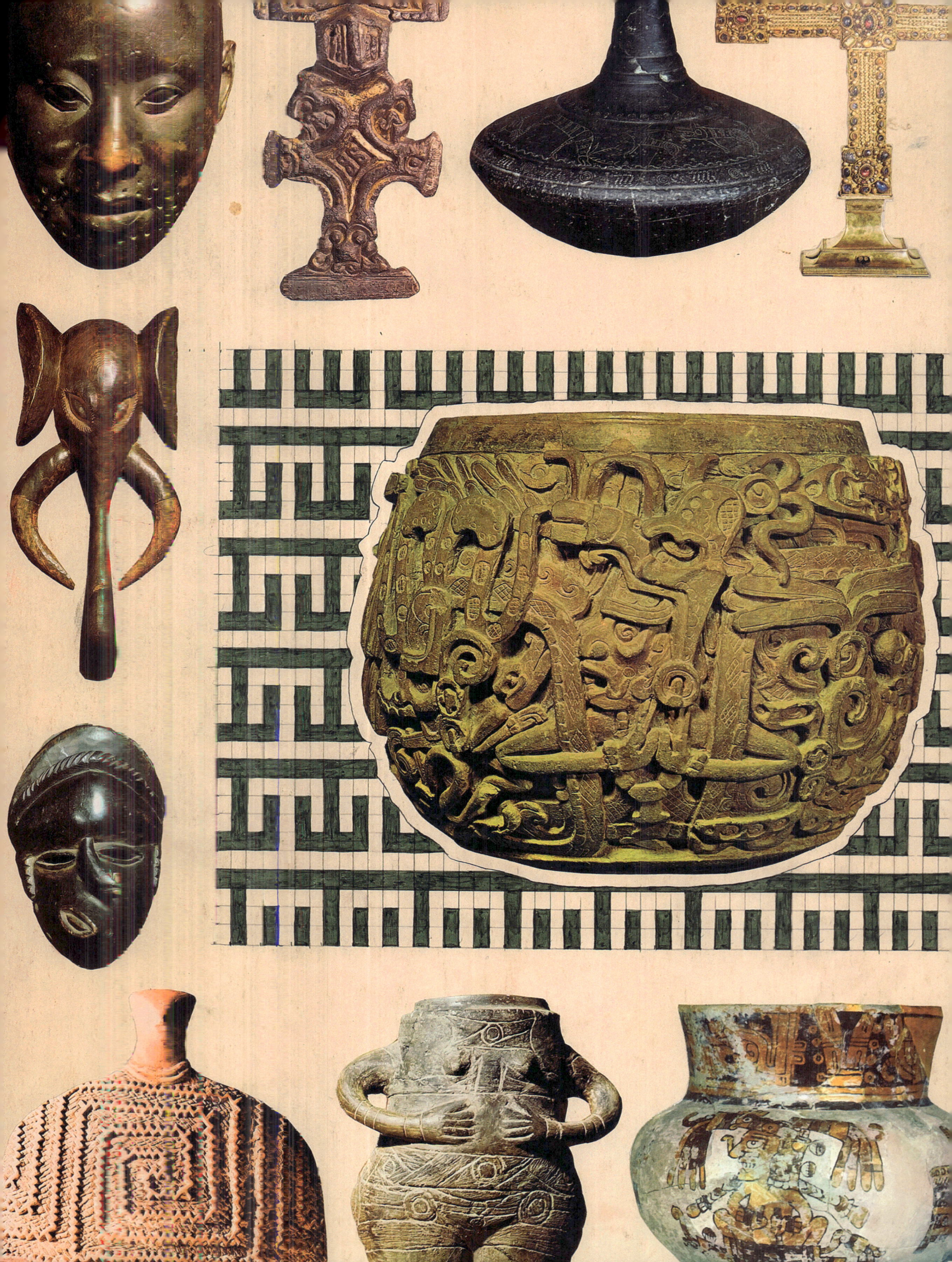

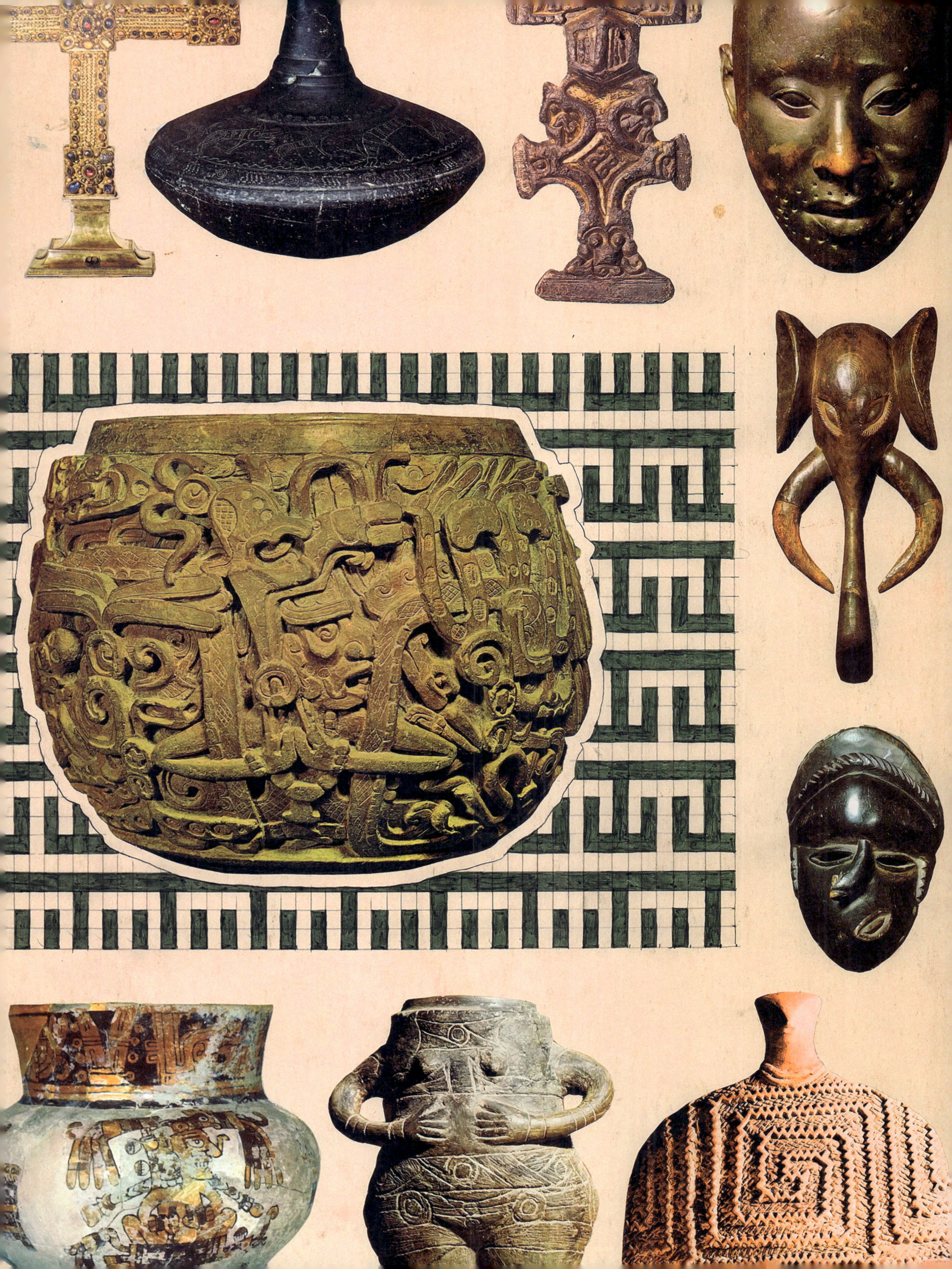

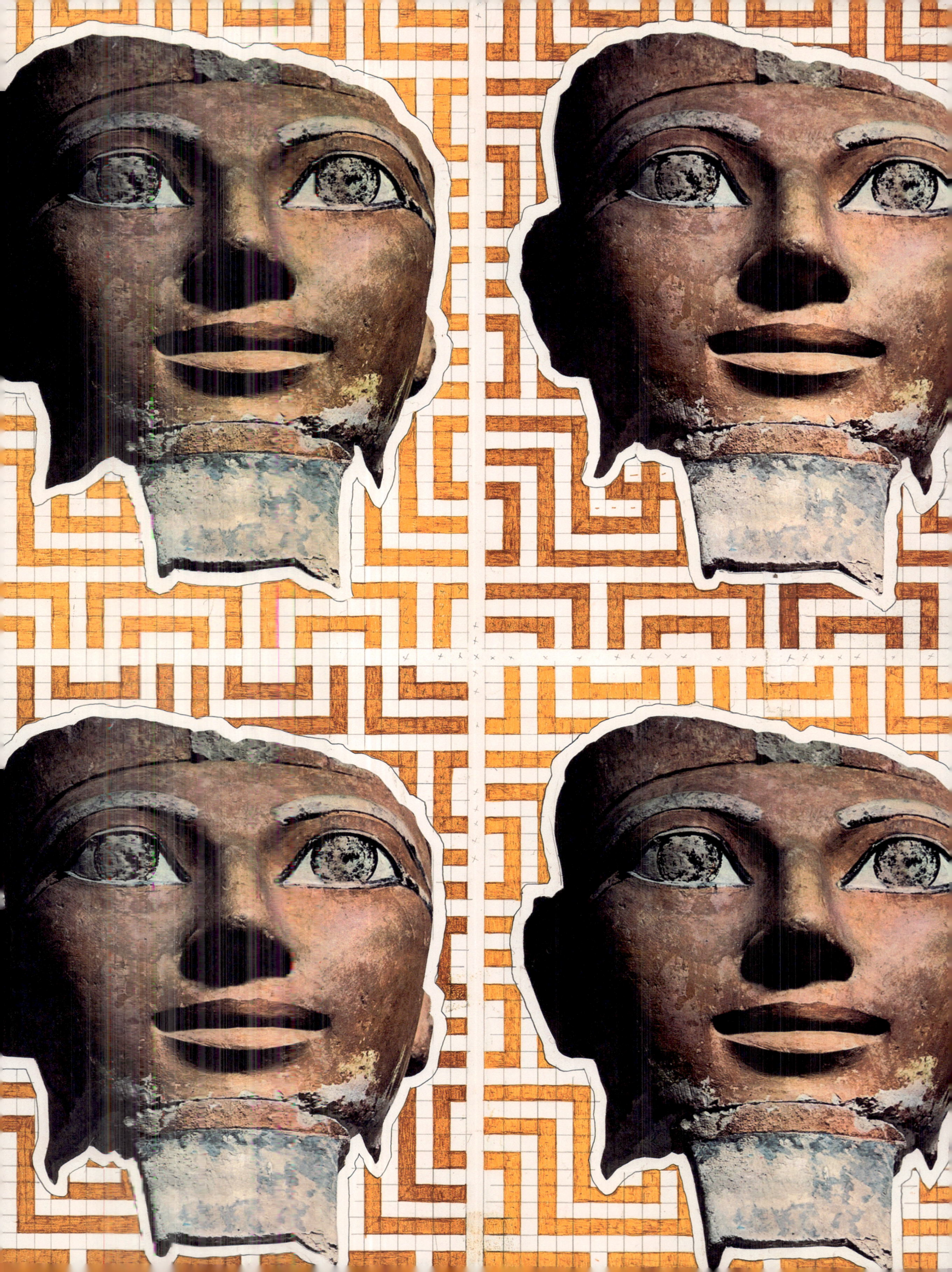

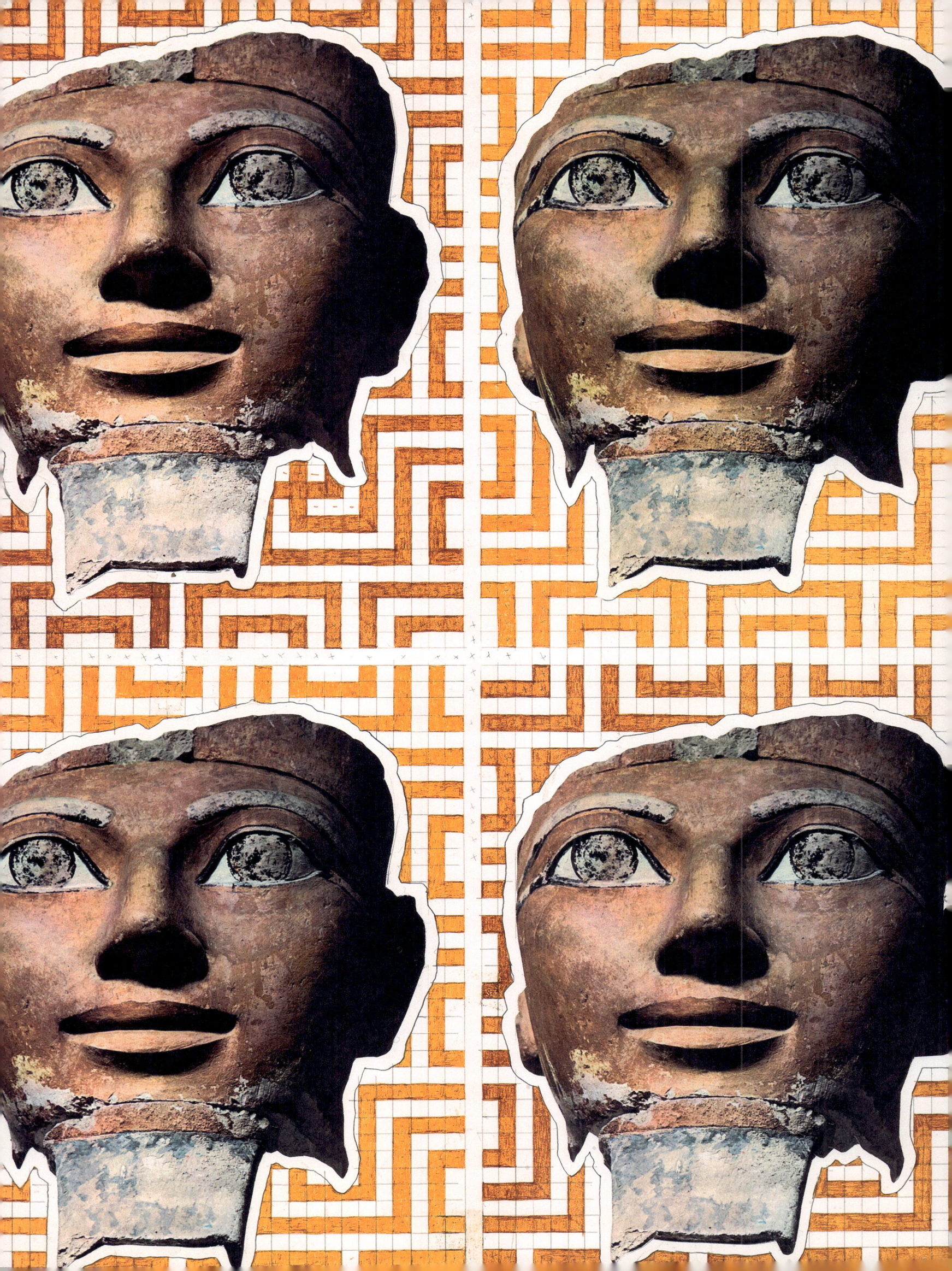

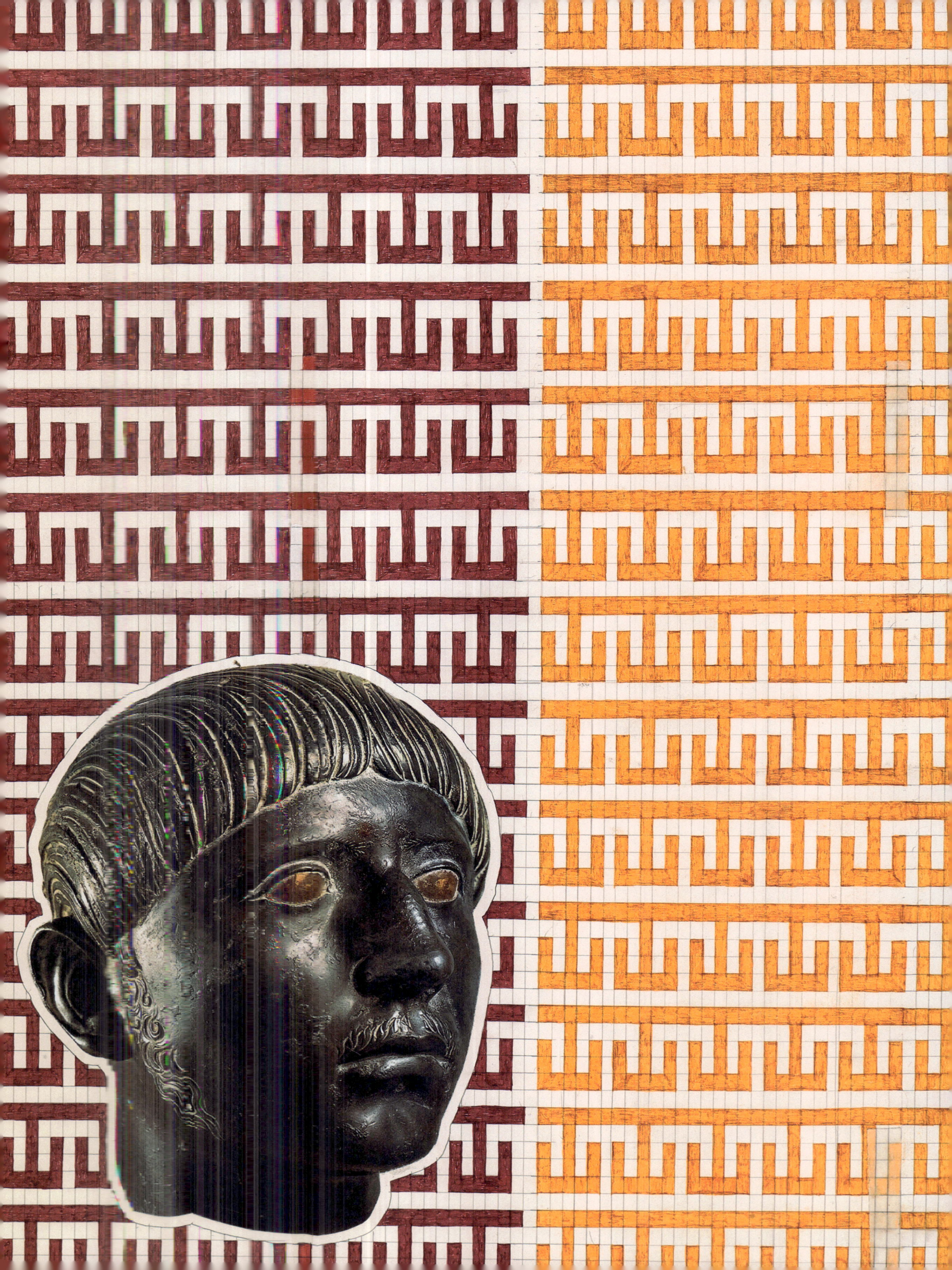

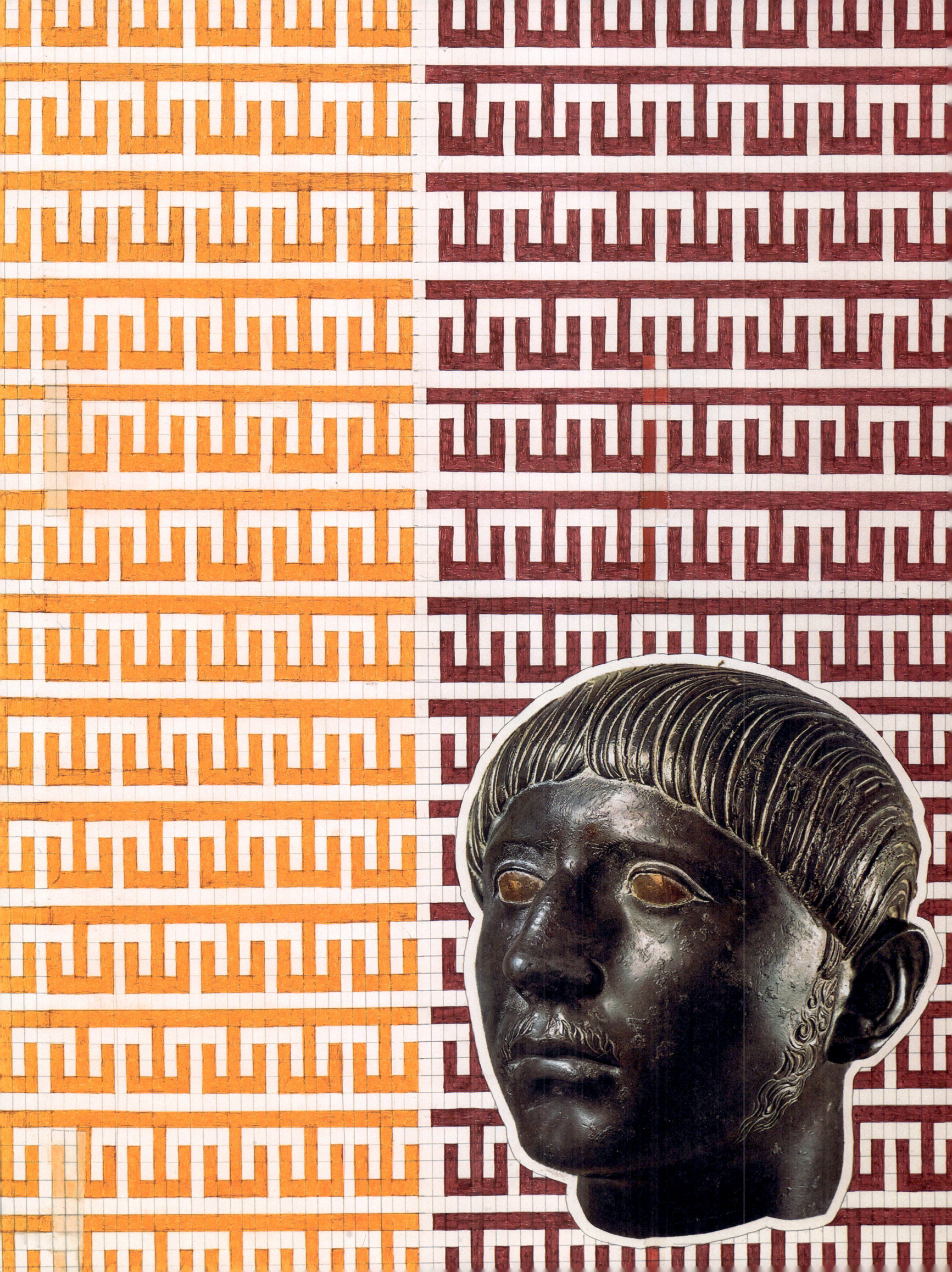

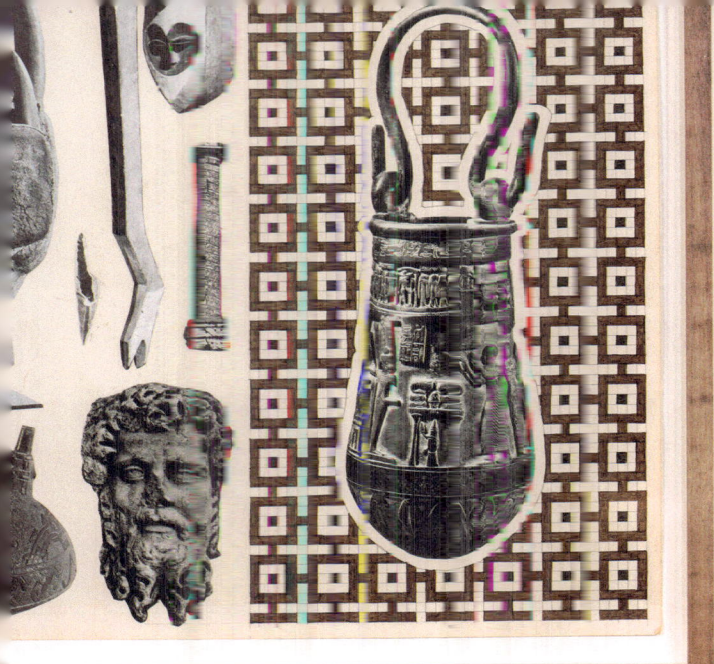
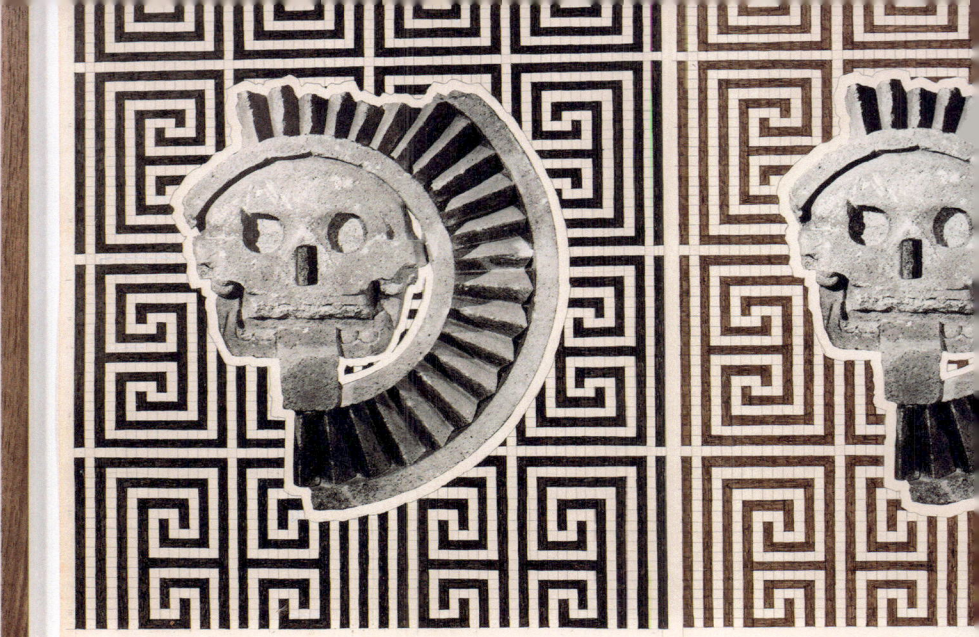
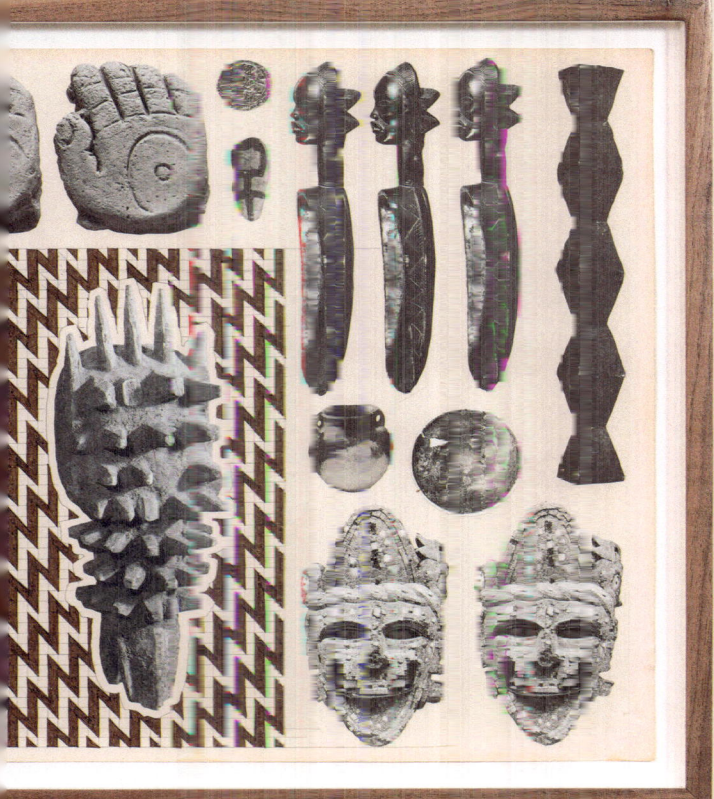
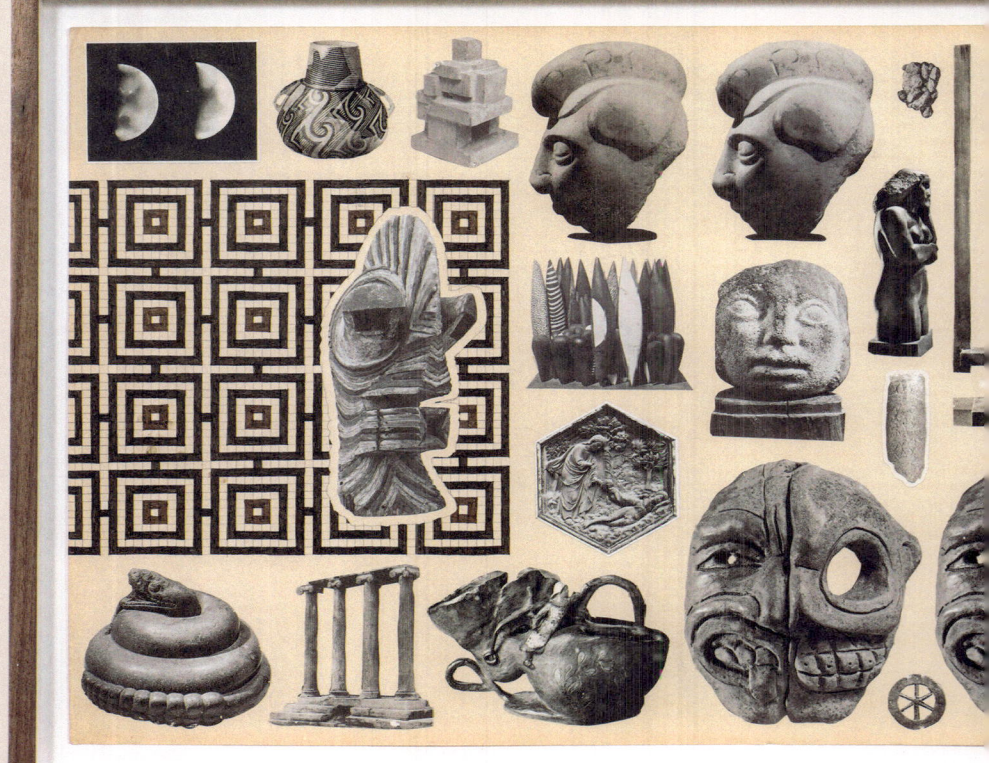
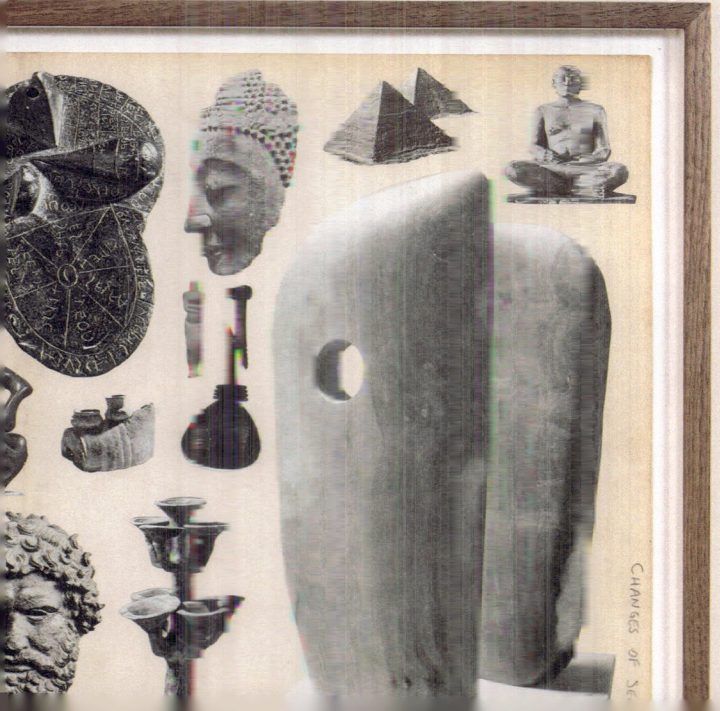
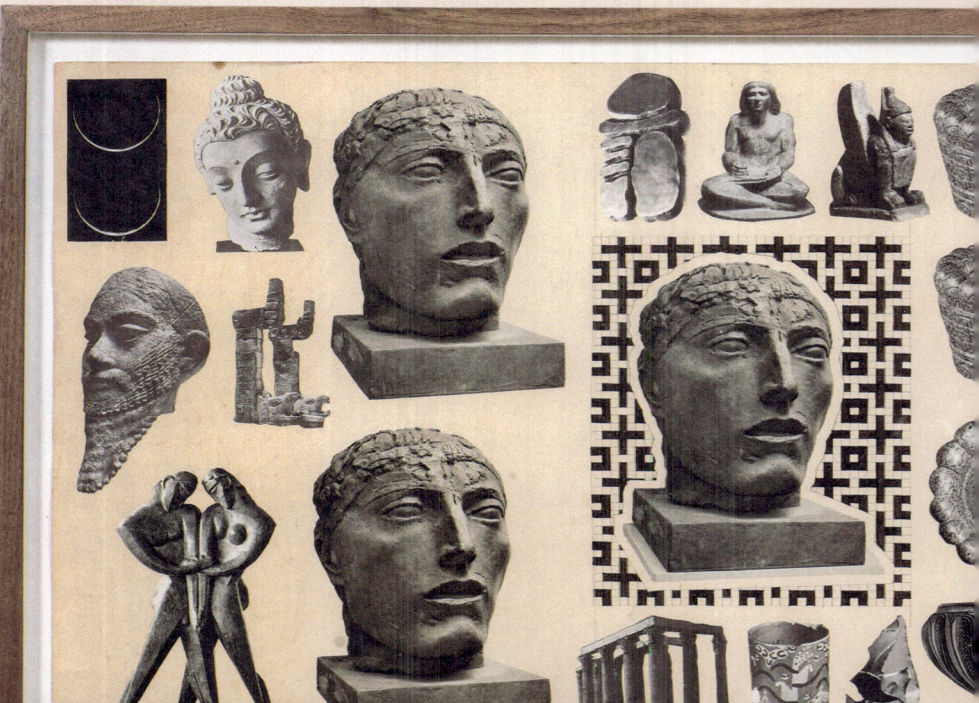

CHANGES OF S

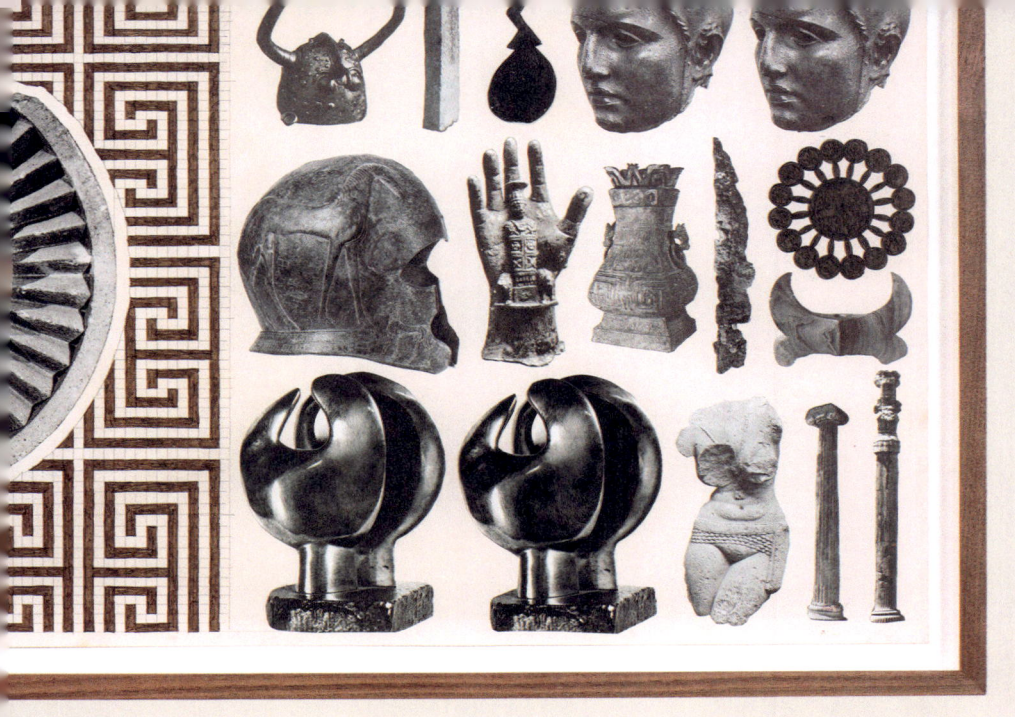
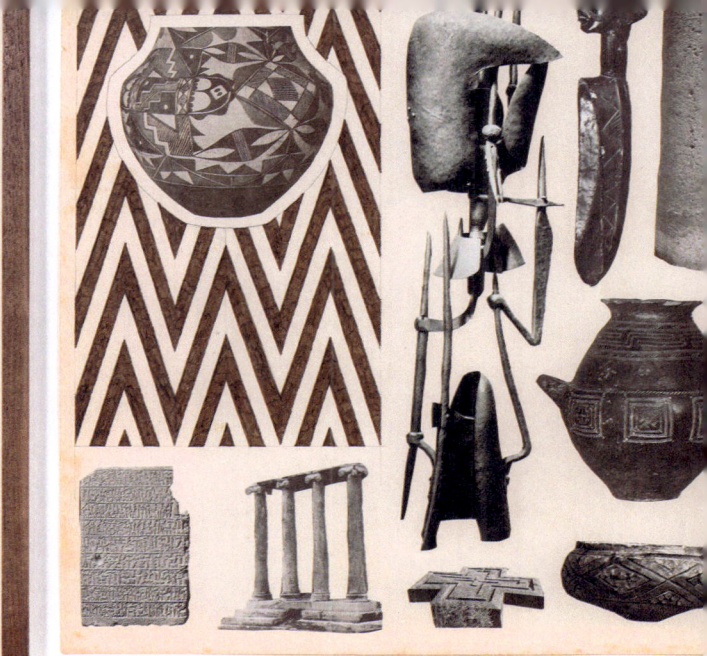
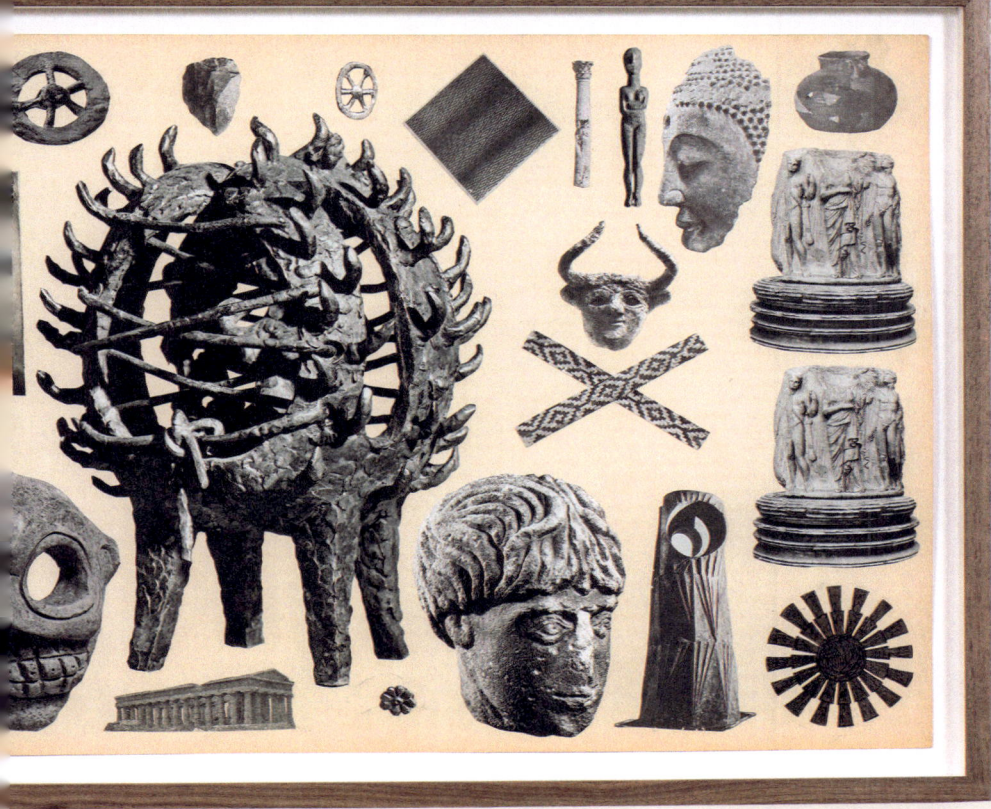
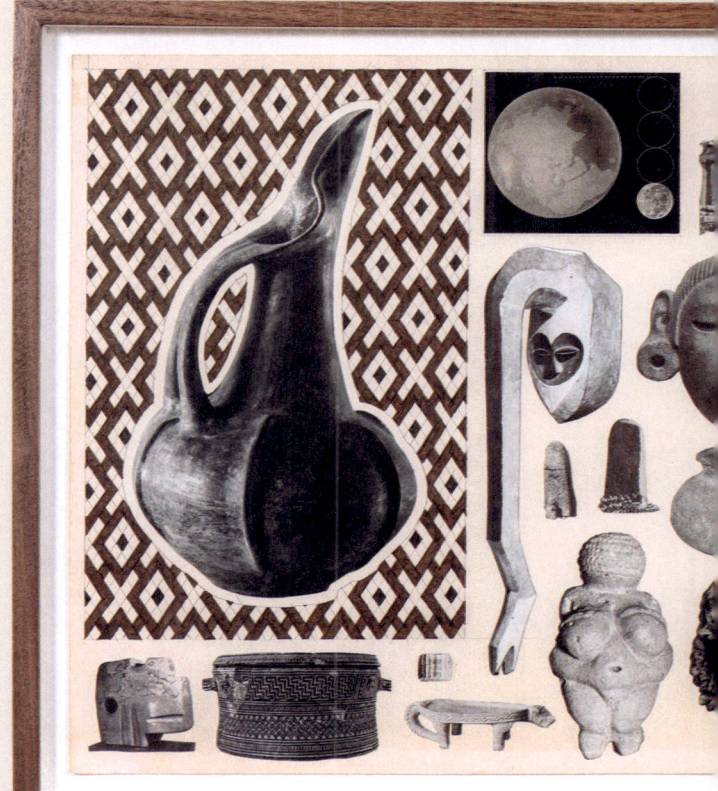
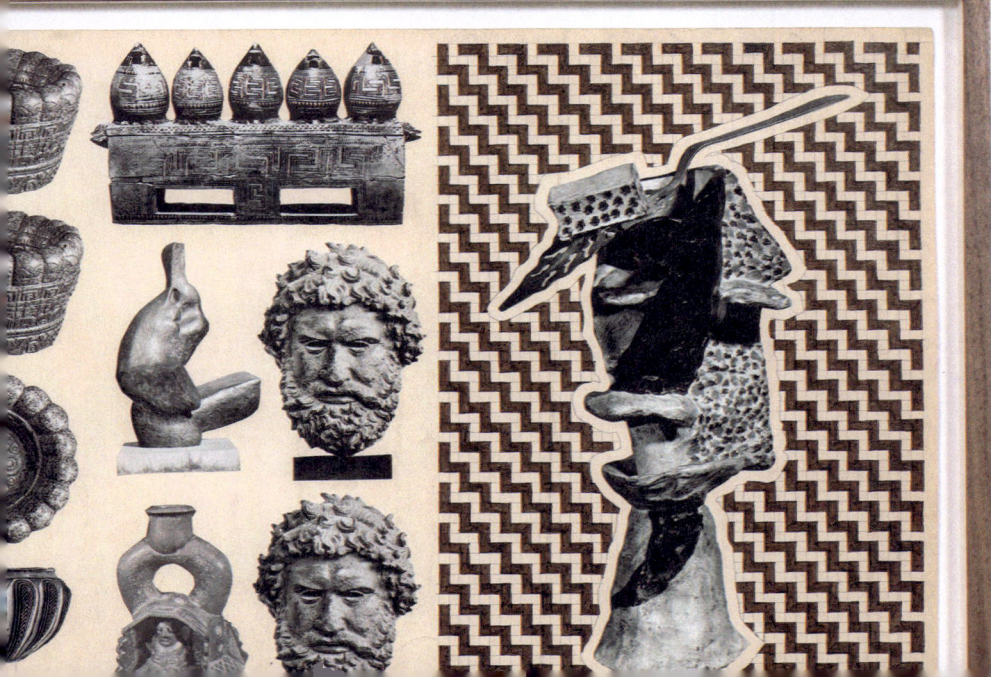
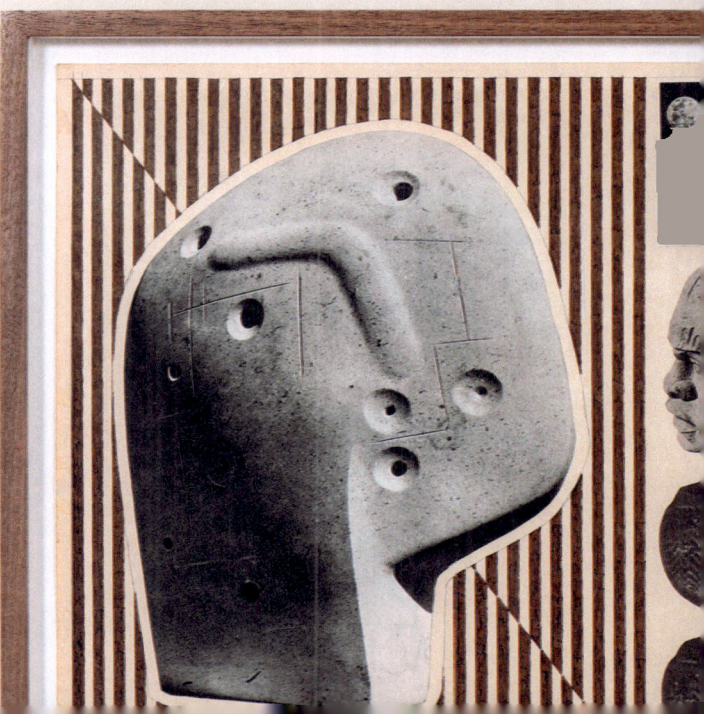

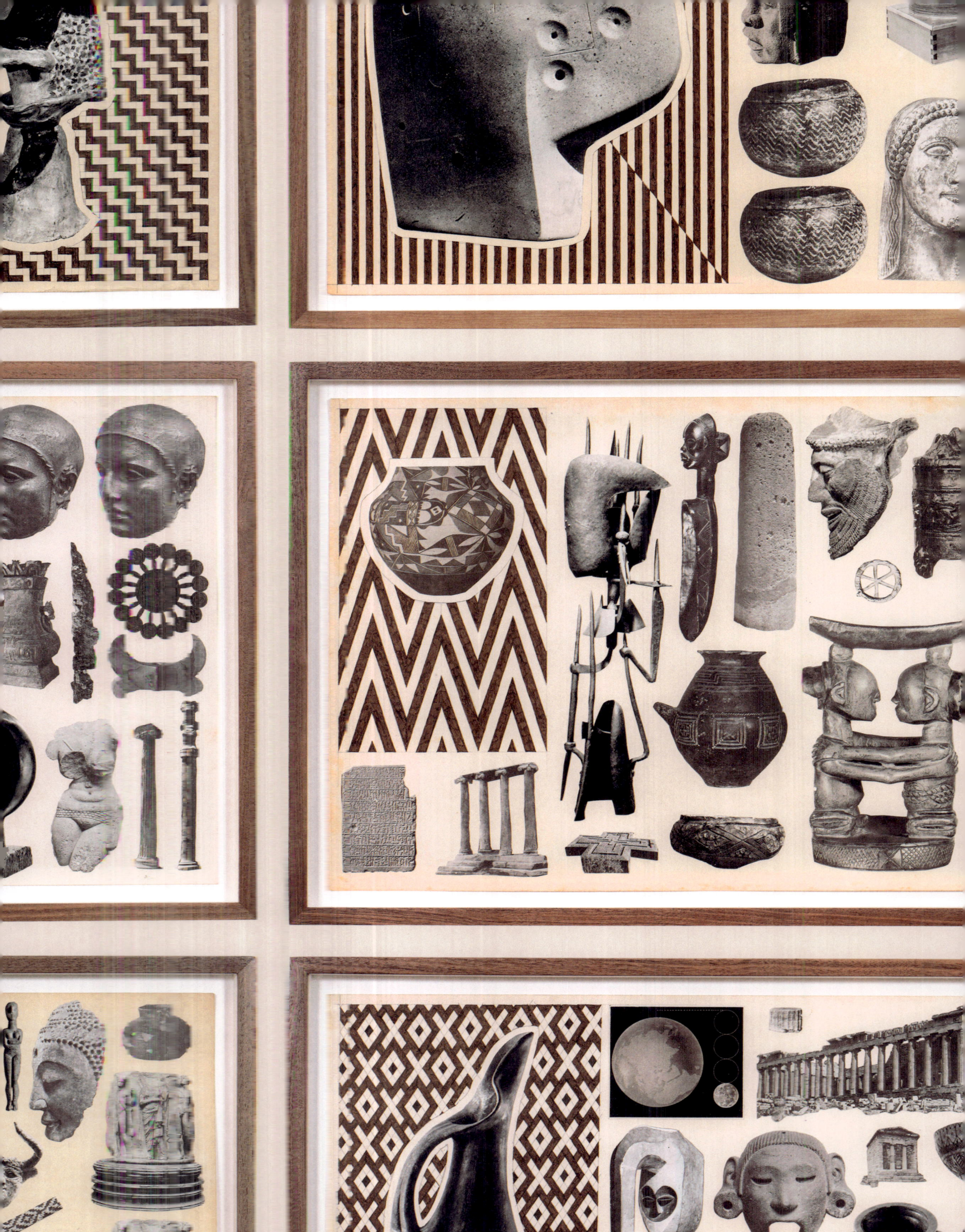

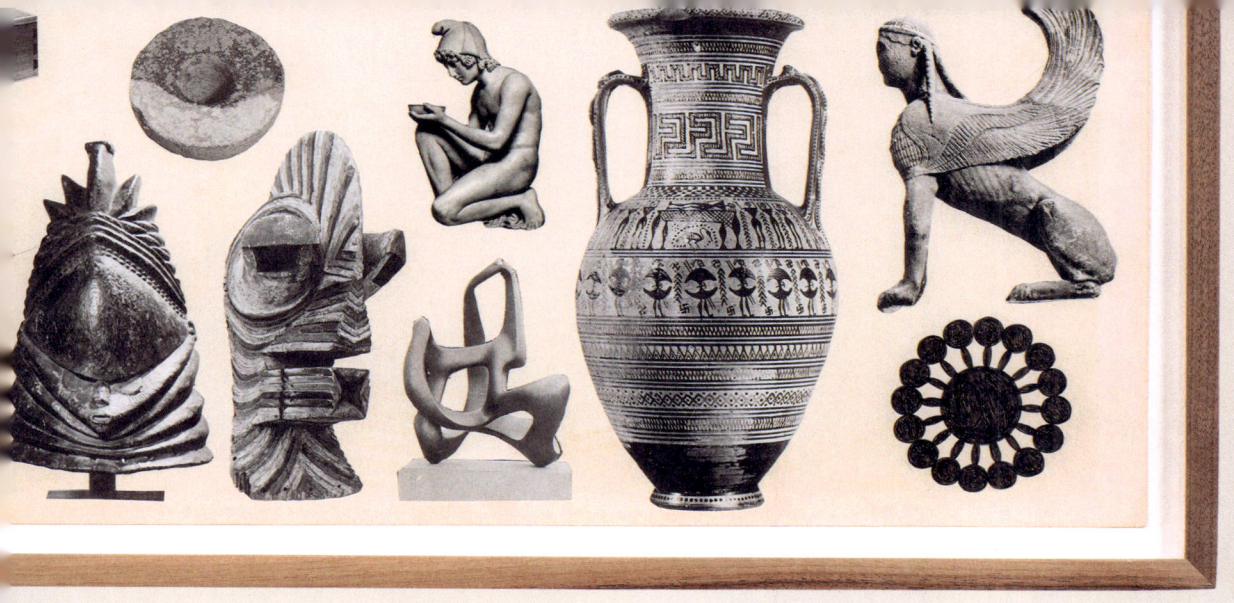
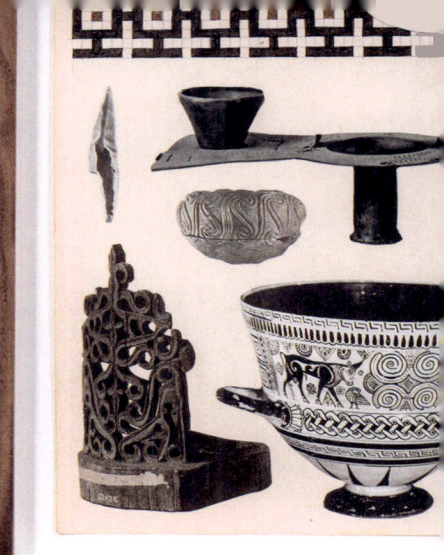
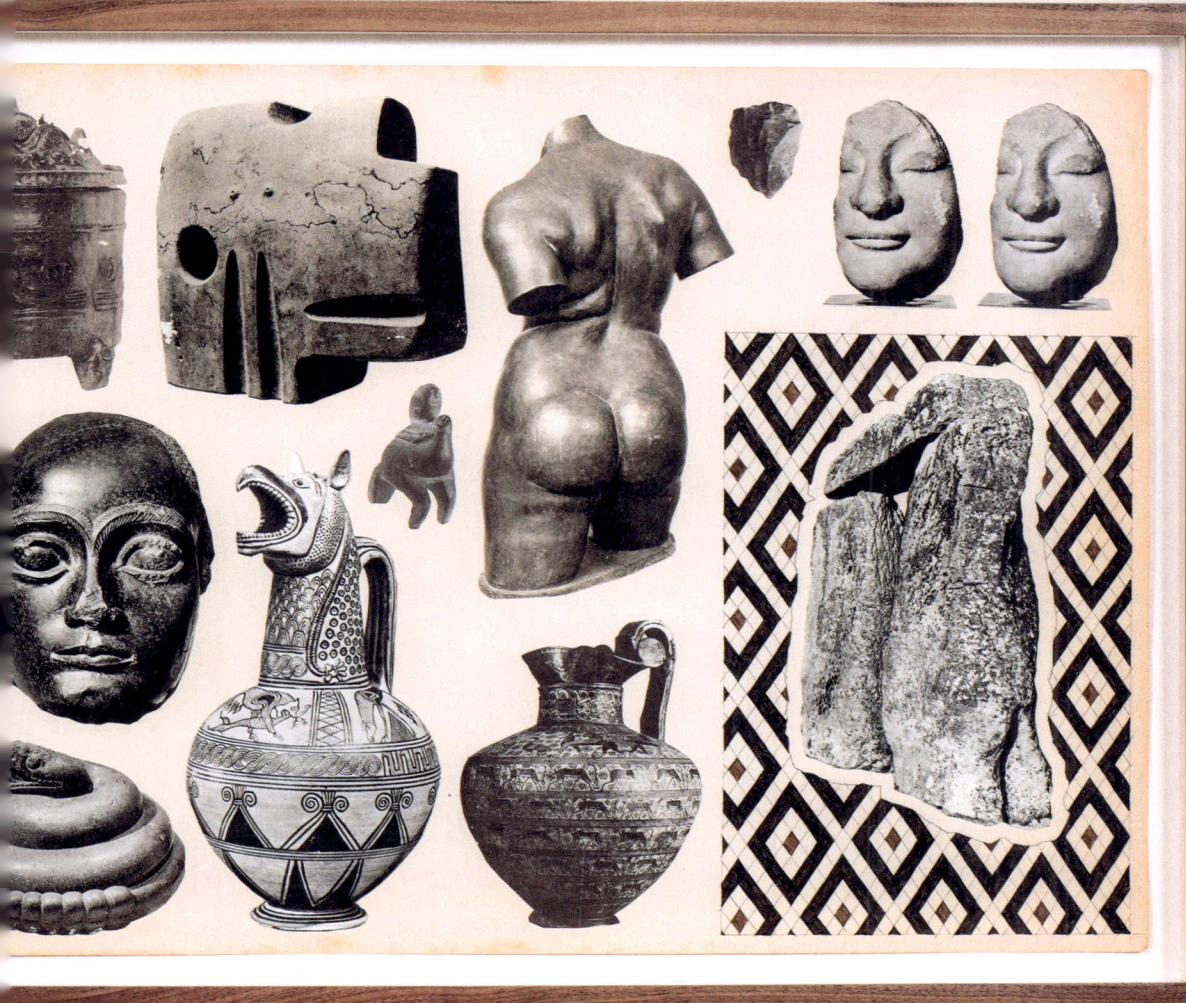
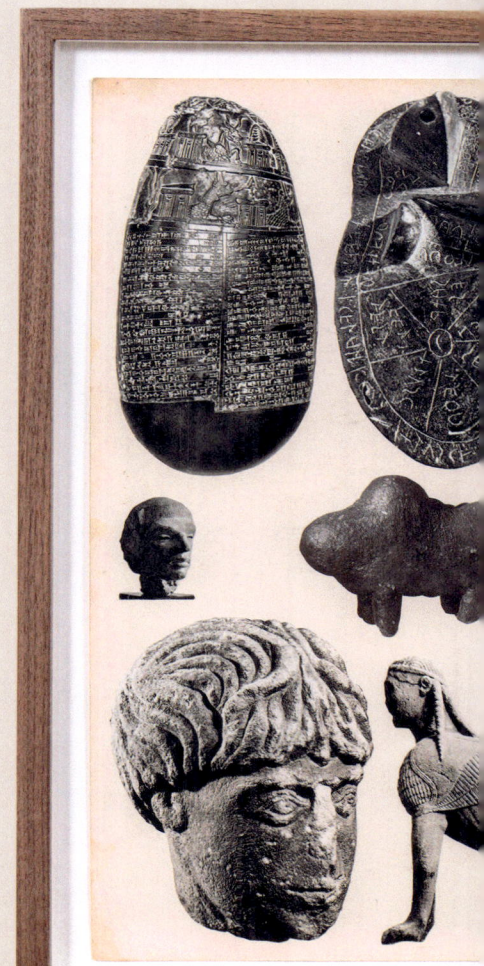
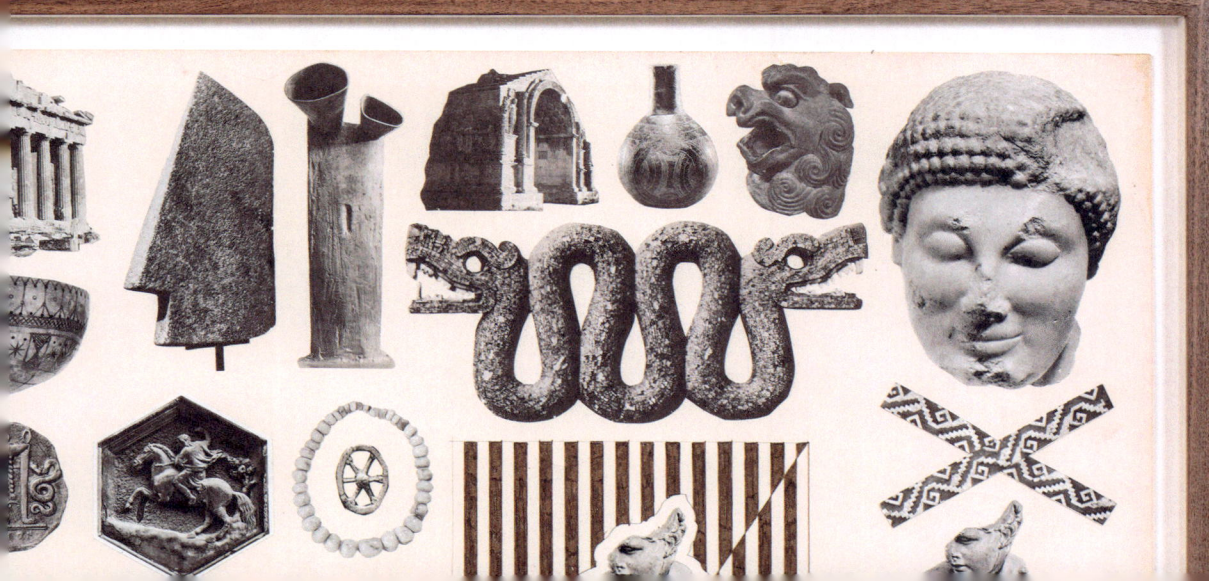
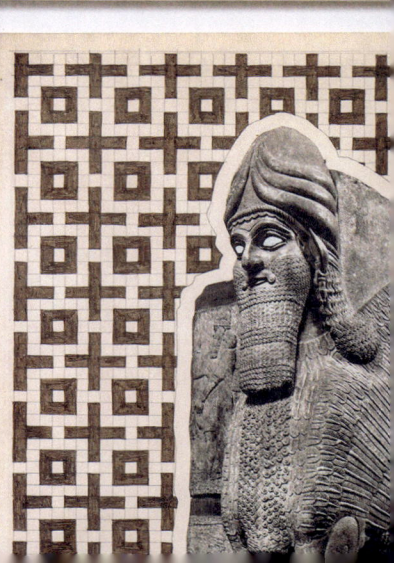

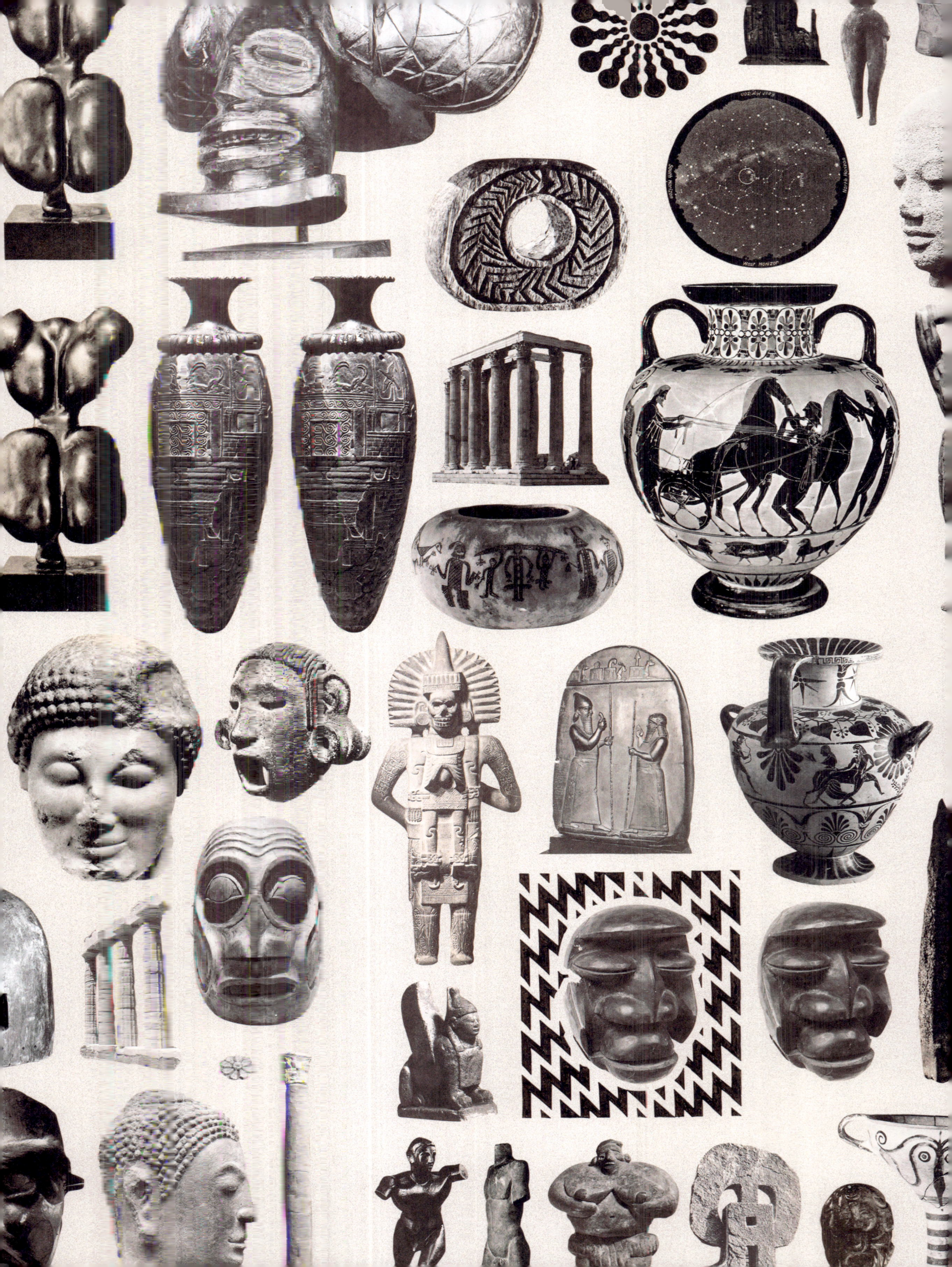

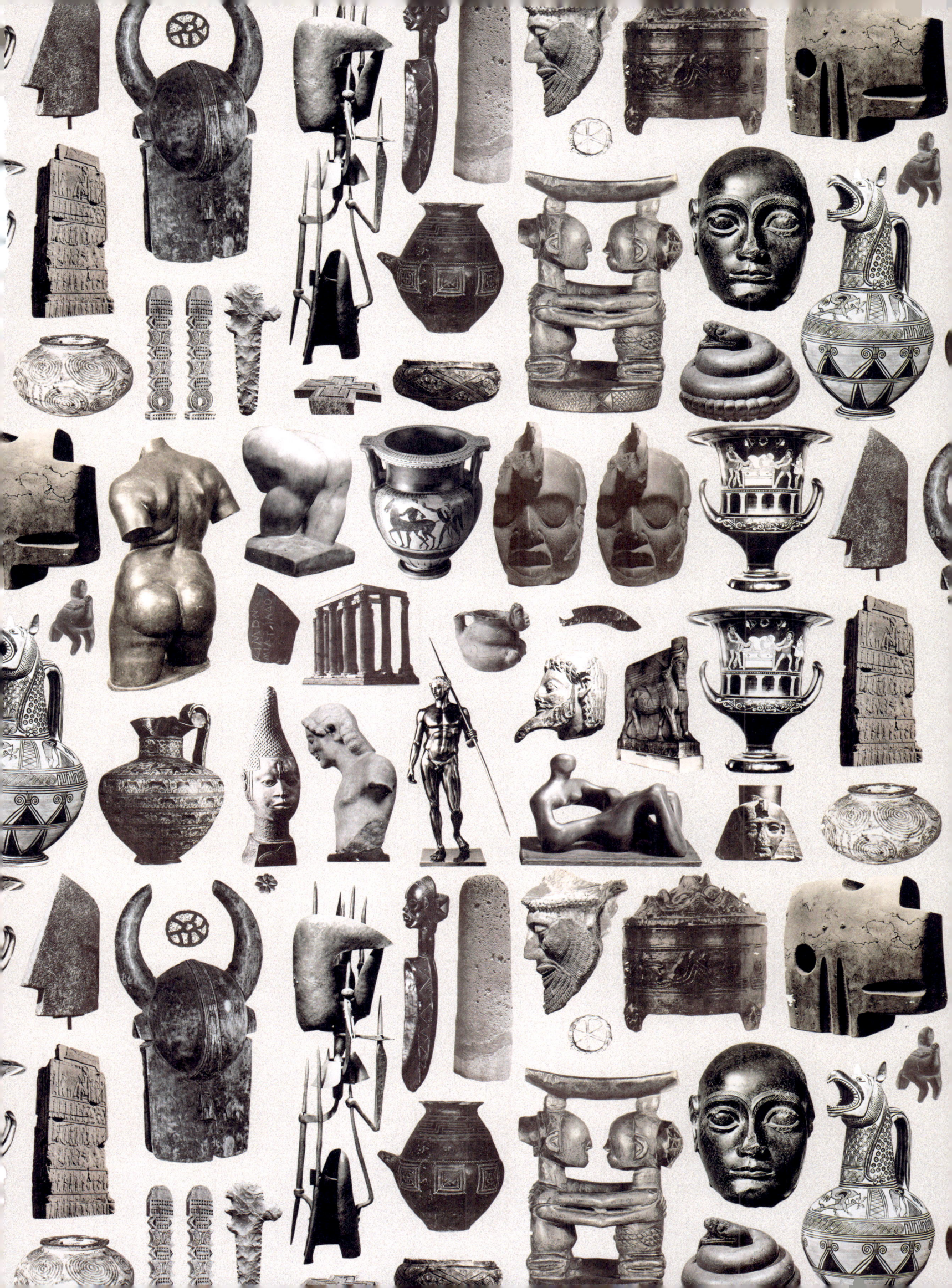

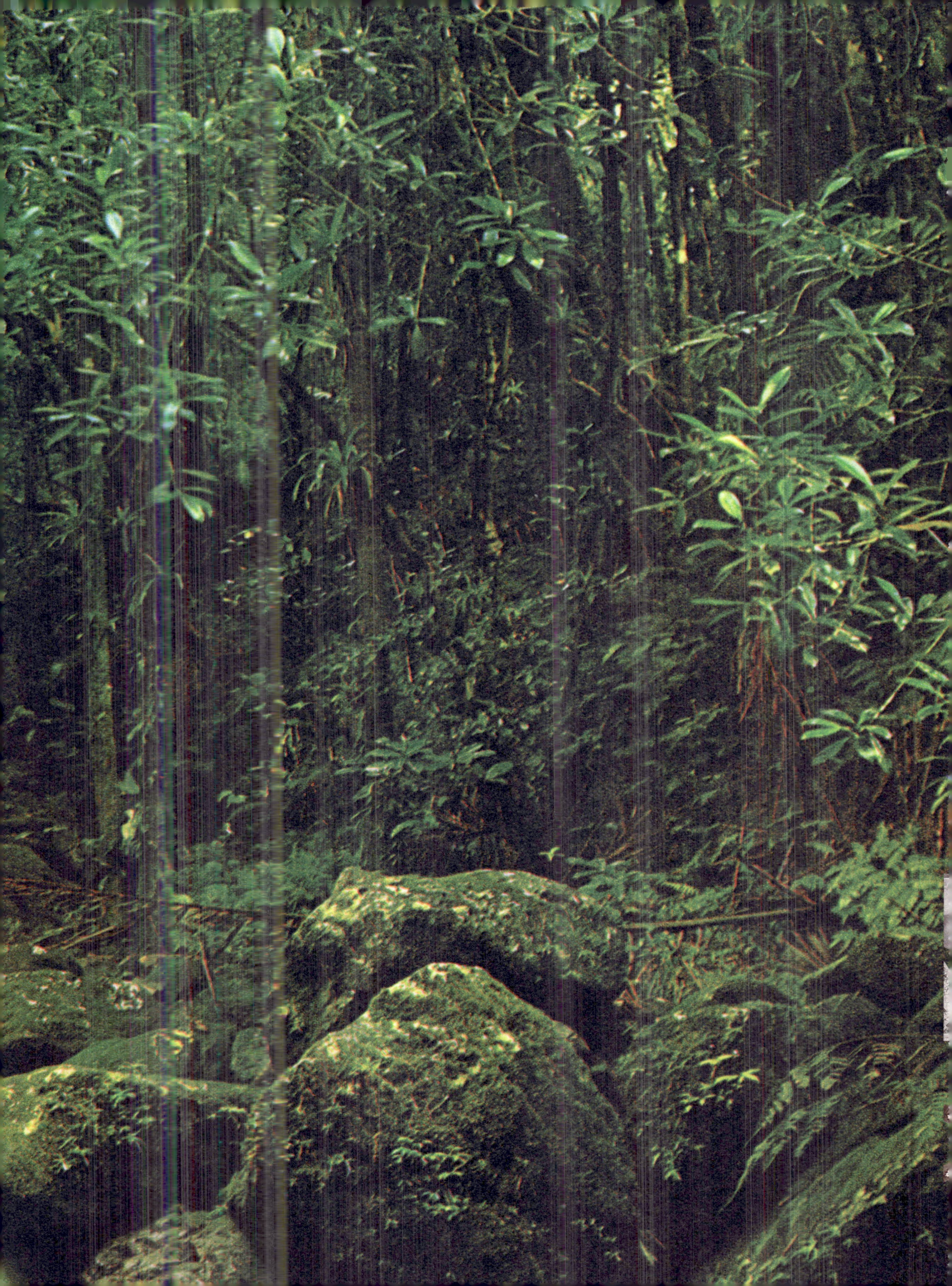

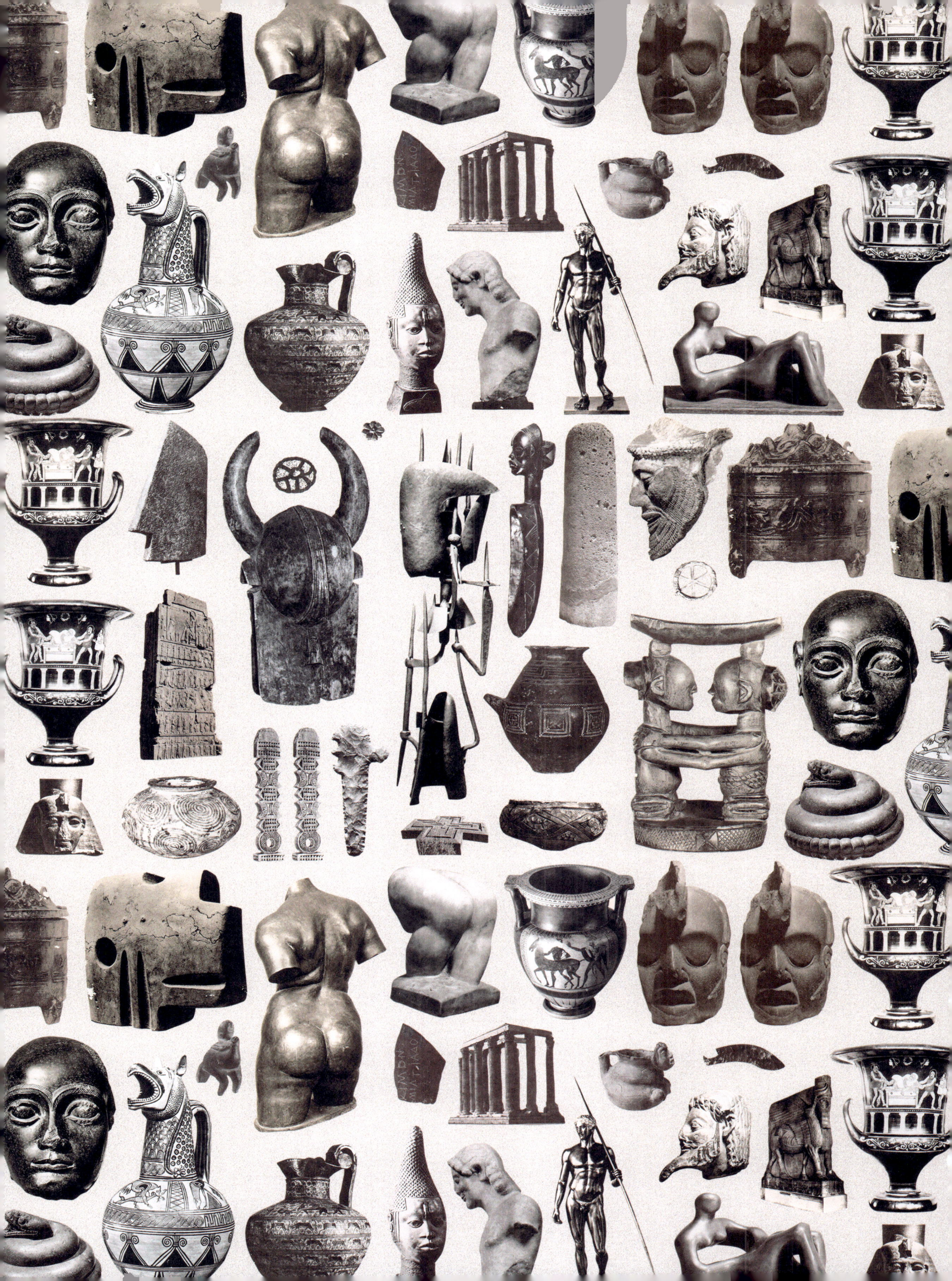

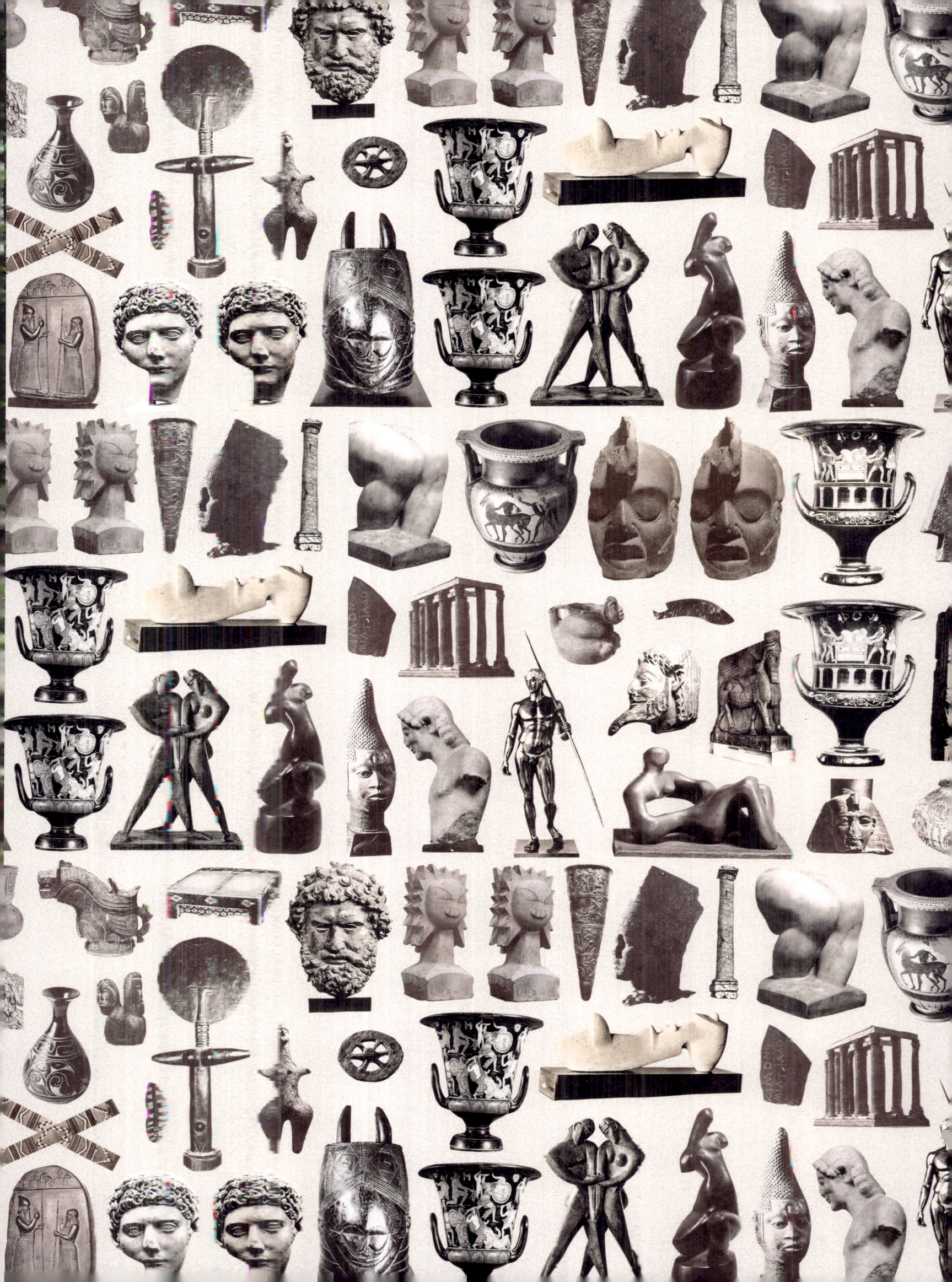

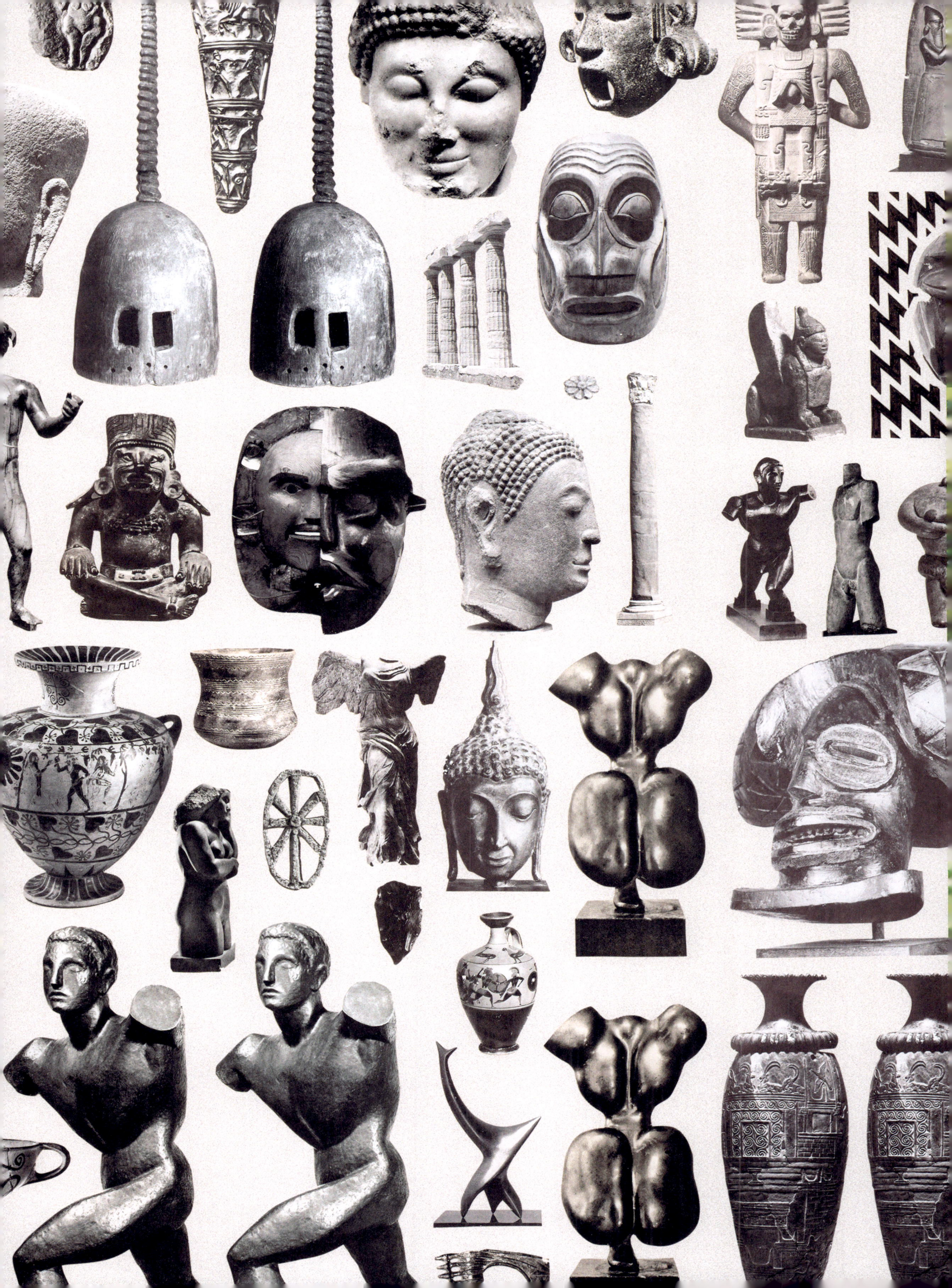

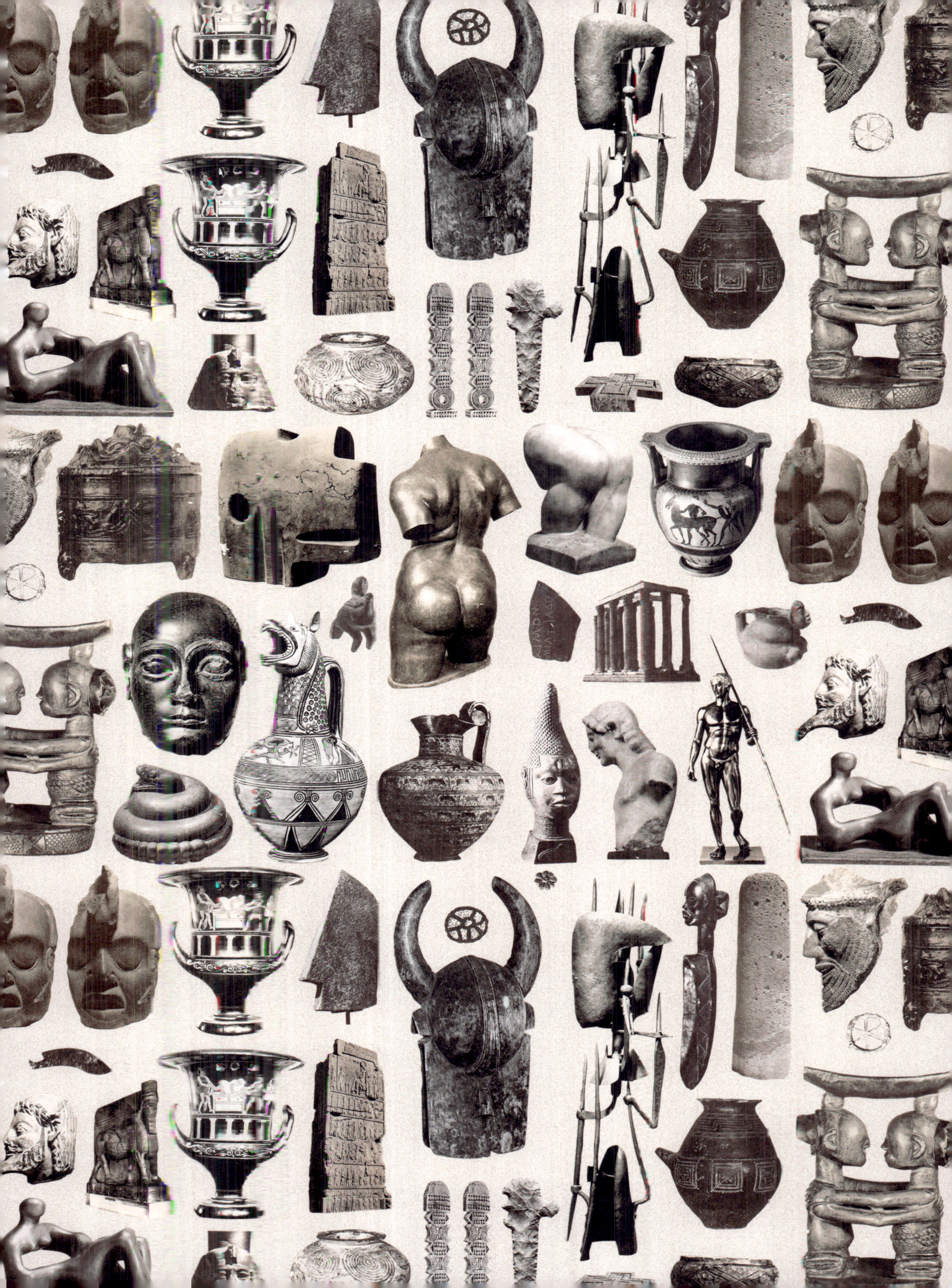

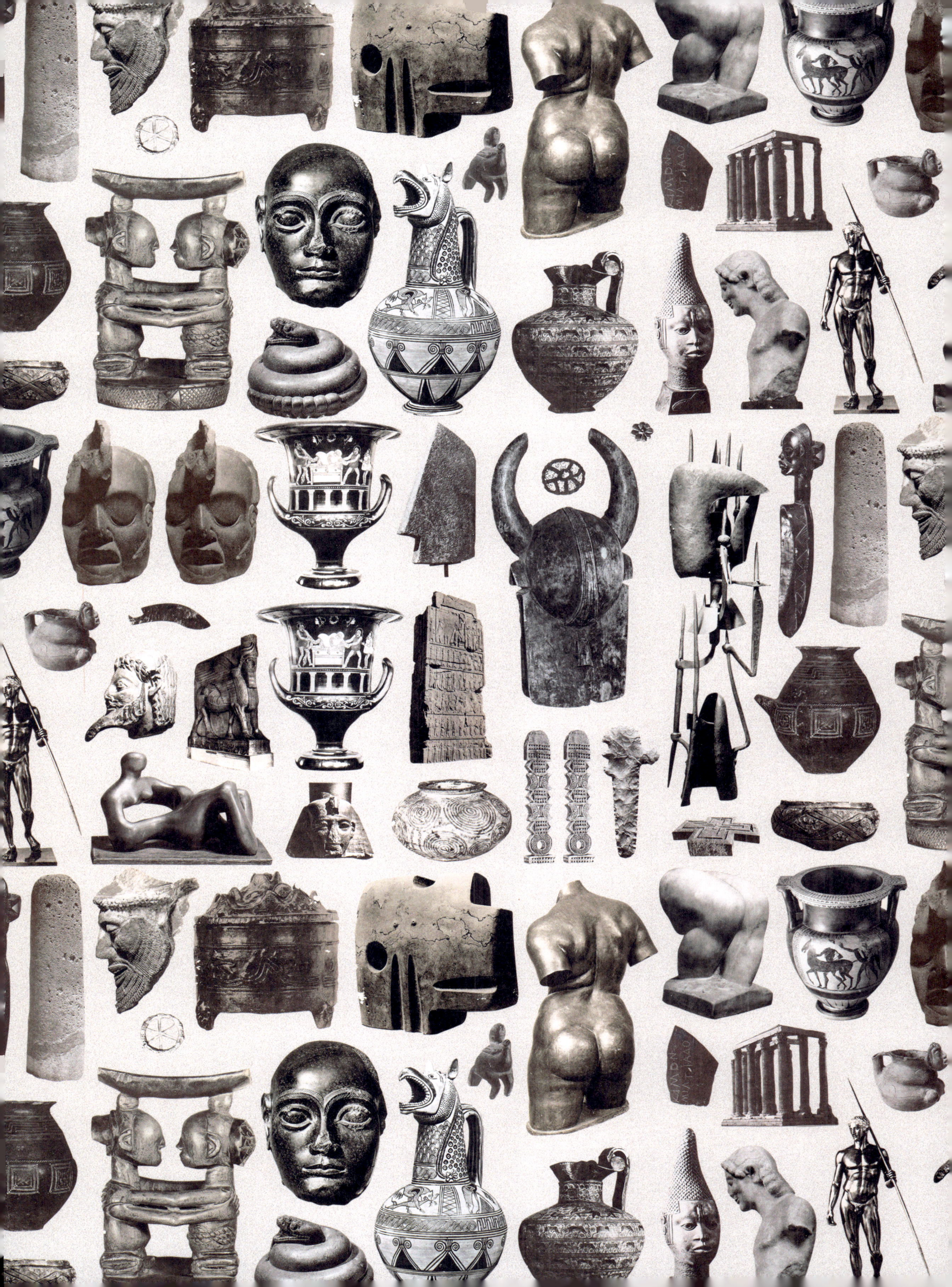

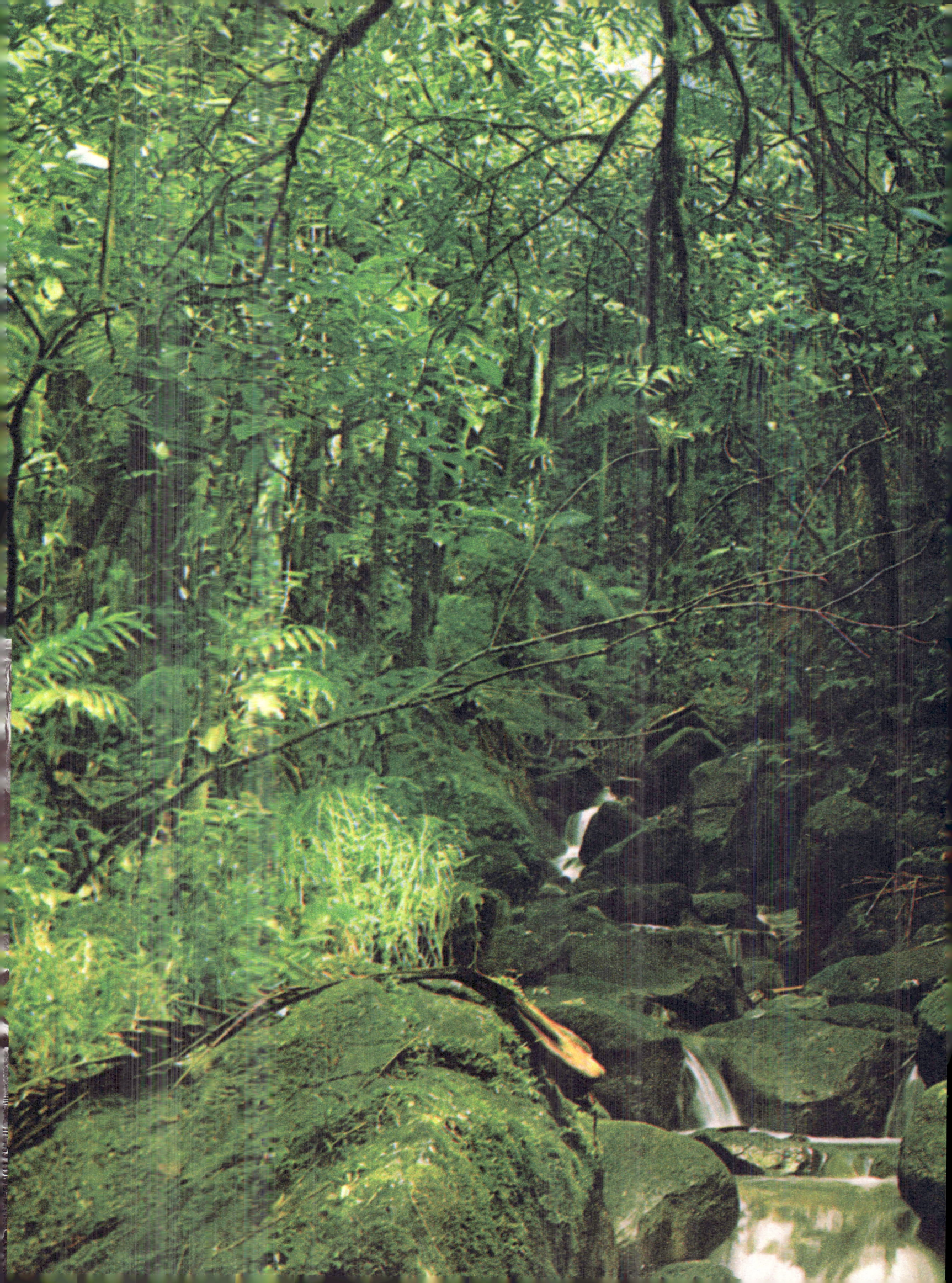

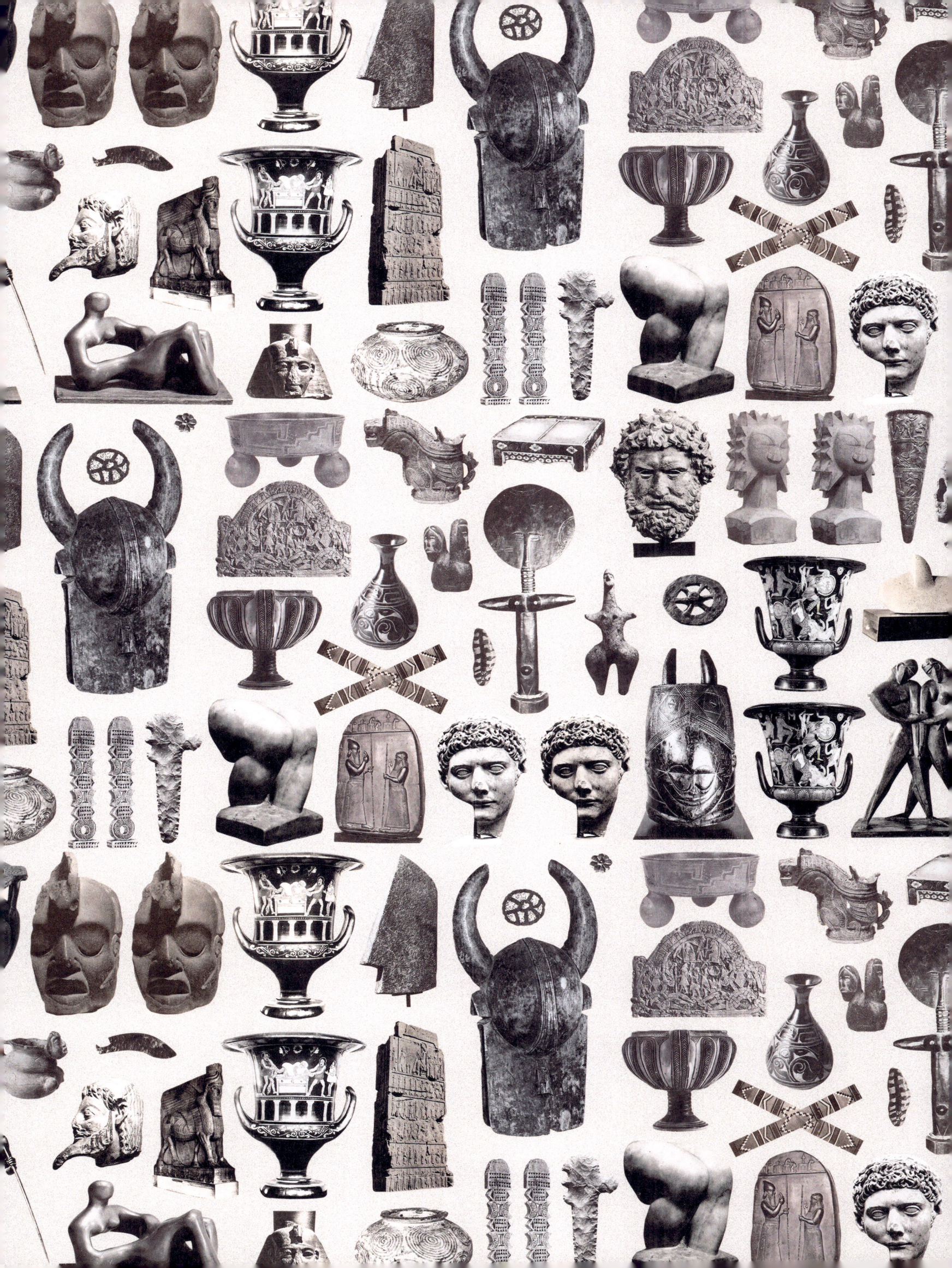

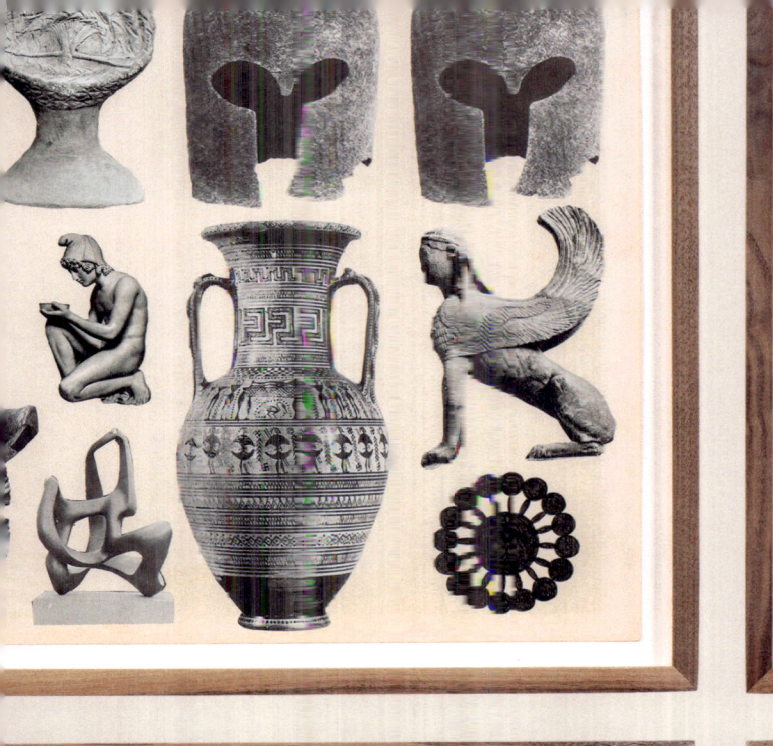
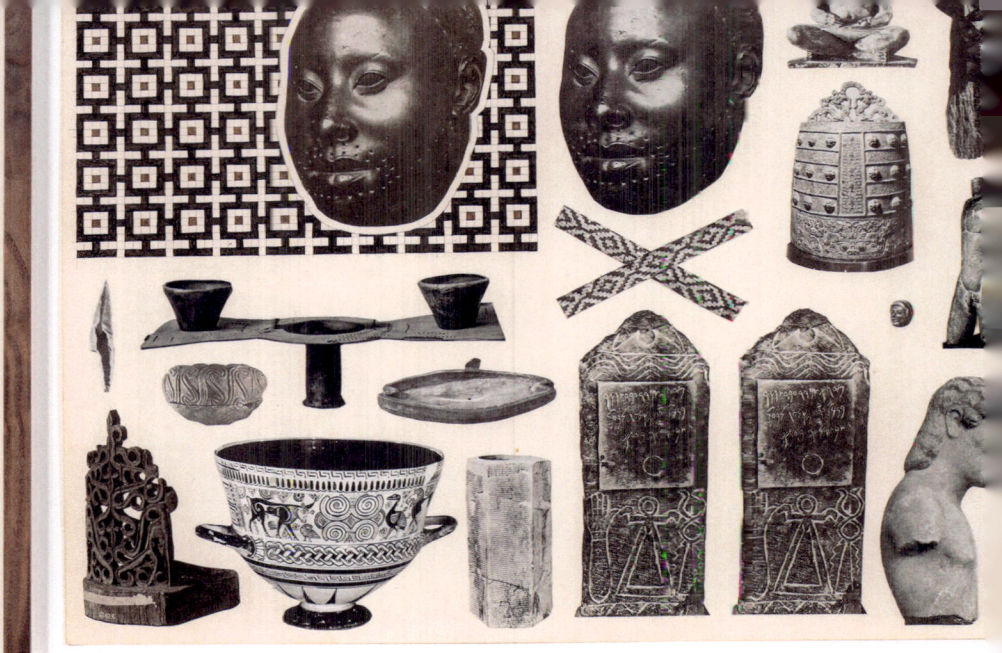
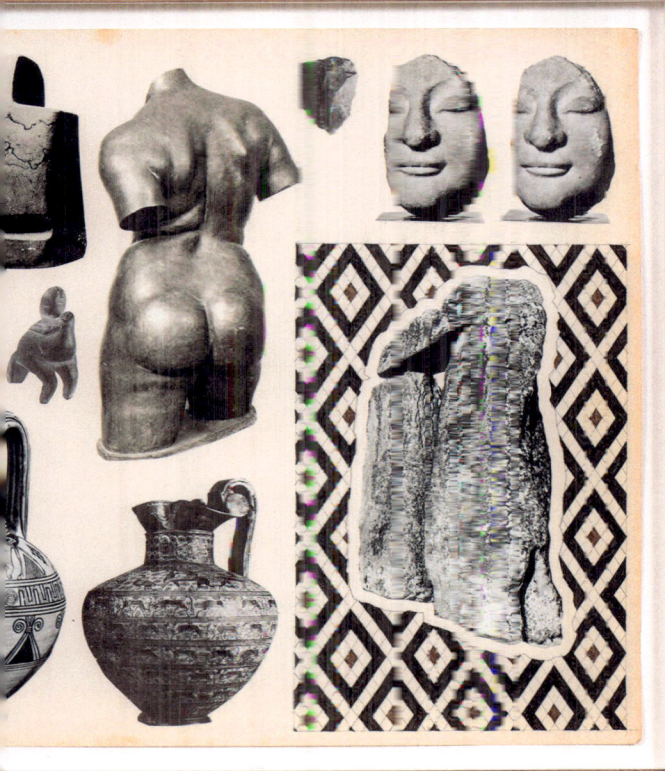
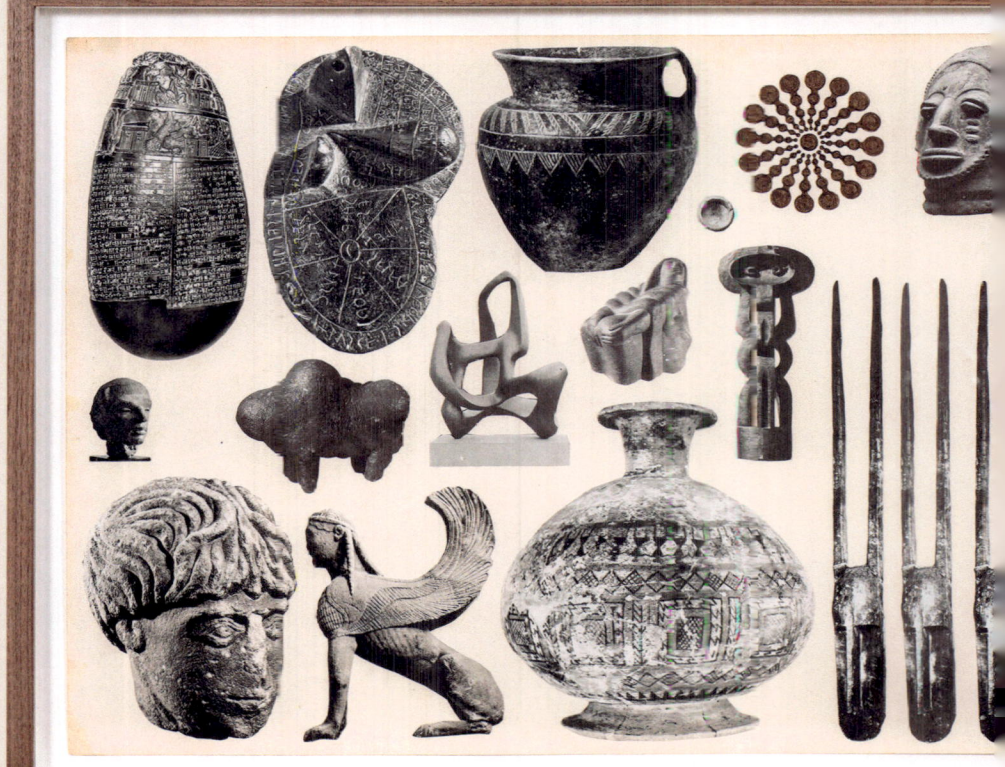
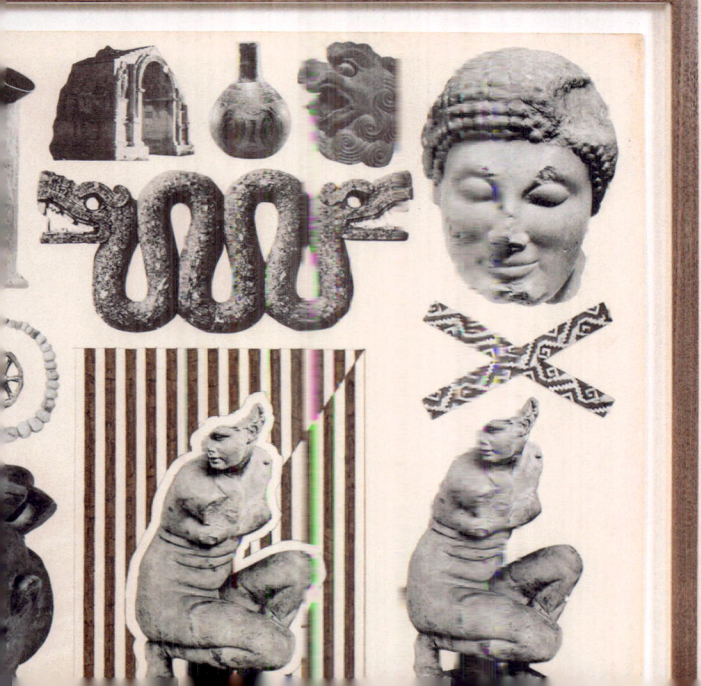
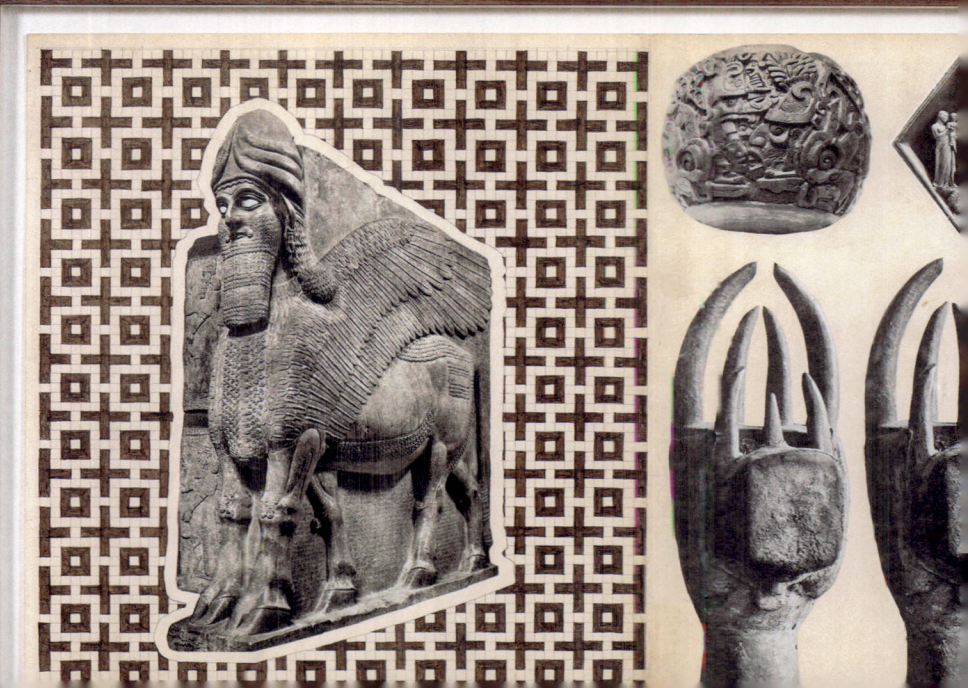

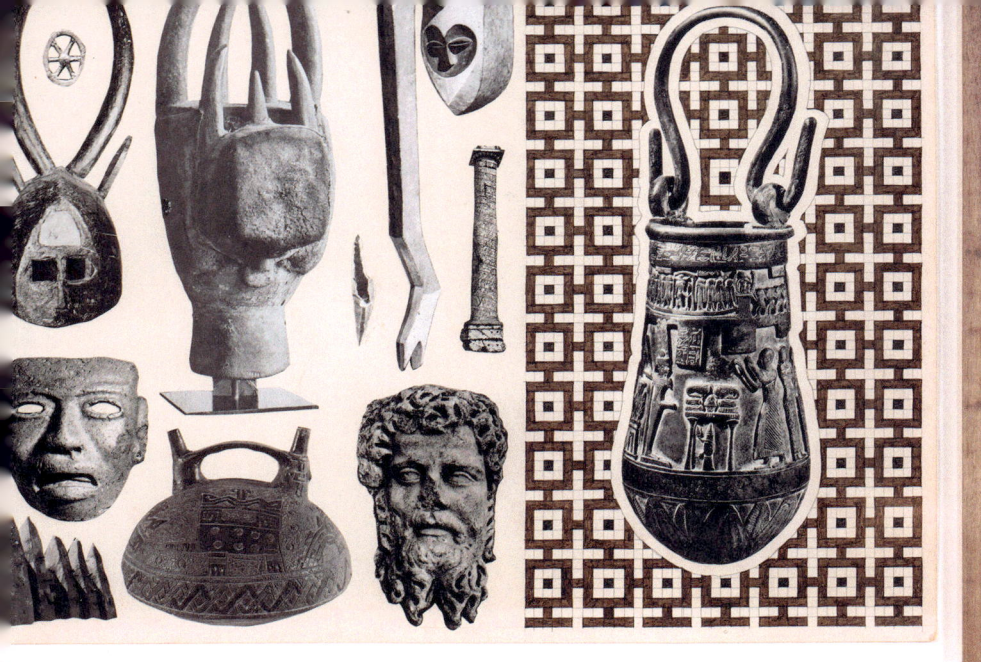

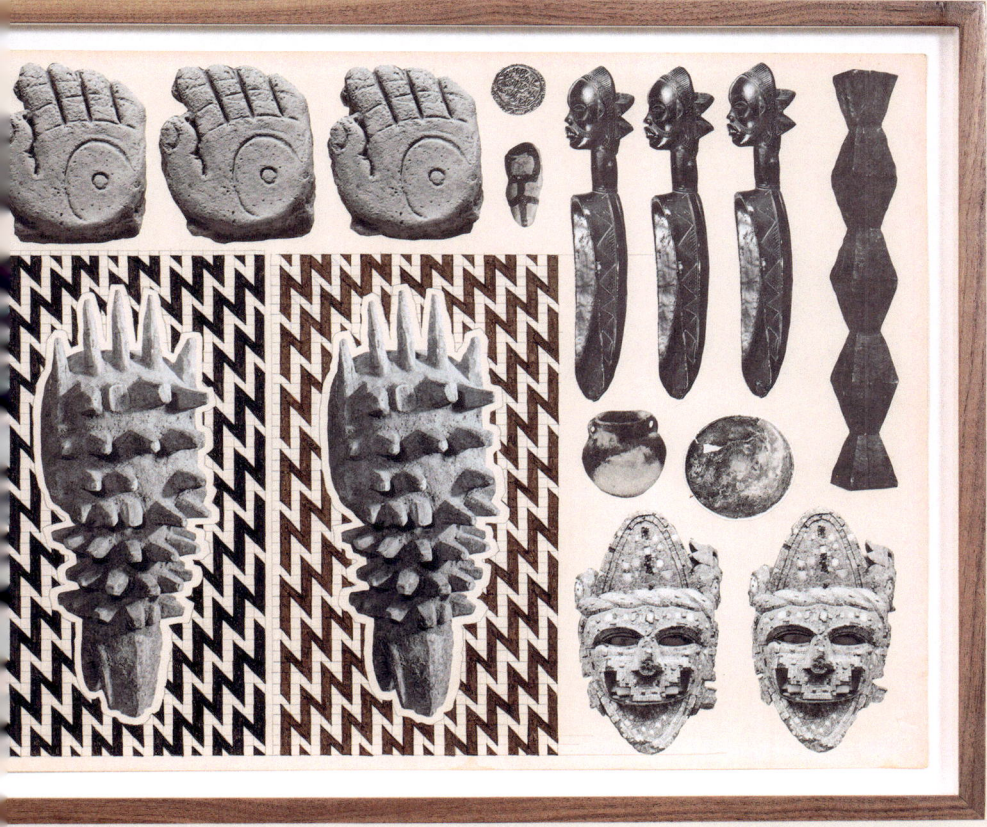
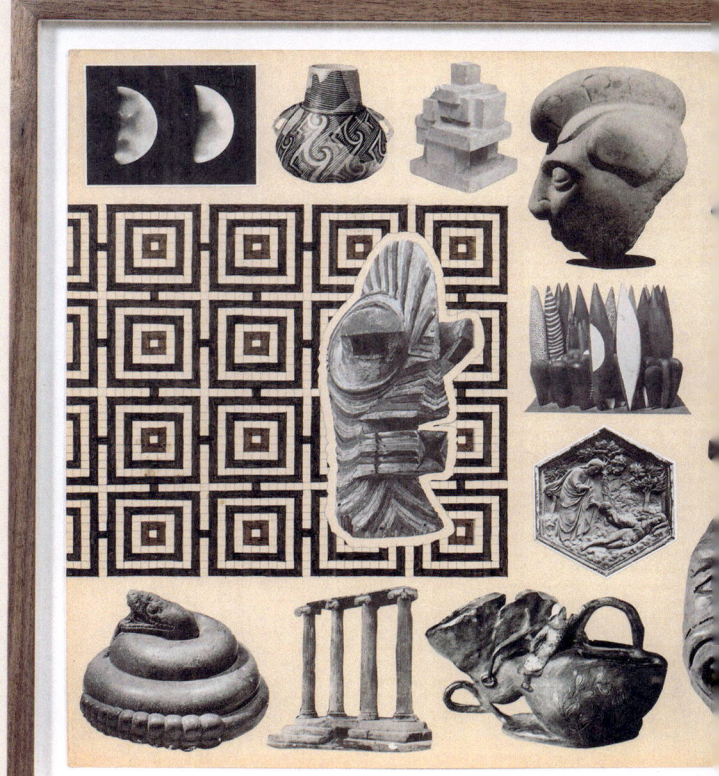
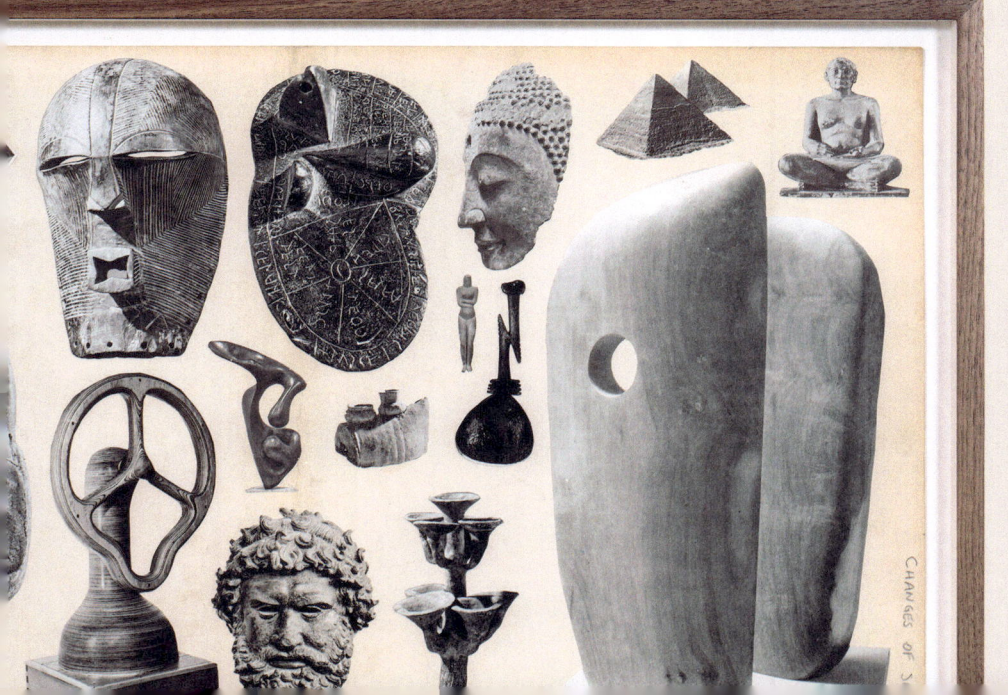
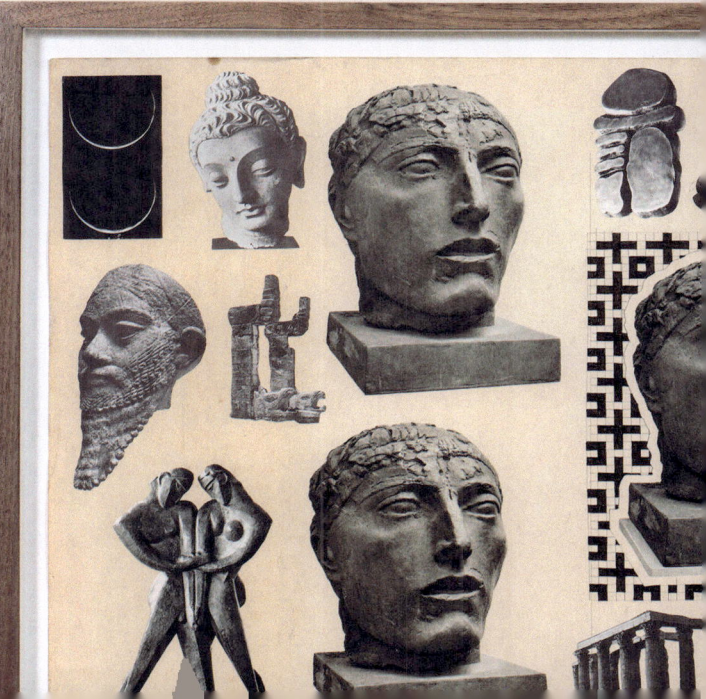

CHANGES OF S

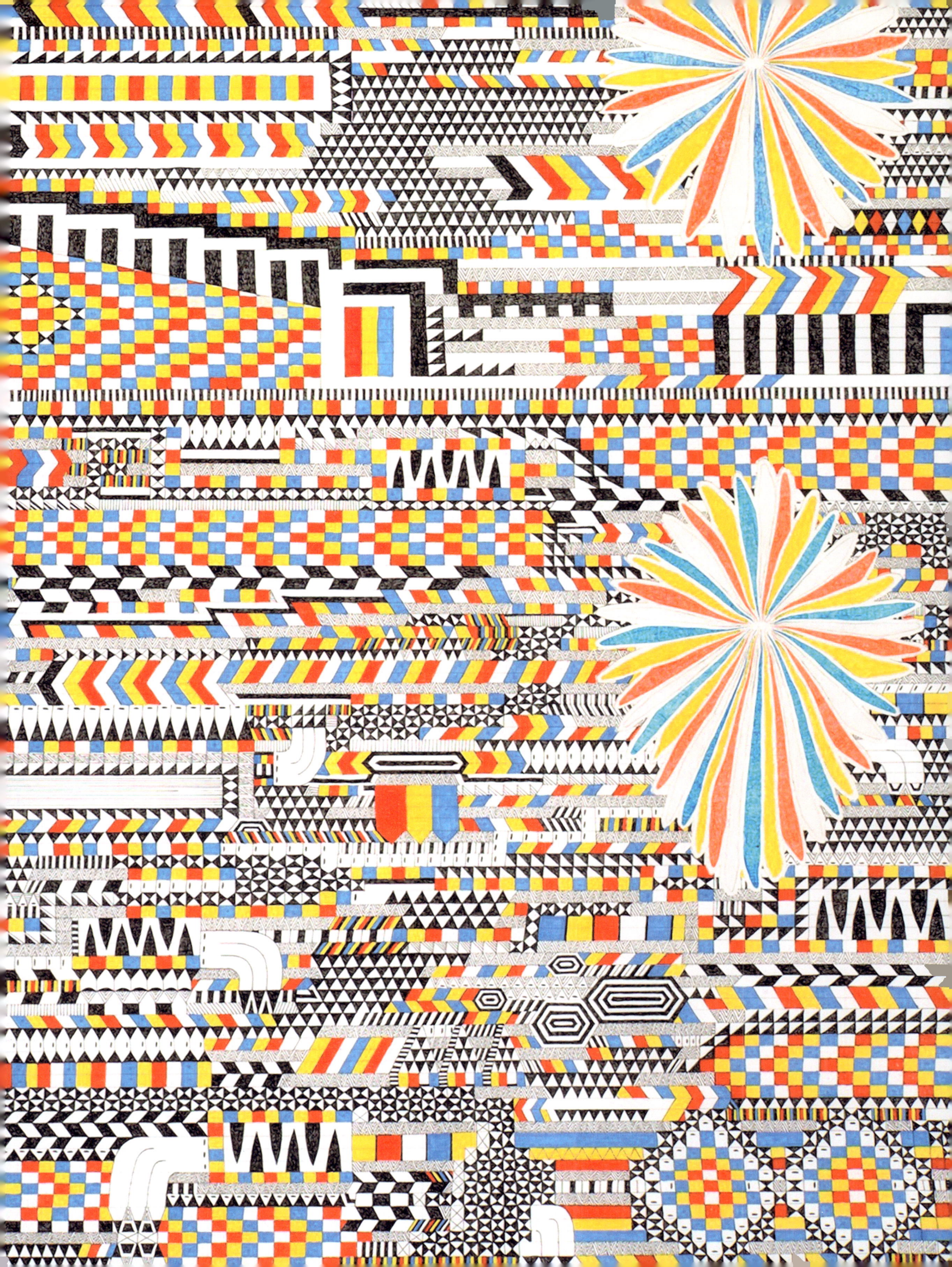

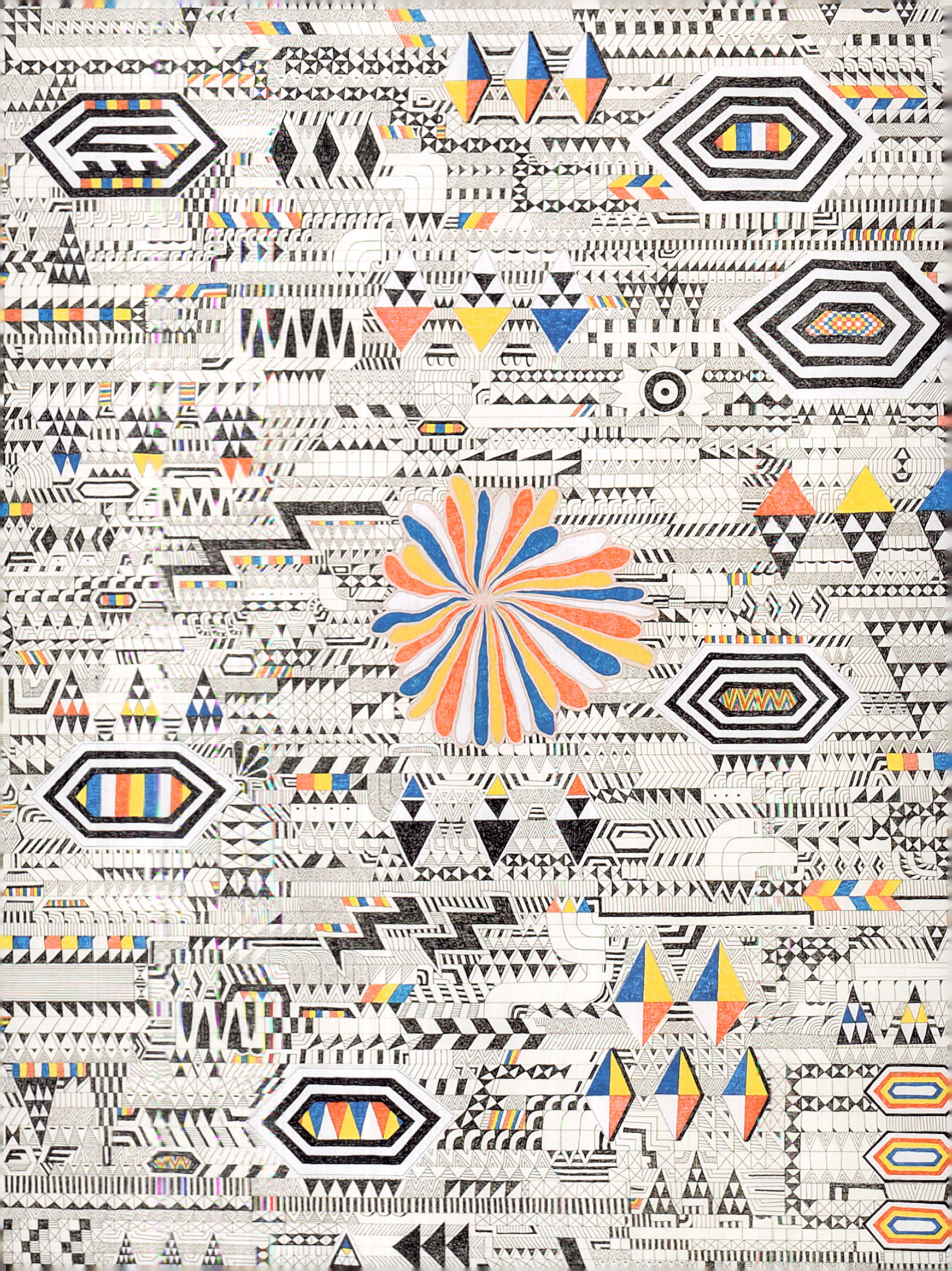

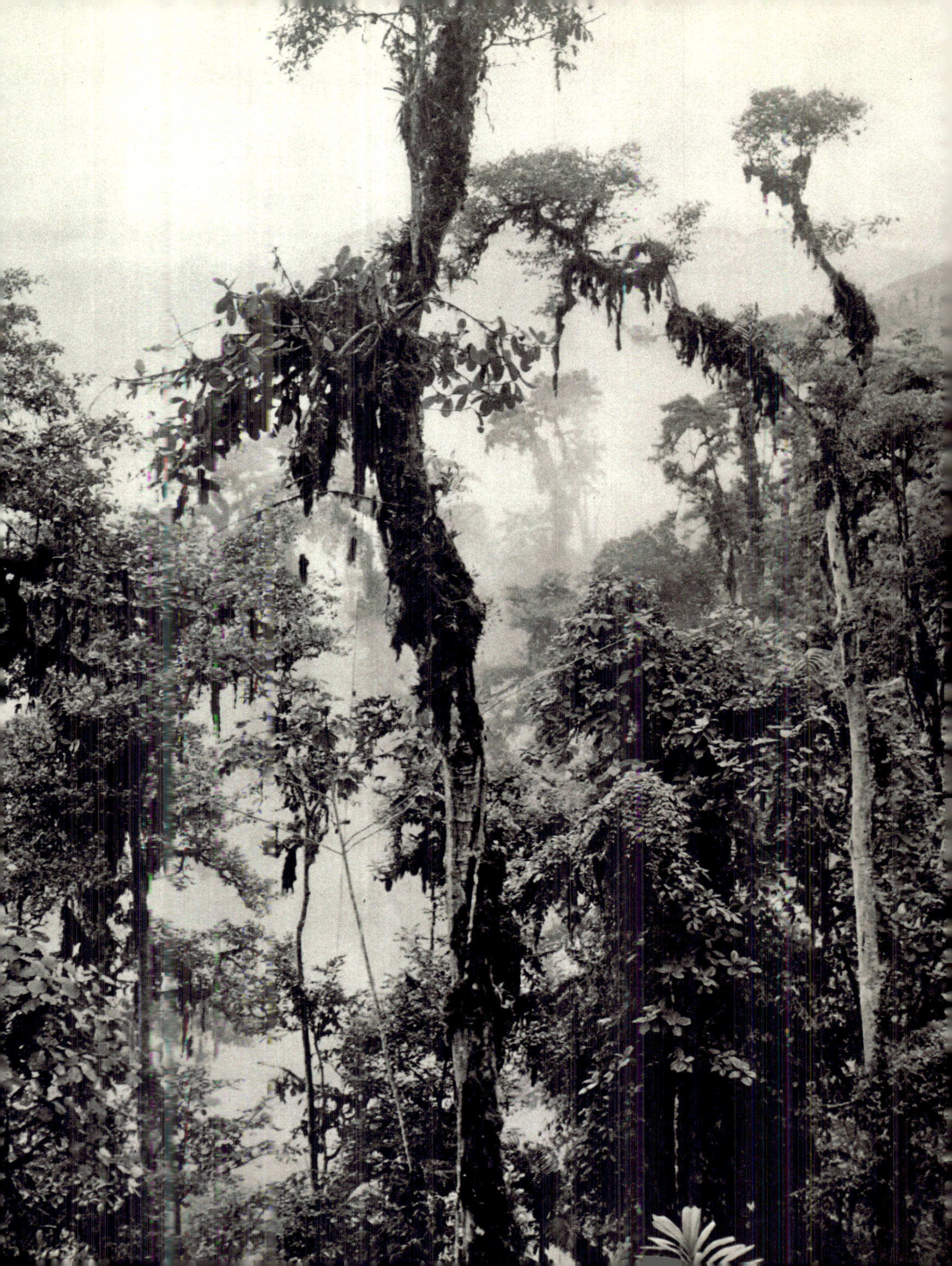

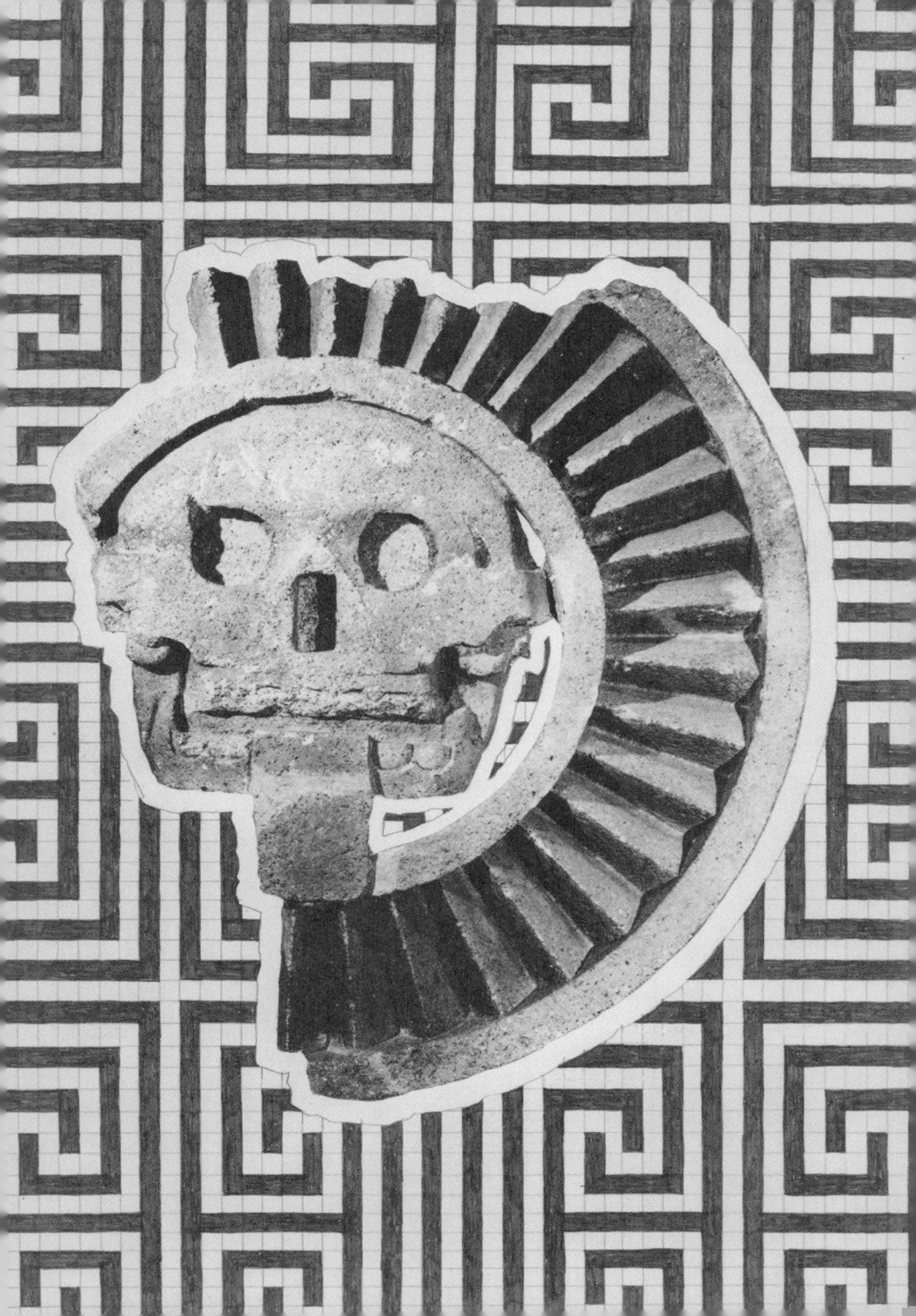

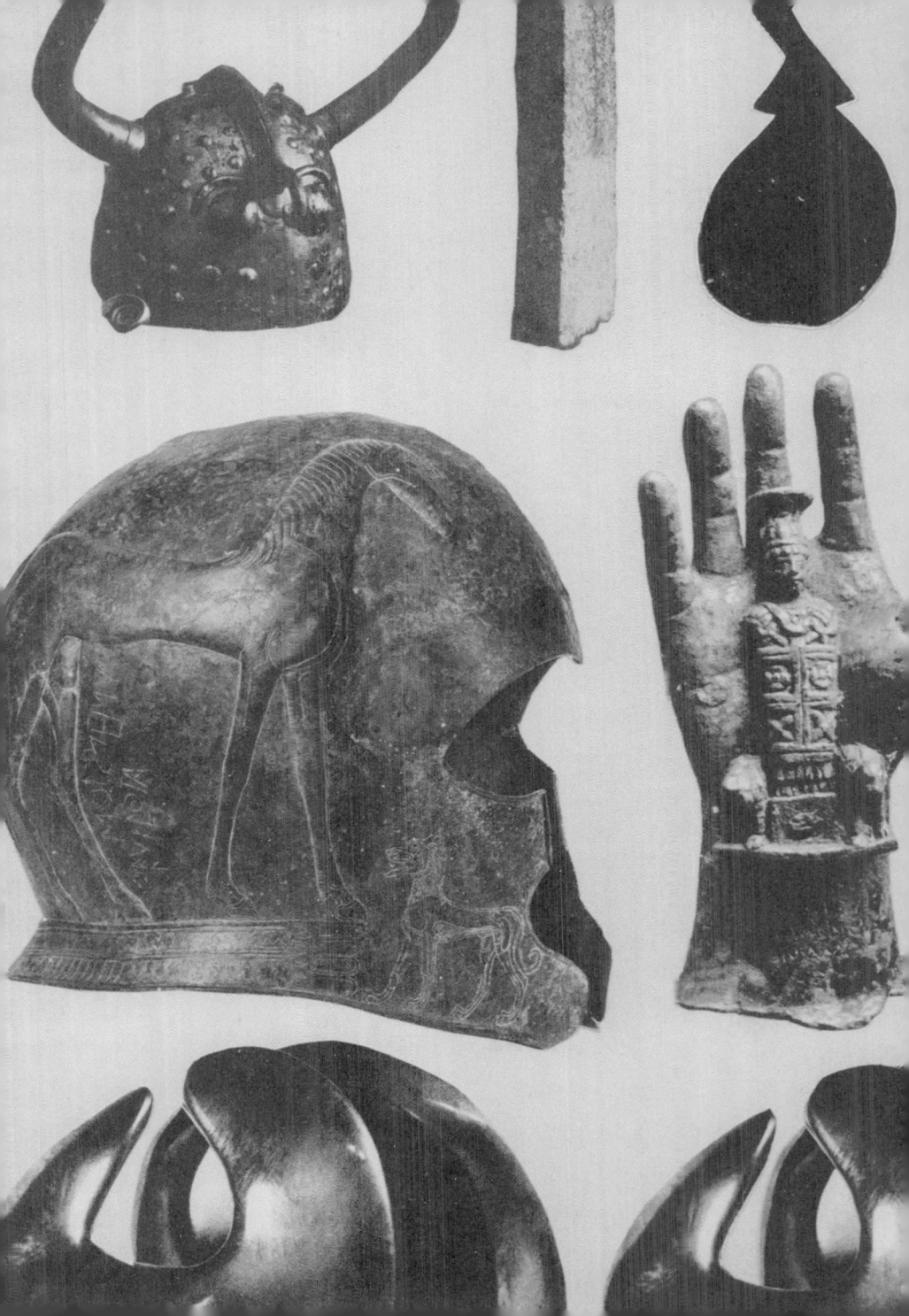

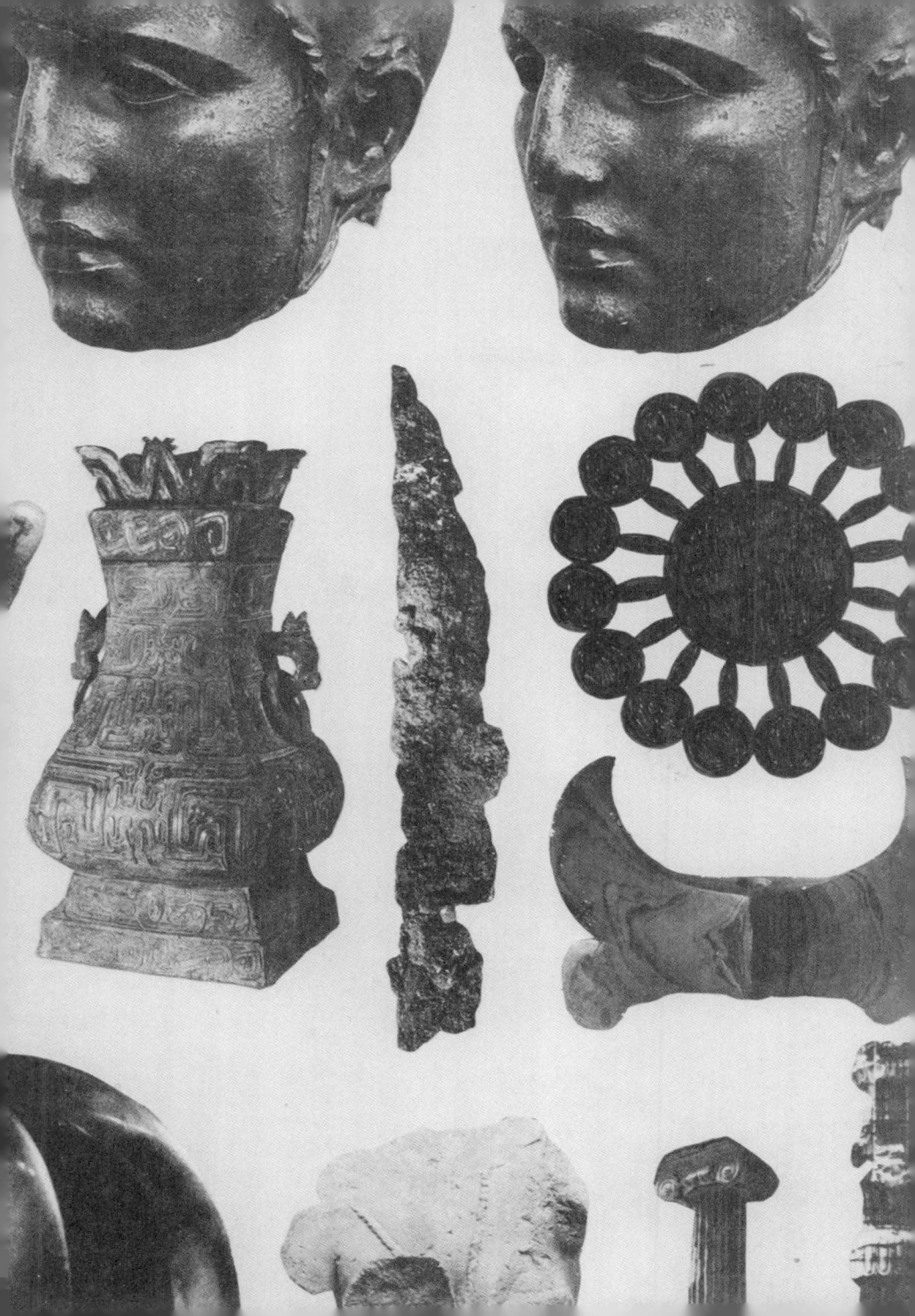

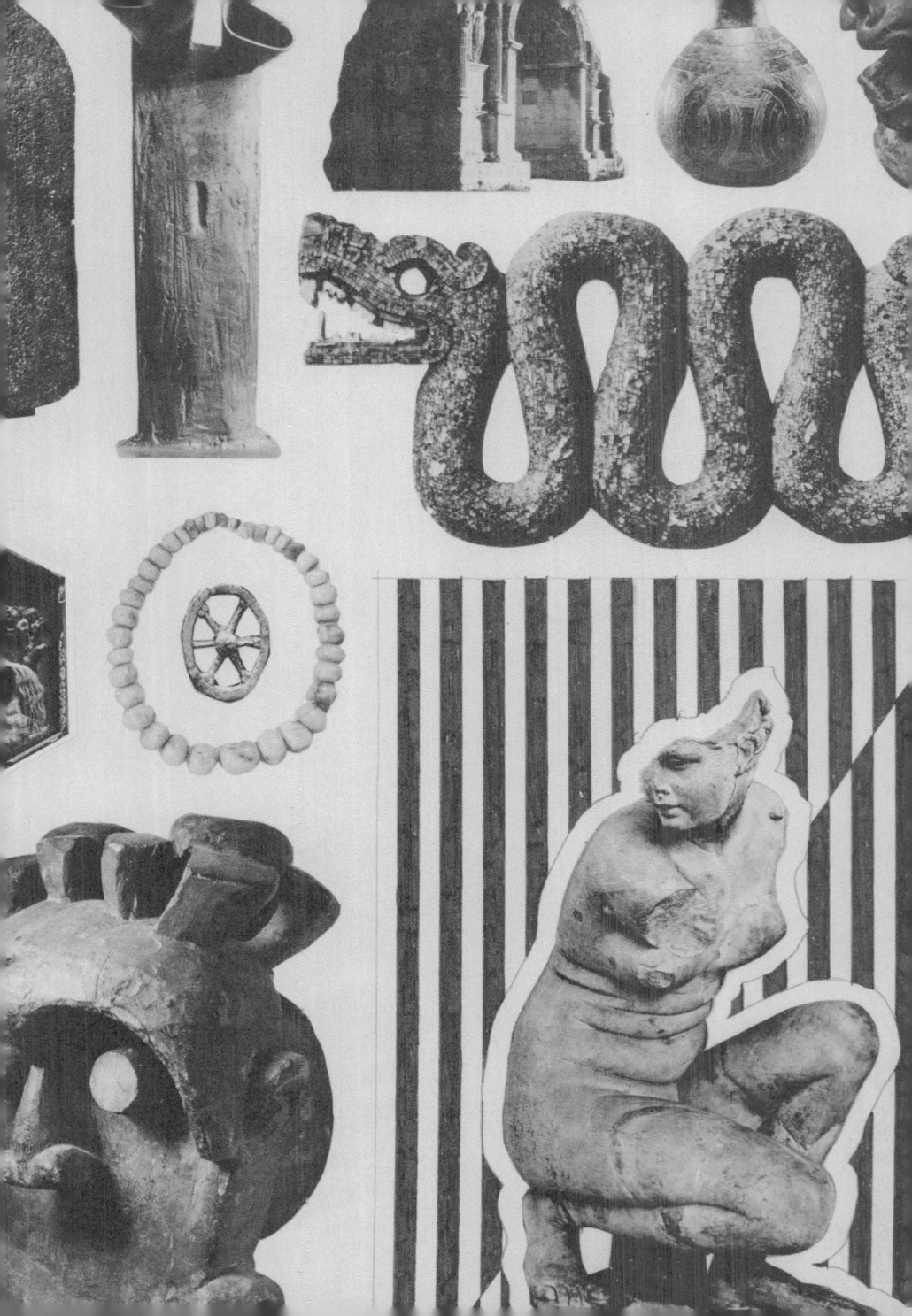

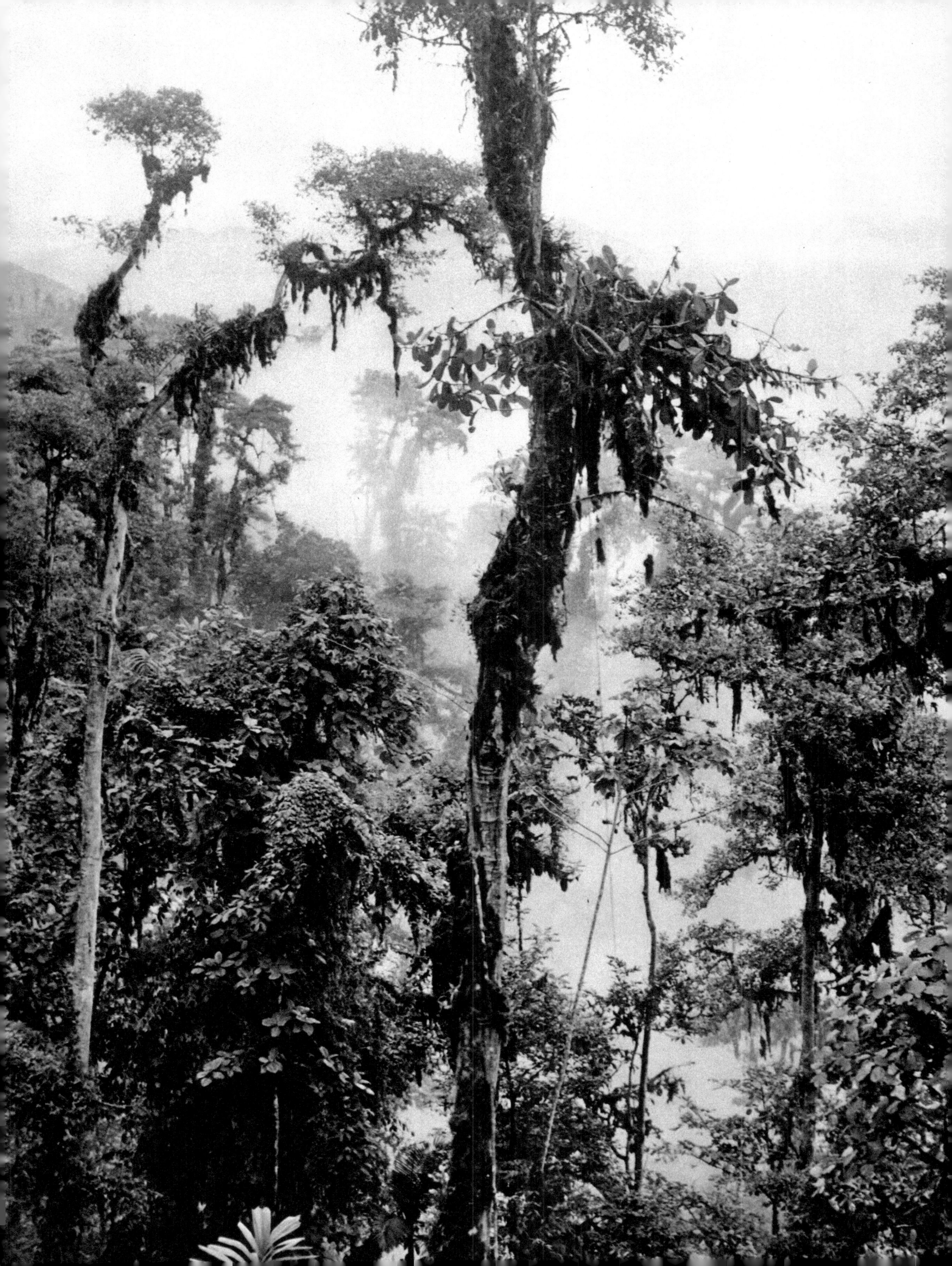

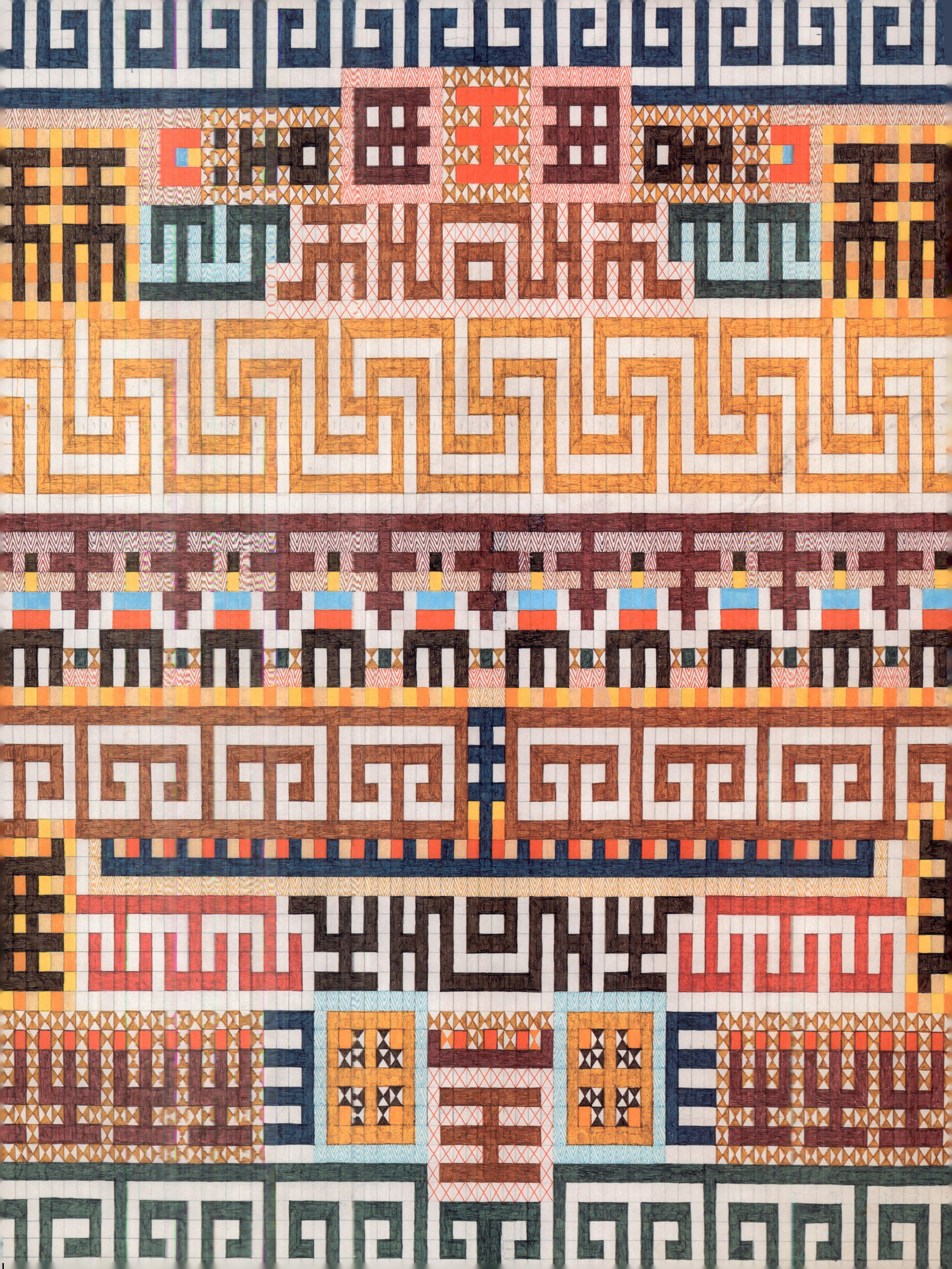

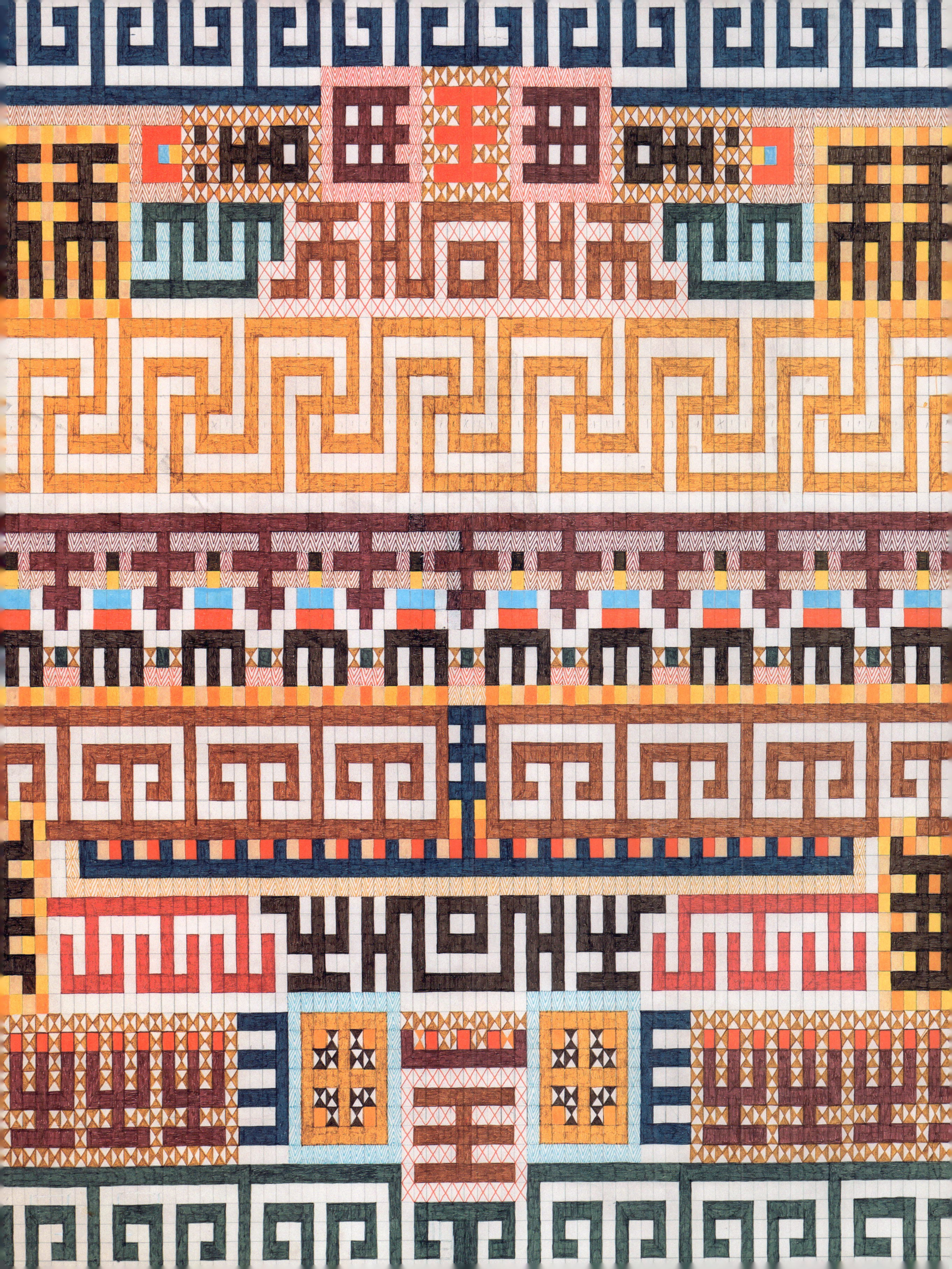

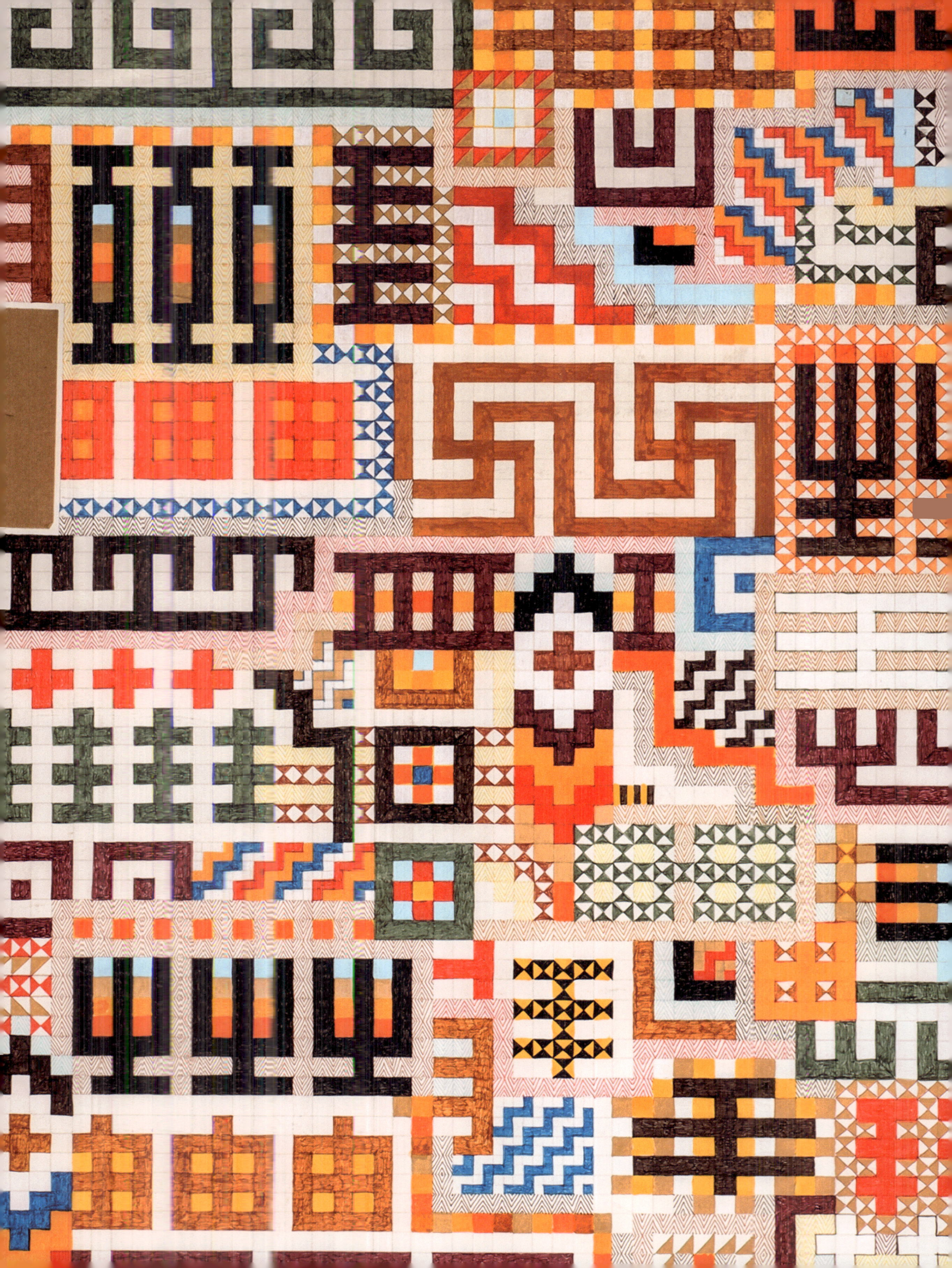

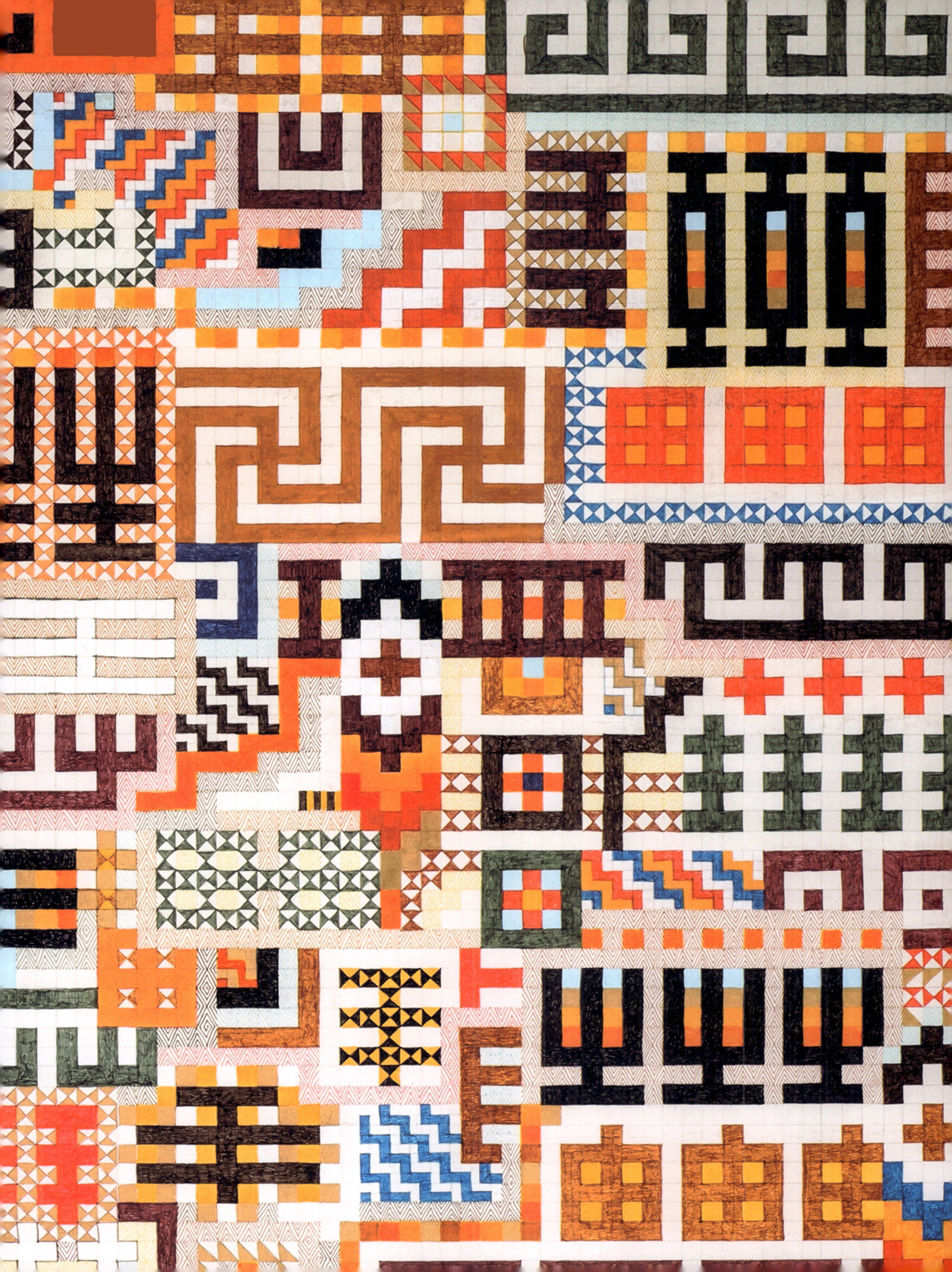

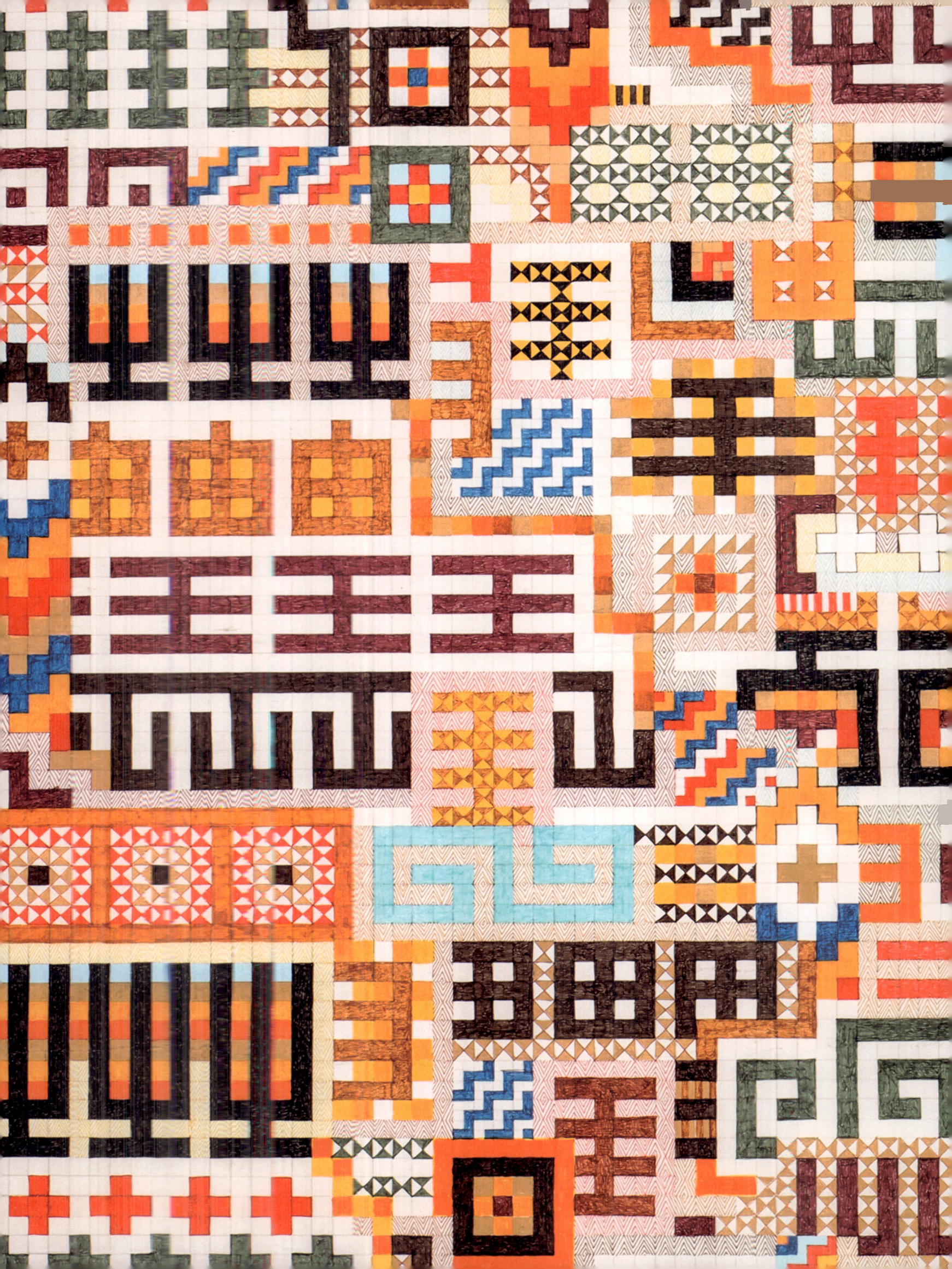

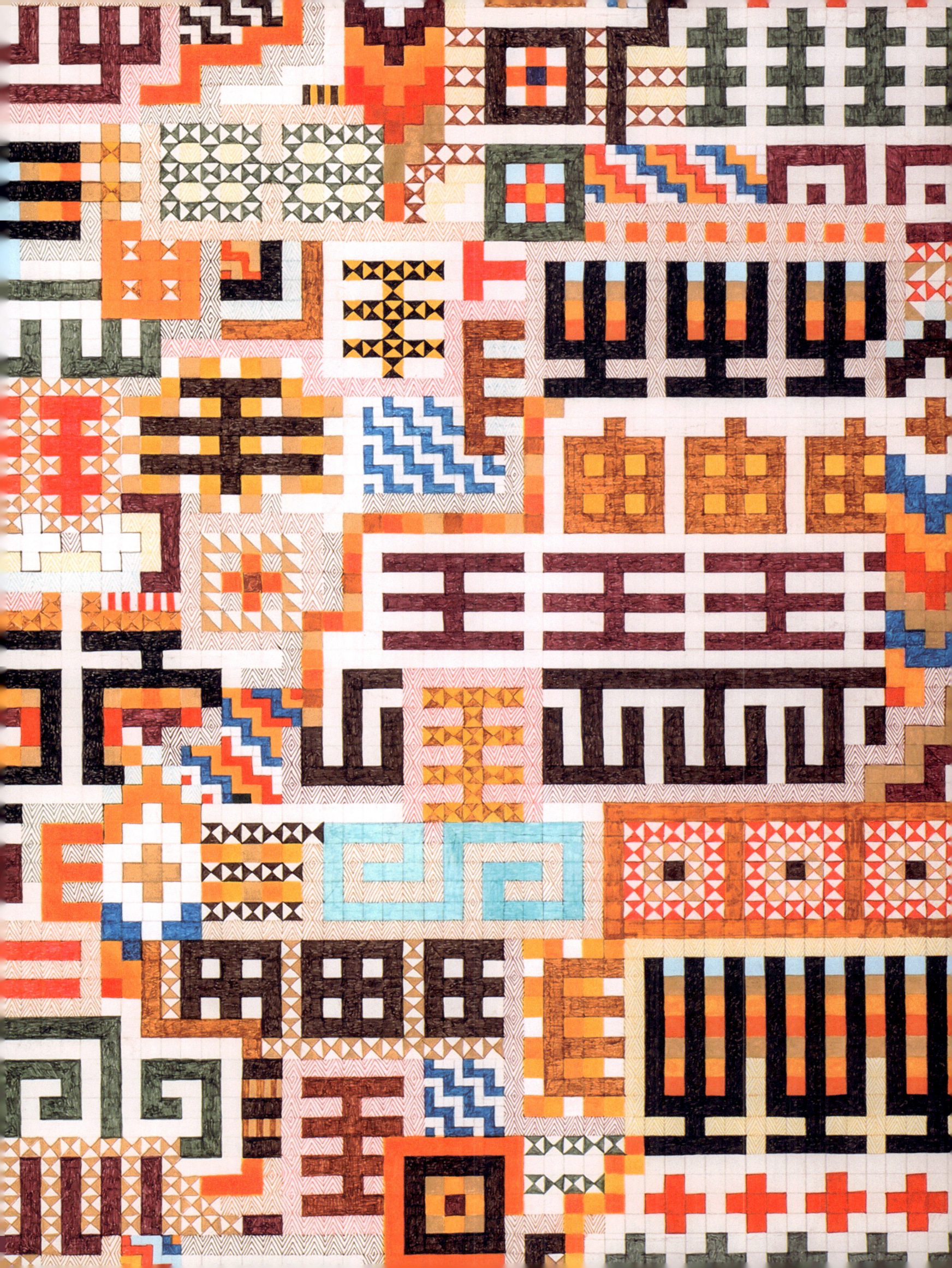

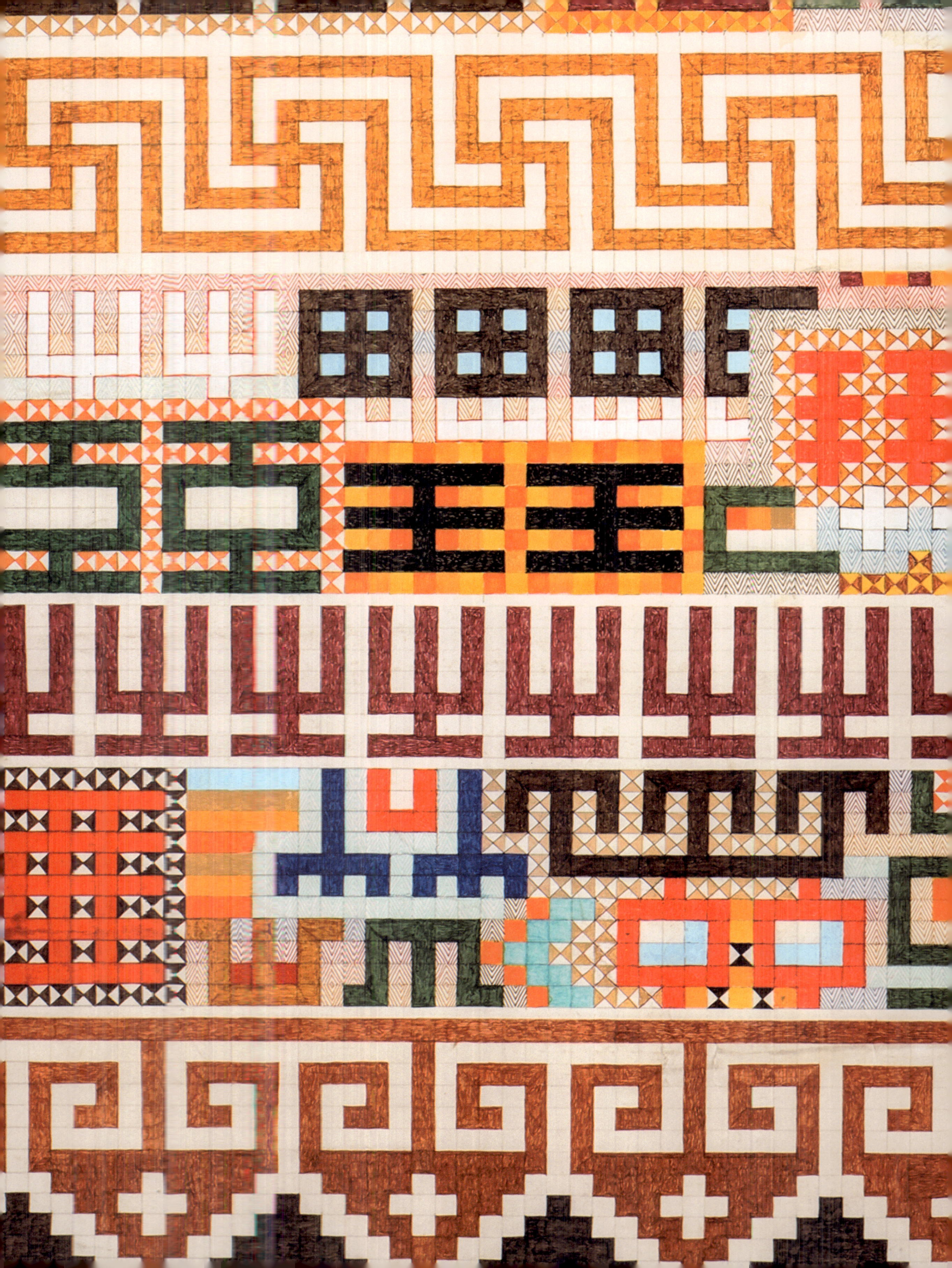

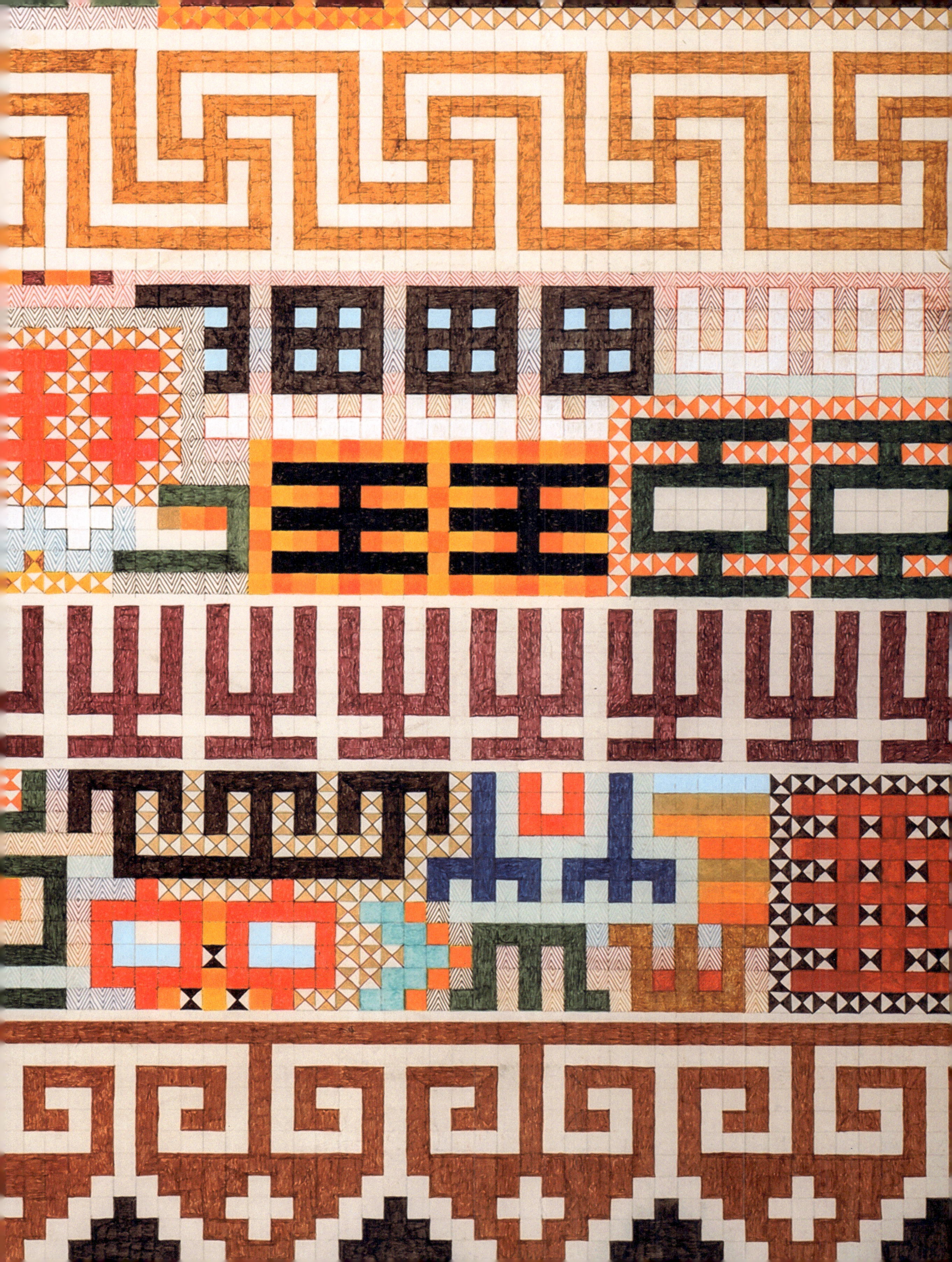

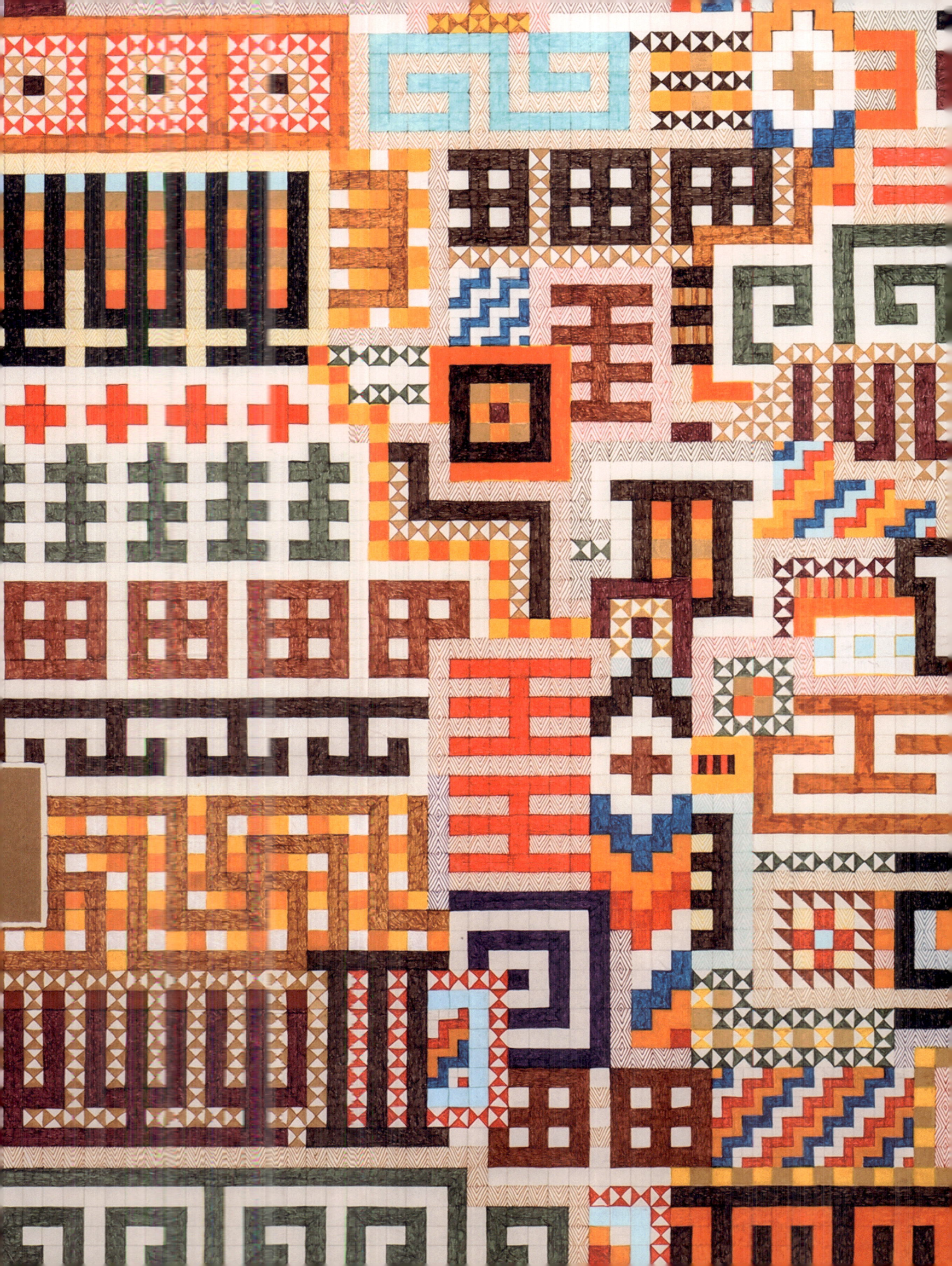

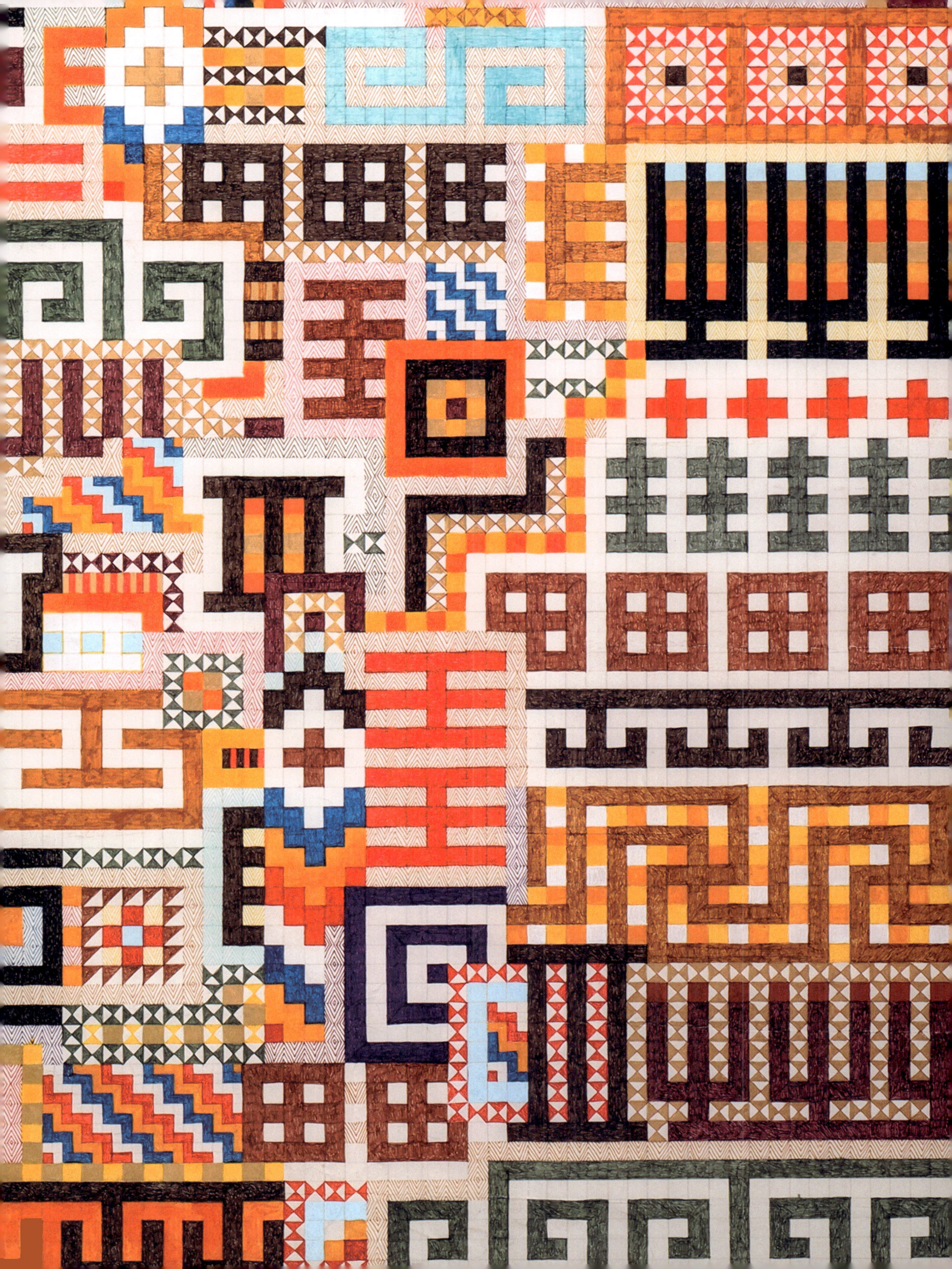

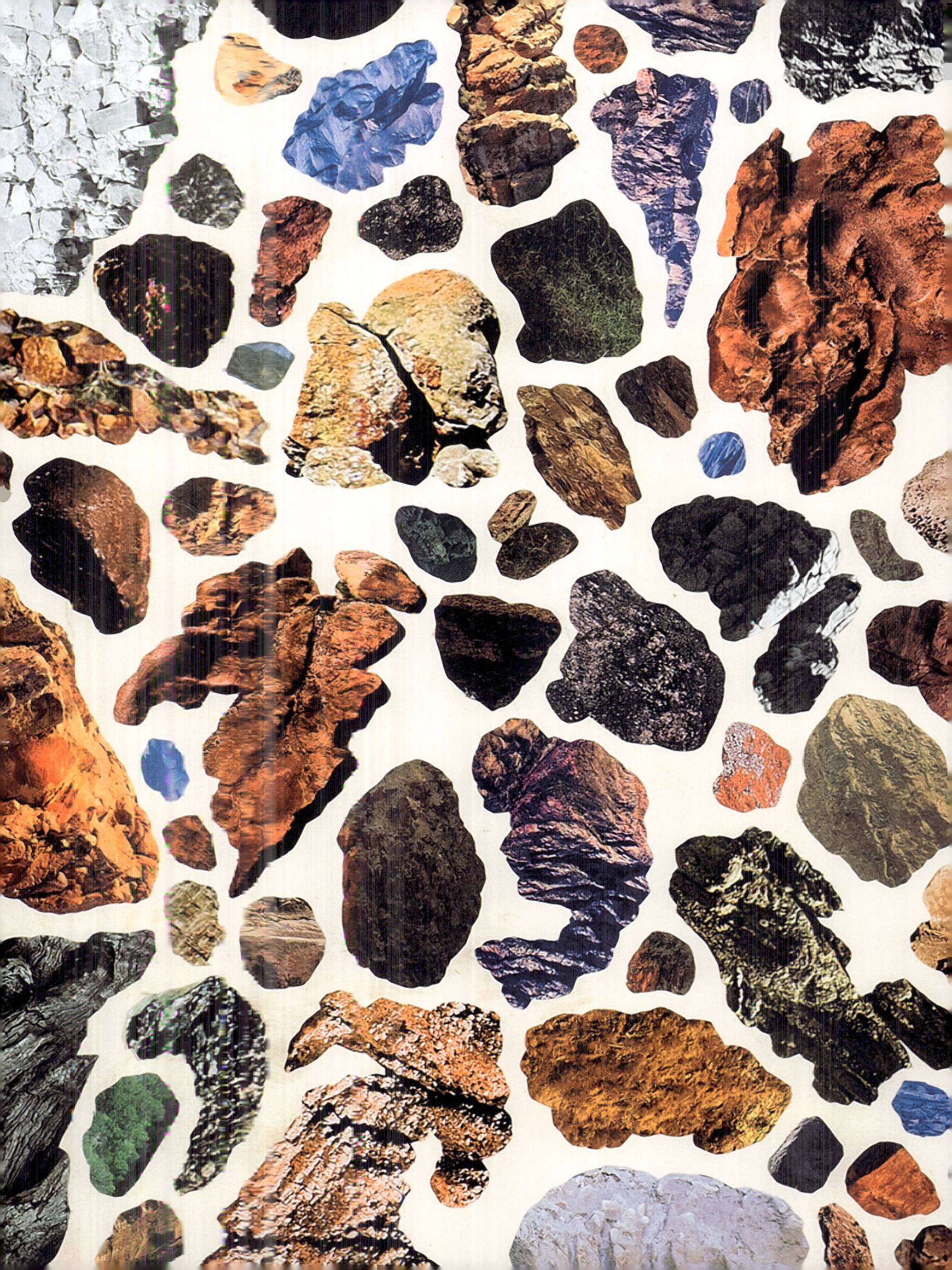

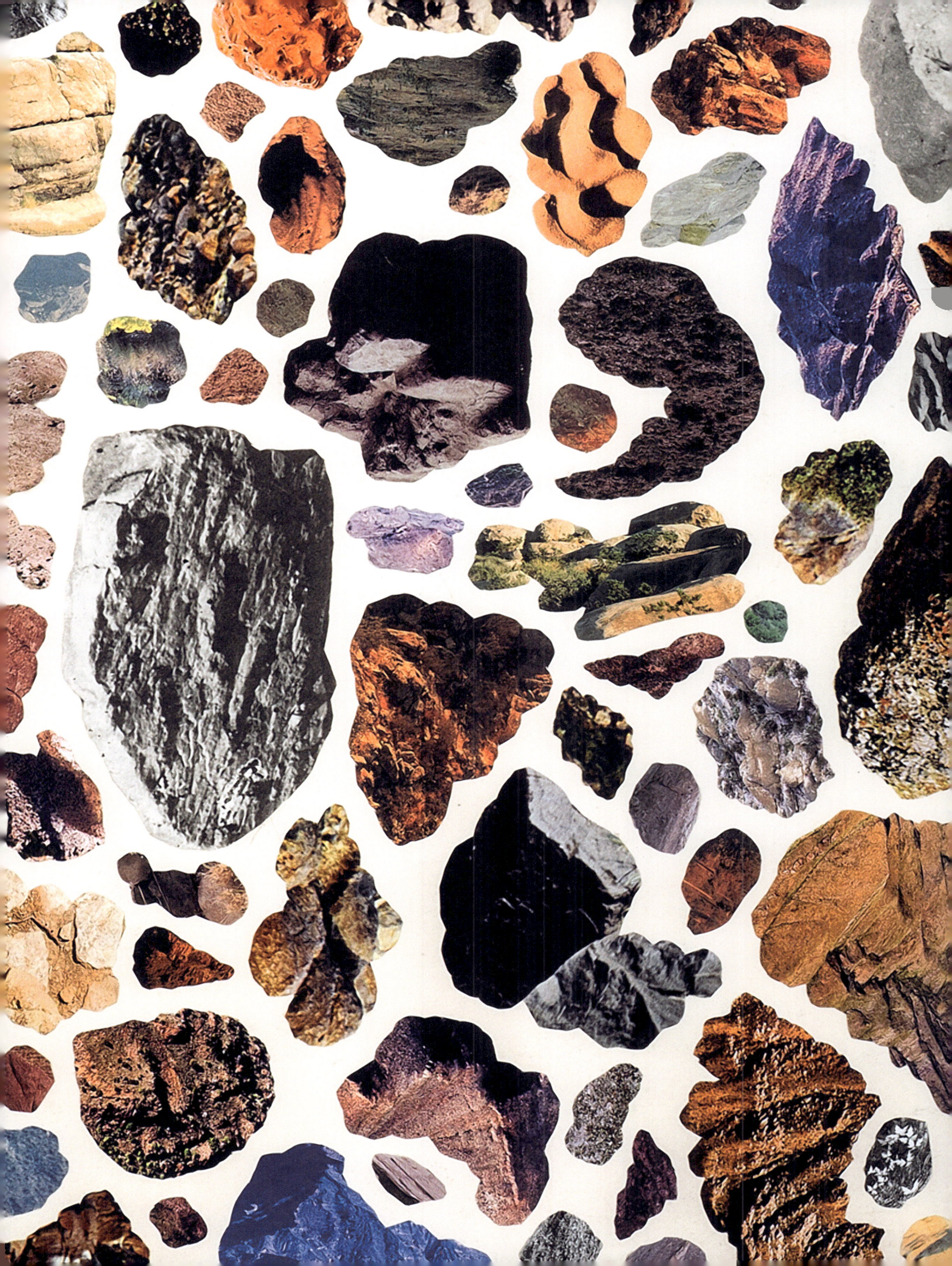

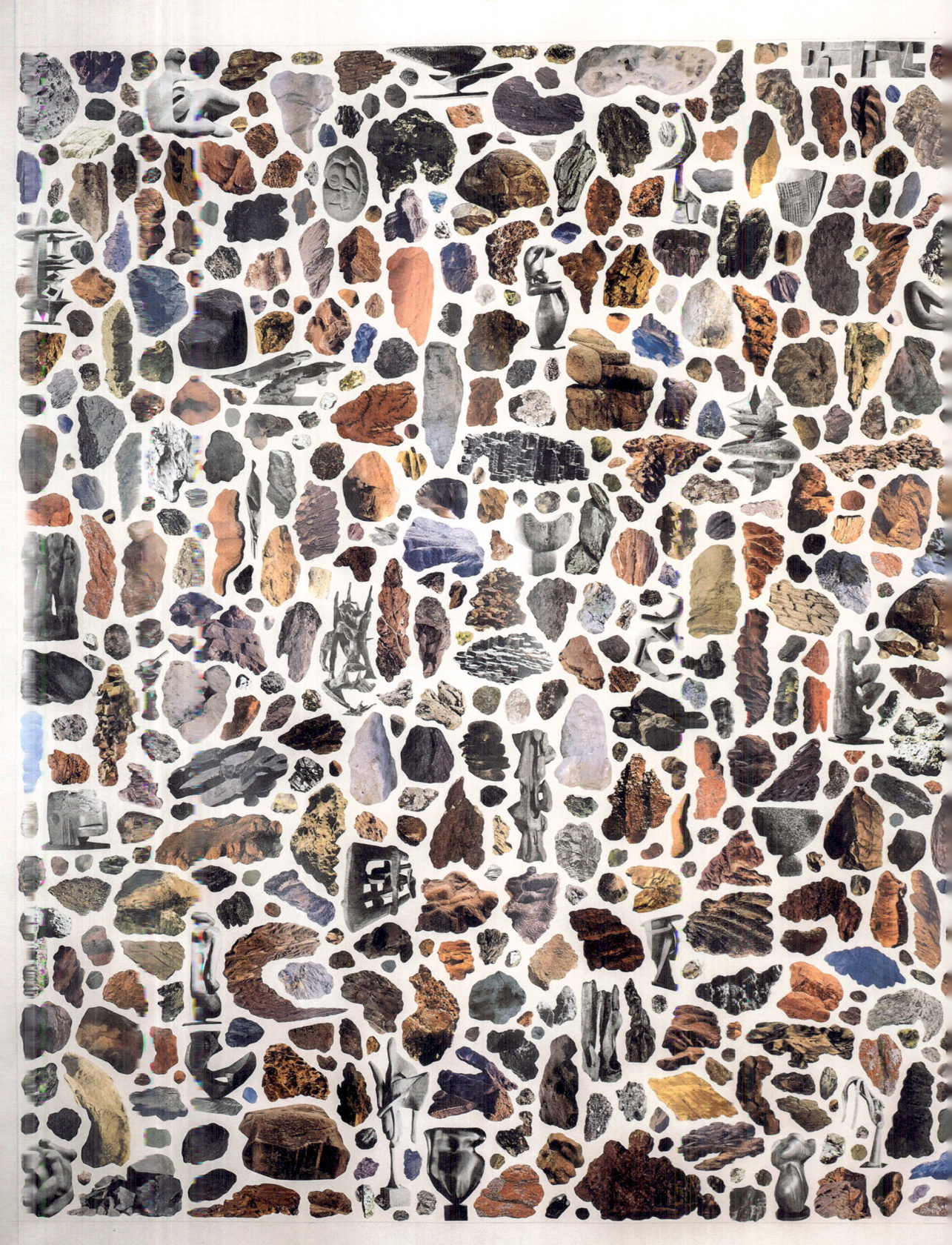

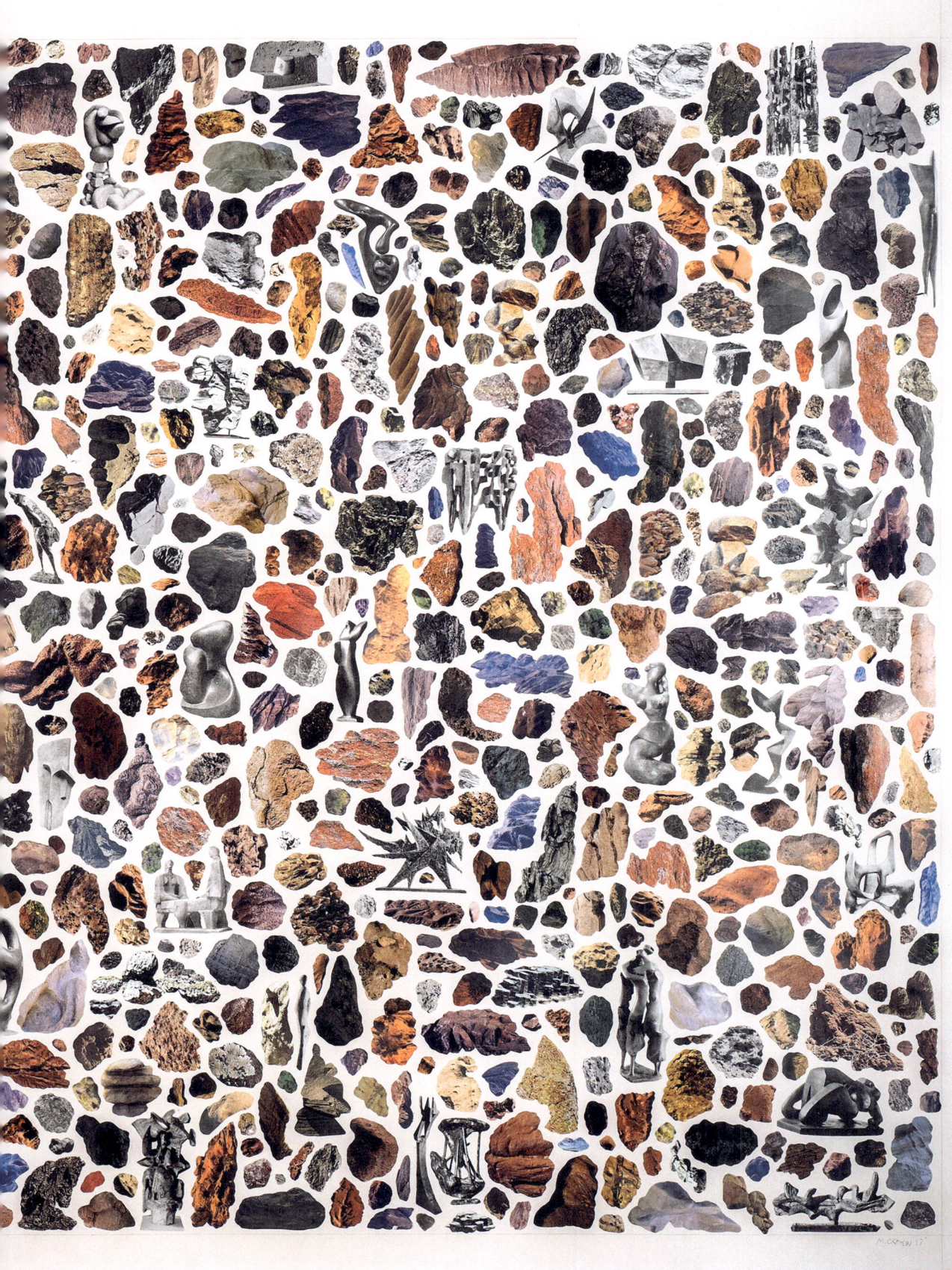

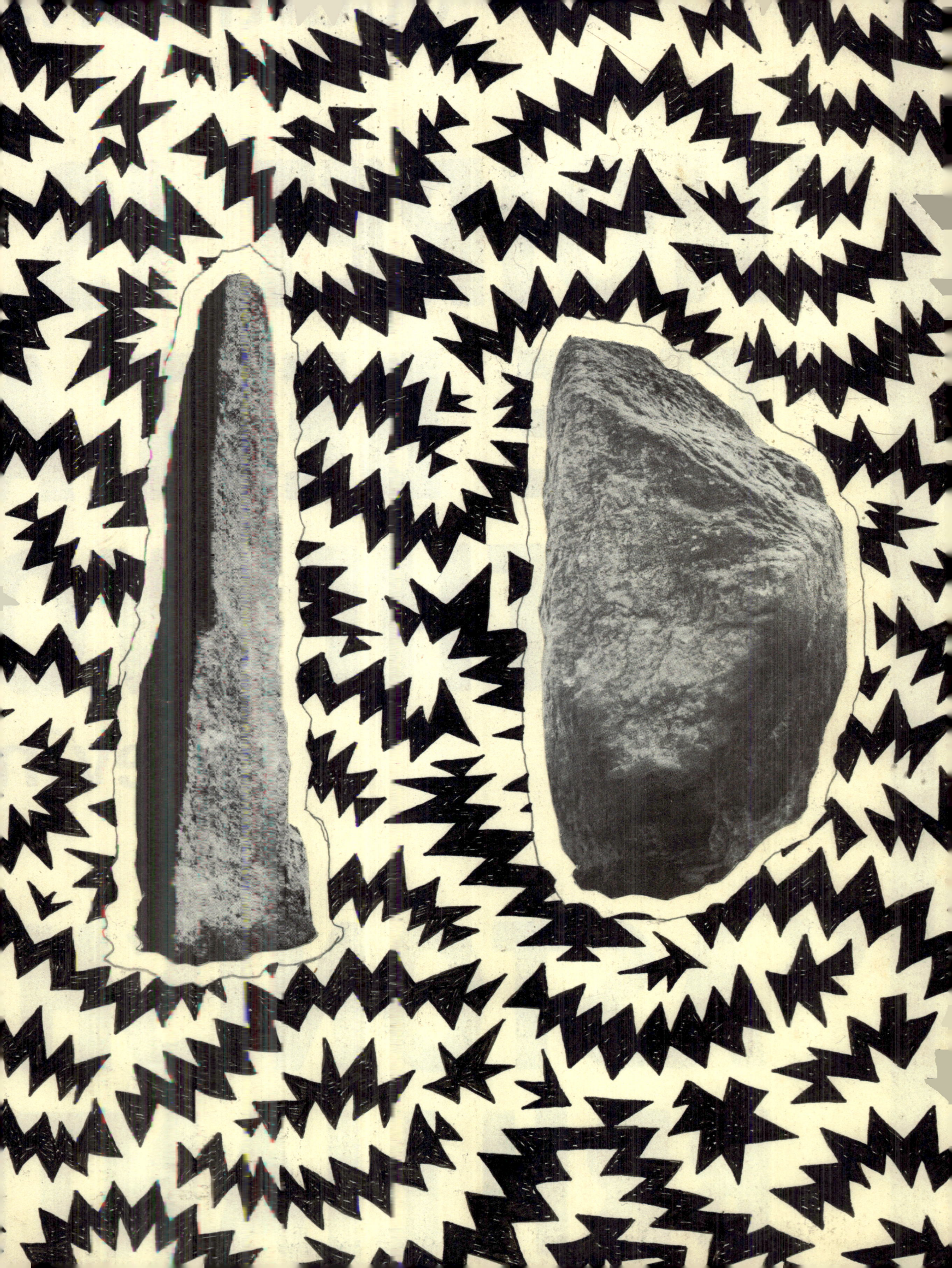

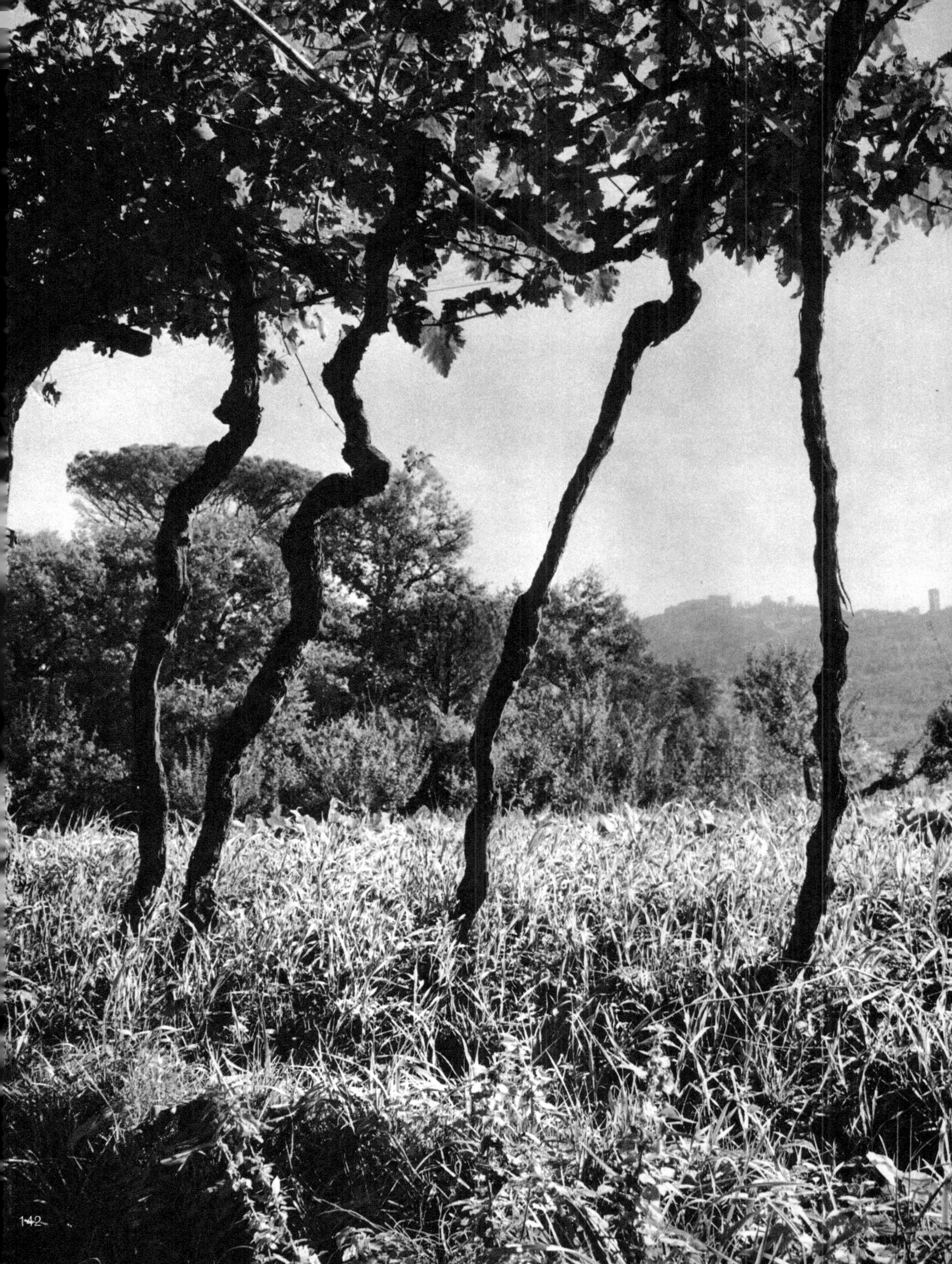

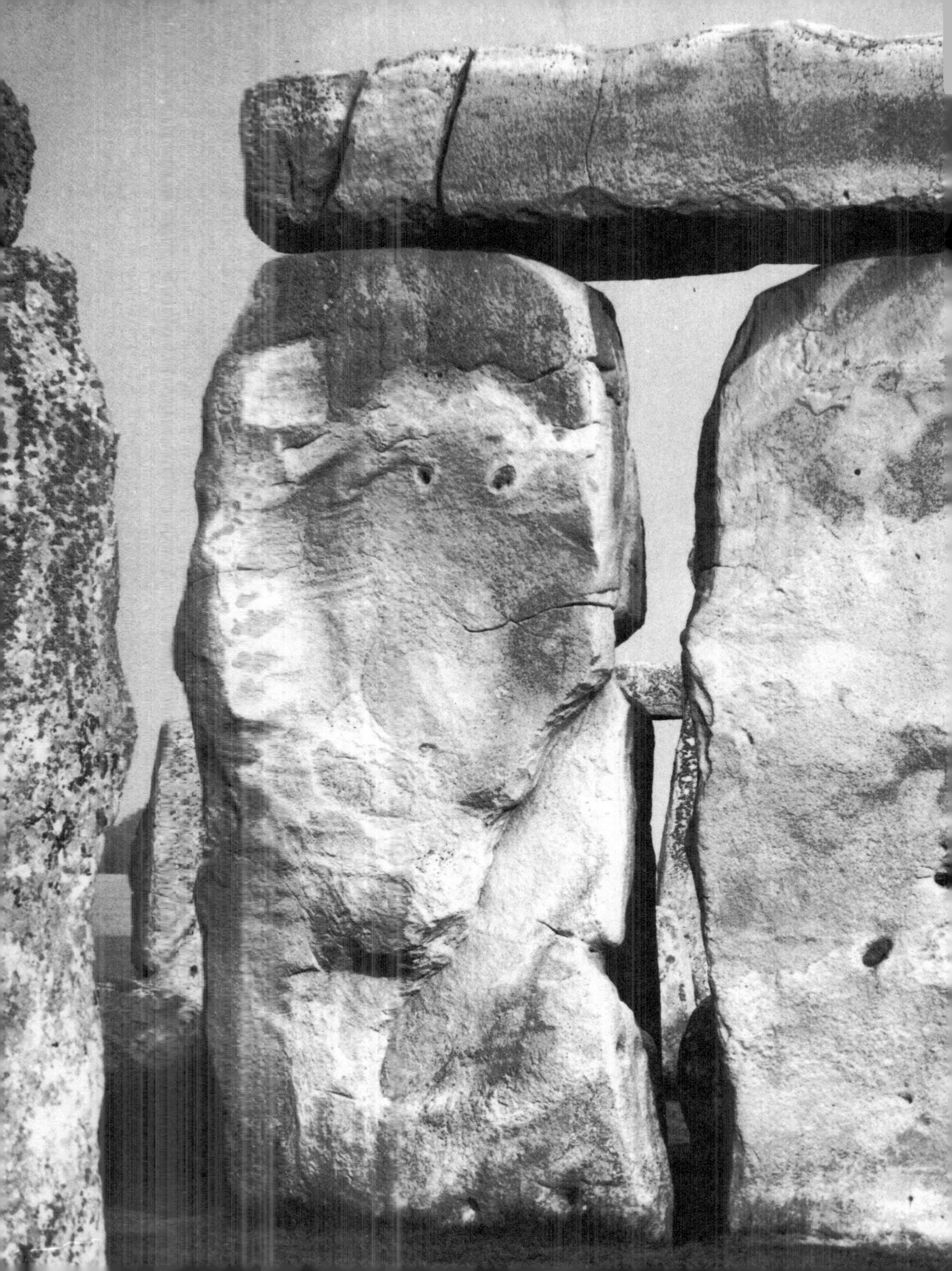

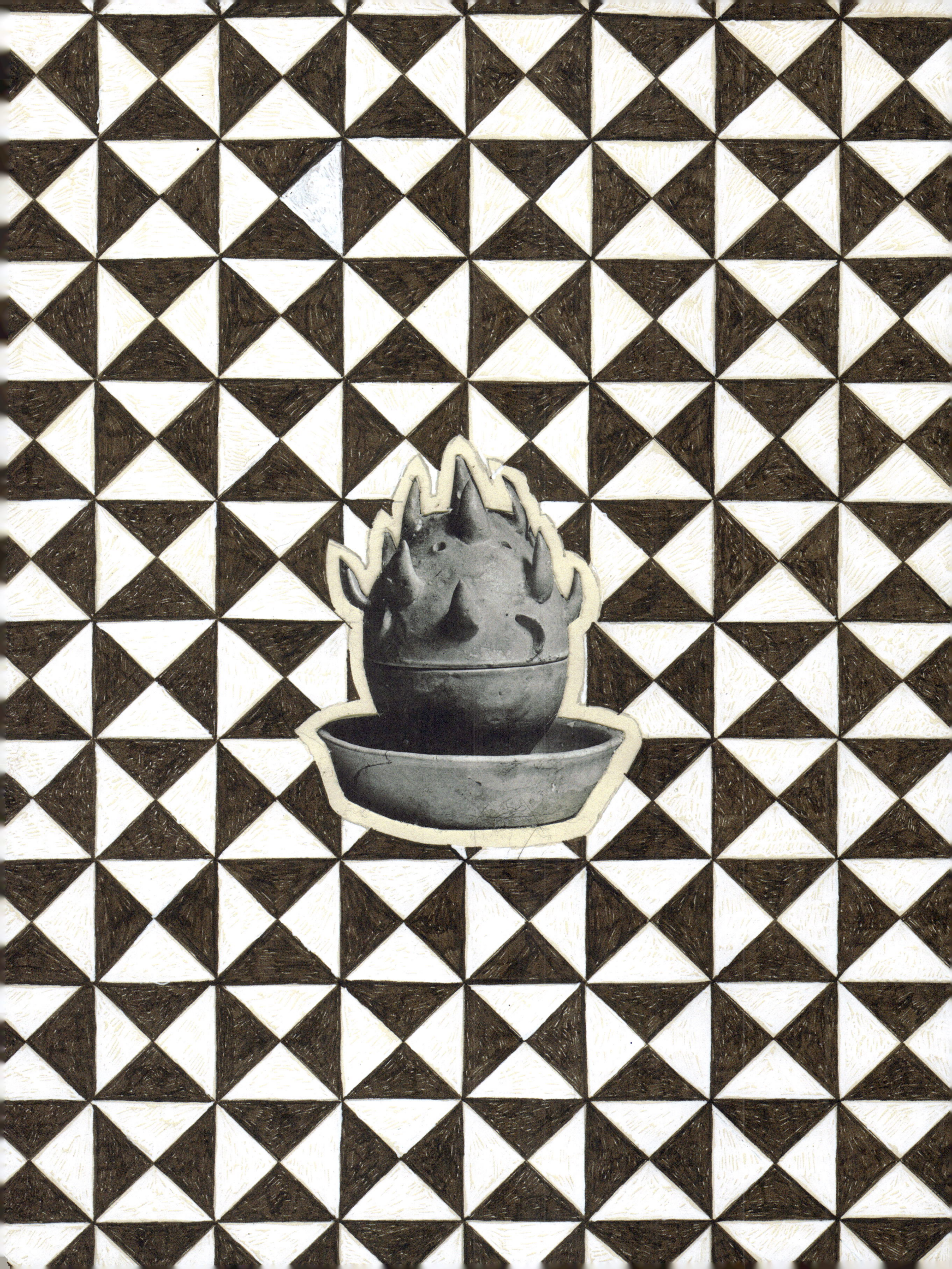

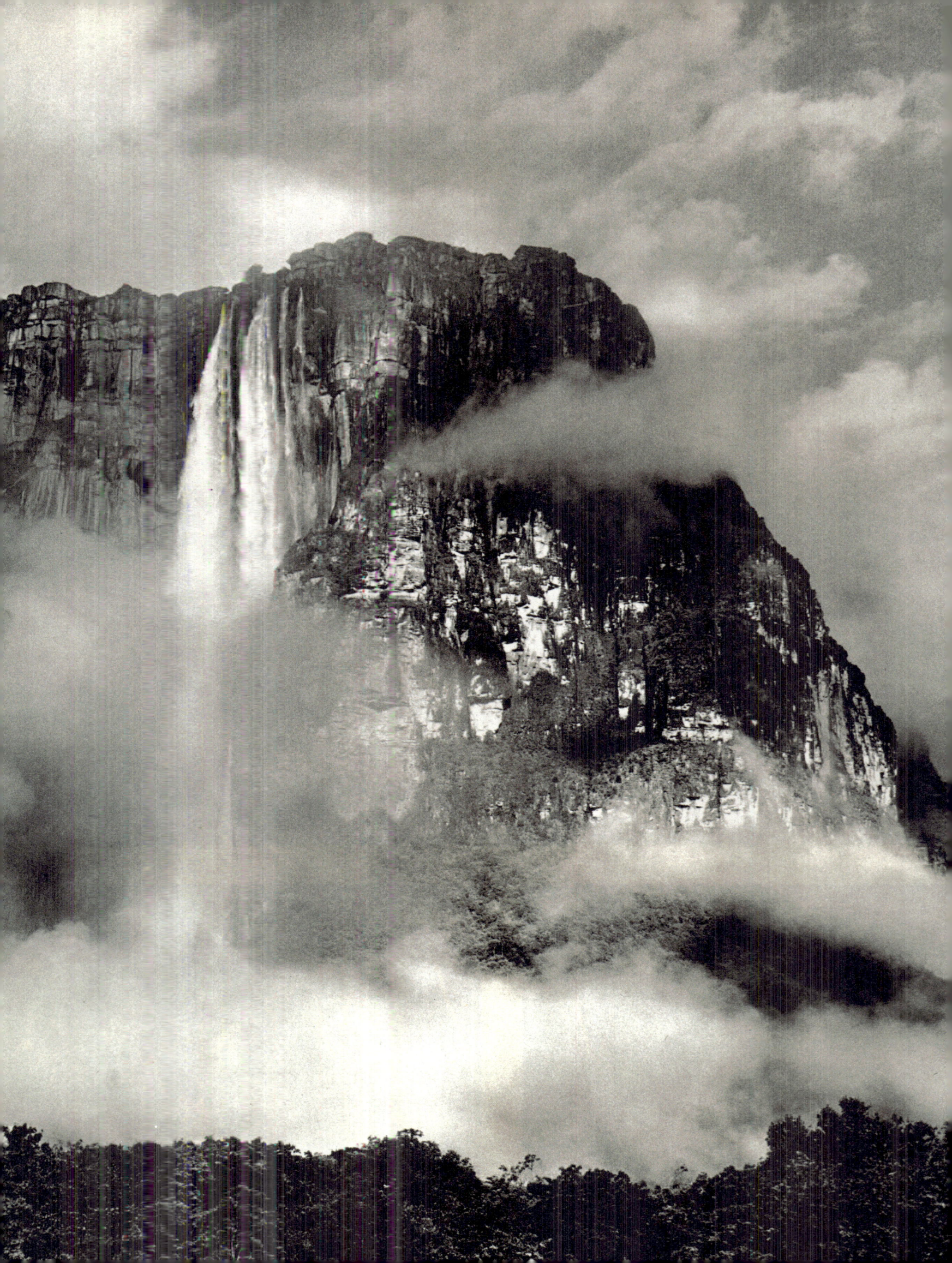

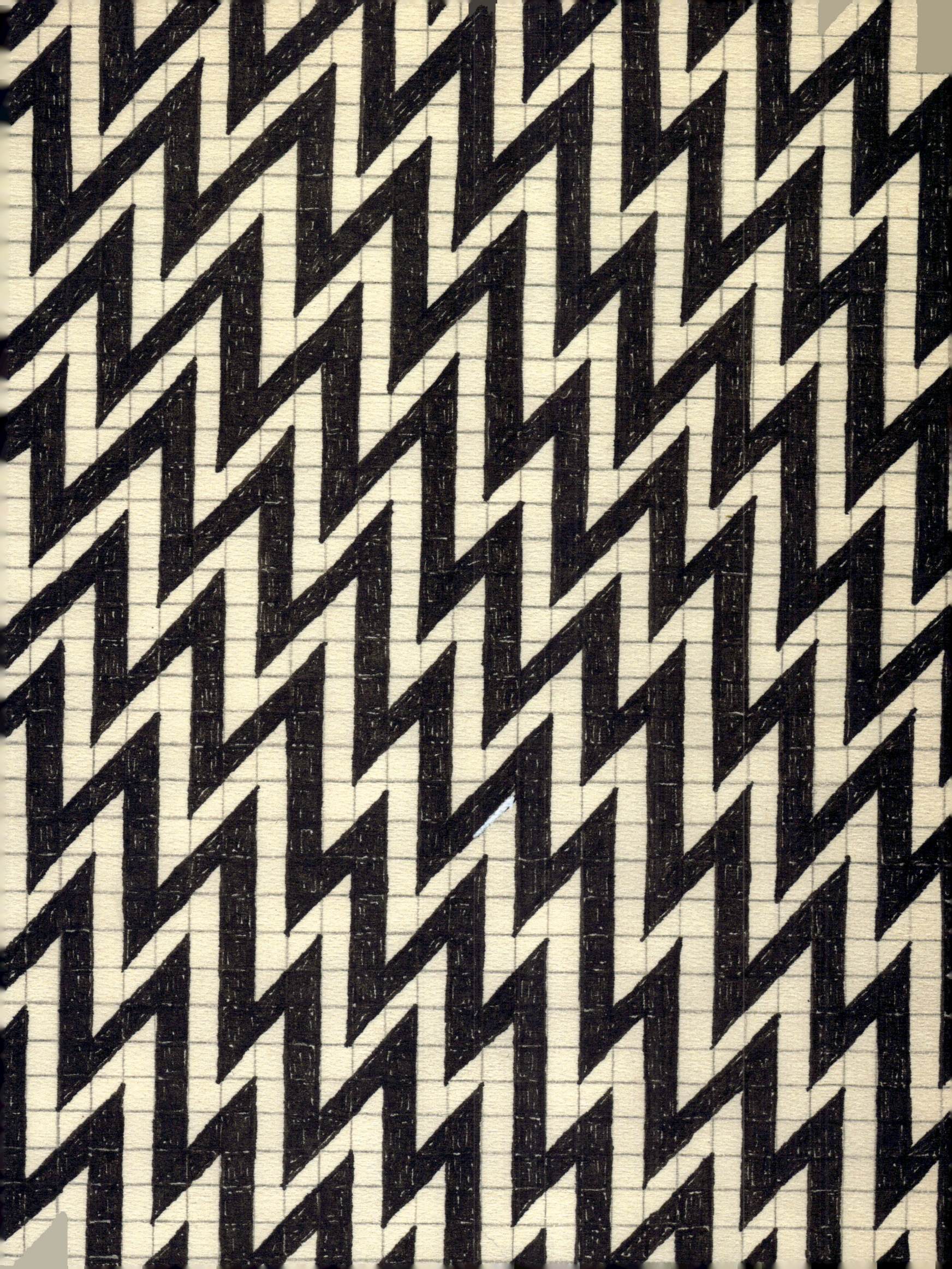

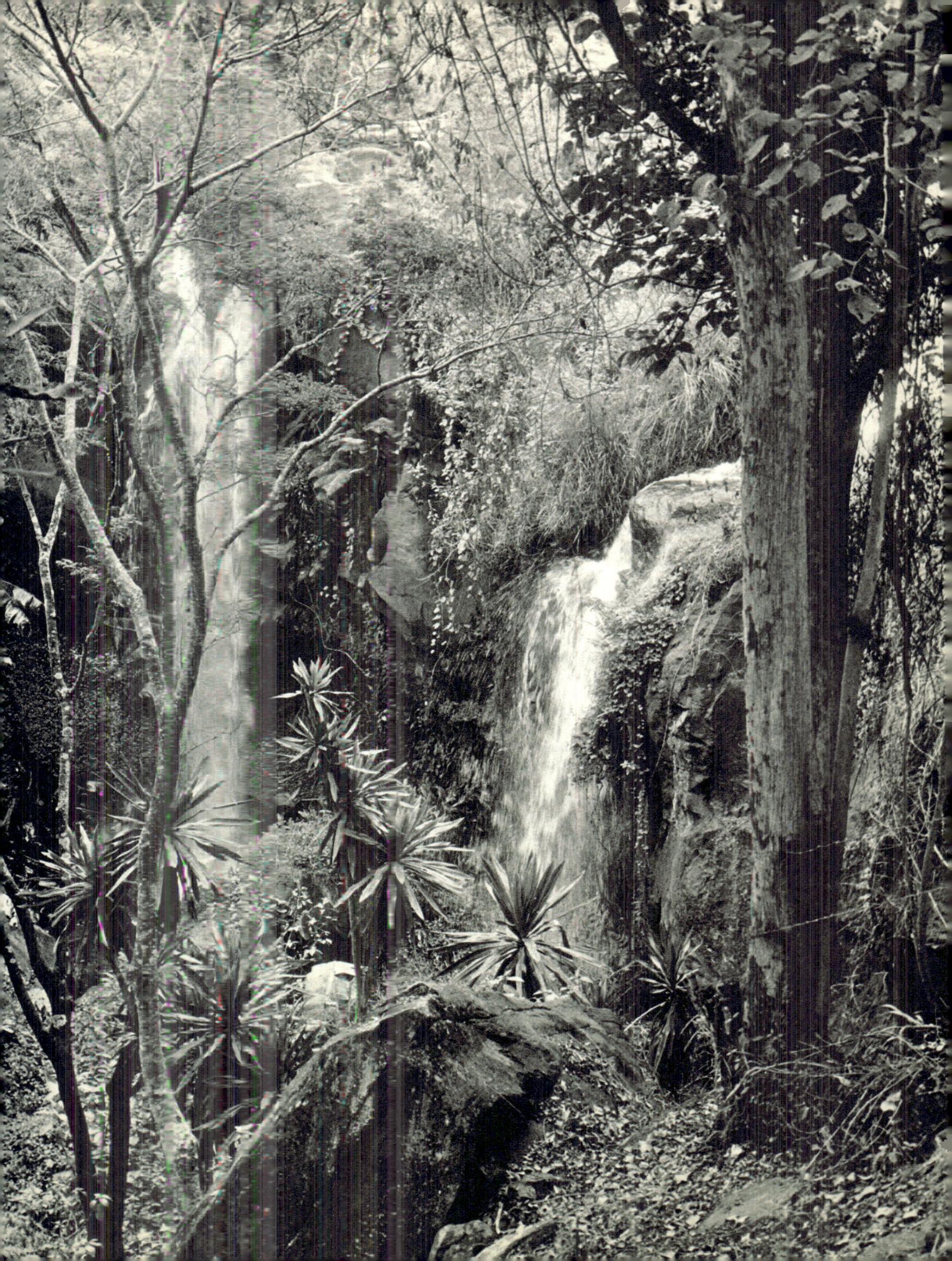

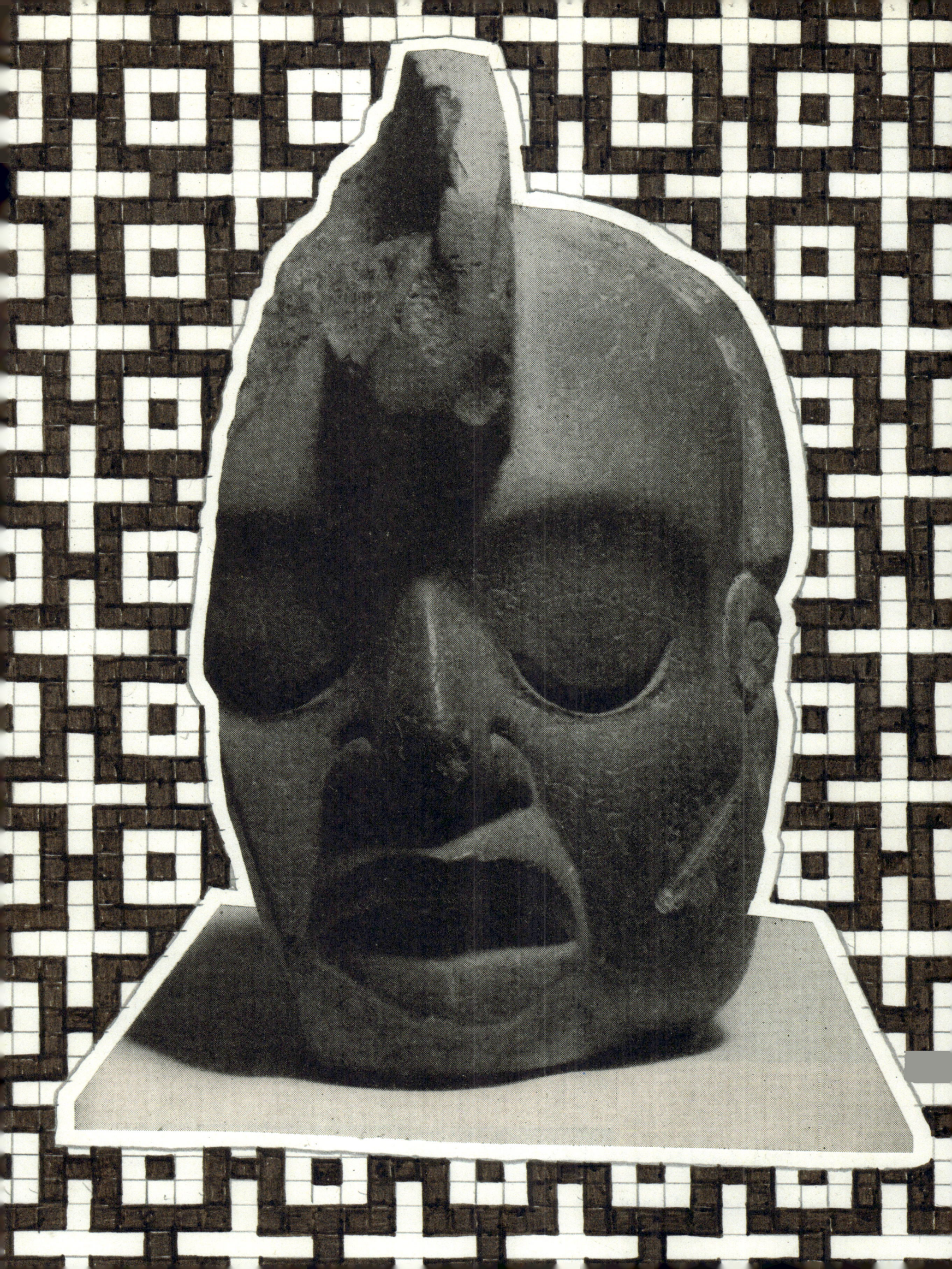

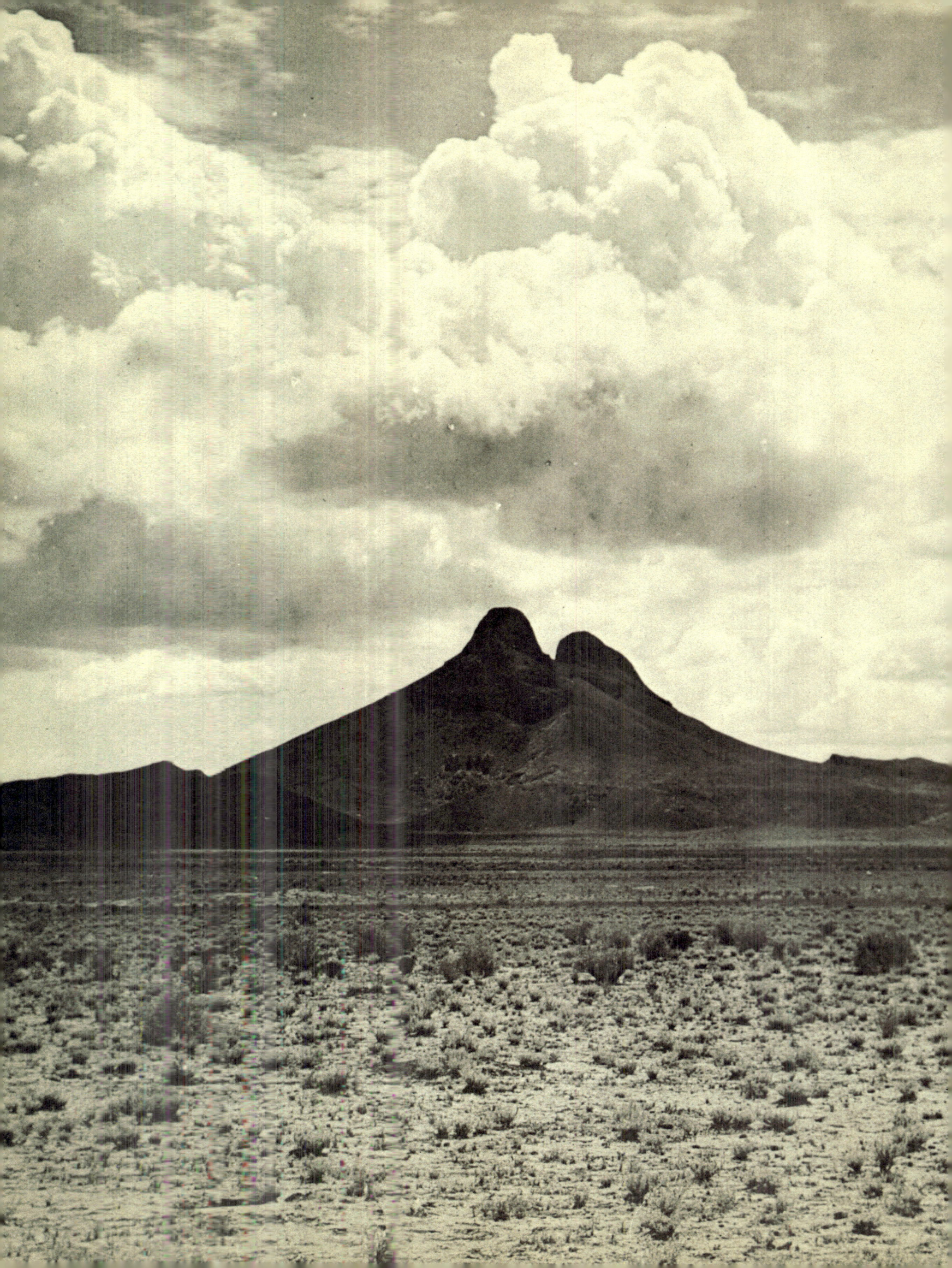

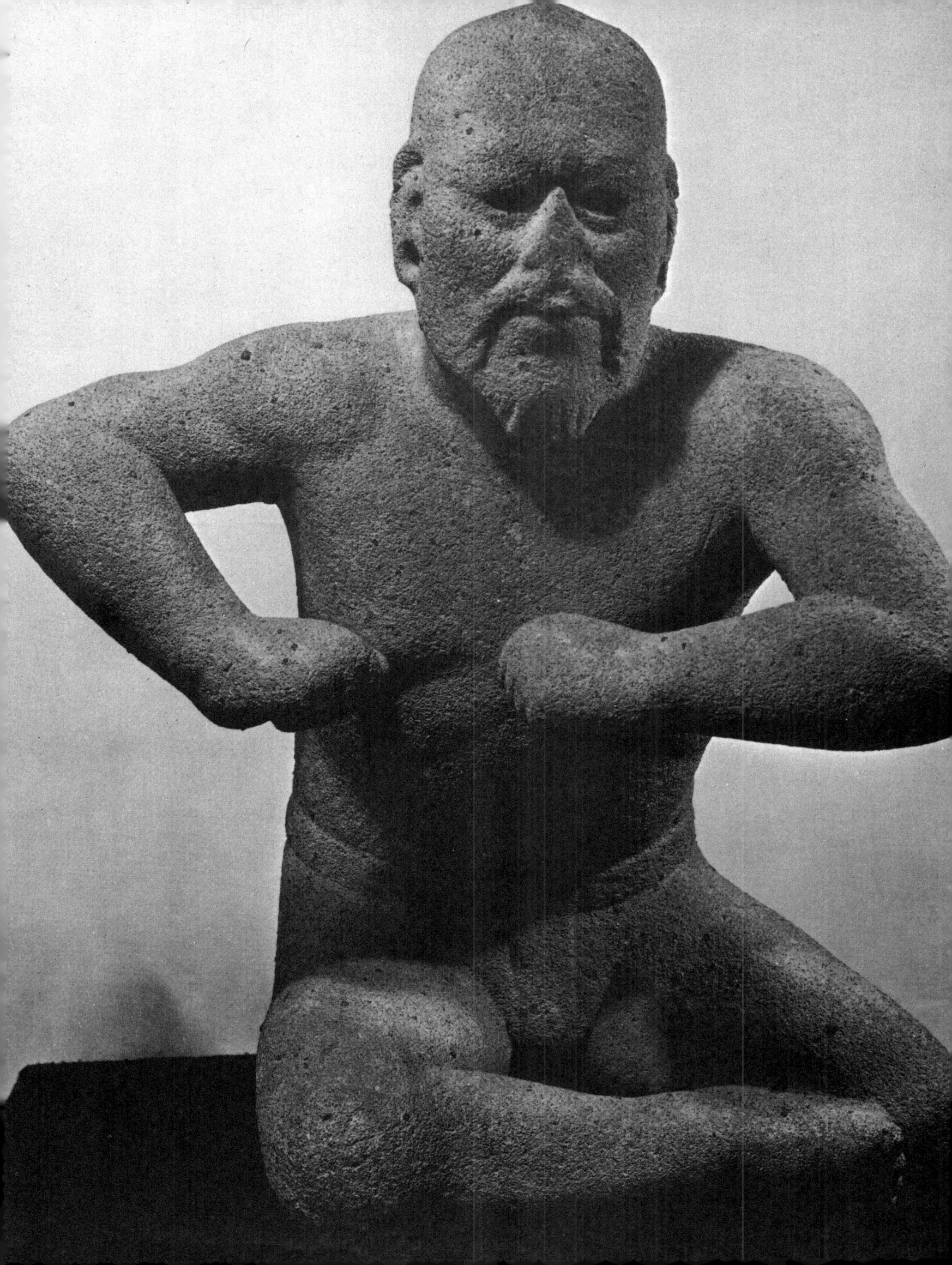

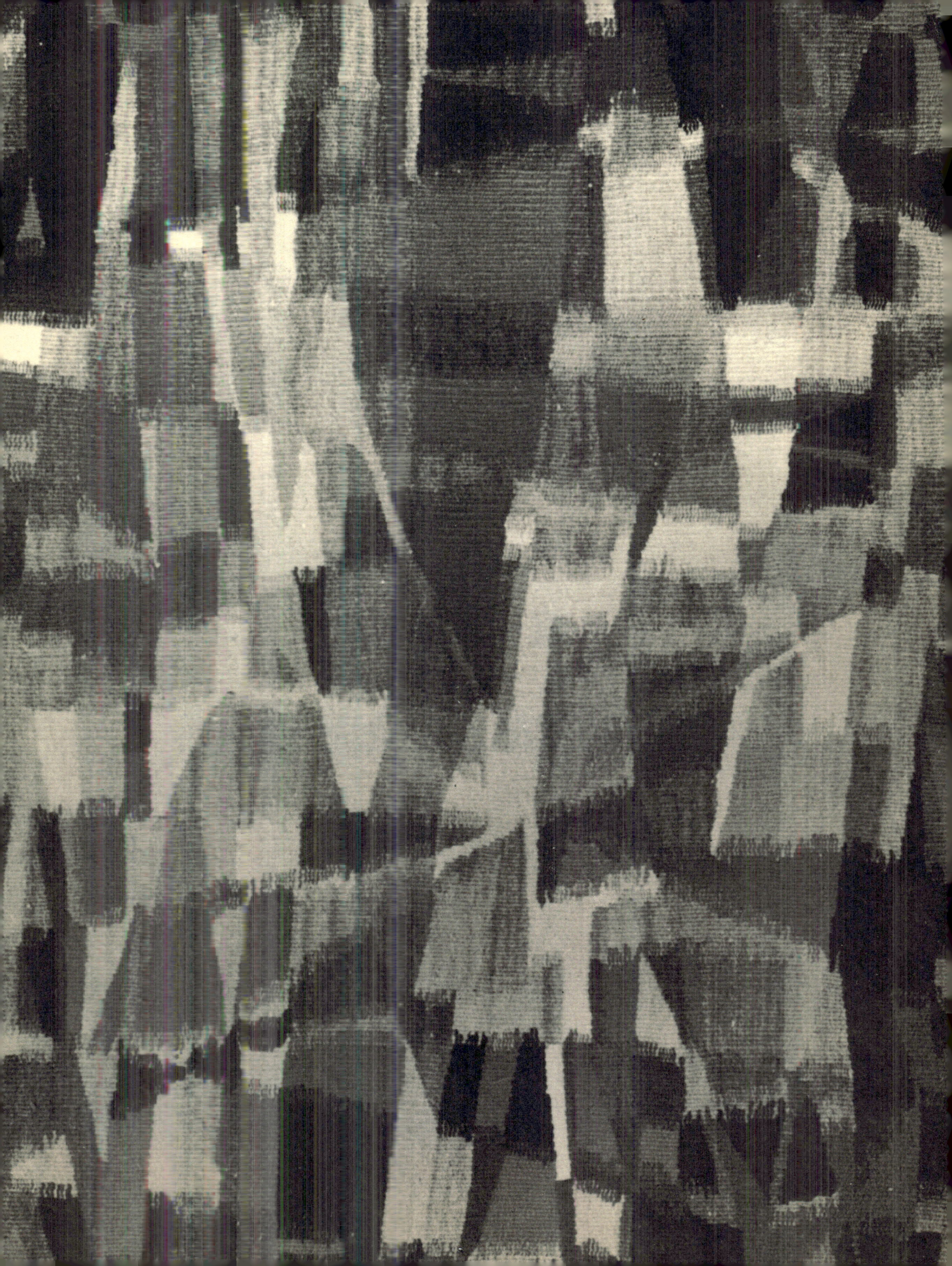

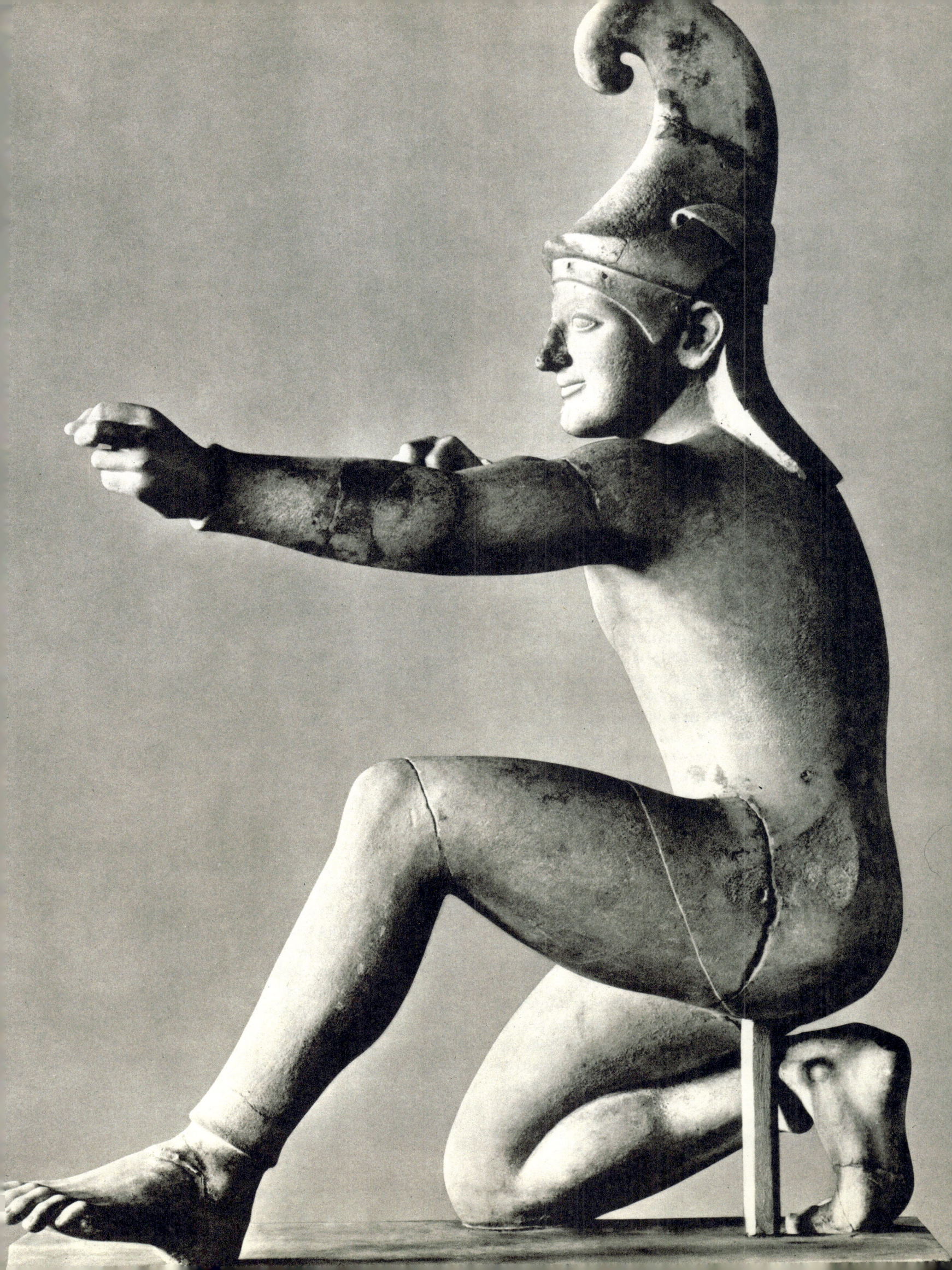

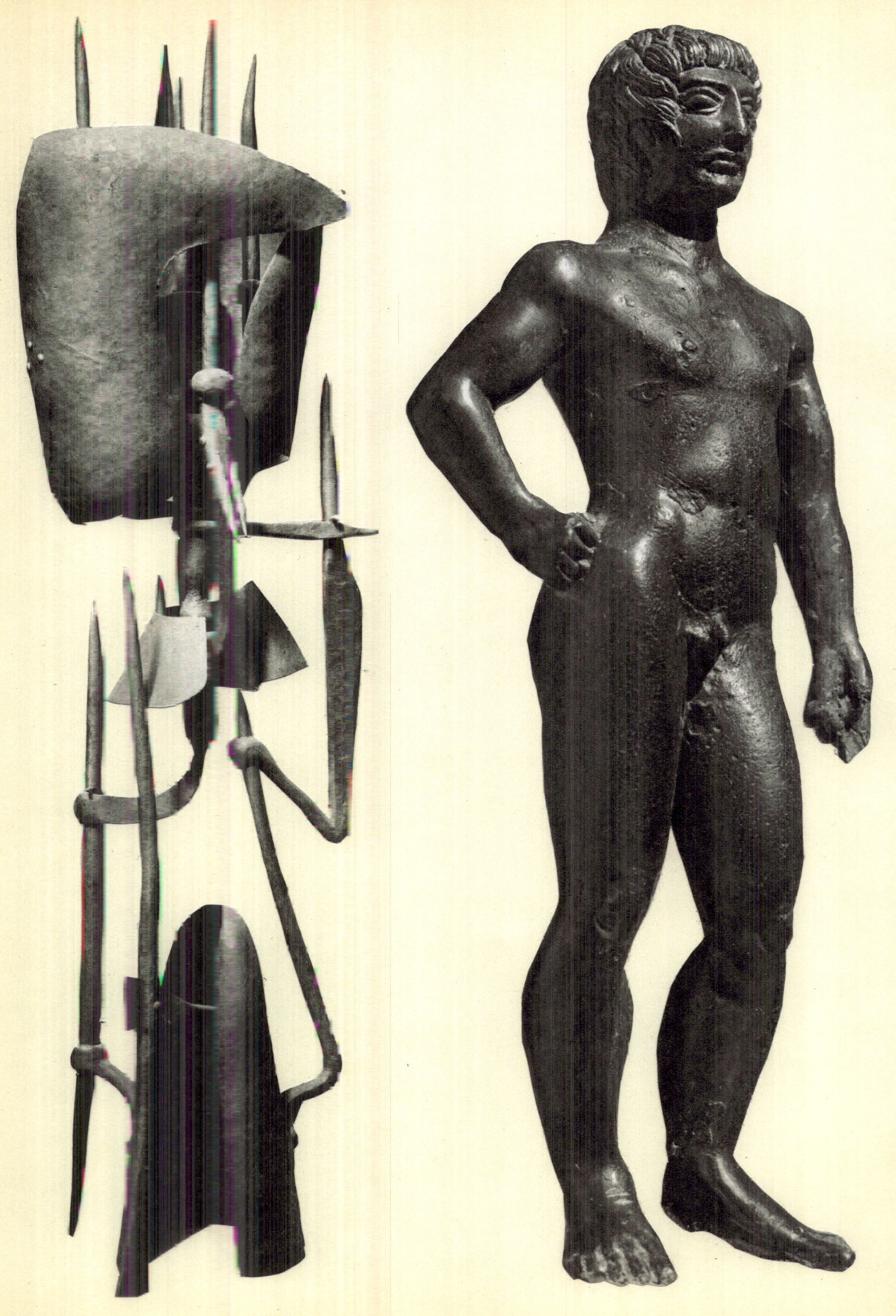

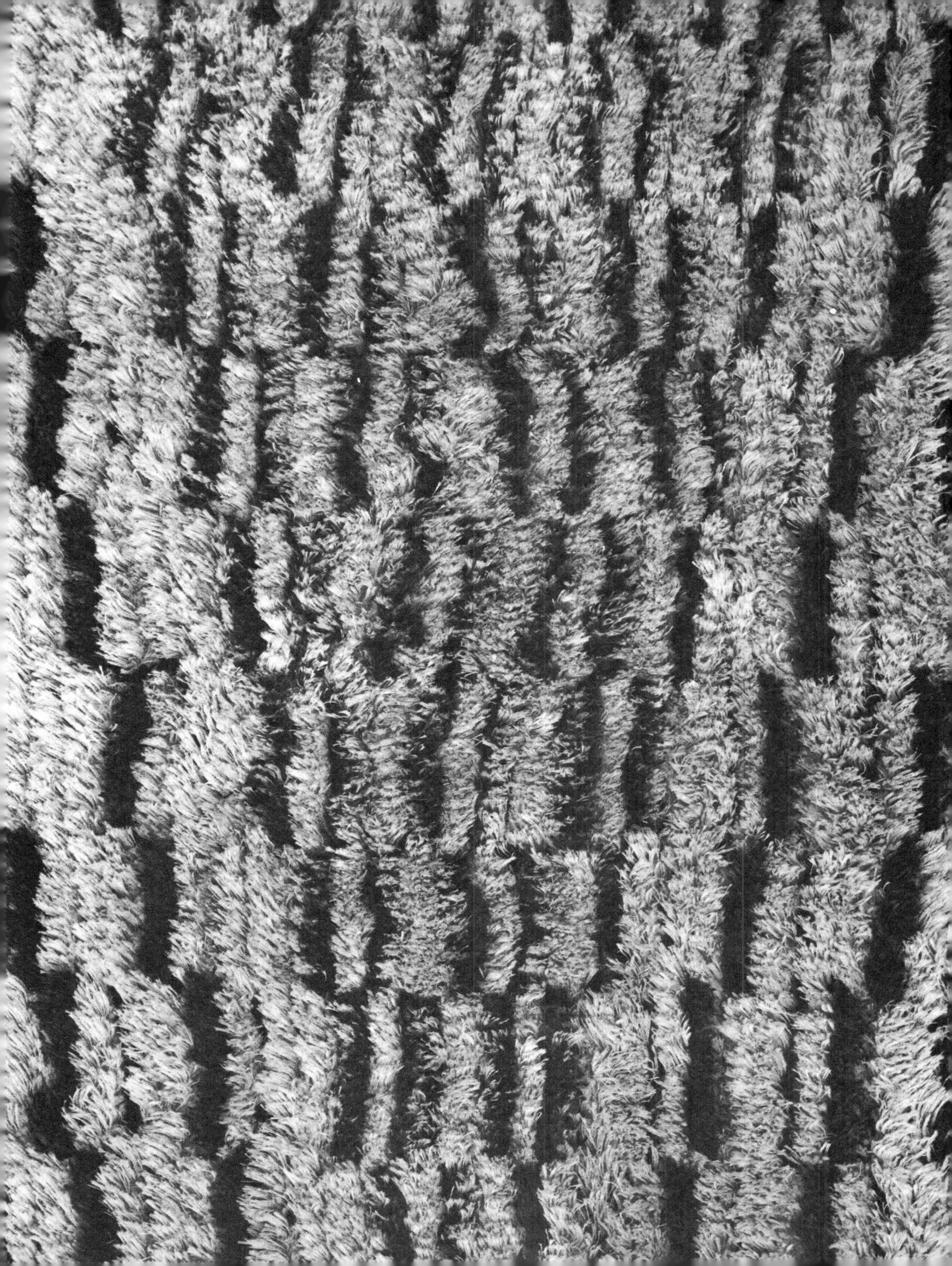

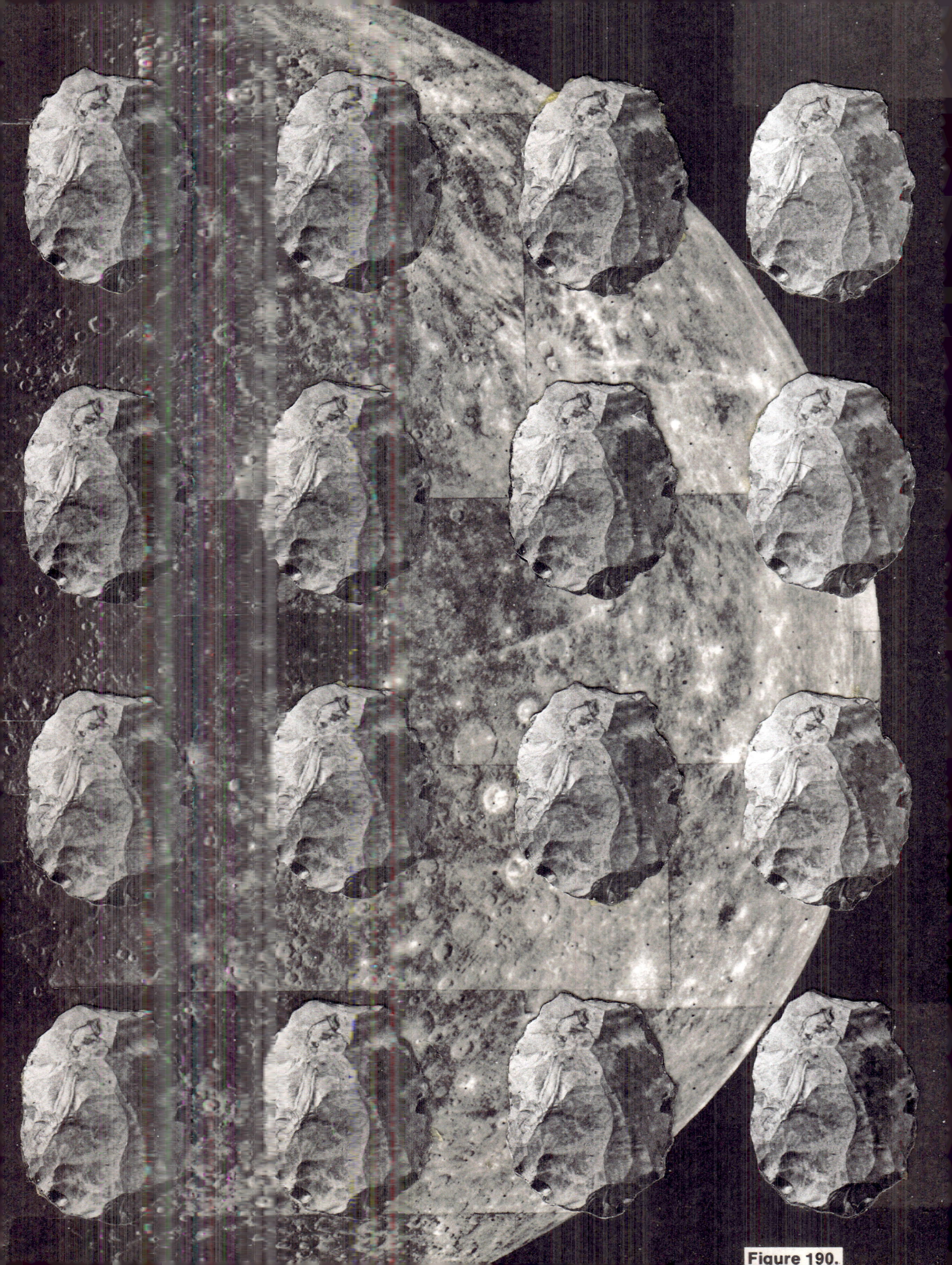

Figure 190.

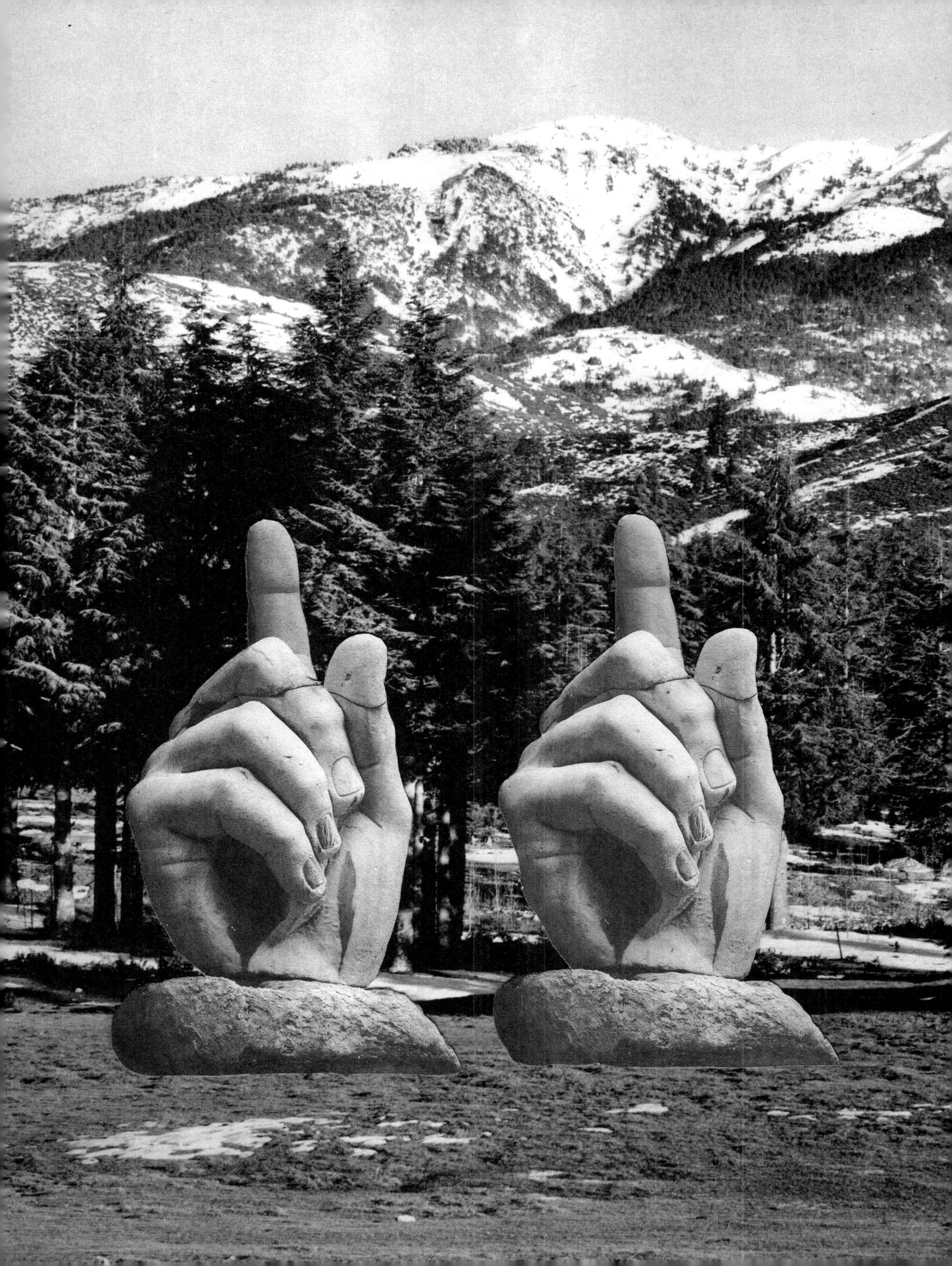

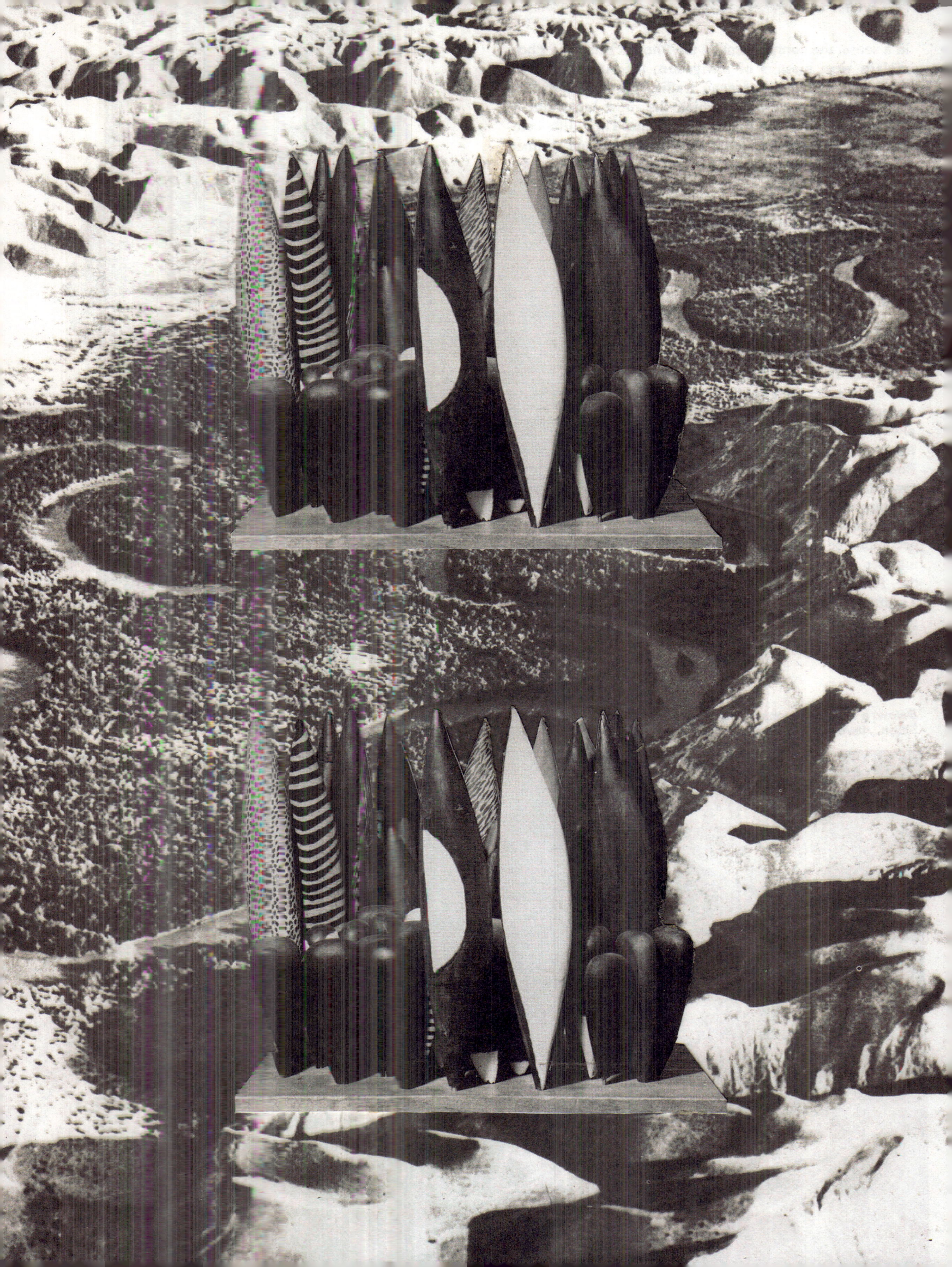

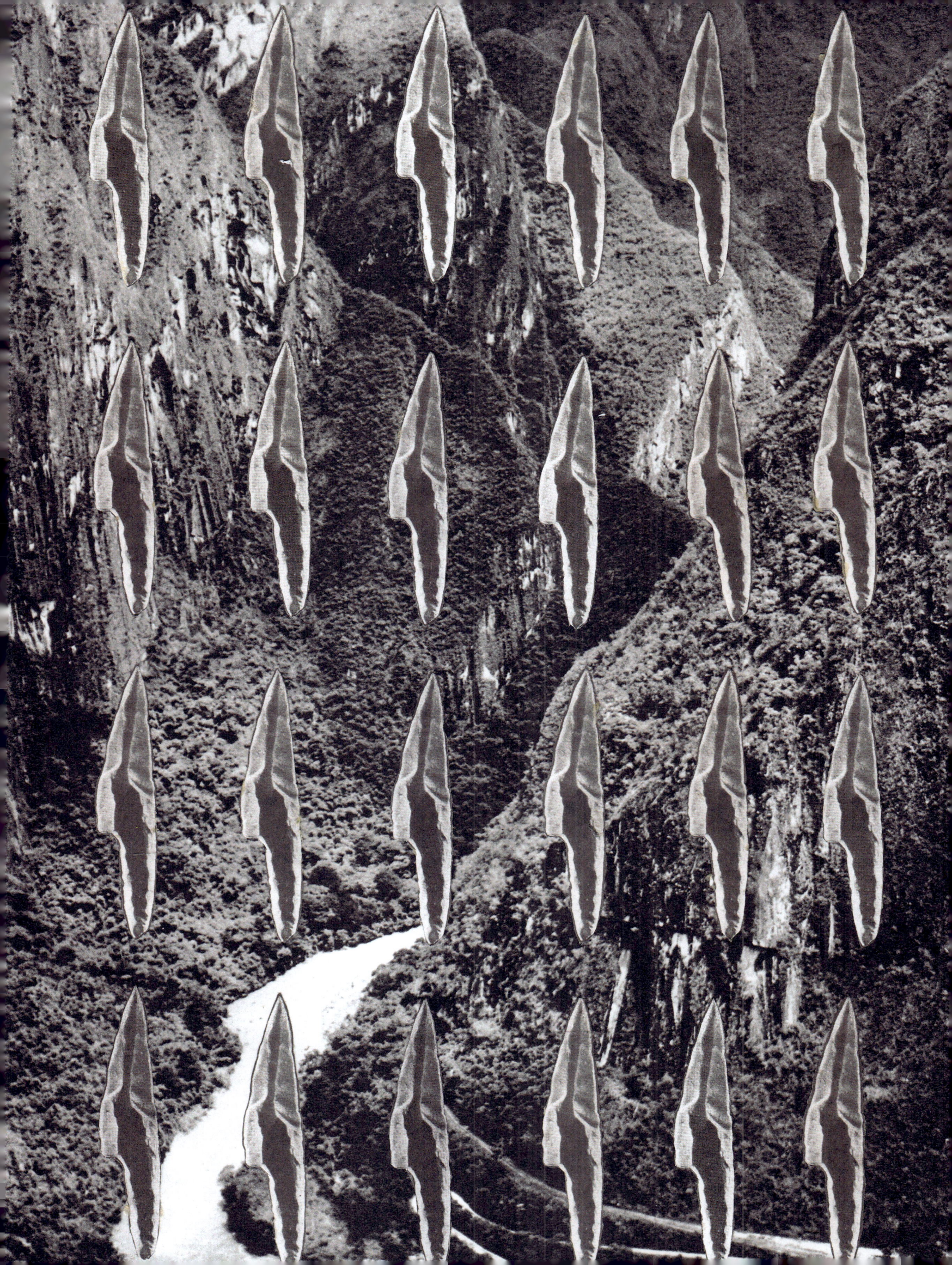

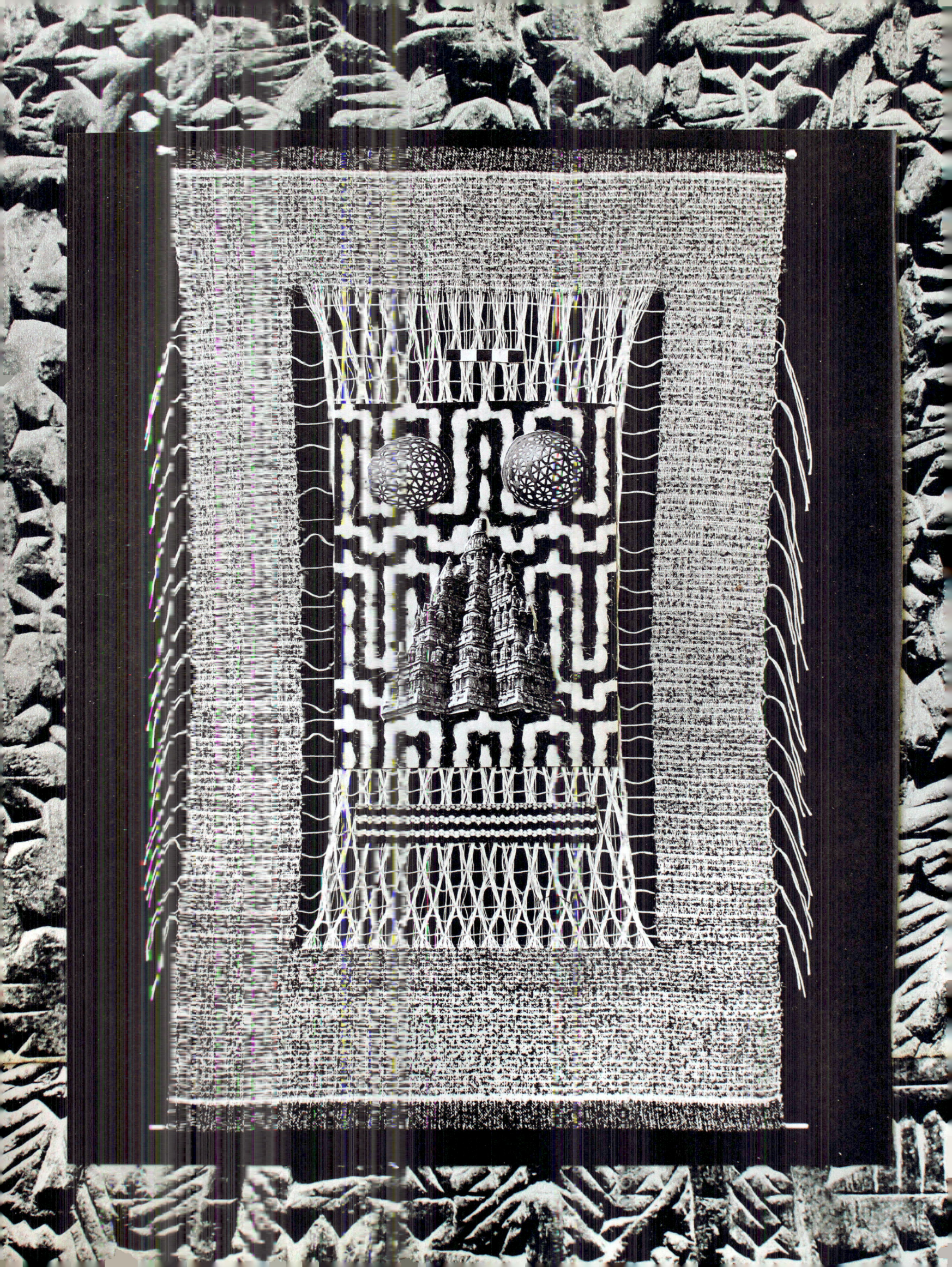

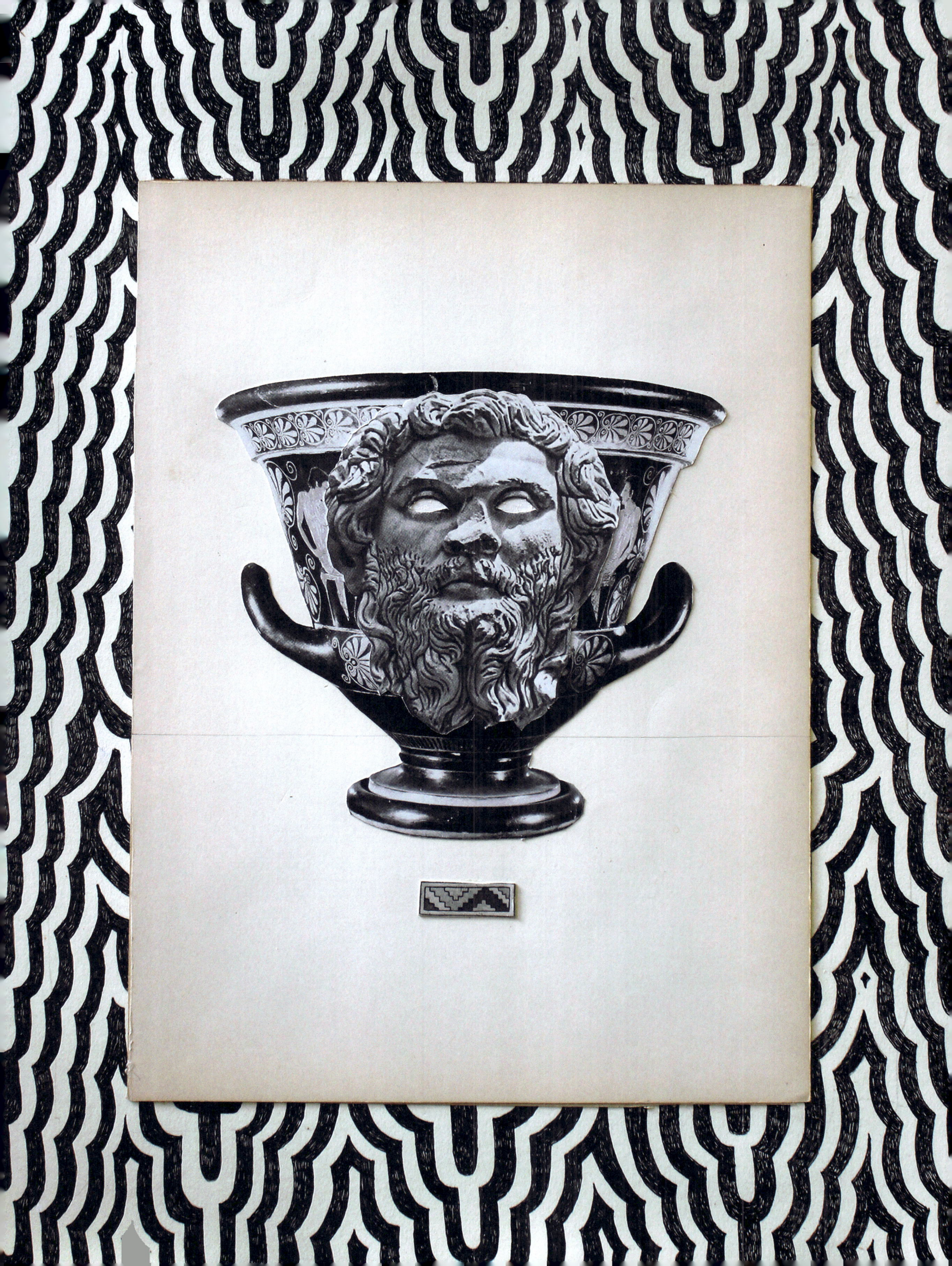

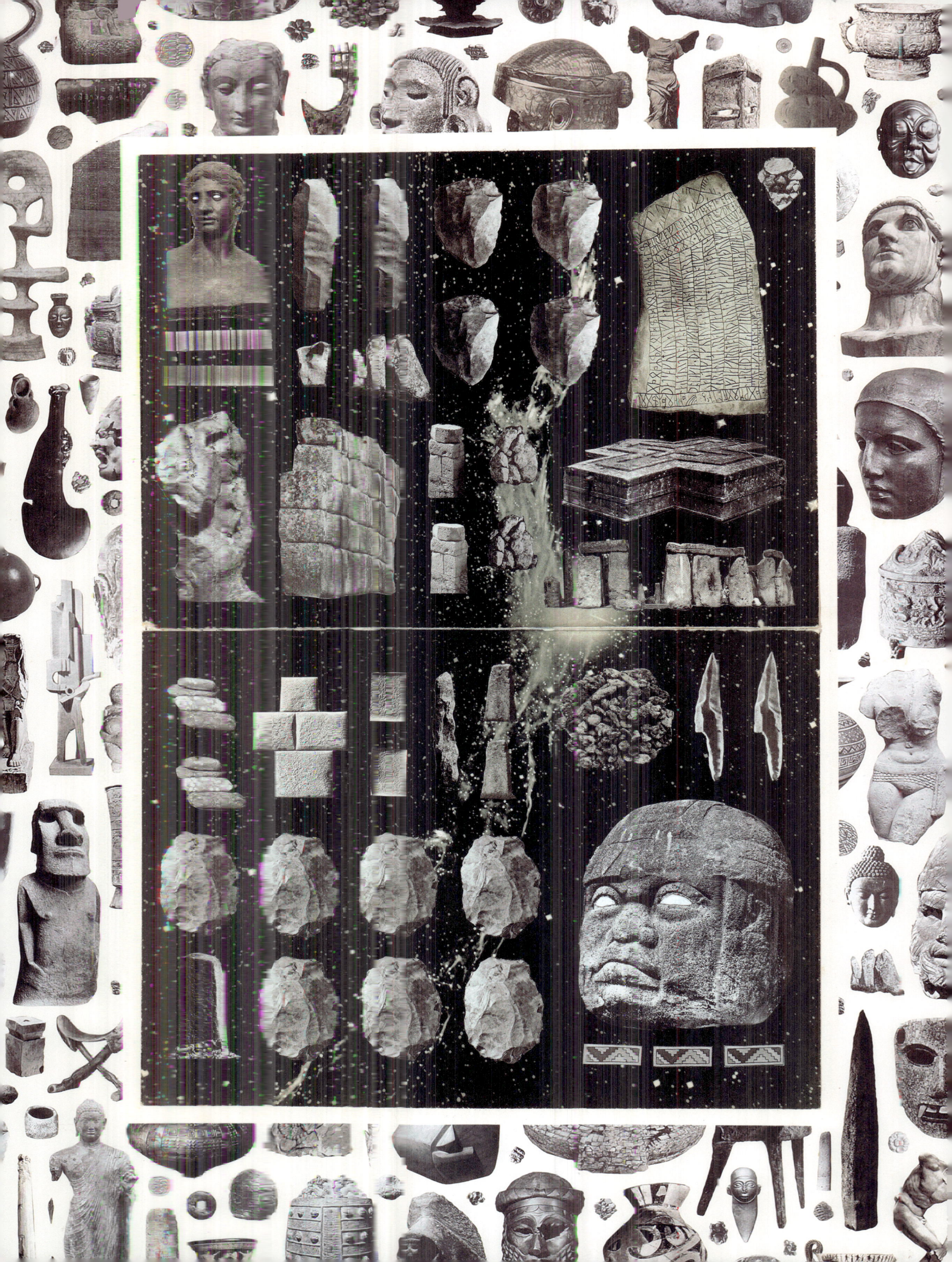

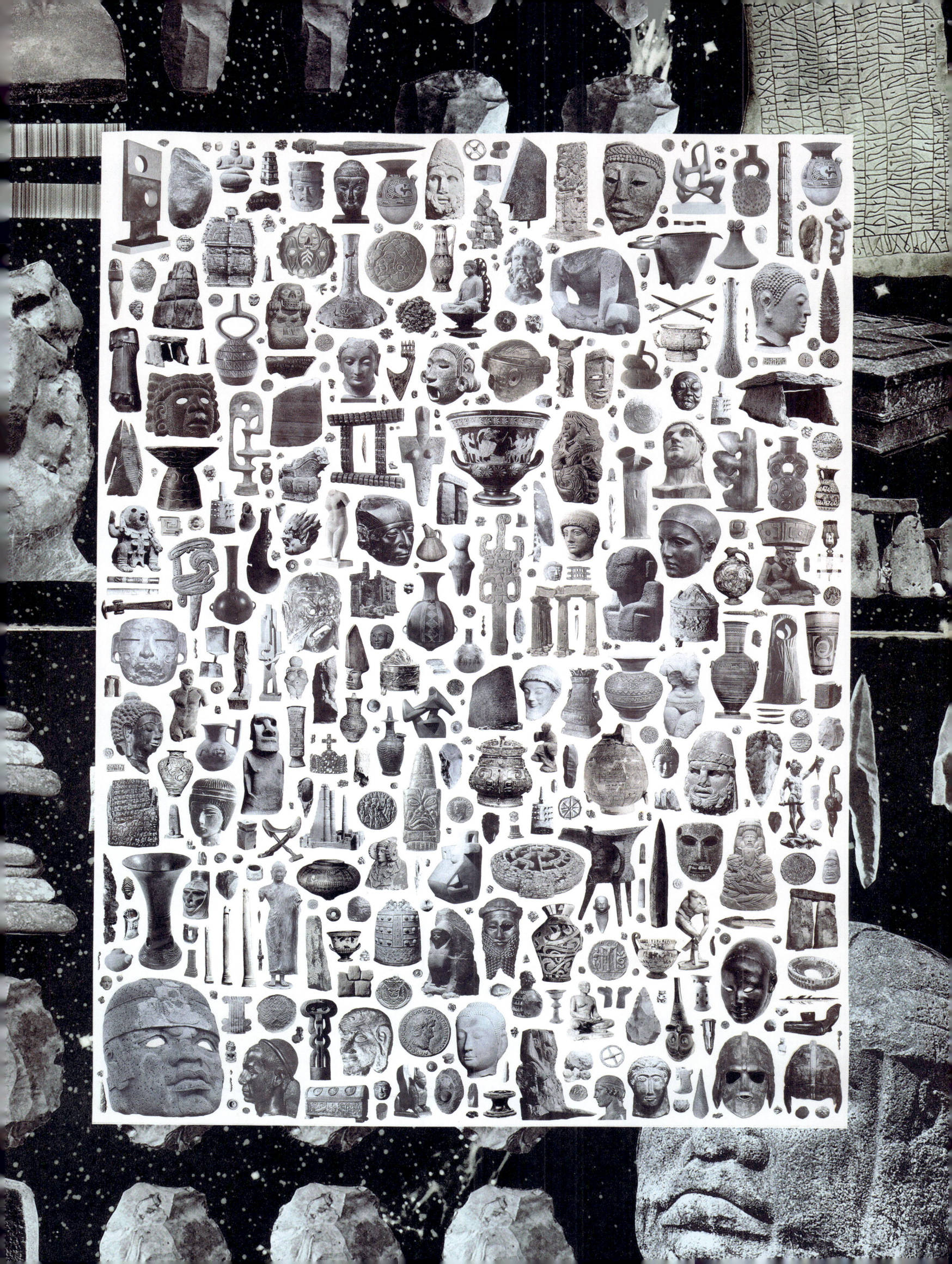

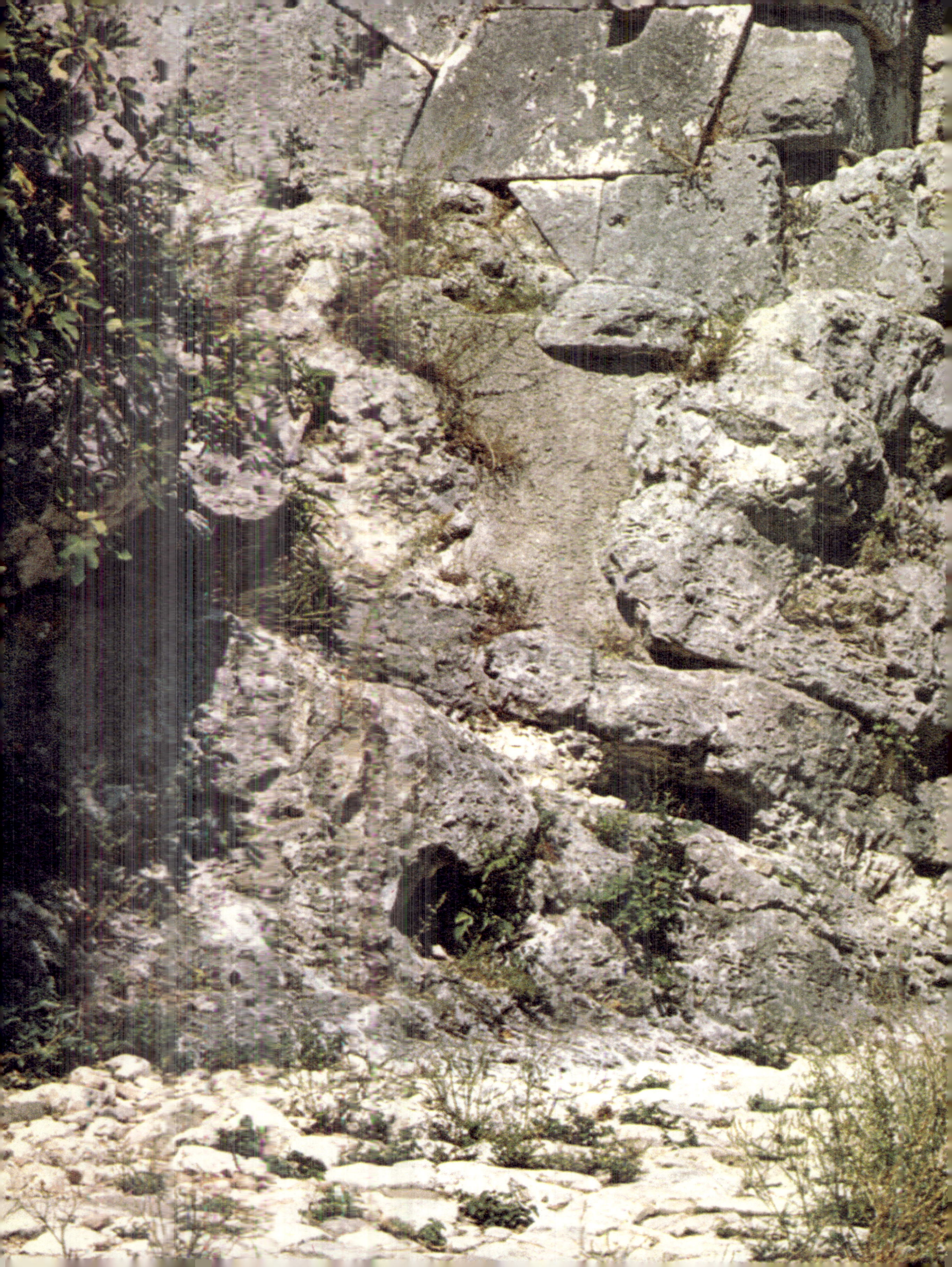

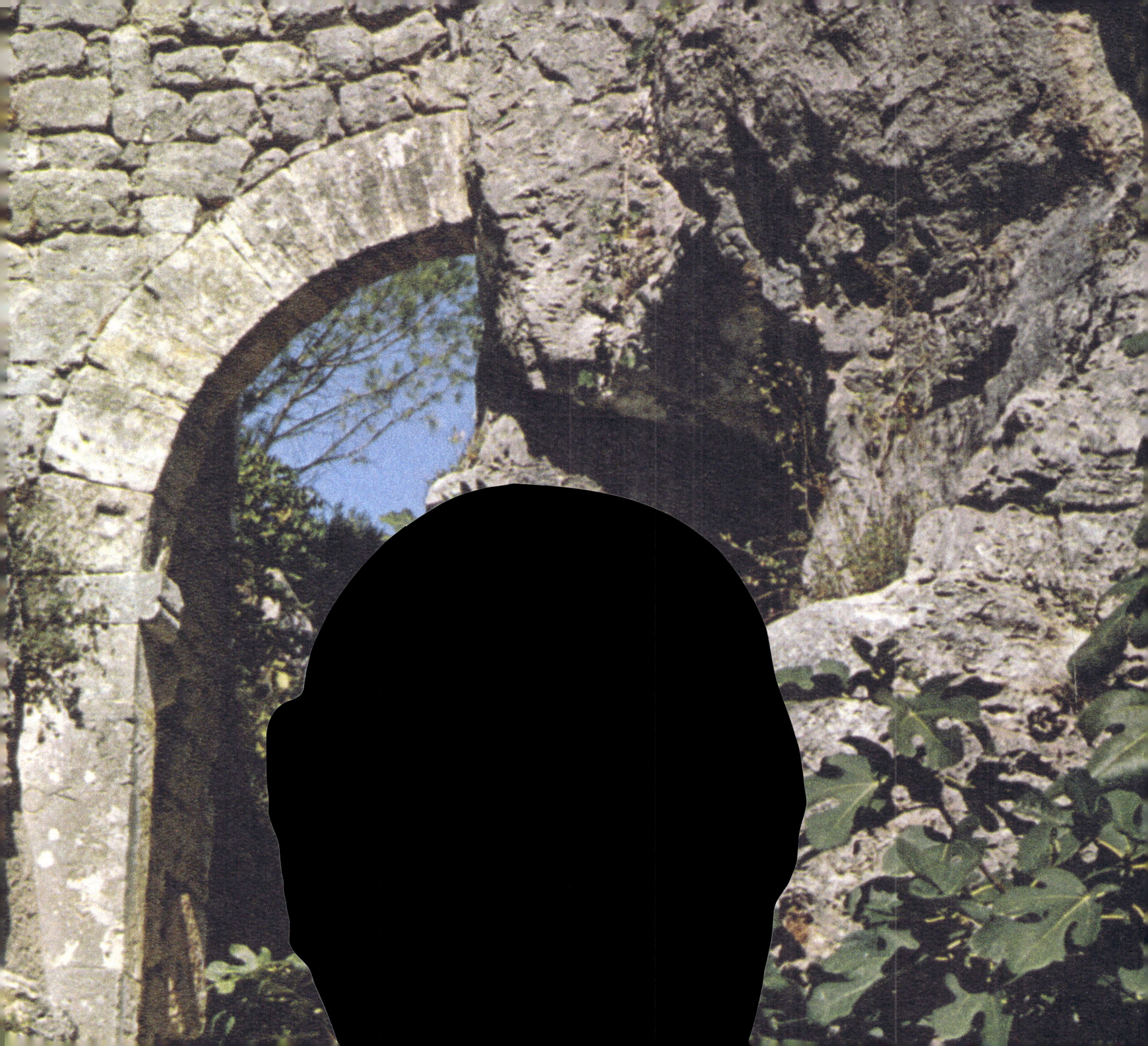

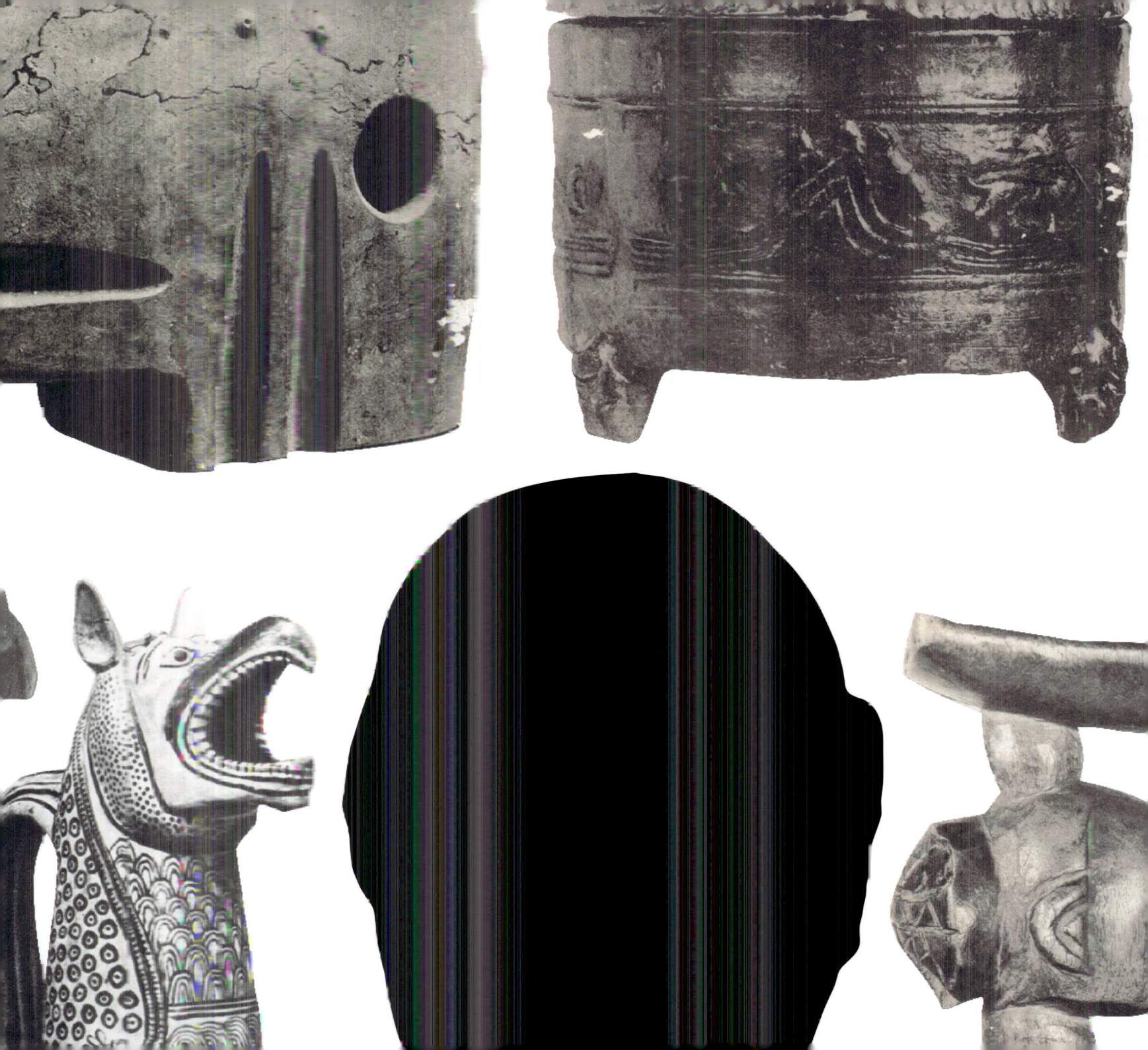

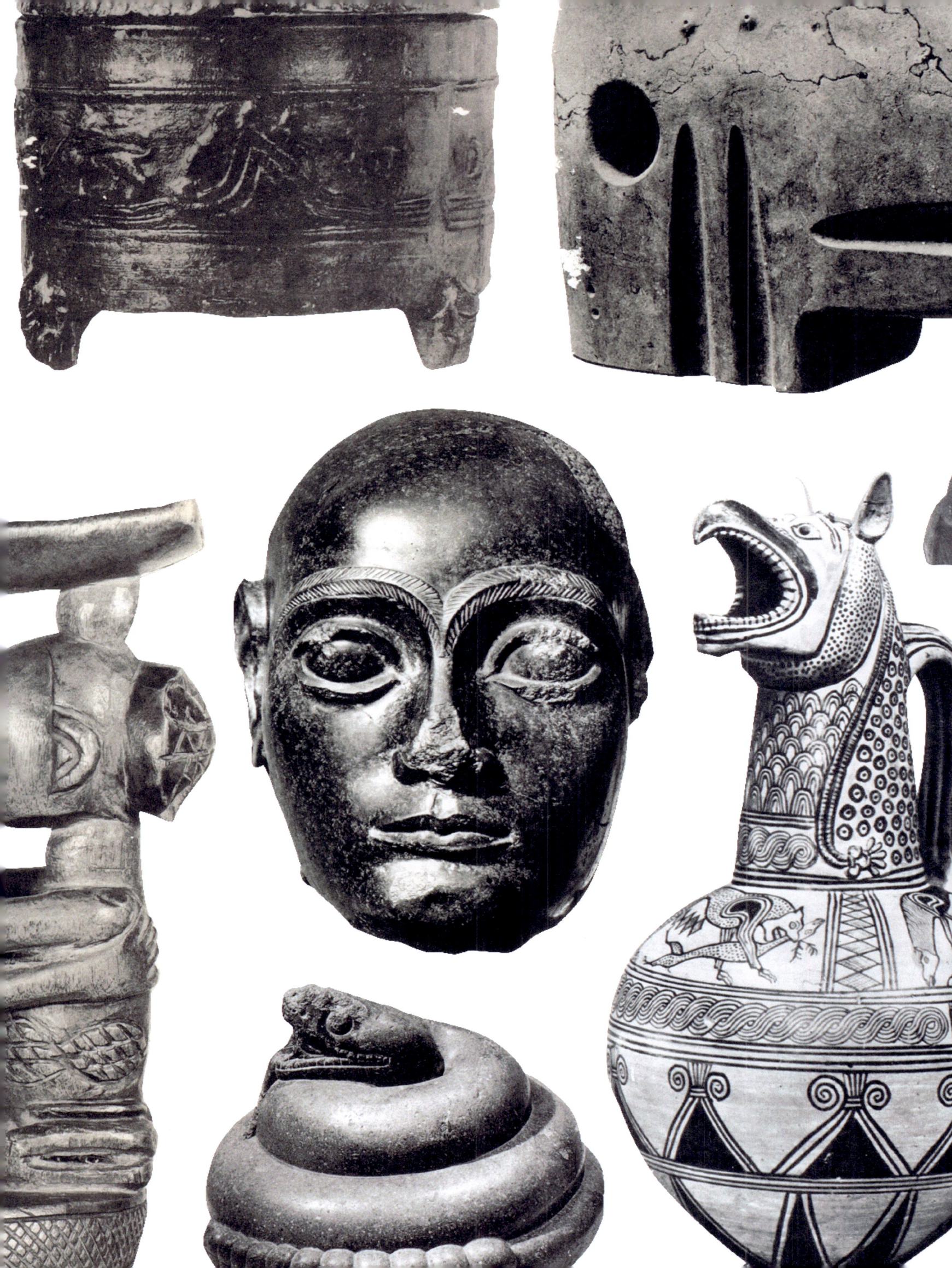

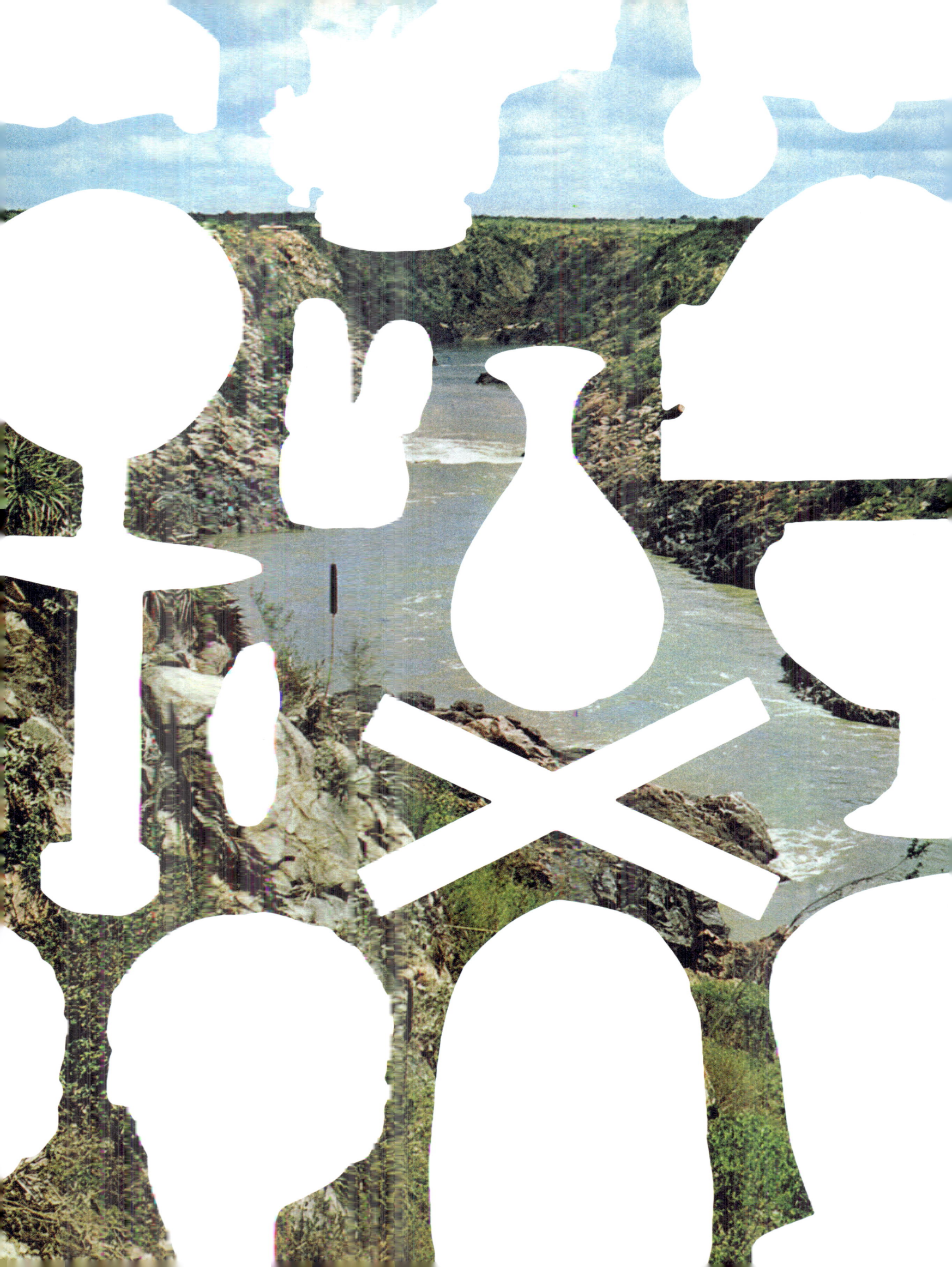

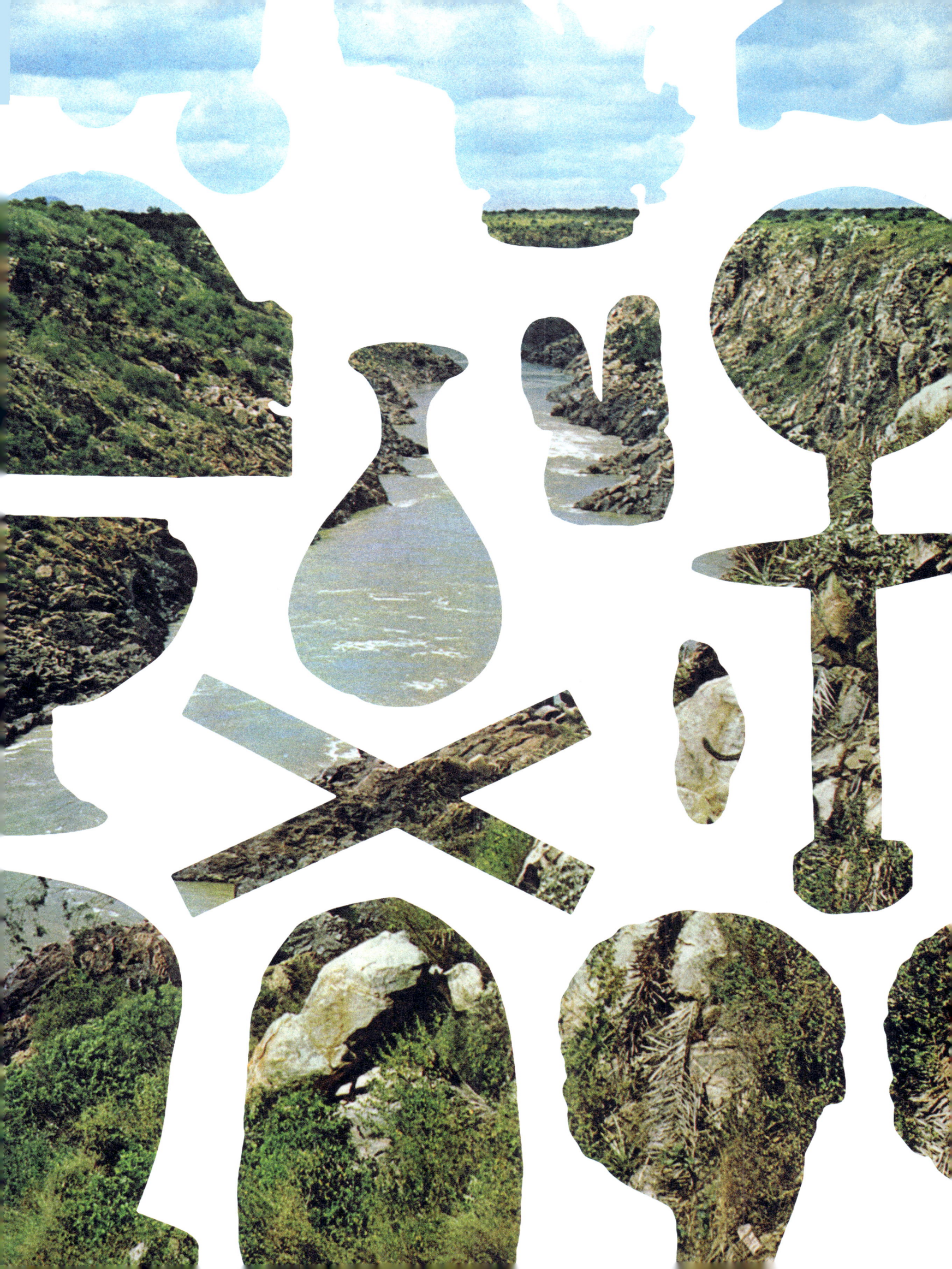

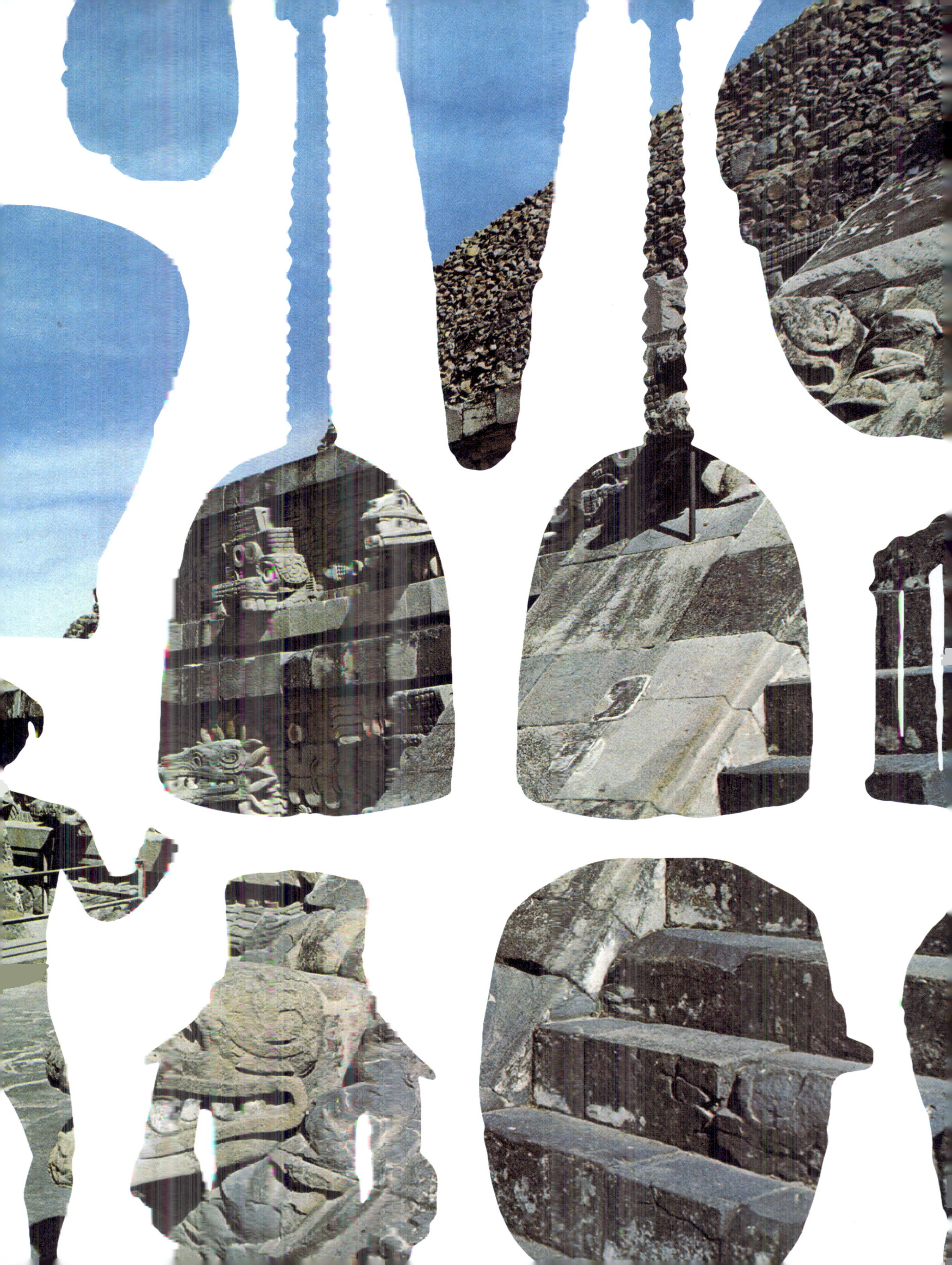

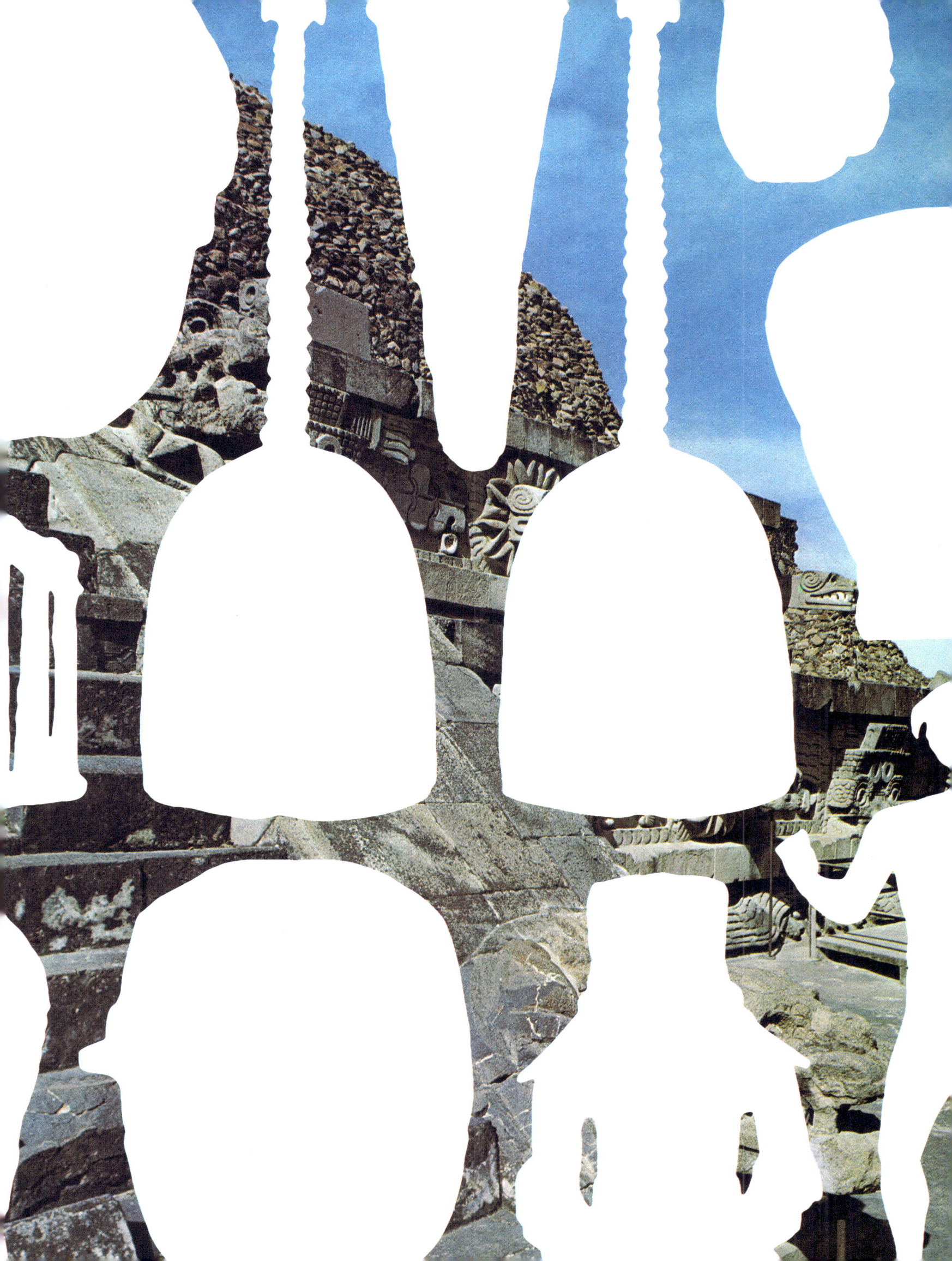

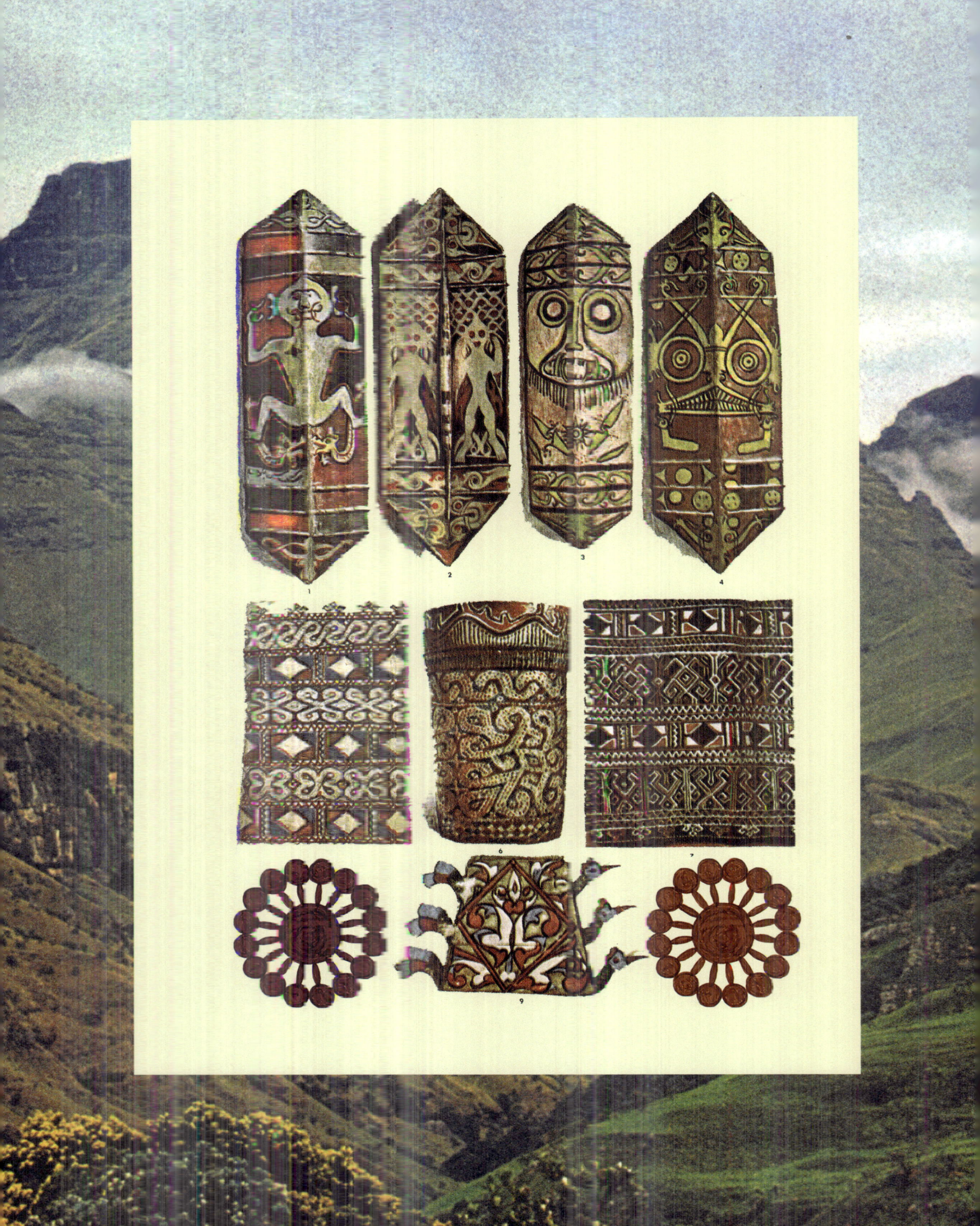

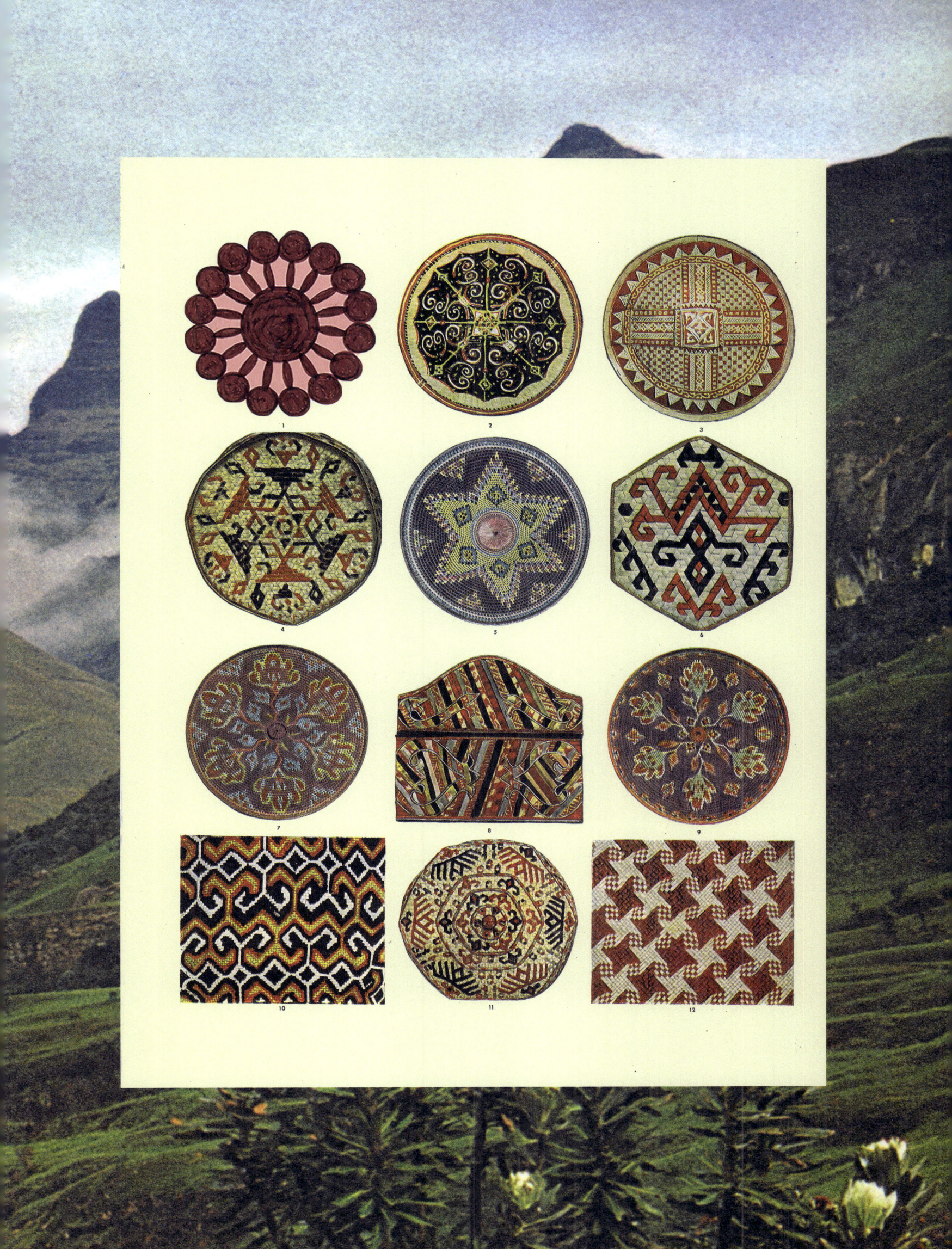

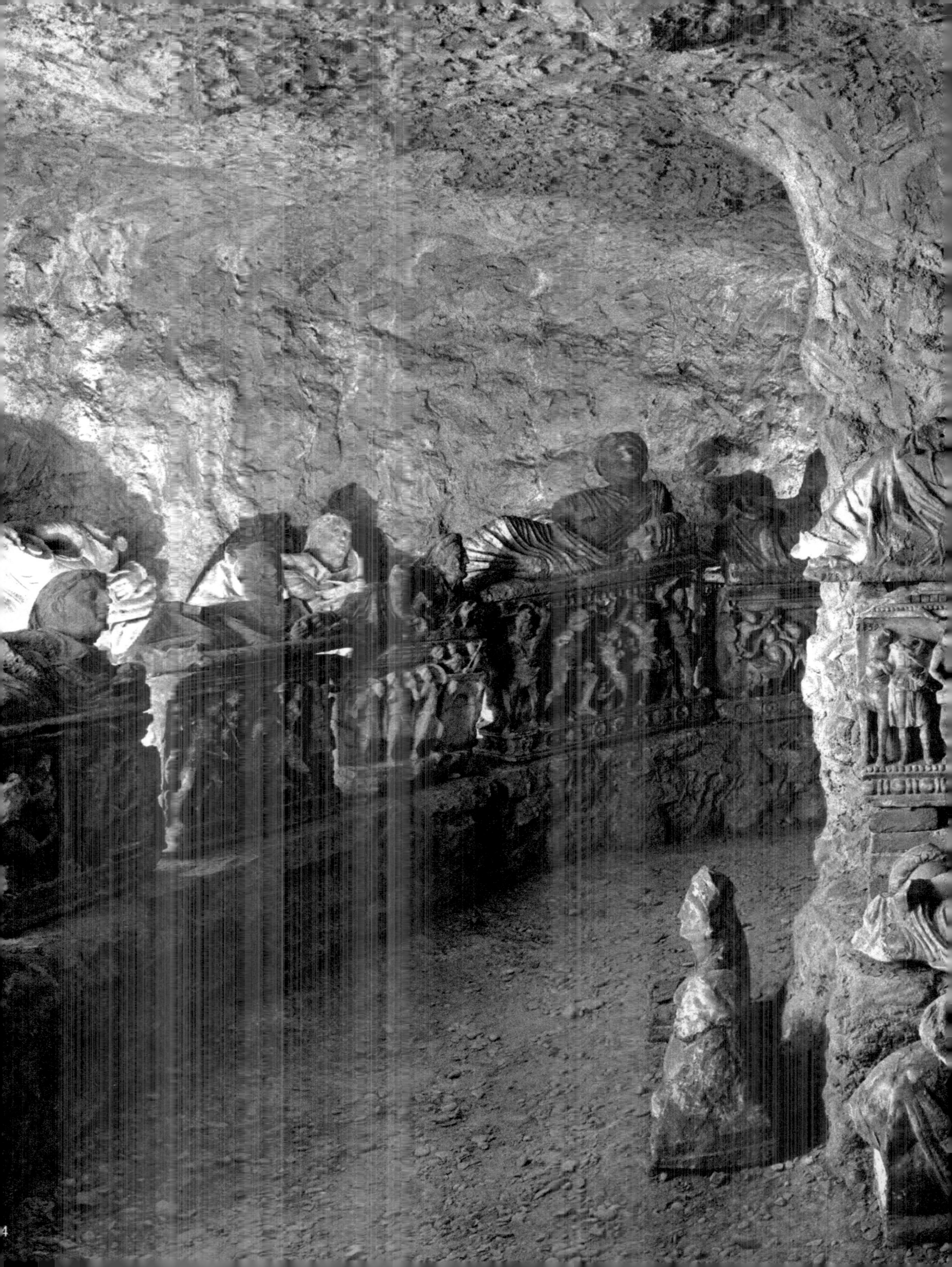

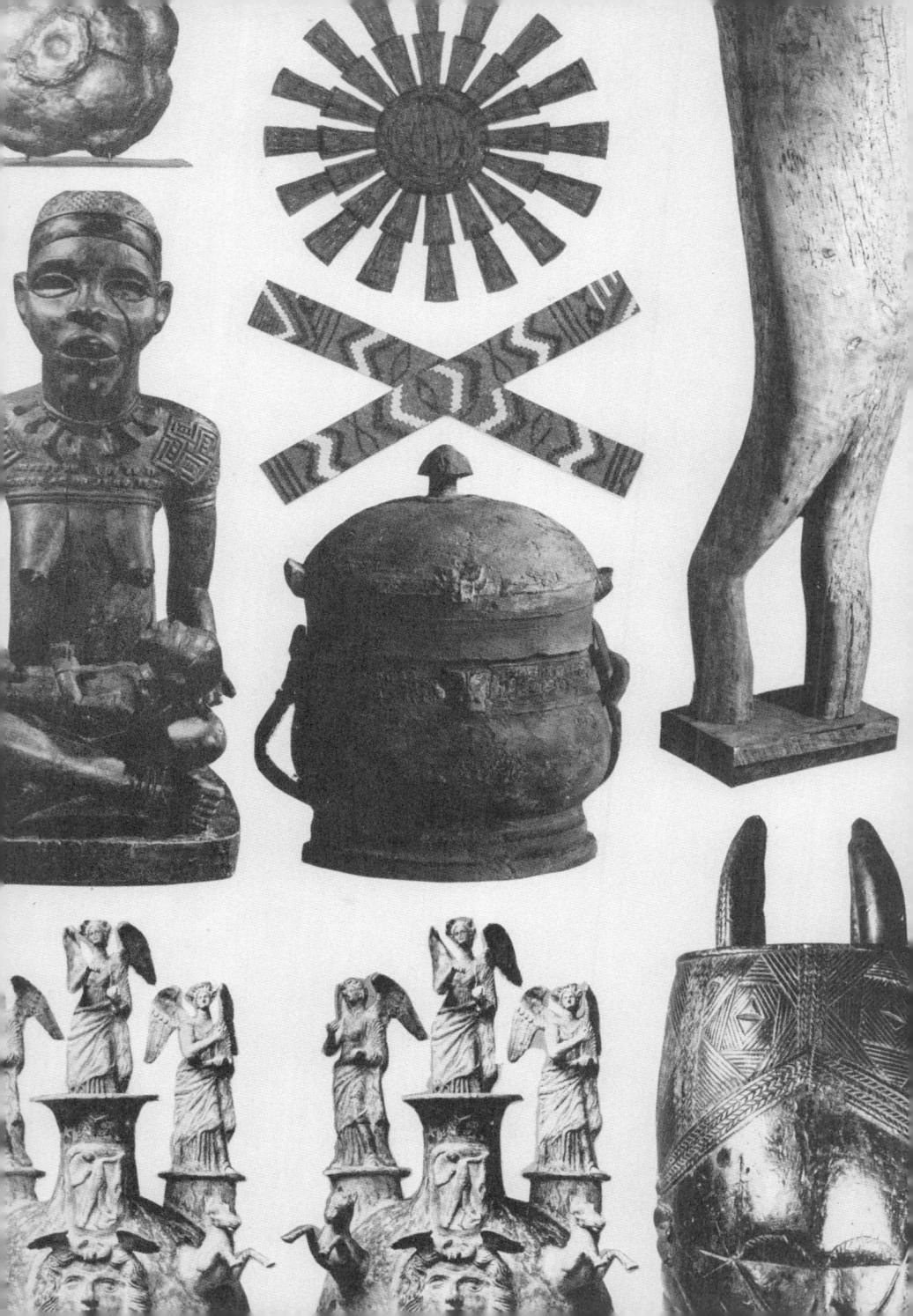

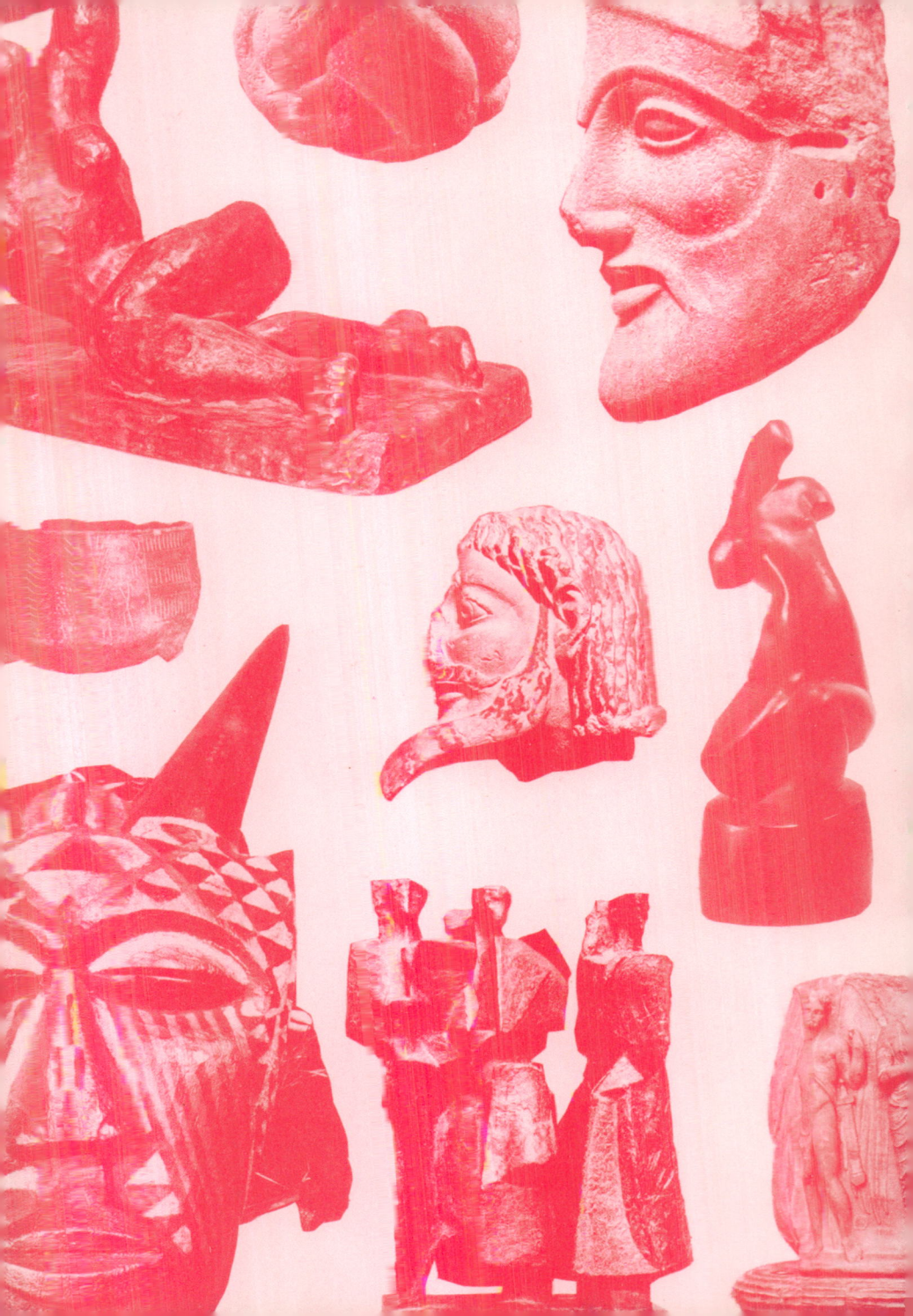

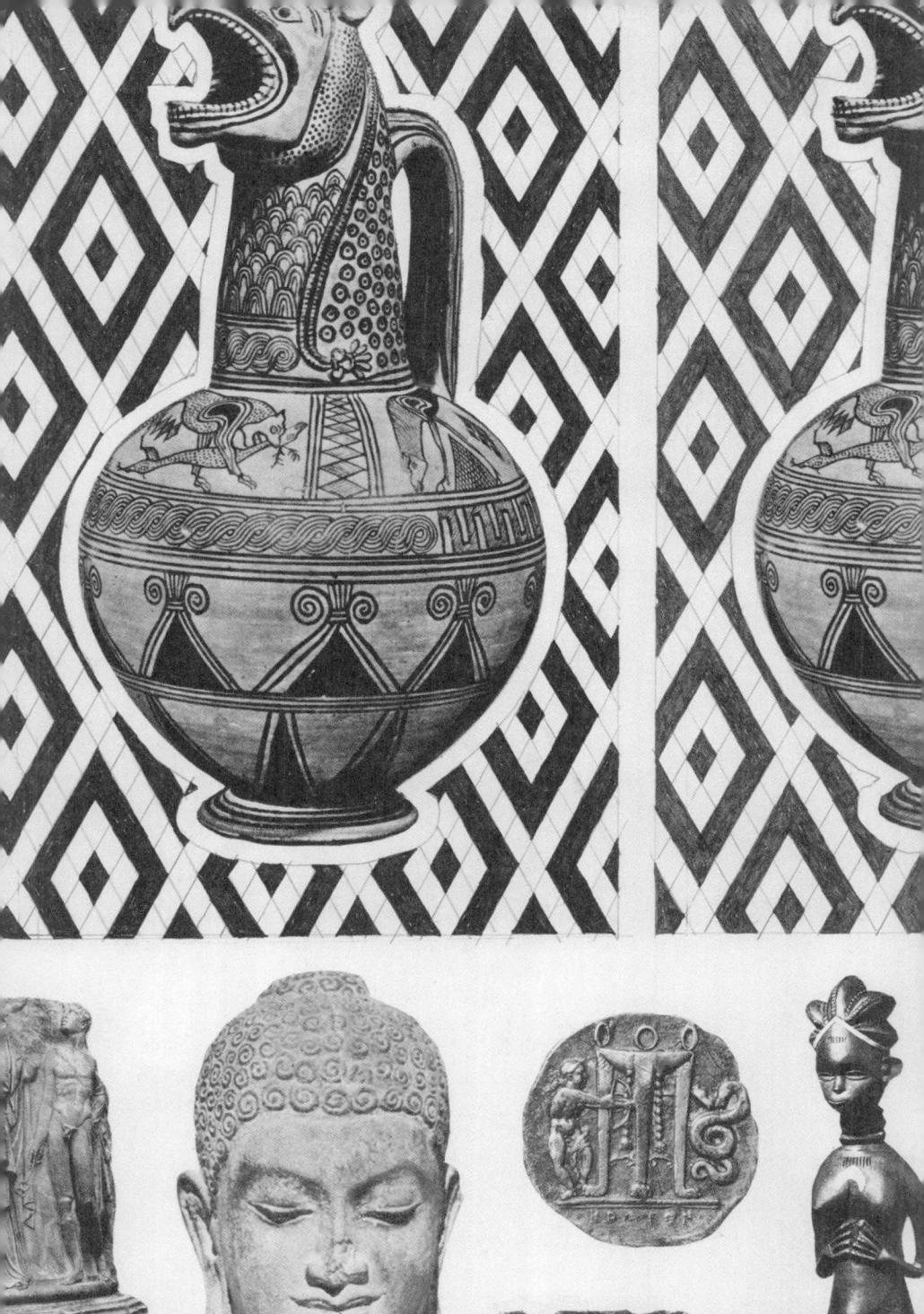

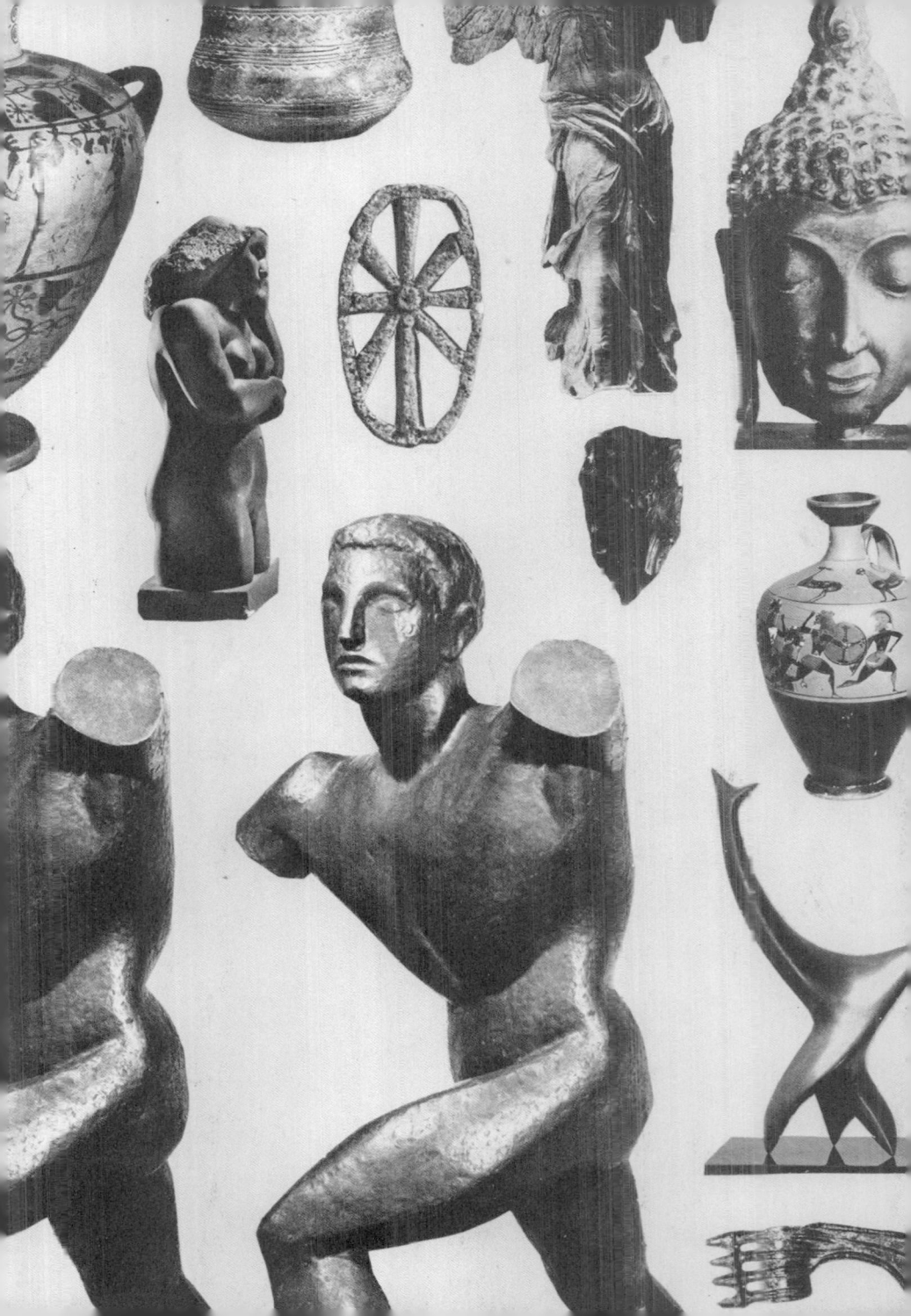

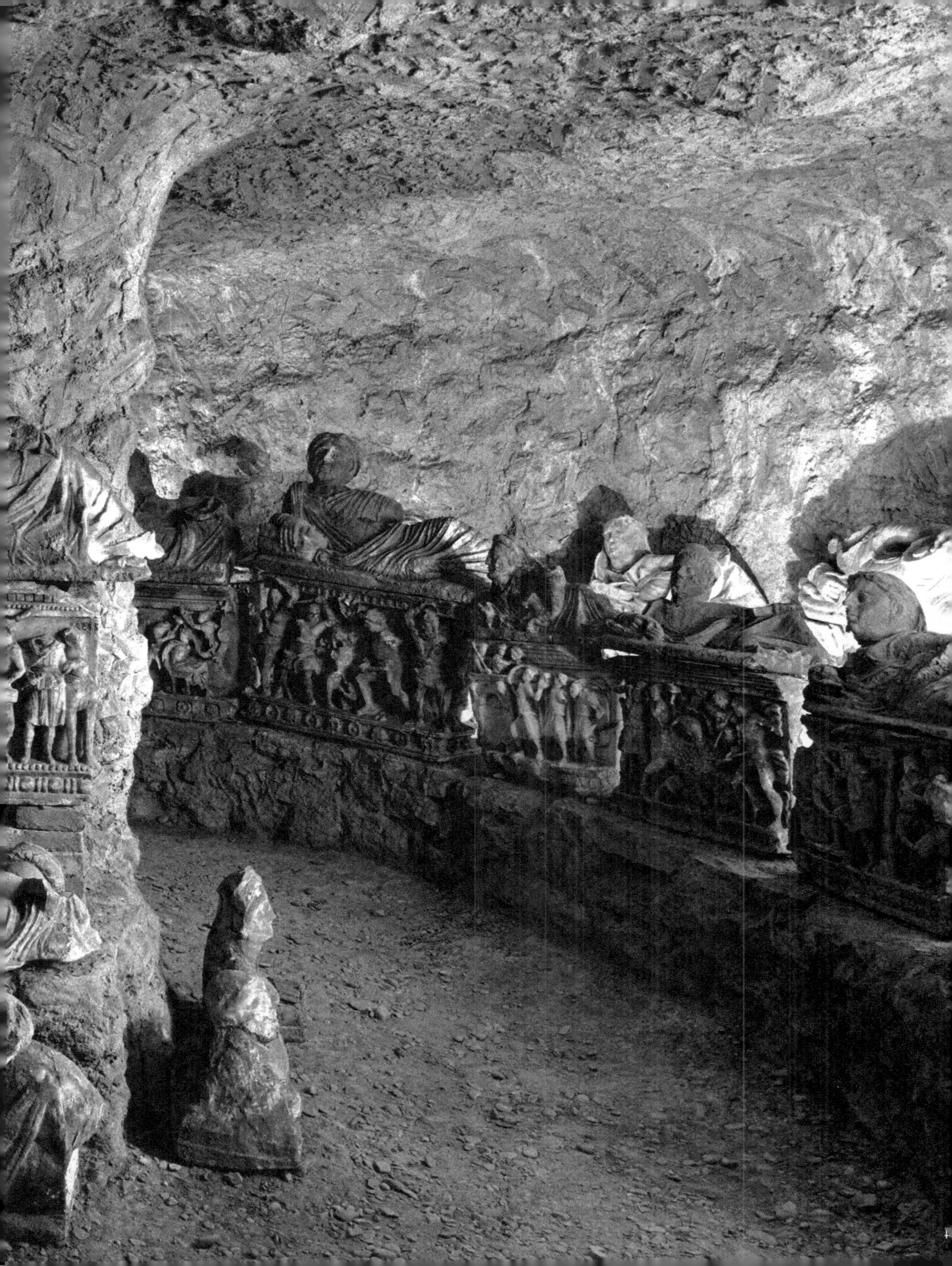

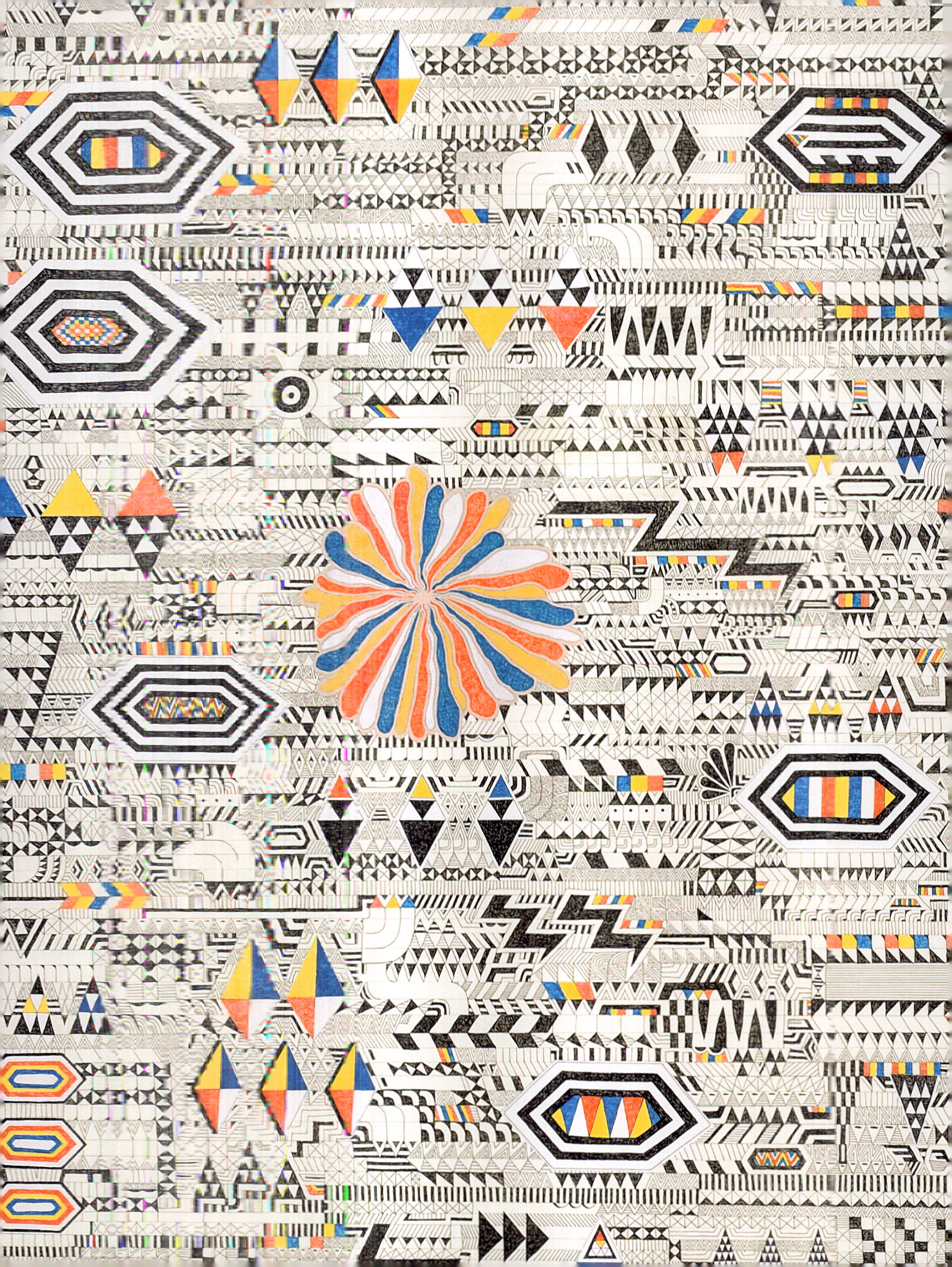

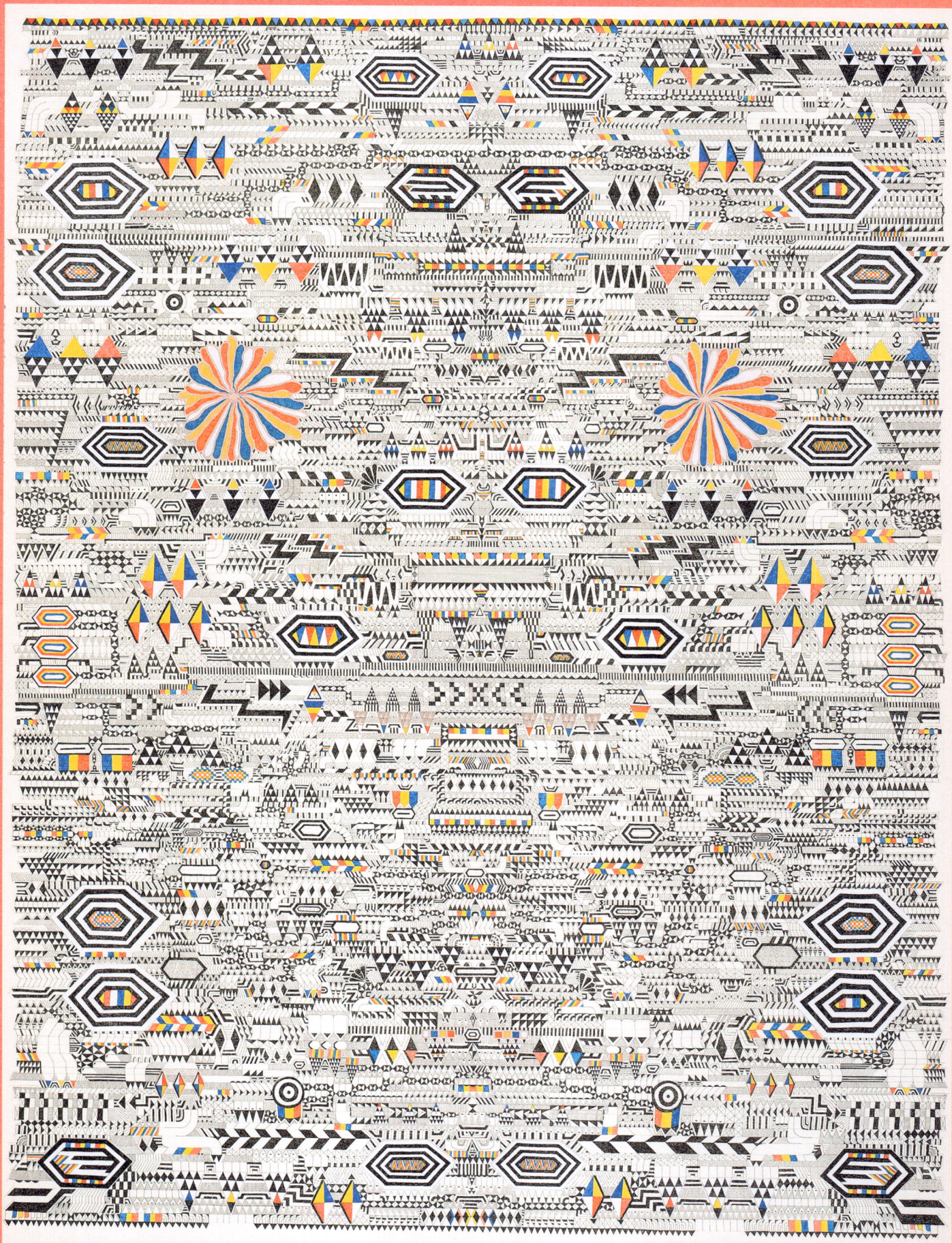

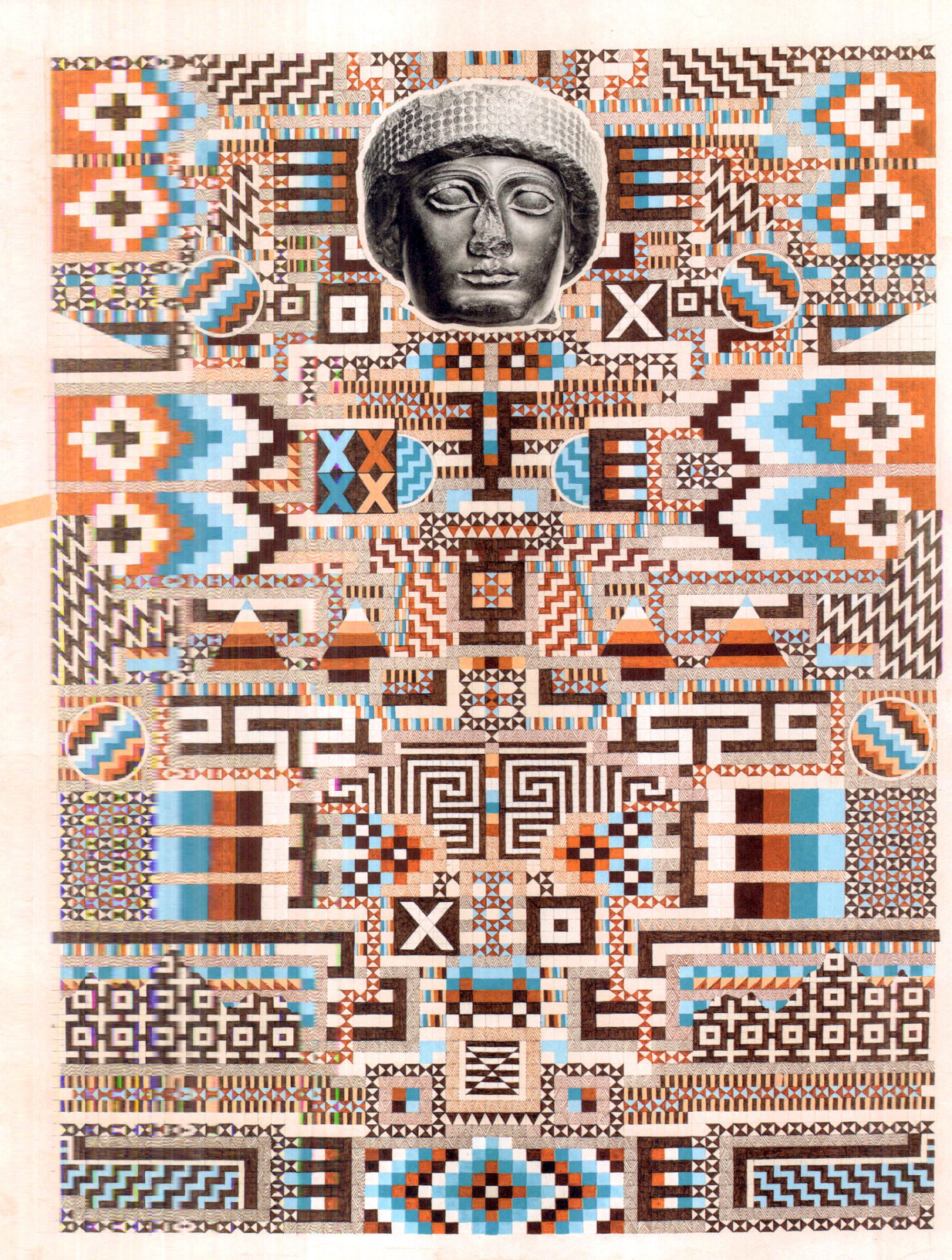

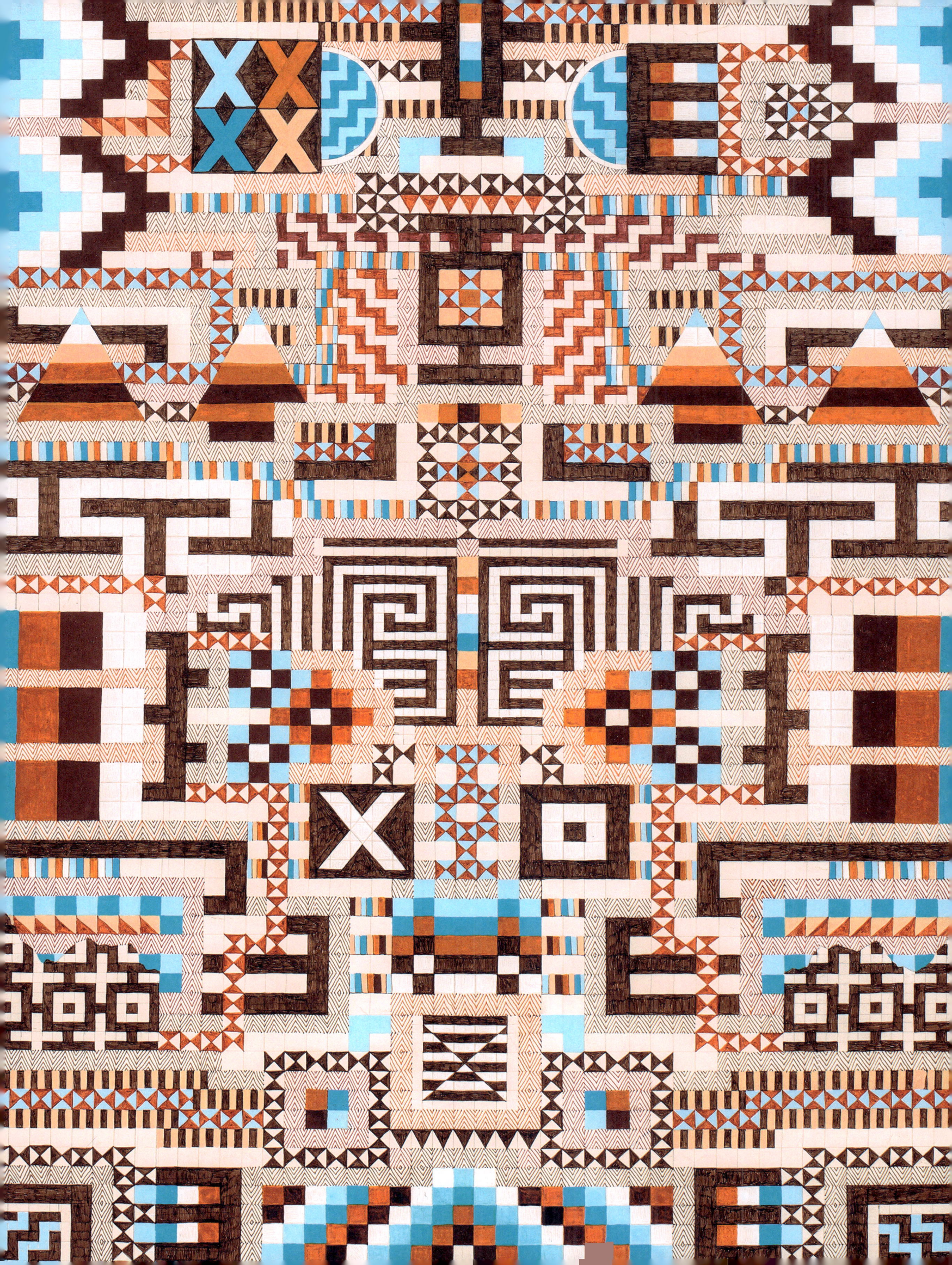

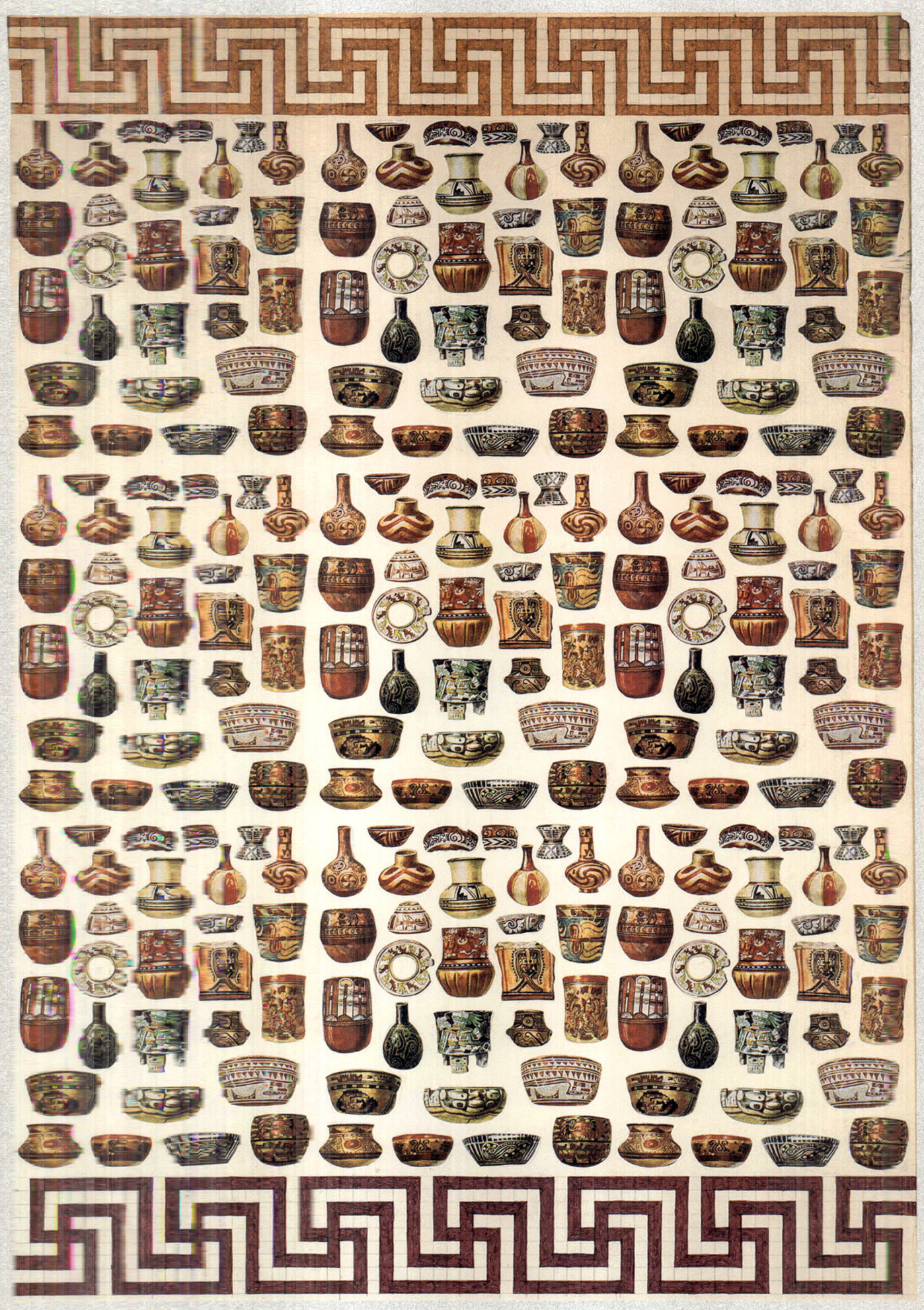

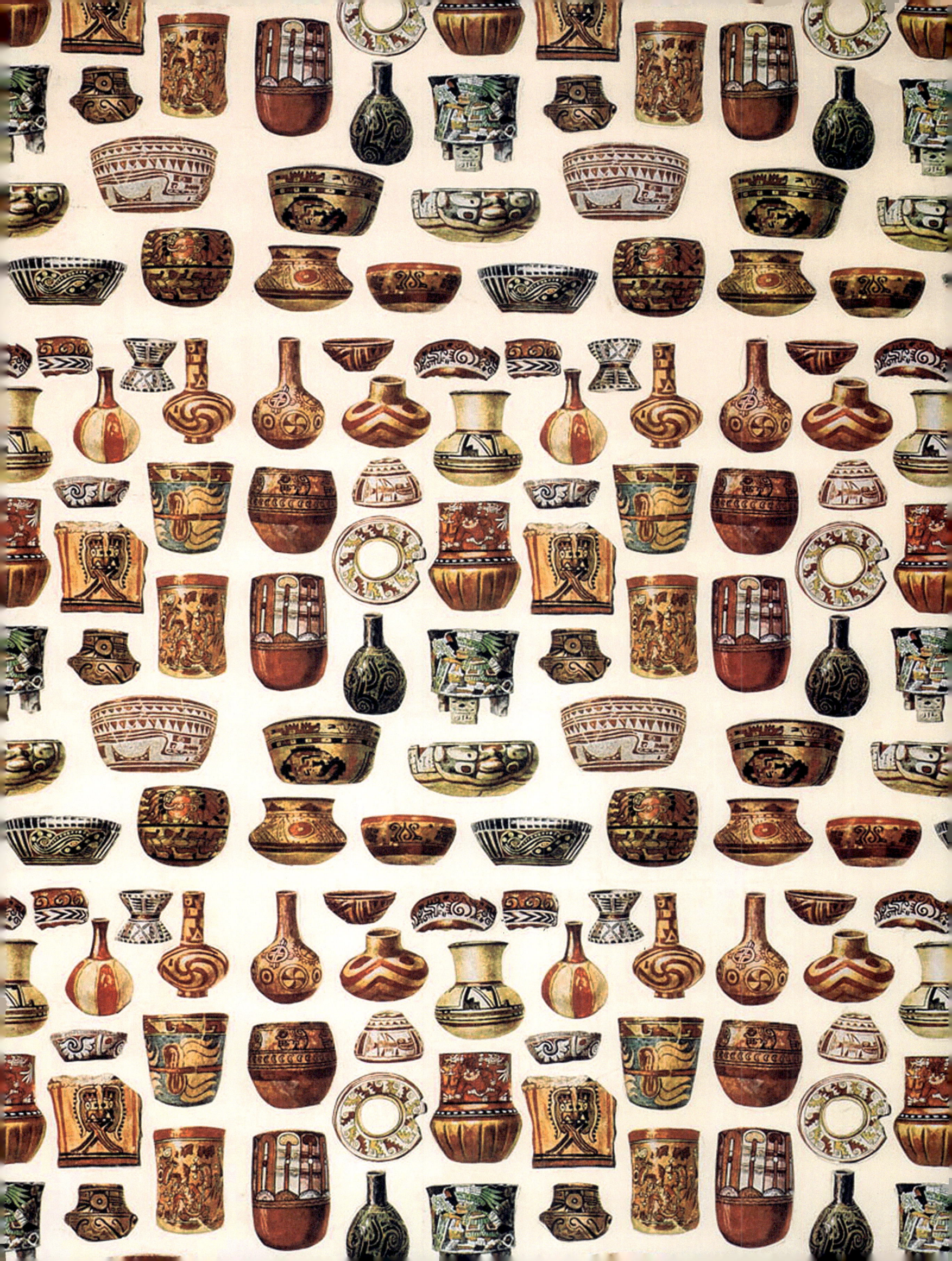

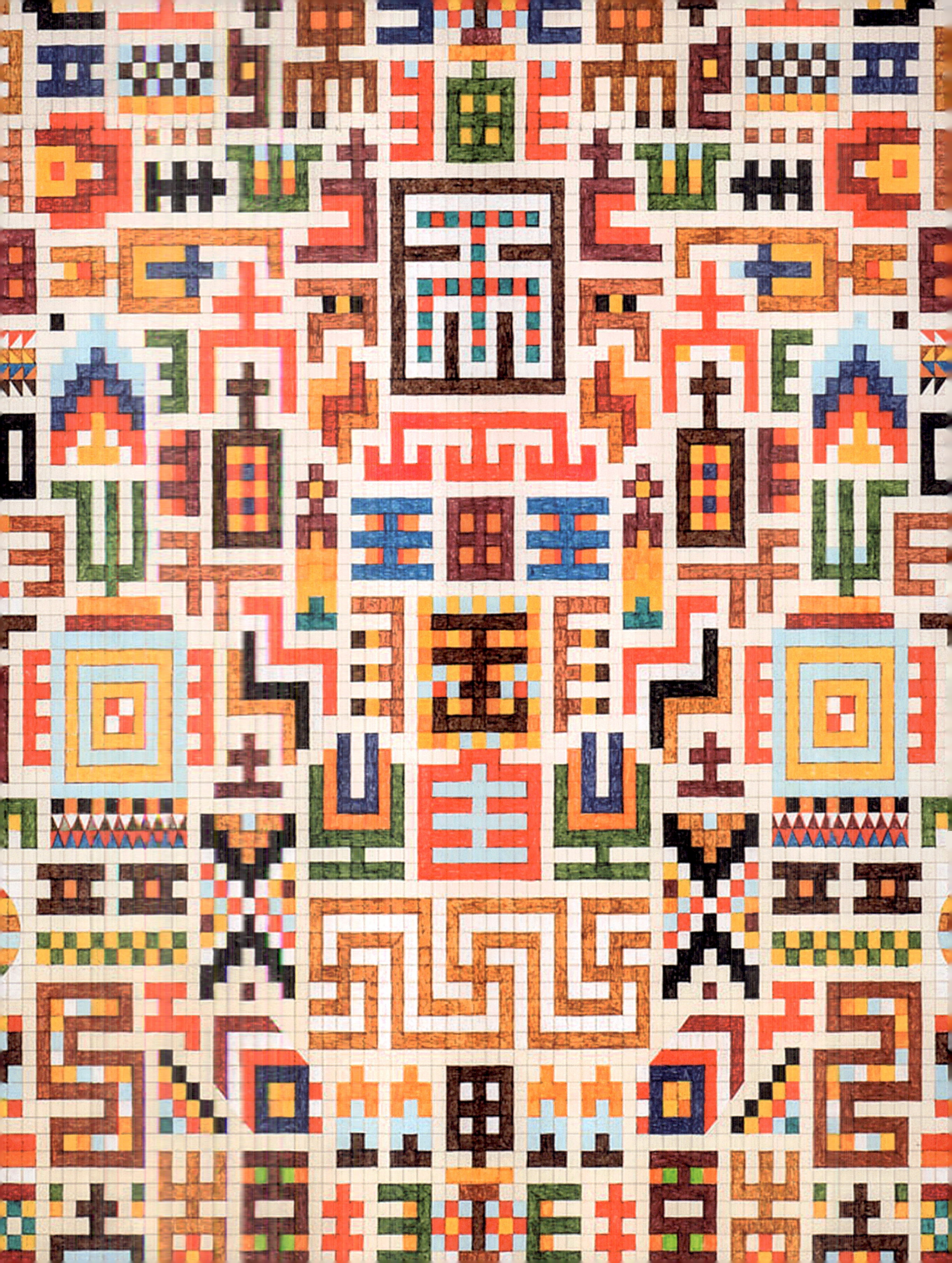

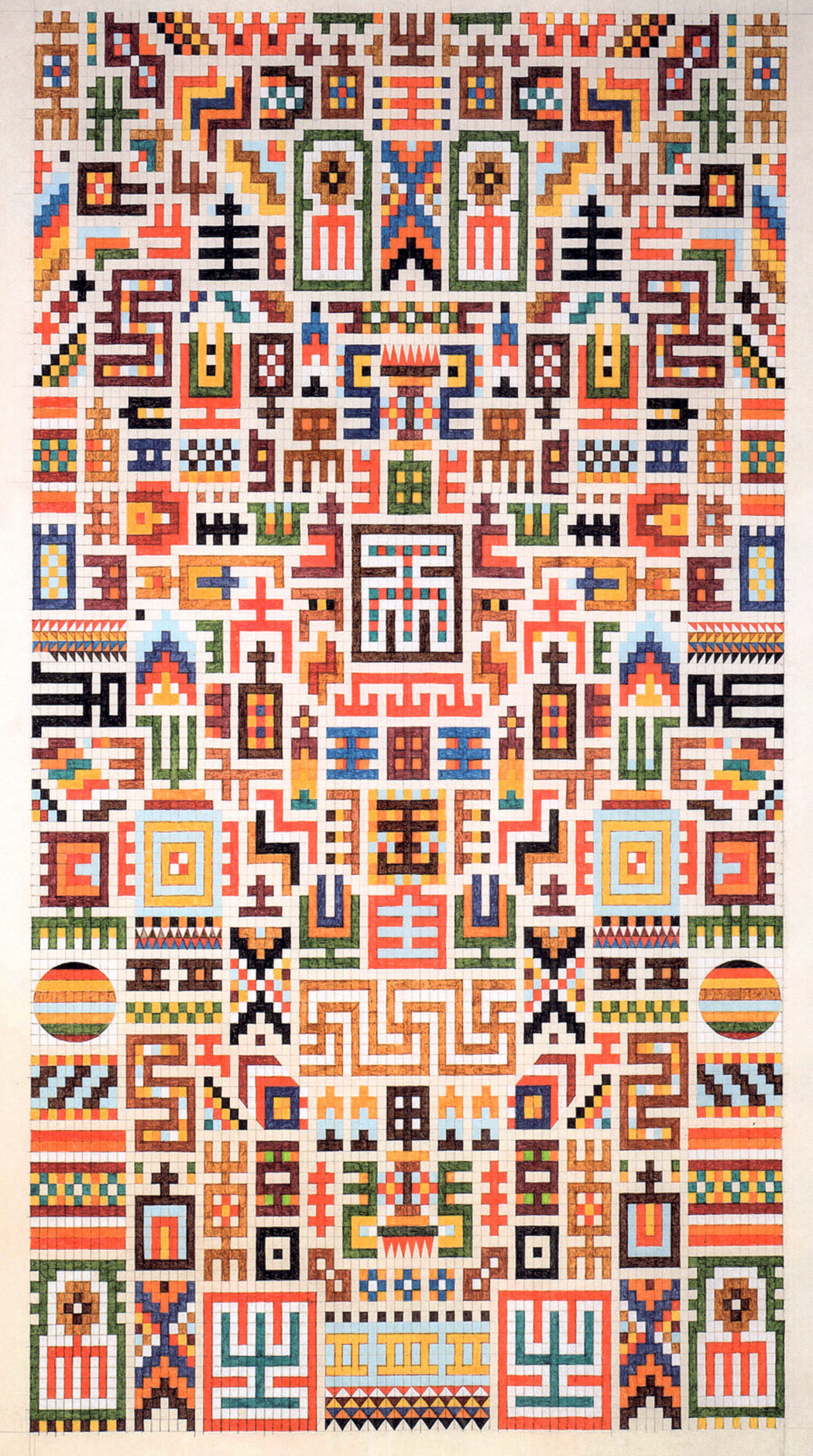

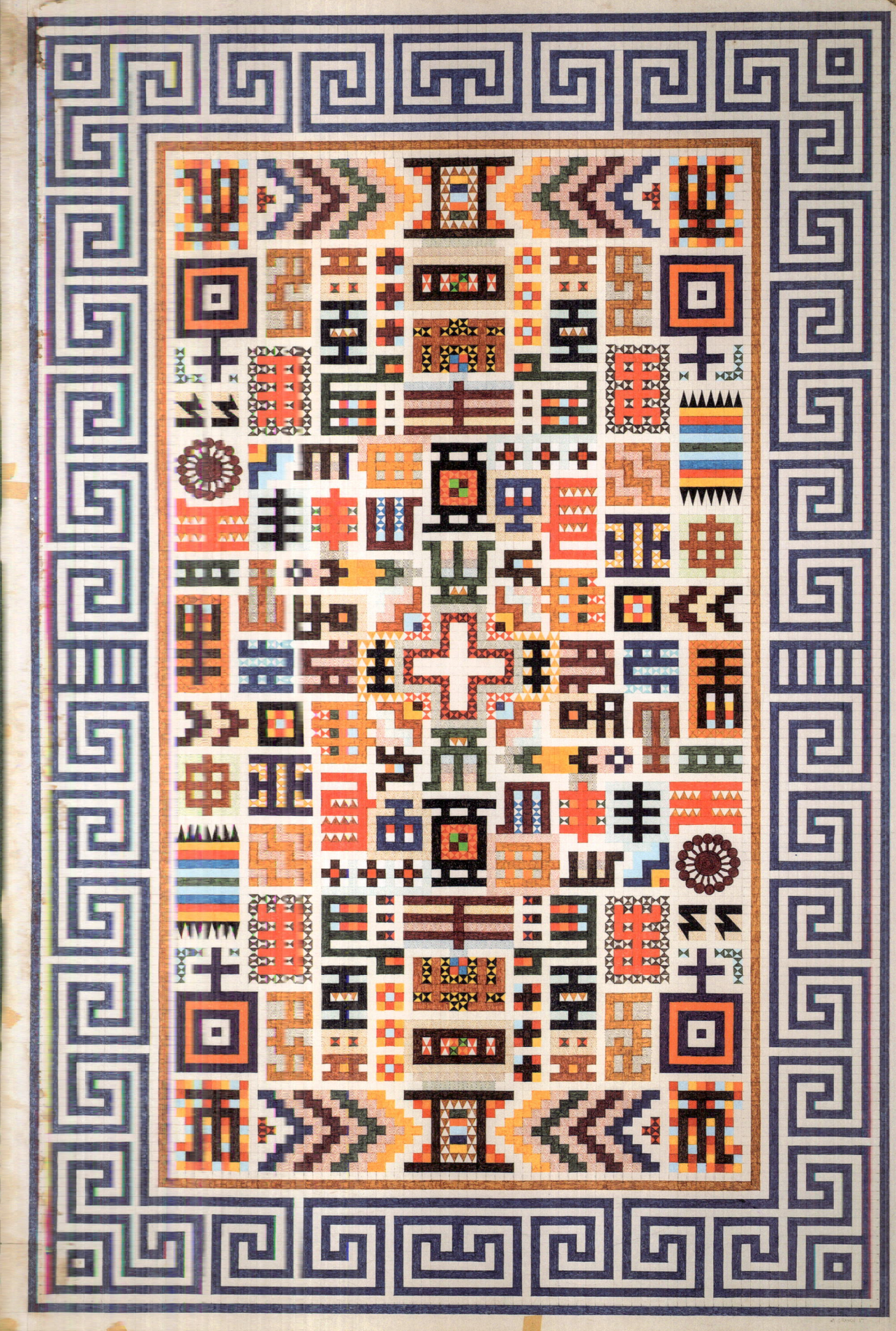

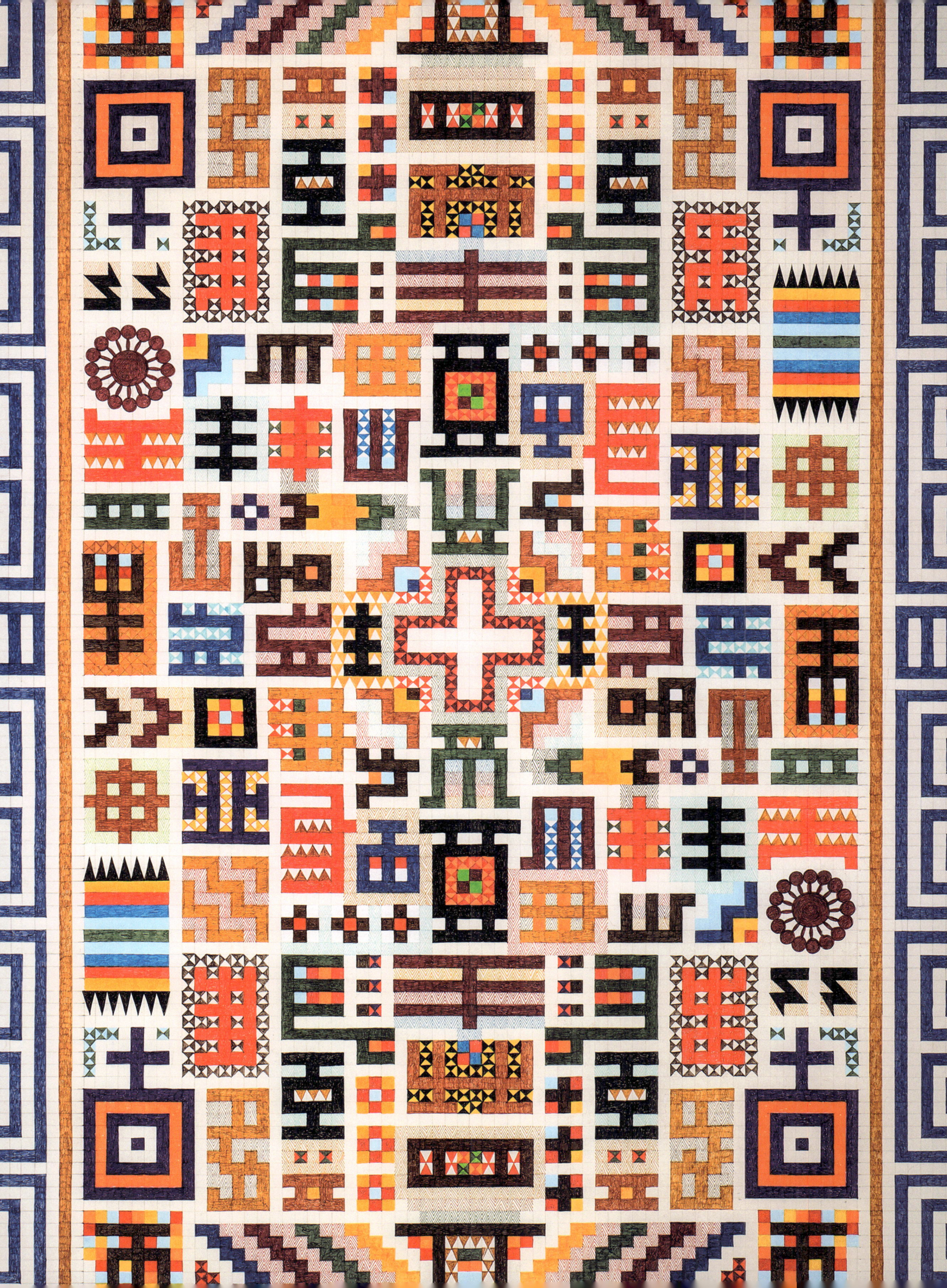

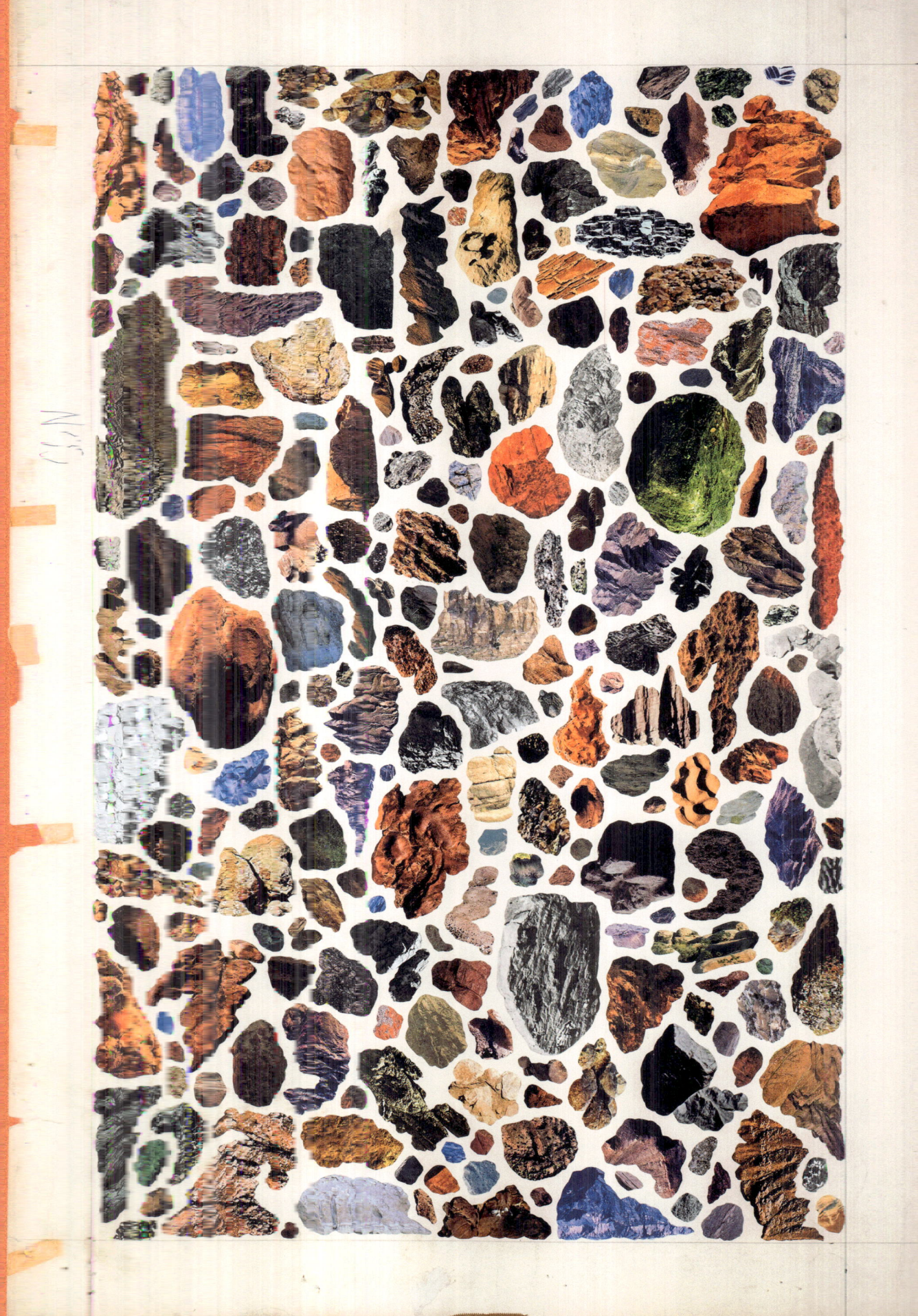

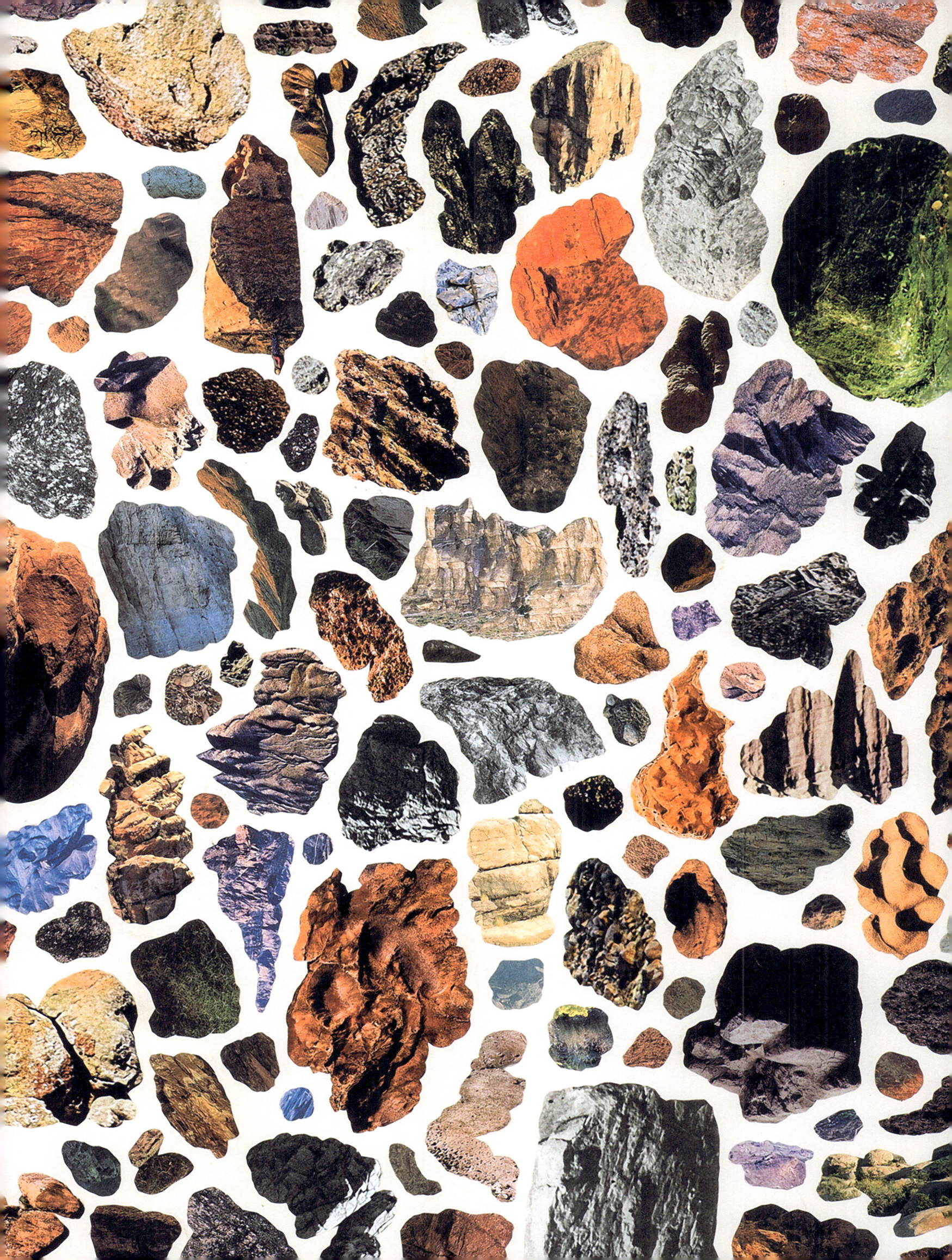

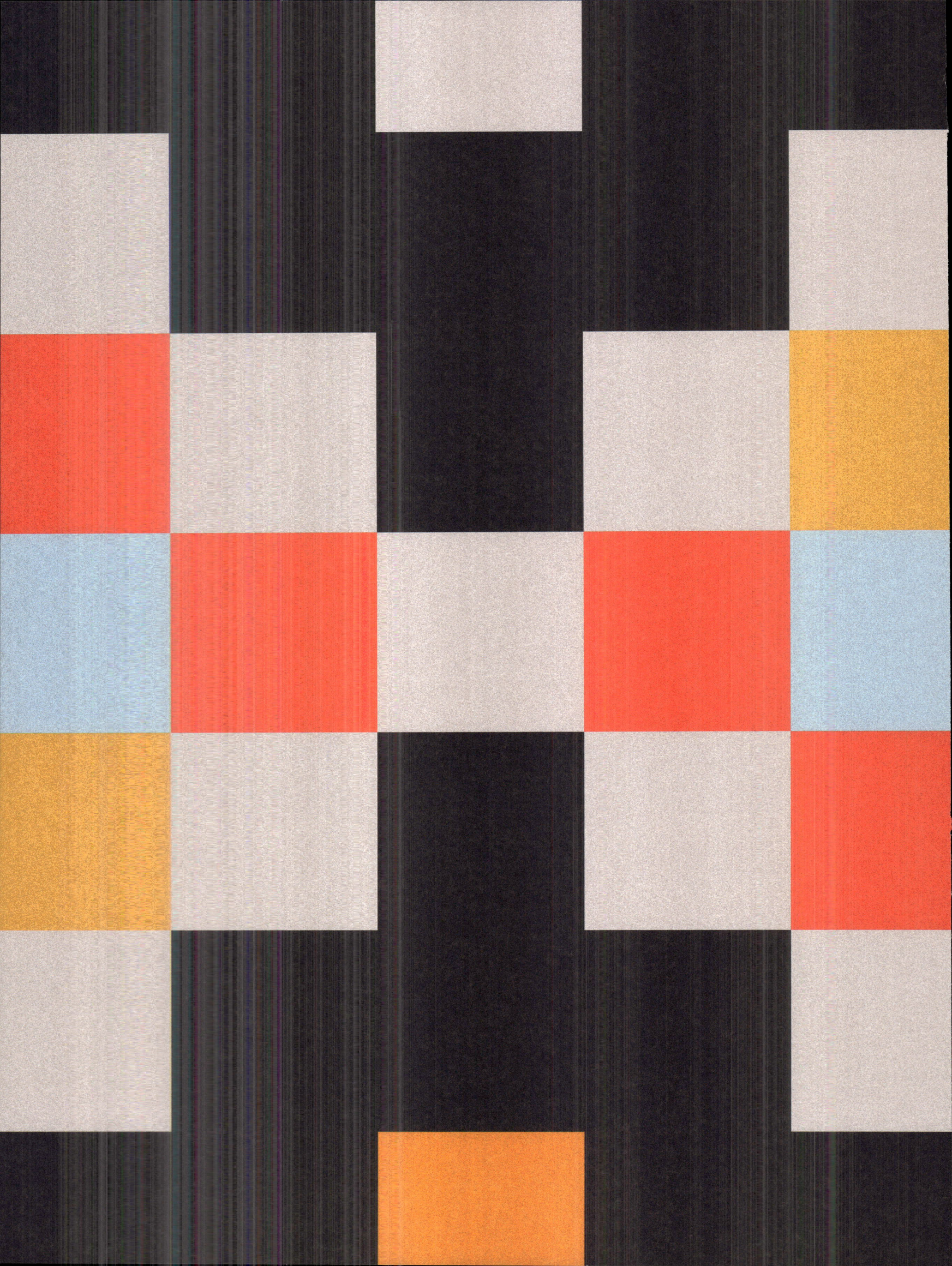

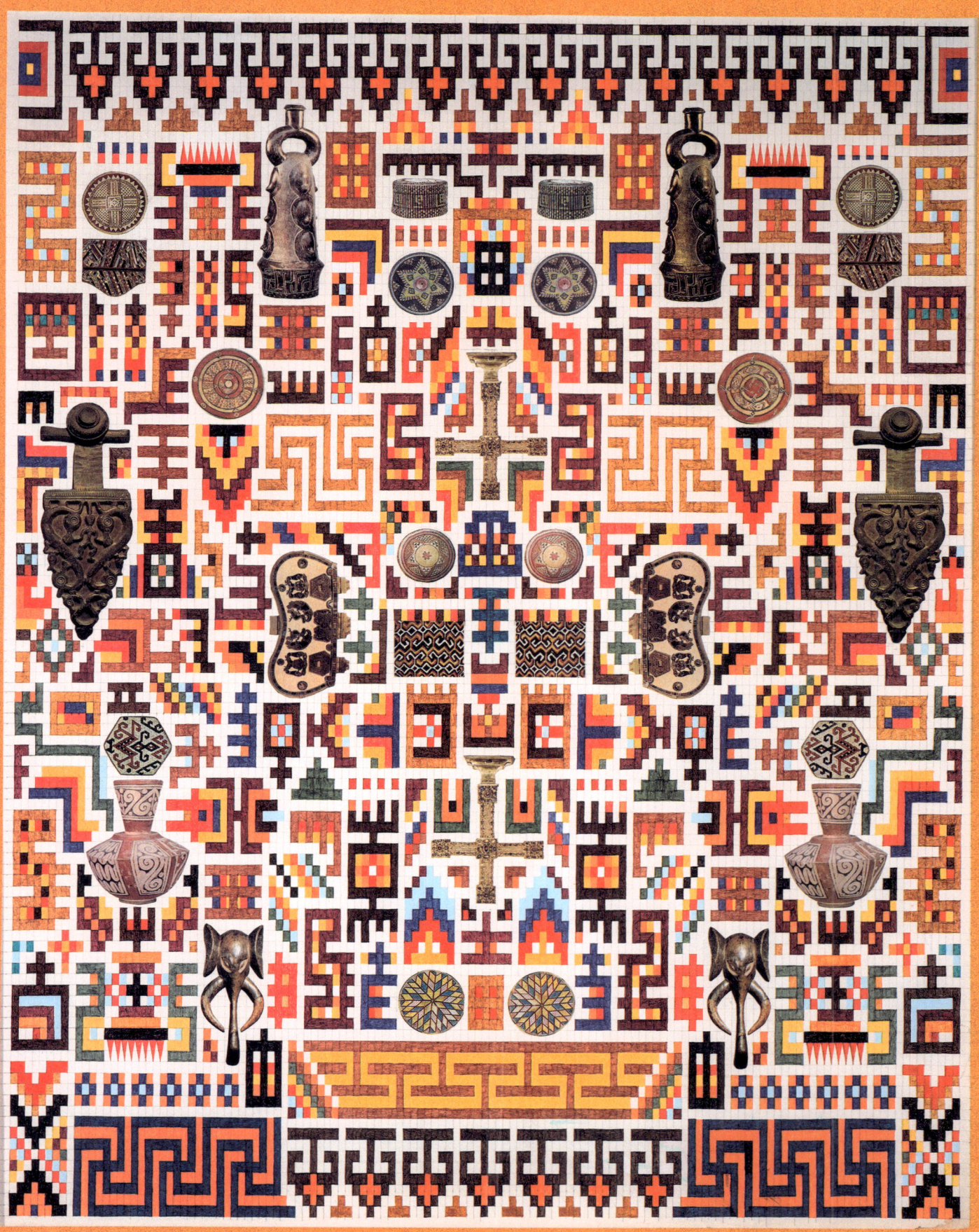

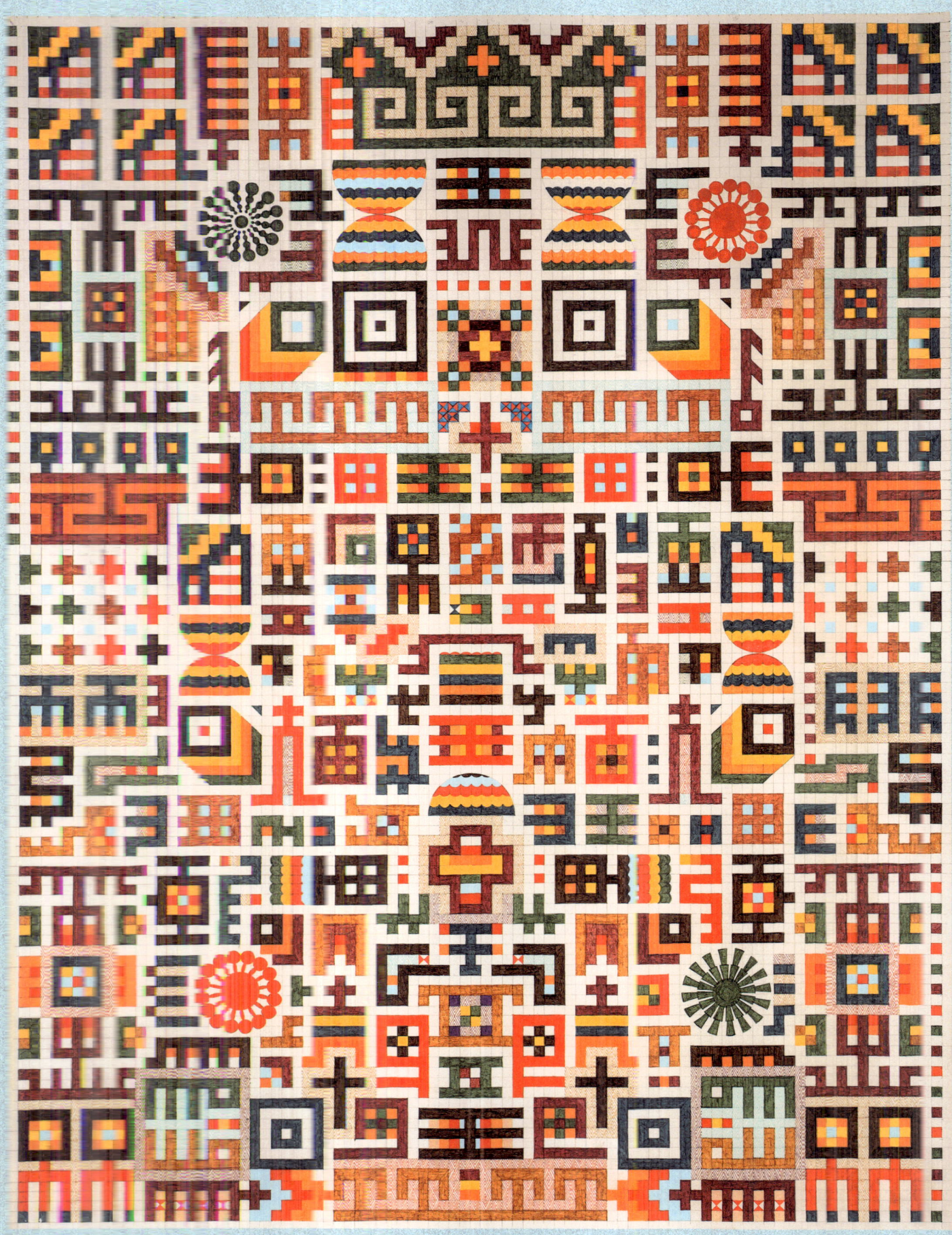

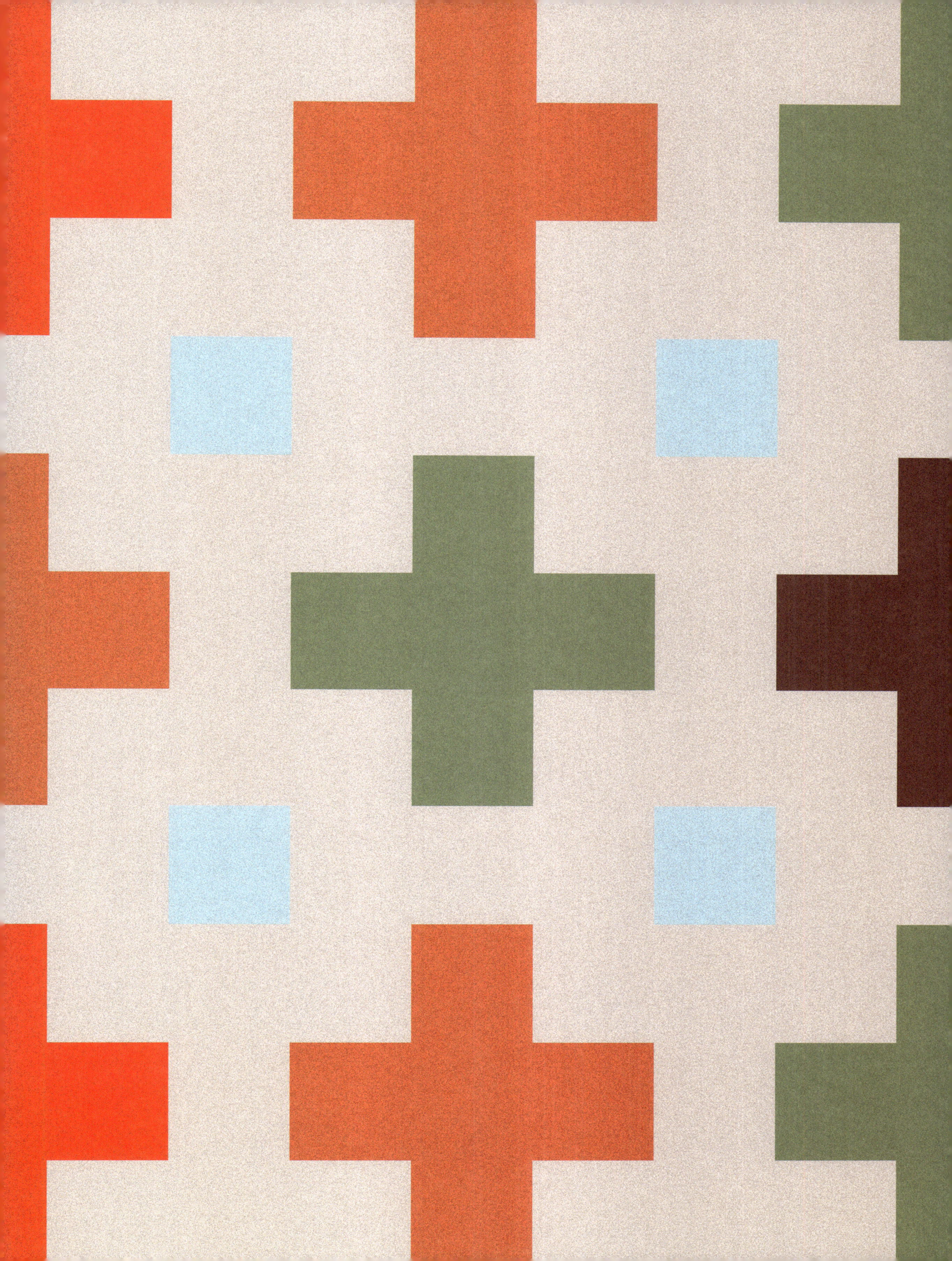

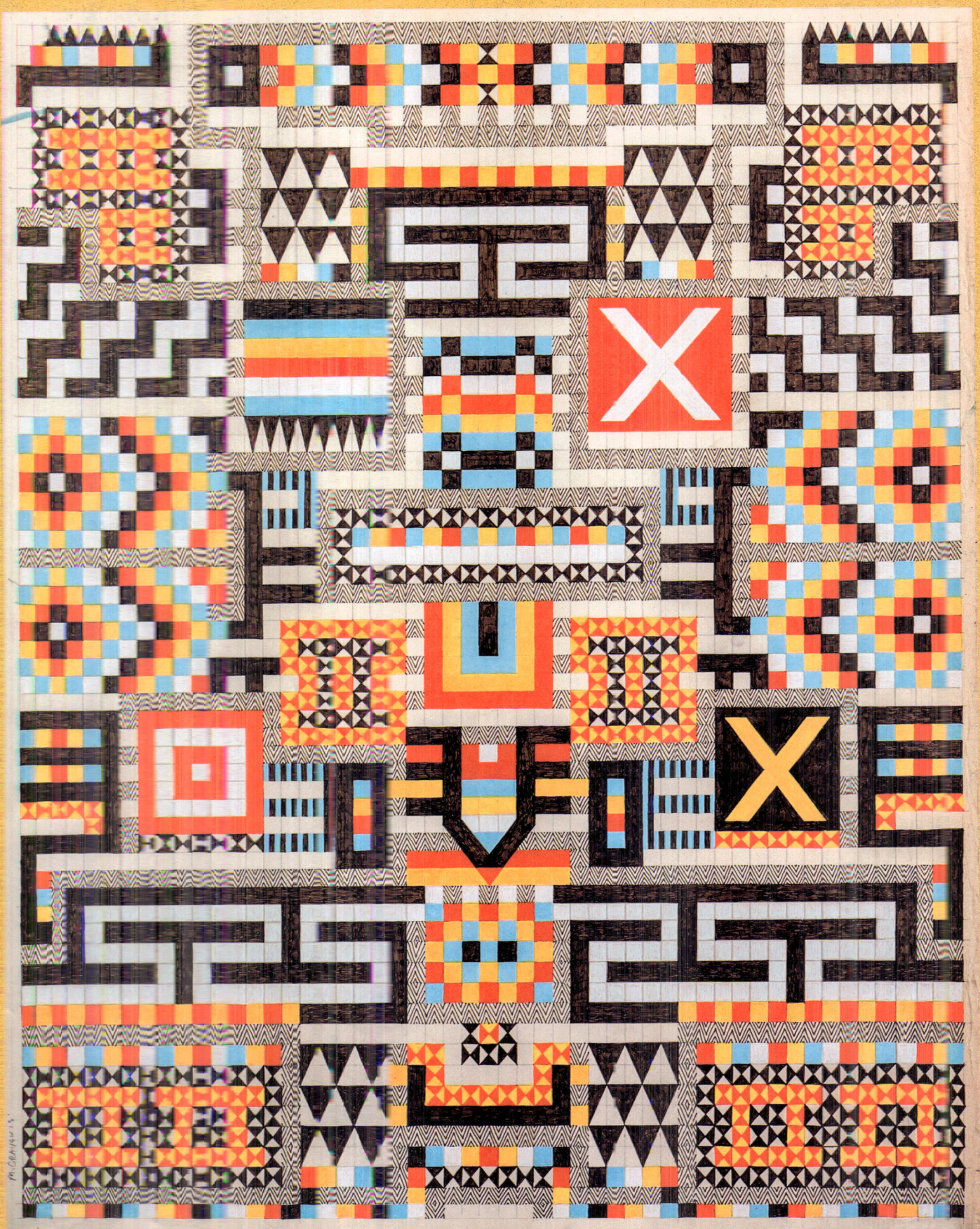

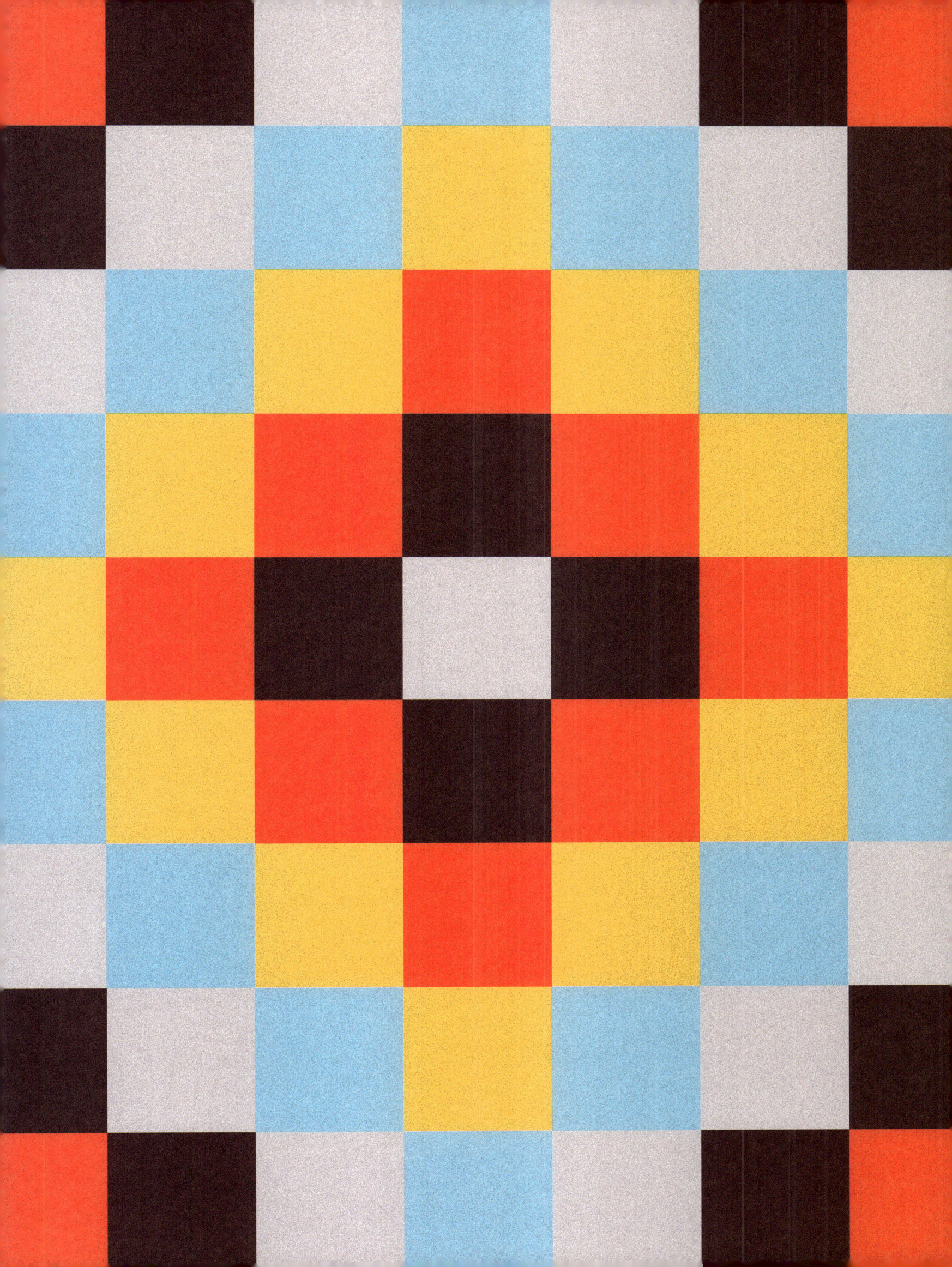

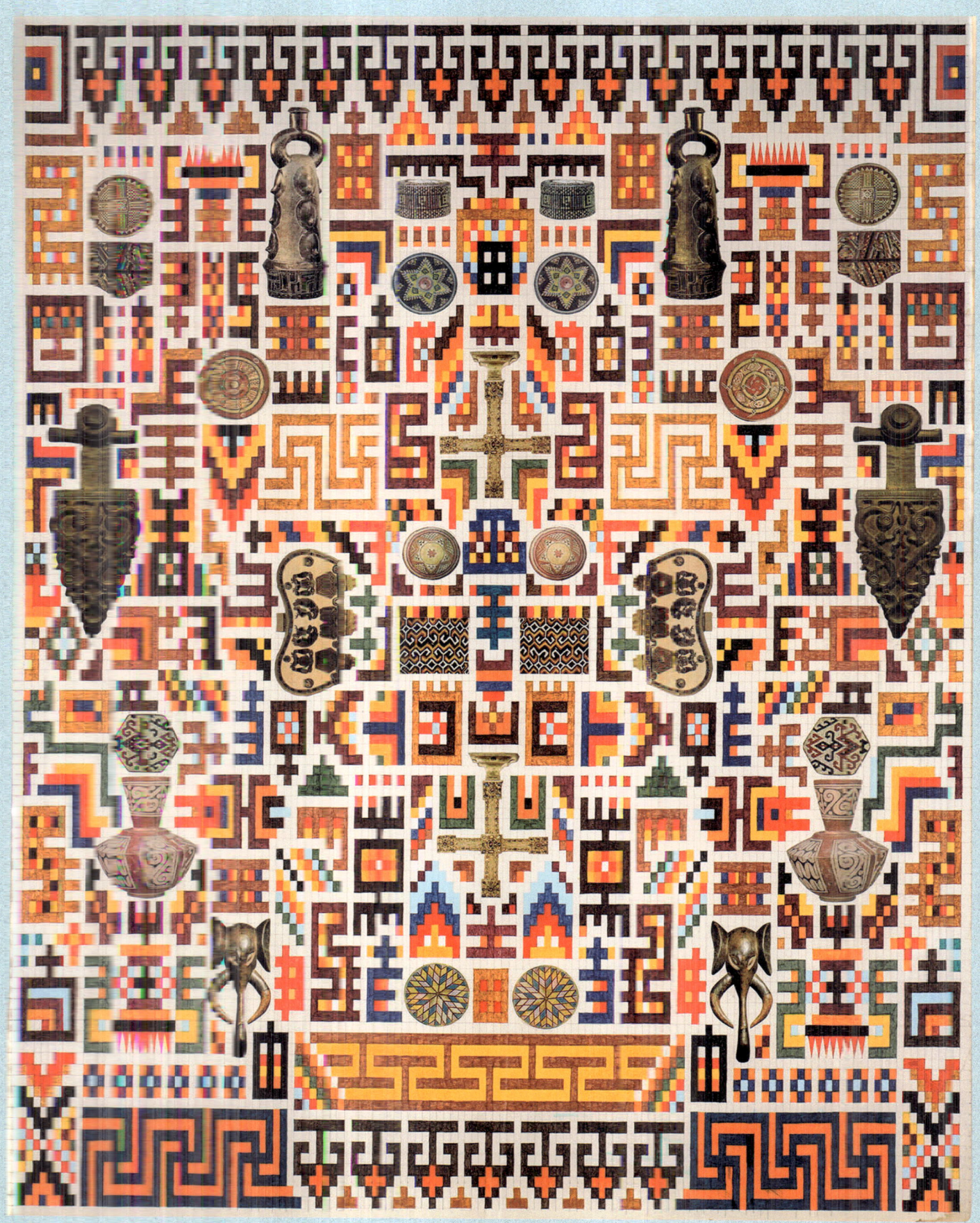

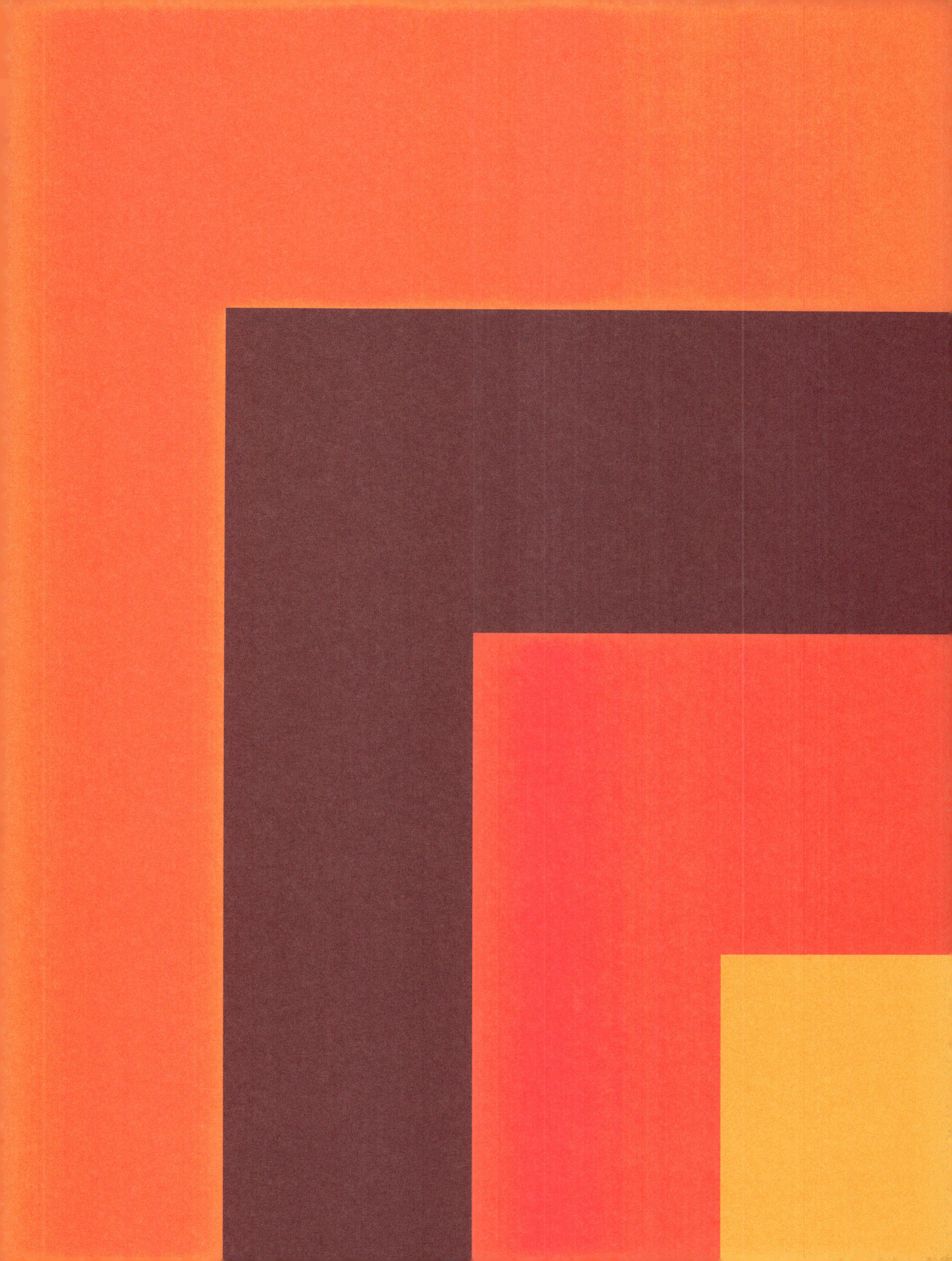

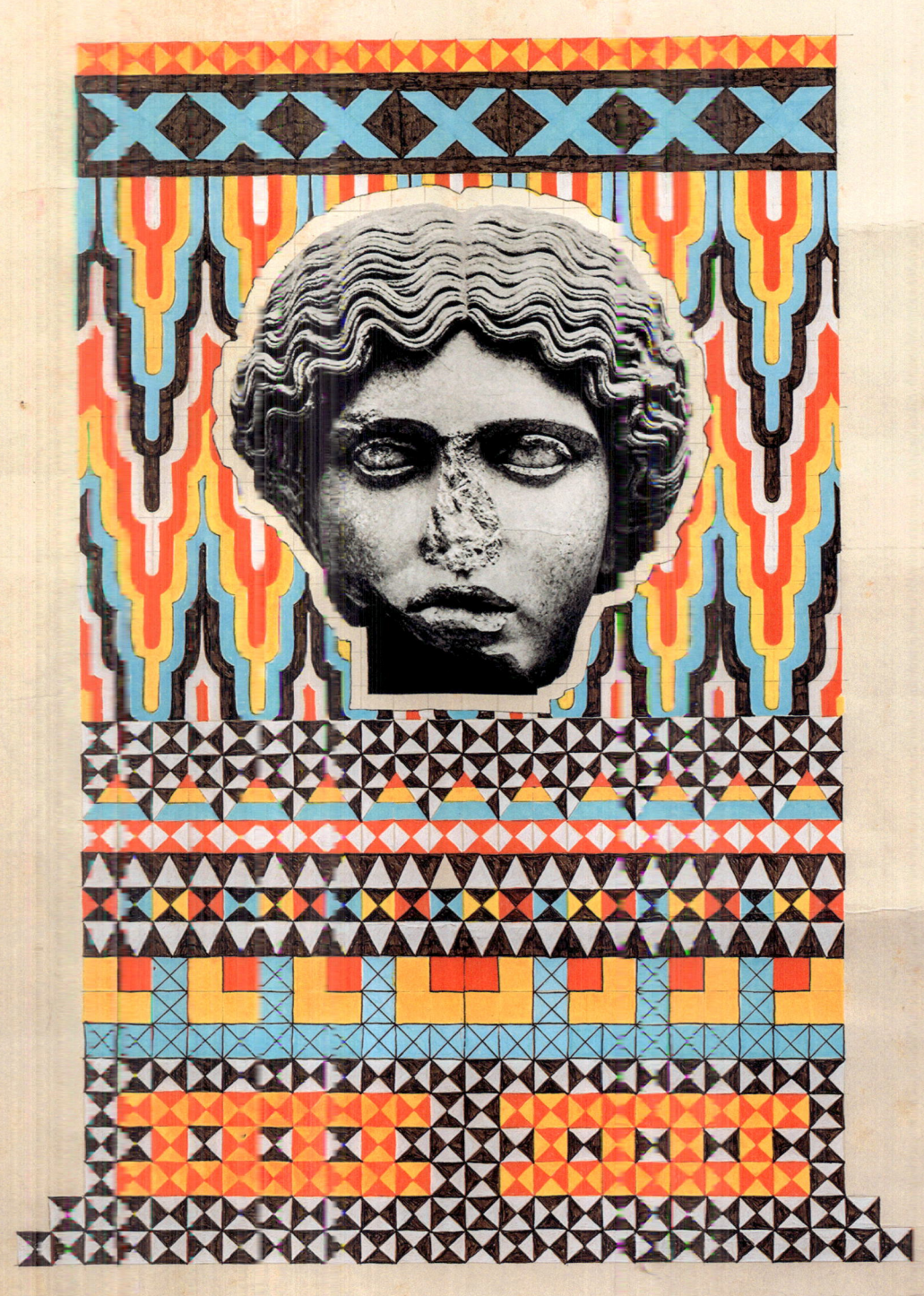

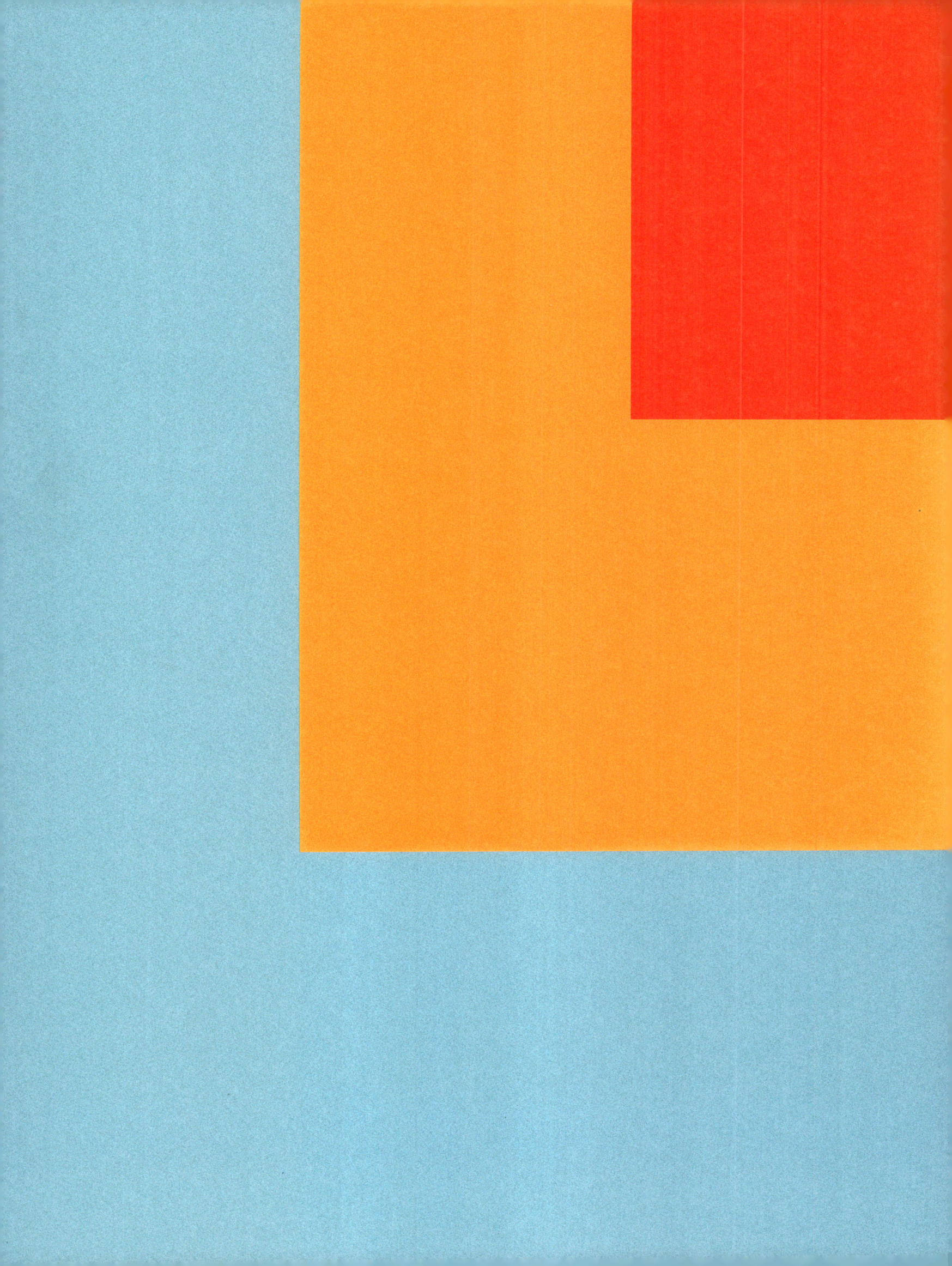

This project represents the accumulation of years of digging through old books in various bookstores across the country, an introspective journey to understand the world in which we live. I would like to thank Anthology Editions for the opportunity to consolidate my inspiration back into its original form. Thank you to the whole Anthology team for helping me fulfill this lifelong dream.

THANK YOU:

Casey Whalen, Mark Iosifescu, Nicholas Law, Bryan Cipolla, Jesse Pollock, Keith Abrahamsson, Matt Werth, Bailey Elder, Grace Srinivasiah, Alexandra Tults, Brian Leeds, Emma Olson, as well as Asya Geisberg, Holly Jarret, Hana Fruchtenicht, David Shelton, Dennis Christie, Ken Tyburski, Amanda Schneider, Sloan Shaffer, Seth Adelsberger, Alex Ebstein, Rob Pruitt, Kevin Stahl, Matt and Rebecca Burns, Christopher and Alice Daniels, Matt Stone, Ben Edmiston, Sam Adams, the Olthouse family, Tosha Stimage, and so many more who have helped me along the way . . .

And finally, thank you to my brother, Joel Craven, and my mother, Jane Geluso.

This book is dedicated to the memory of William Geluso.